DB2 Universal Database in Application Development Environments

MW00965011

ISBN 0-13-086987-2

90000

9 780130 869876

IBM DB2 Certification Guide Series

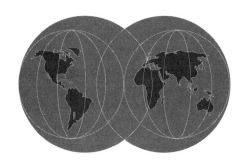

DB2 Universal Database in Application Development Environments
  by Shirai, Barber, Saboji, Naick, and Wilkins

DB2 Universal Database V6.1 Certification Guide, Third Edition
  by Cook, Harbus, and Shirai

DB2 Universal Database in the Solaris Operating Environment
  by Shirai, Michel, Wilding, Logan, and Bauch

DB2 Universal Database Certification Guide, Second Edition
  edited by Janacek and Snow

DB2 Cluster Certification Guide
  by Cook, Janacek, and Snow

DB2 Universal DRDA Certification Guide
  by Brandl, Bullock, Cook, Harbus, Janacek, and Le

DB2 Replication Certification Guide
  by Cook and Harbus

DB2 Universal Database and SAP R/3, Version 4
  by Bullock, Cook, Deedes-Vincke, Harbus, Nardone, and Neuhaus

The Universal Guide to DB2 for Windows NT
  by Cook, Harbus, and Snow

DB2 Universal Database in Application Development Environments

TETSUYA SHIRAI ■ JOHN BARBER ■ MOHAN SABOJI

INDRAN NAICK ■ BILL WILKINS

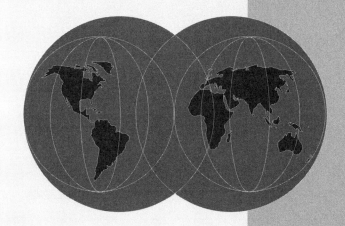

International Technical Support Organization
San Jose, California 95120

PRENTICE HALL PTR, UPPER SADDLE RIVER, NEW JERSEY 07458
www.phptr.com

© **Copyright International Business Machines Corporation 2001. All rights reserved.**

Note to U.S. Government Users — Documentation related to restricted rights — Use, duplication or disclosure is subject to restrictions set forth in GSA ADP Schedule Contract with IBM Corp.

Editorial/production supervision: *Jane Bonnell*
Cover design director: *Jerry Votta*
Cover designer: *Bruce Kenselaar*
Manufacturing buyer: *Maura Goldstaub*
Marketing manager: *Bryan Gambrel*
Acquisitions editor: *Michael Meehan*
Editorial assistant: *Linda Ramagnano*

Published by Prentice Hall PTR
Prentice-Hall, Inc.
Upper Saddle River, NJ 07458

Prentice Hall books are widely used by corporations and government agencies for training, marketing, and resale.
The publisher offers discounts on this book when ordered in bulk quantities.
For more information, contact
        Corporate Sales Department,
        Phone 800-382-3419; FAX: 201-236-7141
        E-mail (Internet): corpsales@prenhall.com
Or Write: Prentice Hall PTR
        Corporate Sales Department
        One Lake Street
        Upper Saddle River, NJ 07458

The following terms are trademarks or registered trademarks of the IBM Corporation in the United States and/or other countries: ADSTAR, Distributed Database Connection Services, DRDA, DATABASE 2, DB2, Distributed Relational Database Architecture, AIX, AS/400, OS/400, VSE/ESA, OS/2, SQL/DS, MVS/ESA, IBM, VM/ESA.

The following terms are trademarks or registered trademarks of other companies as follows: HP-UX, Hewlett-Packard Company; Lotus, 1-2-3, Lotus Development Corporation; ActiveX, Microsoft, Visual Basic, Visual C++, Visual Studio, Windows, Windows NT, Microsoft Corporation; PostScript, Adobe Systems, Incorporated; IPX/SPX, NetWare, Novell, Novell, Inc.; Java, Solaris, Sun Microsystems, Inc.; UNIX, X/Open, X/Open Company Limited.

UNIX is a registered trademark in the U.S. and other countries licensed exclusively through X/Open Company Limited.
DB2 information on the Internet—http://www-4.ibm.com/software/data/db2
DB2 certification information on the Internet—http://www.ibm.com/certify

All other products or services mentioned in this book are the trademarks or service marks of their respective companies or organizations.

All rights reserved. No part of this book may be
reproduced, in any form or by any means,
without permission in writing from the publisher.

Printed in the United States of America
10 9 8 7 6 5 4 3 2 1

ISBN   0-13-086987-2

Prentice-Hall International (UK) Limited, *London*
Prentice-Hall of Australia Pty. Limited, *Sydney*
Prentice-Hall Canada Inc., *Toronto*
Prentice-Hall Hispanoamericana, S.A., *Mexico*
Prentice-Hall of India Private Limited, *New Delhi*
Prentice-Hall of Japan, Inc., *Tokyo*
Pearson Education Asia Pte. Ltd.
Editora Prentice-Hall do Brasil, Ltda., *Rio de Janeiro*

Preface

Windows NT/2000 is the fastest growing platform for IBM's relational database servers, known as DB2 Universal Database (DB2 UDB), and over 74% of all DB2 UDB applications are created using Microsoft Visual Studio. This book is intended for IT architects, systems designers, and programmers who are interested in developing Windows applications for DB2 UDB using Microsoft's application development tools. The focus will be on Microsoft Visual Studio, which includes development environments for Visual Basic and Visual C++.

First, we will introduce supported programming interfaces for DB2 UDB, and server-side features which can be used in the design of your applications.

Then we will discuss application development using Visual Basic and Visual C++. We will focus on the ActiveX Data Objects (ADO) programming model.

We will also talk about multi-tier applications in the Microsoft Transaction Server (MTS) environment, and web applications using Active Server Pages (ASP) and Internet Information Server (IIS).

Finally, we will discuss performance tips relevant to application development for DB2 UDB.

Prior to reading this book, you need to have a basic database, Visual Basic, and Visual C++ knowledge.

This book is based on DB2 UDB Version 7.1, due to become generally available in June, 2000.

How this Book was Created

This book was a joint effort between the San Jose ITSO (International Technical Support Organization) and the IBM Toronto Lab. The ITSO is a group within IBM whose mission is to provide skill transfer on new products and technology worldwide. We provide direct feedback to the IBM software labs as we gather input from various groups of DB2 users, including IBM support personnel, customers and business partners.

The ITSO provides a working environment for interested individuals to work with new IBM software products. These individuals may include IBM employees and customers. The team develops a workshop or a book, known as a redbook.

Note: IBM Redbooks — http://www.redbooks.ibm.com/redbooks

This book was produced by I/T professionals from all over the world, assisted by the expertise of the following people:

- **Tetsuya Shirai** is a Project Leader at the International Technical Support Organization (ITSO), San Jose Center. He worked in Tokyo, Japan before joining the San Jose ITSO. He has been with IBM for 8 years, working for the last 4 years with DB2 UDB products. He has worked in the area of DB2 services, teaching classes to both customers and IBMers. He has also provided consulting services to DB2 customers worldwide.

- **John Barber** has worked in IBM's AS/400 Support Center, in the UK, for the last 3 years. He specializes in supporting customers who are developing Client/Server applications to access DB2/400. For the 28 years prior to joining IBM, John worked for a leading UK Defence Equipment Supplier, where for the last 18 years, he was responsible for developing and implementing defect and test result data collection and analysis systems, on a range of different computer systems.

- **Mohan Saboji** works for IBM Global Services in Bangalore, India. He has many years of experience of working in the Client/Server application development environment. He has extensively worked on the Microsoft development tools such as Visual Basic and Visual Interdev, and the Microsoft BackOffice server products such as IIS and MTS.

- **Indran Naick** is a Project Leader and Senior I/T specialist at the International Technical Support Organization (ITSO), Austin Center. He has 10 years of industry experience. He writes extensively and teaches IBM classes worldwide on a number of client/server topics. Before joining the ITSO in 1999, Indran worked for the IBM Software Group, Southern Africa, in Software Solutions.

- **Bill Wilkins** is a technical specialist in the IBM Data Management Consulting Services group in Toronto. Prior to this he worked in DB2 performance analysis in the IBM Toronto development laboratory for 6 years, including 2 years as manager. He is an IBM Certified Advanced Technical Expert in DB2 UDB and has over 20 years of experience in the IT industry.

Acknowledgments

A special thanks to Steve Sanyal of the IBM Toronto Lab for providing his invaluable assistance.

Thanks also to the following people for their significant contributions to this project:

- Abdul Al-Azzawe, IBM Toronto Lab
- Robert Begg, IBM Toronto Lab
- Darl Crick, IBM Toronto Lab
- Susan Visser, IBM Toronto Lab
- Robert Harbus, IBM Toronto Lab

The following people were invaluable for their expertise:

- Yvonne Lyon, IBM ITSO San Jose
- Emma Jacobs, IBM ITSO San Jose
- Elsa Martinez, IBM ITSO San Jose

Overview

- ◆ D B2 UNIVERSAL DATABASE
- ◆ D B2 PRODUCTS
- ◆ D B2 GUI TOOLS
- ◆ MICROSOFT DNA ARCHITECTURE
- ◆ MICROSOFT VISUAL STUDIO
- ◆ MICROSOFT UNIVERSAL DATA ACCESS

*I*n this chapter, you will be introduced to the DB2 Universal Database (DB2 UDB) and Windows Distributed interNet Applications (DNA) architecture, which is Microsoft's framework of application development. Visual Studio will be introduced as a tool suite to develop Windows DNA applications. The software versions used here are DB2 Universal Database Version 7.1 for Windows NT and Microsoft Visual Studio Version 6.0, hence to be referred as DB2 UDB and Visual Studio respectively. We also show that DB2 UDB is well suited to the Windows DNA architecture. Finally we discuss the benefits of using DB2 UDB as the data store for the Windows DNA applications.

DB2 Universal Database

DB2 Universal Database (DB2 UDB) is IBM's relational database management system that is at the core of many business-critical systems. It is fully scalable from a single processor to symmetric multiple processors and to massively parallel clusters, and features multimedia capabilities with image, audio, video, text, spatial and other object relational support.

Scalable Database

DB2 Universal Database (UDB) is a highly scalable relational database product. DB2 UDB is supported on a wide variety of systems.

DB2 Everyplace on a handheld device running Palm Operating System and Windows CE serves a highly mobile environment.

DB2 UDB Satellite Edition on a mobile laptop PC running Windows 95, 98, and NT also serves a mobile environment.

DB2 UDB Personal Edition on a laptop PC running Windows 95, 98, NT, 2000, OS/2 or LINUX serves the individual user's needs.

DB2 UDB Workgroup Edition on a server system running Windows NT, 2000, OS/2, AIX, Solaris, HP-UX or LINUX supports groups of local end-users accessing the server from a variety of client platforms.

DB2 UDB Enterprise Edition can be run on a server system running Windows NT, 2000, OS/2, LINUX, AIX, Solaris, HP-UX or PTX. DB2 UDB Enterprise Edition is a superset of DB2 UDB Workgroup Edition and includes the DB2 Connect Enterprise Edition product which enables access to host databases such as DB2 for OS/390, DB2 for AS/400, or DB2 Server for VSE/VM.

DB2 UDB Enterprise-Extended Edition supports massively parallel processors which allow a database to be physically partitioned across the same or multiple independent machines, while providing a single logical database interface. SQL operations can operate in parallel on the individual database partitions, thus, increasing the execution speed of a single query. DB2 UDB Enterprise-Extended Edition is supported on Windows NT, 2000, AIX, Solaris, HP-UX, and PTX.

As you have seen, DB2 UDB supports almost all major operating systems. You can select the appropriate platform for your environment and the appropriate DB2 UDB Server product to suit the database size and performance you require.

In Fig. 1–1, all of the DB2 UDB Server products are shown.

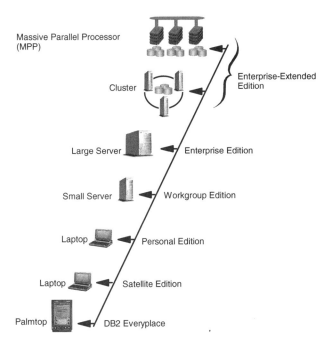

Overview

Fig. 1–1 *DB2 Universal Database (DB2 UDB) Products*

The beauty of DB2 is that you may move from the lower-end Intel platforms such as a laptop to the higher-end UNIX platforms such as the RS/6000 SP without necessarily modifying your application; the database manager has not changed, but has grown with you and your application requirements.

Note: As this book intends to describe application development using Microsoft Visual Studio, we are assuming your database applications are running on the Windows operating system. However, it does not mean your DB2 UDB Server must be a Windows machine. Your application can access DB2 UDB Servers on any supported platform. If you install and configure DB2 Connect, your application can access host databases such as DB2 for OS/390.

Storing Universal Data

DB2 UDB has the ability to store all kinds of electronic information. This includes traditional relational data, as well as structured and unstructured binary information, documents and text in many languages, graphics, images, multimedia (audio and video), information specific to operations, like engineering drawings, maps, insurance claims forms, numerical control streams, or any type of electronic information.

DB2 UDB Object Relational Extenders (DB2 Image Extender, DB2 Audio Extender, DB2 Video Extender, DB2 Text Extender, DB2 Spatial Extender, DB2 XML Extender, Net Search Extender) can take your database applications beyond traditional numeric and character data to these more complex types of data. You can bring any or all of these data types together in one SQL query and manipulate them with powerful built-in functions. DB2 UDB Object Relational Extenders are contained in the DB2 UDB product packages (DB2 Spatial Extender is the separated package).

DB2 UDB also has the ability to access other data sources including the DB2 family, other RDBMS such as Oracle or Sybase, non-relational databases such as VSAM or IMS, and OLE DB providers such as MS-Access or MS-Excel. This means that after establishing a link to those data sources, a simple SELECT statement will access remote data as if it is a local table, without populating a local DB2 table. You can also move the data from a remote database into DB2 UDB using an SQL statement like INSERT INTO...SELECT FROM....

For the DB2 family, the DB2 Client provides the ability to access a DB2 UDB Server installed on Windows, UNIX, or OS/2 machines. The functionality of a DB2 Client is included in the DB2 UDB Server product, or a DB2 Client can be installed as an independent software product. For host databases such as DB2 for OS/390, DB2 UDB (or a DB2 Client) can access them through the DB2 Connect product.

The DB2 DataJoiner product provides the ability to view popular relational data sources (DB2 Family, Informix, SQL Server, Oracle, Sybase, Teradata, and others) and non-relational data sources (IMS and VSAM) as if they were local data.

DataJoiner has been partly integrated into DB2 UDB since in Version 7.1 as a separately priced feature, DB2 Relational Connect. DB2 Relational Connect provides native read access to Oracle databases.

For OLE DB providers such as MS-Access, MS-Excel, and Intersolv Connect OLE DB for Notes, you can define OLE DB table functions to access these data sources as if they were local read-only DB2 tables.

These various possibilities are depicted in Fig. 1–2.

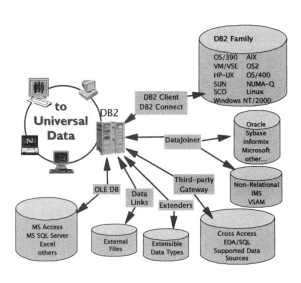

Fig. 1–2 *Universal Access to a Universe of Data*

DB2 UDB Products

There are three main DB2 Universal Database Version 7.1 products:

- **DB2 Universal Database**

  There are five product packages for DB2 Universal Database V7.1, as shown in Fig. 1–1 on page 3: Satellite Edition, Personal Edition, Workgroup Edition, Enterprise Edition, and Enterprise-Extended Edition.

- **DB2 Connect**

  This product provides the ability to access a host database using the DRDA protocol. There are two product packages: DB2 Connect Personal Edition and DB2 Connect Enterprise Edition. DB2 Connect Personal Edition provides access to host databases only from the system where it is installed. DB2 Connect Enterprise Edition routes each database request from DB2 Clients to the appropriate DRDA Application Server and provides the ability for multiple clients to access host data. The functionality of DB2 Connect Enterprise Edition is also contained in the DB2 UDB Enterprise Edition.

- **DB2 UDB Developer's Edition**

This product provides the ability to develop and test a database application. It is designed to give application developers all necessary data access tools and DB2 UDB Server code for developing database applications. There are two versions of the product packaging: Personal Developer's Edition and Universal Developer's Edition. Personal Developer's Edition includes DB2 UDB Personal Edition and DB2 Connect Personal Edition for each platform. Universal Developer's Edition includes DB2 UDB Personal Edition, DB2 UDB Workgroup Edition, DB2 UDB Enterprise Edition, DB2 Connect Personal Edition, and DB2 Connect Enterprise Edition for each platform.

Note: DB2 UDB Personal Developer's Edition can be downloaded freely from IBM Data Management Web site. The URL is:
```
http://www-4.ibm.com/software/data/db2/udb/
downloads.html
```

DB2 UDB Clients

Whether you are developing or running DB2 applications, at least one DB2 UDB Server needs to be accessed locally or remotely through the DB2 Client. The DB2 Client is a point of contact to DB2 databases for DB2 applications. If your DB2 application is working on each client workstation, a DB2 Client needs to be installed on each of them. If you have a Web application accessing a DB2 UDB database and each client is using it through the Web browser, a DB2 Client should be installed on the Web server. The functionality of the DB2 Client is included in the DB2 UDB Server product, or a DB2 Client can be installed as an independent software product.

All DB2 UDB products and product packages have three common client components:

- DB2 Runtime Client
- DB2 Administration Client
- DB2 Software Developers Kit (SDK) Client

Once a DB2 UDB application has been developed, the DB2 Runtime Client
component must be installed on each workstation executing the application.
Fig. 1–3 shows the relationship between the application, the DB2 Runtime Client,
and the DB2 UDB Server. If the application and database are installed on the same
system, the application is known as a *local client*. If the application is installed on a
system other than the DB2 UDB Server, the application is known as a *remote
client*.

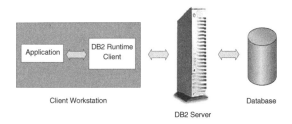

Client Workstation   Database

DB2 Server

Fig. 1–3 *Application, Client, and Server Relationships*

The Runtime Client provides functions other than the ability to communicate with
a DB2 UDB Server or DB2 Connect Server machine. For example, you can do any
of the following:

- Issue an interactive SQL statement on a remote client to access data on a DB2
  UDB Server.
- Run applications that were developed to comply with the Open Database
  Connectivity (ODBC) standard.
- Run applications that were developed to comply with the OLE DB interface.
- Run Java applications that access and manipulate data in DB2 UDB databases
  using Java Database Connectivity (JDBC).

If you need to graphically administer and monitor a DB2 UDB Server, then you
should install the DB2 Administration Client. It includes all the graphical DB2
UDB administration tools in addition to all of the functionality of the DB2 Runtime
Client.

 Note: The native OLE DB Provider for DB2 UDB is supported from
Version 7.1. For DB2 UDB Version 6.1, you should use the OLE
DB-ODBC Bridge provider for applications using OLE DB interface.

DB2 Software Developer's Kit (SDK) Client

To develop DB2 UDB applications, you must install the DB2 Software
Developer's Kit (SDK) Client and configure that client to access a DB2 UDB
Server either remotely or locally. The SDK Client contains the Software
Developer's Kit (SDK), which is a collection of developer's tools that are designed
to meet the needs of database application developers. It includes the necessary
programming libraries, header files, code samples and precompilers for the
supported programming languages. Several programming languages, including
COBOL, FORTRAN, C, C++, and Java are supported by DB2 UDB. The compiler
for these programming languages needs to be installed in addition to the SDK. The
DB2 SDK Client includes all of the graphical DB2 UDB administration tools and
the DB2 Runtime Client functionality.

> **Note:** The DB2 Software Developer's Kits (SDKs) for a specific
> platform are also included with each DB2 UDB Server package (DB2
> Personal Edition, Workgroup Edition, Enterprise Edition, and Enterprise-
> Extended Edition). When you install the server product, you can also
> install the DB2 Software Developer's Kit for that platform.

There are no licensing requirements to install the DB2 Runtime, DB2
Administration or DB2 SDK Client components. Licensing is controlled at the
DB2 UDB Server.

The DB2 client product that you install is dependent on your requirements and the
operating system on the client machine. For example, if you have a database
application developed for AIX, and you do not require the DB2 UDB
administration or application development tools, you should install the DB2
Runtime Client for AIX.

DB2 Universal Database V7.1 client support includes: Windows NT, Windows
2000, Windows 95, Windows 98, OS/2, Linux, AIX, HP-UX, Solaris, SGI-IRIX,
SCO UnixWare 7, and PTX.

DB2 UDB GUI Tools

DB2 UDB Servers and DB2 Administration Clients provide GUI tools which allow
you to administer your databases, manipulate and access data, and perform various
complex tasks easily. You can start the GUI tools on the DB2 UDB Server machine
and administer the database locally. You can also start the GUI tools on the DB2
Client or other DB2 Servers and administer databases remotely.

The Control Center

The Control Center is the central point of administration for DB2 UDB. The Control Center provides the user with the tools necessary to perform typical database administration tasks. It allows easy access to other server administration tools, gives a clear overview of the entire system, enables remote database management and provides step-by-step assistance for complex tasks. Even if you are a DB2 application developer and not a database administrator, you can use the Control Center to see database object names, the contents of the database, and so on. Fig. 1–4 is an example of the information available from the Control Center.

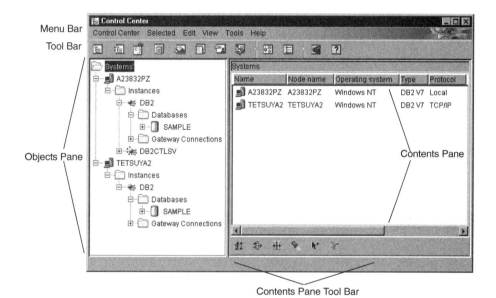

Fig. 1–4 *DB2 UDB Control Center*

The Systems object represents both local and remote machines. To display all the DB2 UDB systems that your system has cataloged, expand the object tree by clicking on the plus sign (+) next to **Systems**. The left portion of the screen lists available DB2 UDB systems (local and remote). We can see from the figure that the system A23832PZ contains a DB2 UDB instance, DB2, in which the database SAMPLE is located. When **Systems** is highlighted, details about each system is shown in the Contents Pane. We can see that A23832PZ is a Windows NT system. The other system that is shown is a remote Windows NT system.

The main components of the Control Center are listed below:

- Menu Bar - Used to access Control Center functions and on-line help.
- Tool Bar - Used to access the other administration tools.
- Objects Pane - Shown on the left-hand side of the Control Center window, and contains all the objects that can be managed from the Control Center, as well as their relationship to each other.
- Contents Pane - Shown on the right-hand side of the Control Center window, and contains the objects that belong or correspond to the object selected on the Objects Pane.
- Contents Pane Toolbar - Contains icons which are used to tailor the view of the objects and information in the Contents pane. These functions can also be selected in the View menu.

Hover Help is also available in the Control Center, providing a short description for each icon on the tool bar as you move the mouse pointer over the icon.

Other Tools Available from the Control Center

By using the Control Center Tool Bar, you can access other administration tools to help you manage and administer databases in your environment:

- **Satellite Administration Center** - Used to manage the satellite environment.
- **Command Center** - Provides an interactive window allowing input of SQL statements or DB2 UDB commands, viewing of execution results, and an explanation of the information. The graphical command utility is the preferred method for text commands, as it provides enormous flexibility and function and interacts with the Script Center.
- **Script Center** - Used to create, schedule and manage scripts that can contain SQL statements, DB2 UDB commands, or operating systems commands.
- **Alert Center** - Used to view performance variables that have reached a threshold. Use the Alert Center to work with alerts generated by DB2 UDB, for example.
- **Journal** - Keeps a record of all script invocations, all DB2 UDB messages, and the DB2 UDB recovery history file for a database. It is used to show the results of a job or the contents of a script, and also to enable or disable a job.
- **License Center** - Used to manage licenses and check how many connections are used.
- **Tools Settings** - Allows you to configure the DB2 UDB graphical tools and some of their options.
- **Information Center** - Provides the user with quick access to the DB2 UDB product documentation. Information is available about common tasks, problem determination, DB2 UDB on-line manuals, and the sample programs provided with DB2 UDB.

The graphical tool set provided with DB2 UDB is full functioned and very powerful, allowing you to administer and access your DB2 UDB system from graphical interfaces. We urge you to investigate all the facets of the DB2 UDB graphical tools to see how beneficial they can be to your environment and to understand all that they can do for you.

The SmartGuides

SmartGuides are tutors that help you to create objects and perform other database operations. Each SmartGuide has detailed information available to help the user. The DB2 UDB SmartGuides are integrated into the administration tools, and assist you in completing administration tasks. For example, the Add Database SmartGuide is used to set up communications on a DB2 client to a database on a DB2 UDB Server and is invoked from the Client Configuration Assistant (CCA).

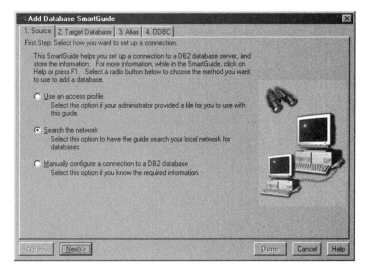

Fig. 1–5 *Client Configuration Assistant - Add Database SmartGuide*

Fig. 1–5 shows that there are a number of ways to add a remote database. You don't have to know the syntax of commands, or even the location of the remote database server. One option searches the network, looking for valid DB2 UDB Servers.

Other DB2 UDB SmartGuides provided for your use include:

- Backup Database
- Configure Multi-Site Update
- Create Database
- Create Table
- Create Table Space
- Create Index
- Restore Database
- Performance Configuration

DB2 Stored Procedure Builder

DB2 Stored Procedure Builder (SPB) is a graphical application that supports the rapid development of DB2 stored procedures. Using SPB, you can create and build stored procedures on local and remote DB2 servers. SPB also allows you to modify and rebuild existing stored procedures, and run stored procedures for testing and debugging the execution of installed stored procedures. From a single development environment that SPB provides for you, you can build stored procedures for the entire DB2 family, ranging from the workstation to System/390. Fig. 1–6 shows you an example of Java stored procedure code generated by SPB. You can then build, register and test the stored procedure. We will discuss SPB in detail in Chapter 4.

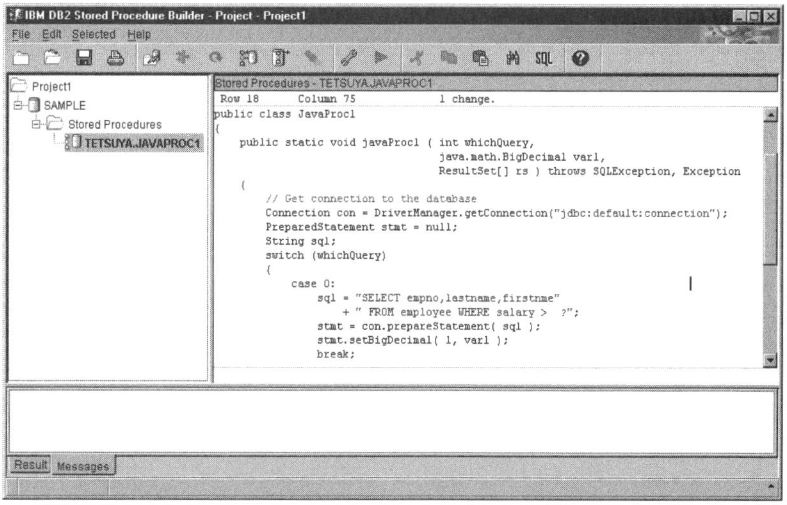

Fig. 1–6 *Stored Procedure Builder*

Microsoft Universal Data Access and DB2 UDB

We have been discussing DB2 UDB, which is IBM's relational database product with high scalability, and the ability to store all kinds of electronic information. This can be called the 'universal database' strategy.

Microsoft advocates a Universal Data Access (UDA) architecture as a strategy for providing access to data. In UDA, any client should be able to use data regardless of where and how it is stored rather than storing all data in the 'universal' database. Data can be retrieved from spreadsheets and e-mail applications, and also from database servers. This is a different approach from using database servers which contain the business logic and centralize all data access via one interface, and one point of control.

Microsoft's UDA is included in the Microsoft Windows Distributed interNet Application (DNA) architecture, which is the application framework describing how to build distributed applications for the Windows platform based on Web servers and Web browsers.

Windows DNA is based on the concept that distributed applications should be logically separated into three tiers. That makes the application easier to manage and update. Those three tiers are:

- Presentation (or user interface) tier service
- Business logic tier service
- Data tier service

For the data service tier, Microsoft's Universal Data Access (UDA) architecture is used. As already introduced, UDA provides access to a variety of information sources, including relational and non-relational data.

Developers can take advantage of UDA through the Microsoft Data Access Components (MDAC), which is a set of redistributable technologies. MDAC consists of OLE DB, ActiveX Data Objects (ADO), and Open Database Connectivity (ODBC), and can be downloaded from the following Web site:

```
http://www.microsoft.com/data/
```

OLE DB

In the UDA architecture, any client should be able to use data regardless of where and how it is stored. Data can be retrieved from spreadsheets, e-mail, and an SQL database. This can be done without independent APIs or tools for the particular data source. OLE DB is designed to provide a common API that can be used to present data to an OLE DB data consumer (an application). At the data source side, the OLE DB provider should manipulate a particular type of data and expose data to the OLE DB consumer in a tabular format.

An OLE DB provider for each data source should be implemented by vendors; therefore, programmers don't need to implement that part. What programmers need to do is learn OLE DB and write their programs as OLE DB consumers. By directing OLE DB to use a particular OLE DB provider and then issuing retrieval commands, you can get the data into a format that is easy to use in an application. Even if a DBMS does not have the same capability as an OLE DB data provider, Microsoft provides an OLE DB-ODBC bridge so that applications can access that database using the OLE DB interface.

ActiveX Data Objects (ADO)

Though OLE DB implements Universal Data Access, you need to write a C++ program to use the OLE DB interface. As all Windows application programmers don't work with C++ but may use Visual Basic or other high-level languages, Microsoft thought there should be a higher level programming interface, and then introduced a component-based architecture to provide an easy-to-use interface to OLE DB. This is called ActiveX Data Objects (ADO). ADO is a set of Component Object Model (COM) objects that are readily usable from Windows programming languages, and which provides a lightweight, high level of performance.

As shown in Fig. 1–7, any data can be accessed though the OLE DB interface as long as the data source can perform as an OLE DB provider, and an application can use the OLE DB interface or the higher level programming interface, ADO. Note: ADO will be explained in detail in Chapter 3.

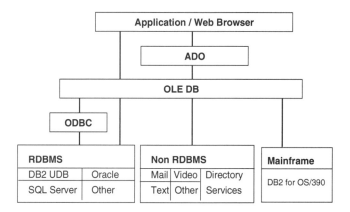

Fig. 1–7 *Universal Data Access Architecture*

Universal Access of DB2 UDB

If your system is critical and high performance is required, consolidating your data into the DBMS is better than directly accessing distributed data in a different data store. Using a DBMS provides you good performance with effective data management such as indexing or prefetching. You can also ensure the integrity of the data and ensure that the data conforms to your business rules, since data access and manipulation is done through the DBMS.

This approach usually brings good results. But in some cases, you might want to leave your data in the original source. One reason is the maintenance cost of moving data. To consolidate your data into the DBMS, you are required to move the data into the DBMS from the original data source. If easy maintenance is required rather than the highest performance, or if you have various data sources and want to use them casually, leaving them in the original data source and accessing them through the OLE DB interface can be the choice as long as the data source can be an OLE DB data provider.

DB2 UDB has the ability to access OLE DB data providers. You can define OLE DB table functions to access them as if they are local read-only DB2 tables. You don't need to change the configuration between the DB2 Client and Server. Instead, you need to define an OLE DB table function at the DB2 UDB Server using the CREATE FUNCTION statement. When you define an OLE DB table function, you can specify the cardinality, which is an estimate of the expected number of rows to be returned by the function. The DB2 optimizer uses this value to find the best access path. OLE DB table functions will be explained in Chapter 4.

Even DB2 UDB itself can be accessed through the OLE DB interface, since DB2 UDB Version 7.1 supplies a native OLE DB provider for DB2 UDB. For DB2 UDB Version 6.1 or the prior releases, an OLE DB (or ADO) application can access a database through the OLE DB-ODBC bridge which Microsoft provides.

If you install DB2 DataJoiner, it provides the ability to view popular relational data sources (DB2 Family, Informix, SQL Server, Oracle, Sybase, Teradata, and others) and non-relational data sources (IMS and VSAM) as if they were local data.

DB2 UDB is not only a *universal database* which can store many types of data, but it also has the ability of *universal access*. Regardless of where and how the data is stored, DB2 UDB can access it in the same manner as a local DB2 table using OLE DB table functions or DB2 DataJoiner.

It is likely that storing all data in DB2 UDB databases will result in good performance; however, even if your data is distributed into other OLE DB providers, you can expect the DB2 optimizer to find the best access path, since the data is regarded as DB2 tables.

Microsoft Visual Studio

Visual Studio Version 6.0 provides a suite of tools that addresses all aspects of Windows DNA application development. Visual Studio includes the following as core development tools:

- Visual Basic 6.0

  A popular tool for building application programs for accessing both local and remote databases, on the Windows operating system platforms.
- Visual C++ 6.0

  A popular C++ tool for creating high performance applications on the Windows operating system platforms.
- Visual J++ 6.0

  A development tool which provides the Microsoft Virtual Machine. Developers can use Windows Foundation Classes for Java (WFC) and make the Microsoft Win32 API encapsulated (applications using WFC are not 100% pure Java).

- Visual InterDev 6.0

  A Web application development tool. Web application can be based on HTML, Script, and components written in any languages.

All visual tools in the Visual Studio support the Component Object Model (COM). This means you can create a component in any of these tools, and can reuse it in any other tool. Some examples of building applications in Visual Basic will be given in Chapter 5.

Add-In Tools

Microsoft Visual Studio has an add-in concept which allows third party software houses to produce both improvements to the development interface, and additional types of components for users to add to their toolbox.

DB2 UDB provides a collection of add-ins to simplify the building and deployment of DB2 applications from within the Microsoft Visual Studio integrated development environment (IDE). These include:

- DB2 UDB Tools Add-In for Visual C++
- DB2 UDB Project Add-In for Visual C++
- DB2 Stored Procedure Builder Add-In for Visual Basic and Visual C++

Fig. 1–8 shows the Microsoft Visual C++ IDE, including the three DB2 UDB Add-In tool bars.

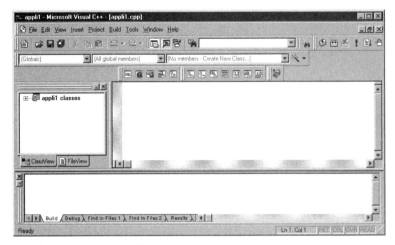

Fig. 1–8 *DB2 UDB Add-Ins*

The DB2 UDB Tools Add-In for Visual C++ is a tool bar that enables the launch of some of the DB2 administration and development tools from within the Visual C++ integrated development environment (IDE). The supported DB2 graphical tools include:

- **SQL Statement Assistant** - Launches DB2 SQL Assist wizard to build/generate SQL statements.
- **Information Center** - Launches the DB2 Information Center to access the DB2 on-line help library.
- **Context Sensitive SQL Help** - Launches the Web browser with the appropriate DB2 SQL help for the currently highlighted text.
- **Client Configuration Assistant** - Launches the Client Configuration Assistant to manage DB2 clients (see "The SmartGuides" on page 11).
- **Control Center** - Launches DB2 Control Center to administer instances and databases (see "The Control Center" on page 9).

The DB2 UDB Project Add-In for Visual C++ is a collection of management tools and wizards that plug into the Visual C++ component of the Visual Studio integrated development environment (IDE) to automate and simplify the various tasks of developing applications for DB2 using embedded SQL. The Project Add-In may be used to develop, package, and deploy:

- One or more stored procedures written in C/C++ for a DB2 UDB Server on a Windows 32-bit operating system
- Windows 32-bit C/C++ embedded SQL client applications accessing the DB2 family of servers
- Windows 32-bit C/C++ client applications that invoke stored procedures defined in the DB2 family of servers using C/C++ function call wrappers

Some of the Project Add-In development tasks may include:

- Generating skeletal embedded SQL modules
- Generating sample SQL code
- Using the SQL Assistant to generate live insertable SQL statements
- Automatically pre-compiling embedded SQL C/C++ modules to C/C++ modules
- Managing pre-compiler options of embedded SQL modules
- Generating native code function wrappers for imported (called) stored procedures
- Generating skeletal embedded SQL code for exported (built) stored procedures
- Automatically defining the exported stored procedures into the database using generated DDL
- Packaging the DB2 components of the application for deployment
- Deploying the packaged DB2 components of the application to production systems and databases

The goal of the DB2 Project Add-In is to allow developers to focus on the design and logic of their DB2 applications rather than the actual building and deployment, while using the Visual C++ integrated development environment. We will discuss the application development using these add-ins in detail in Chapter 6.

As described in "DB2 Stored Procedure Builder" on page 12, the DB2 Stored Procedure Builder provides an easy-to-use development environment for creating, installing, and testing stored procedures, allowing you to focus on creating your stored procedure logic rather than the details of registering, building, and installing stored procedures on a DB2 UDB Server. The DB2 Stored Procedure Builder can be started from the Start menu, and also can be an add-in for Visual Studio. You can launch the DB2 Stored Procedure Builder from within the Visual Studio integrated development environment (IDE).

Overview

Using Microsoft Technology

Since DB2 UDB can be accessed through the OLE DB interface, you can develop Windows DNA applications using Visual Studio for DB2 UDB without any unique techniques. As for other OLE DB data providers such as Microsoft Access or Microsoft SQL Server, you can write programs with ADO to access DB2 UDB using the language you are familiar with, such as Visual Basic or Visual C++. You need to specify DB2 UDB as a property of the ADO connection object in the code. In Chapter 5, the BookSale sample application that the MSDN library supplies is used to demonstrate that DB2 UDB works well when accessed using ADO.

Fig. 1–9 shows how DB2 UDB works in the Microsoft framework. You can use Visual Studio to build COM/COM+ components that access DB2 UDB using ADO, and deploy and manage them using Microsoft Transaction Server (MTS). You can set up a Web server with Internet Information Server (IIS) and create Active Server Pages (ASP) to run dynamic and interactive Web applications.

The model of the application or the method of the application development is basically same whether the data source is DB2 UDB or another OLE DB provider. You should use ADO as the interface to the data source. Chapter 7 and Chapter 8 will show you that DB2 UDB works well with Microsoft products such as MTS or IIS.

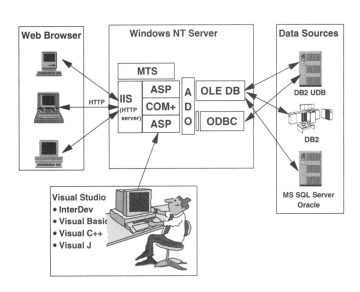

Fig. 1–9 *Building DB2 Applications using Microsoft Technology*

Now we understand that DB2 UDB works as well as other OLE DB providers in the Microsoft application development framework. So, what is the advantage in using DB2 UDB? If you use DB2 UDB as a data source for your application, you get various benefits, including:

- **High scalability**

  You can select from the various supported platforms for DB2 UDB, from the Intel based desktop to higher-end UNIX platforms such as the RS/6000 SP. You may move from the lower-end platform to the higher-end platform, or add new hardware resources such as a new node of the RS/6000 SP, without necessarily modifying your application; the database manager has not changed, but has grown with you and your application requirements.

- **Server-side features**

  DB2 UDB provides many server-side features such as Constraints, UDTs, UDFs, or Triggers. These server-side features can make the programming simpler and improve the performance of the applications. Server-side features of DB2 UDB will be introduced in Chapter 4.

- **Global optimization**

  Based on the statistical information of each table and index, the DB2 optimizer finds the best access path for the submitted query. Even if the data is not in the DB2 database, it acts as a DB2 table, and the DB2 optimizer can handle it. You can get a significant performance gain, particularly for large scale data and complex queries.

2

Set Up Application Development Environment

+ INSTALL PRODUCT

+ CREATE SAMPLE DATABASE

+ MICROSOFT DATA ACCESS COMPONENTS

+ SET UP CONNECTIONS

+ DB2LOOK UTILITY

*T*his chapter deals with installing DB2 UDB and the setting up of connections to local and remote databases. These are the steps that are required before you can create a DB2 UDB database and access the database using the development tools in Visual Studio. There are a number of different packages for DB2, from simple clients up to the Enterprise-Extended Edition. Our description will use the Enterprise Edition.

This book is intended for application developers, so it is not intended to cover all the aspects of installation, as these are the responsibility of database administrators. This chapter is intended to allow a developer to get his environment set up and working as quickly as possible.

Once the DB2 UDB products have been installed, the Sample database is created so that the developer can use the example code which has been provided, and which is mostly based on this database.

Then, Microsoft's Visual Studio, Data Access Components, and Component Checker Tool are discussed, followed by an explanation of how to set up ODBC connections to both local and remote databases.

Installing the DB2 UDB Product

This section describes the installation of DB2 Universal Database V7.1 on Windows NT version 4. DB2 UDB can also be installed on Windows 2000 or Windows 95/98, but obviously, Windows 95/98 would be for database clients or the Personal Edition product.

The installation process detects the active communication protocols on your system and configures them to work with DB2 UDB. Two instances are created when DB2 UDB is installed. A global instance called the DB2 Administration Server (DAS) instance is created. The DAS instance is used by the DB2 UDB administration tools, including the Control Center and the Client Configuration Assistant, to satisfy the requests. The second instance, called DB2, is used to create and manage user databases.

Note: You can get a 60-day trial code of the DB2 UDB Enterprise Edition and Personal Edition on a free CD-ROM from the IBM Data Management Web site. Go to the following Web site:

```
http://www-4.ibm.com/software/data/db2/udb/
downloads.html
```

You can also download a free copy of DB2 UDB Personal Developer's Edition from the same site.

Installing on Windows NT

This section discusses installing DB2 UDB Enterprise Edition on Windows NT. Even if you choose to install a free copy of DB2 UDB Personal Developer's Edition, the steps are basically the same.

Before beginning the installation on a Windows NT machine, make sure that the user account that will be used to perform the installation is:

- Defined on the local machine
- A member of the Local Administrator's group
- Given the *Act as part of the operating system* advanced user right

To install, insert the CD-ROM into the drive. The auto-run feature automatically starts the setup program. The setup program will determine the system language and launch the setup program for that language. If the setup program failed to auto-start, execute the following command from an operating system window:

```
x:\setup.exe
```

x represents the CD-ROM drive.

Fig. 2–1 *DB2 UDB Welcome Screen for Windows NT Installation*

Fig. 2–1 shows the Welcome window. Click on **Next** to continue.

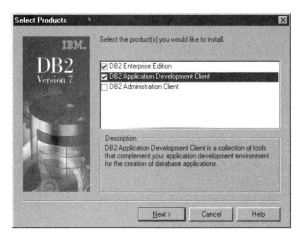

Fig. 2–2 *DB2 UDB Product Selection Screen for Windows NT*

Fig. 2–2 shows you the products you can install. The example used is the Enterprise Edition. For development purposes, select both the DB2 Enterprise Edition and the DB2 Application Development Client.

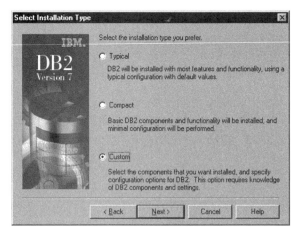

Fig. 2–3 *Windows NT Selection Screen for Installation Type*

There are three types of installation, as shown in Fig. 2–3:

- **Typical** installs those DB2 UDB components that are used most often, including all required components, ODBC support, documentation, and commonly-used DB2 UDB tools such as the Control Center, Client Configuration Assistant, the Information Center, and more. The DAS instance and the DB2 instance are created during this install.
- **Compact** installs only the required DB2 UDB components and ODBC support. The DAS instance and DB2 instance are also created.
- **Custom** installs only the components that you select. You are given the option of when to start the DAS and DB2 instances as part of the Custom installation process.

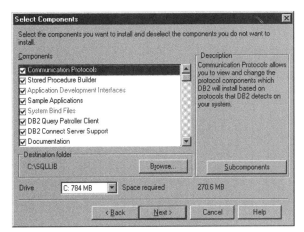

Fig. 2–4 *DB2 UDB Component Screen*

Fig. 2–4 illustrates some of the choices available with a custom install. Notice that the amount of disk required for this installation (270 MB) is given. You can also see the amount of space that is available on the drive. The products will be installed in the `C:\Program Files\SQLLIB` directory. You can change the drive and the install directory from this window. Highlight a component and click **Details** to select subcomponents. Our example is Communication Protocols.

Fig. 2–5 *DB2 UDB Subcomponents*

Fig. 2–5 shows the available subcomponents and disk requirements for the selected installation. Notice that once an item is selected, a description of that item is provided. Click **Continue** to go back to the previous window (Fig. 2–4) and, then, by clicking on **Next**; the following window appears:

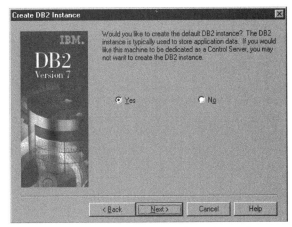

Fig. 2–6 *Select If Instance Should Be Created*

The screen shown in Fig. 2–6 is only required when a Control Server option is involved. A Control Server is used to manage mobile workstations on which DB2 UDB Satellite Editions work. If the current installation is a dedicated Control Server, then it will not contain user databases, and therefore will not require a user instance to be created. However, because you will be using it for development, you should select that a DB2 instance is required, so that you can create local databases to work with.

Set Up Application Development Environment

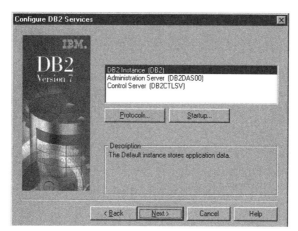

Fig. 2–7 *Configure DB2 UDB Services*

Fig. 2–7 shows instances that are being created, a DB2 instance for managing databases, the DB2 Administration Server instance (DAS) and the Control Server instance. The setup program customizes DB2 UDB to use the communication protocols detected on your system. Highlight the DB2 Instance and Click **Protocols**; the following window appears:

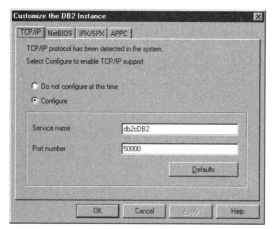

Fig. 2–8 *DB2 UDB Instance Protocols Configuration (TCP/IP)*

The DB2 UDB installation utility examines your system to see what communication protocols are installed and configured to use with the DB2 instance and the DAS. If you select Typical or Compact install (Fig. 2–3 on page 26), communication protocol configuration is done automatically. The Custom install option allows you to explicitly configure communication protocols. Fig. 2–8 shows that TCP/IP has been detected. The values shown in Fig. 2–8 will be used for TCP/IP settings with the DB2 instance, unless changed at this time. Click OK to go back to the previous window (Fig. 2–7). Now you can customize the communication protocols for the DAS instance.

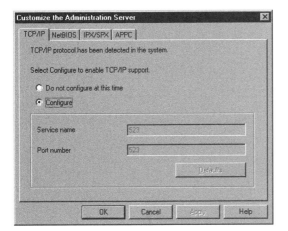

Fig. 2–9 *Administration Server Protocols Configuration (TCP/IP)*

The protocol configuration for the DAS instance is similar to that of the DB2 instance. Notice that the same protocols were detected on your system. Changes can be made at this time. However, notice that TCP/IP settings for the DAS instance cannot be altered. These are indicated by the gray-shaded areas in the communication-specific windows (Fig. 2–9). You are not allowed to change the port number for TCP/IP or the socket number for IPX/SPX for the DAS instance, since these values are reserved within DB2 UDB.

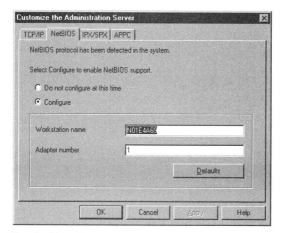

Fig. 2–10 *Administration Server Protocols Configuration (NetBIOS)*

Notice that you can change the communication settings for NetBIOS (Fig. 2–10).

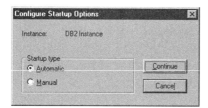

Fig. 2–11 *Select Start Options (DB2 Instance)*

Clicking **Startup** on the Configure DB2 Services window (Fig. 2–7 on page 30) brings up the window shown in Fig. 2–11. By default, the DB2 instance will be automatically started when your server boots. You can choose to have the DB2 UDB instance started automatically or not. You can also change these start options after DB2 UDB has been installed.

Fig. 2–12 *Select Start Options (Administration Server Instance)*

Fig. 2–12 shows the start option for the DAS instance. Notice that you are not allowed to change the start option for the DAS instance. You may change these start options after DB2 UDB has been installed.

Set Up Application Development Environment

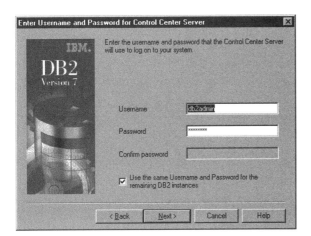

Fig. 2–13 *Username and Password for the Control Center Server*

After setting up communication for the DAS and DB2 instances, the Control Center Server logon screen appears (Fig. 2–13). From here, you can change the default username and password used by the DAS instance. The username you specify here must conform to DB2 UDB's naming rules (20 characters or less, and so on). See the manual *DB2 UDB Quick Beginnings Guide* for more information about the naming rules. If you want to specify an existing user account, it must:

- Be defined on the local machine
- Belong to the Local Administrator's group
- Have the *Act as part of the operating system* advanced user right

Note: All DB2 UDB manuals including *DB2 UDB Quick Beginnings Guide* are available in the DB2 Product and Service Technical Library at the following URL:

    http://www-4.ibm.com/software/data/db2/library

The manual *DB2 UDB Quick Beginnings Guide* is also included in the install CD-ROM.

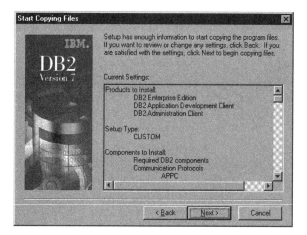

Fig. 2–14 *DB2 UDB Component Summary*

Once you have entered values for username and password, the installation utility displays a summary report (Fig. 2–14). The summary report shows the selections that you have made. After viewing your choices, you can continue with the installation or make changes. The DB2 UDB products are then installed on your system. When the installation of the DB2 UDB product is completed, DB2 UDB is ready to use without rebooting your system. Upon completion, the First Steps screen appears. How to use the First Steps will be discussed in the section "Using First Steps" on page 37.

DB2 Instance Considerations on Windows NT

Installing DB2 UDB for Windows NT creates a default instance called DB2. The DB2 instance is defined as a Windows NT service. Therefore, the DB2 instance name must adhere to any naming rules for Windows NT services. The DAS instance is defined as a Windows NT service as well. Another service created during installation is called the *DB2 Security Server*. When the authentication type is set to CLIENT, and TRUST_CLNTAUTH is set to CLIENT, and you specify a user ID/password on the connect, the DB2 security server needs to be started on the client machine. You can configure these services to start automatically. Click the **Services** icon located in the Windows NT Control Panel to verify the existence and status of these services.

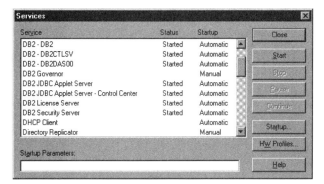

Fig. 2–15 *Windows NT Services*

Fig. 2–15 shows the Control Panel for Windows NT Services. The instance can be started from this control panel or from an operating system window using the command NET START DB2. The DB2 for Windows NT Security service can be started with the command NET START DB2NTSECSERVER. The Administration Server can be started by using NET START DB2DAS00, where DB2DAS00 is the name of the DAS instance.

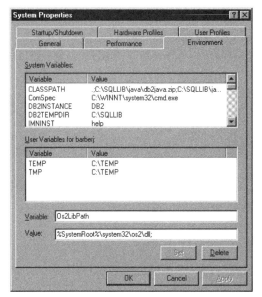

Fig. 2–16 *Environment Variable Screen (Windows NT Only)*

The environment variables are set during installation (Fig. 2–16). To verify these environment variables, examine the System folder of the Program Manager Control Panel.

Starting the DB2 Instance

Now that a DB2 instance has been created, you must initialize or start the instance. The process of starting an instance is similar to starting a network file server; until the instance is started, the clients will not be able to access the databases on the server.

The command to start a DB2 instance is called db2start. This command will allocate all of the required DB2 UDB resources on the server. These resources include memory and communications support.

```
db2start
SQL1064N DB2START processing was successful.
```

On Windows NT, you may also start an instance with the command:

```
net start instance_name
```

Stopping the DB2 Instance

The command to stop the current database manager instance is `db2stop`. Messages are sent to standard output indicating the success or failure of the `db2stop` command.

```
DB2STOP
SQL1064N DB2STOP processing was successful.
```

On Windows NT, you may also stop an instance with the command:

```
net stop instance_name
```

Creating the Sample Database

The Sample database can be created using the command line or using the First Steps application which was installed with DB2 UDB. The following description uses First Steps.

Using First Steps

First Steps is a graphical tool that helps you get started using DB2 UDB. On Windows NT, for instance, one of the options is to create the Sample database. Click on **Start** and select **Programs** → **IBM DB2** → **First Steps**. This will bring up the First Steps main screen.

In DB2 8.1 click Start and select Programs →IBM DB2 → Set-up tools → First Steps

Set Up Application
Development
Environment

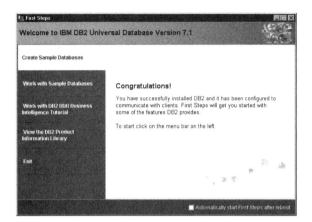

Fig. 2–17 *First Steps Main Menu*

First Steps has a number of options; all are available by clicking on the icon next to the action (Fig. 2–17). You can:

- Create the Sample database.
- Work with the contents of the Sample database. This starts the Control Center which is a graphical tool which enables you to carry out administrative tasks on the databases.
- Work with the DB2 UDB Business Intelligence Tutorial.
- View the DB2 product information library. This is helpful in finding out what DB2 UDB information is available on-line and how it is organized.

Click on **Create the Sample database**. While the Sample database is being created, the program will display a progress indicator. When it has finished, it will display a message to confirm this.

Click on **Work with Sample Database**. This will bring up the Control Center.

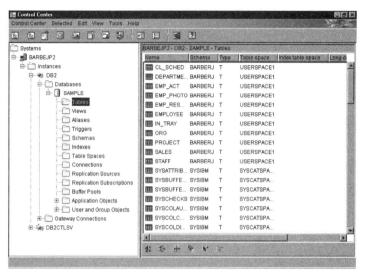

Fig. 2–18 *Control Center*

Fig. 2–18 shows you a list of tables defined in the Sample database. If you want to see some of the contents of each table, click the right mouse button on one of the tables, it will bring a pop-up menu; then select **Sample Contents**.

On Windows NT, the Control Center can also be started by entering the db2cc command at a command prompt or clicking on **Start** and selecting **Programs →** **IBM DB2 → Control Center**.

Once First Steps has finished creating the Sample database, another graphical tool, the Command Center, can be used to connect to the database or issue other DB2 UDB commands and SQL statements. To start the Command Center, click the Command Center icon on the toolbar from the Control Center.

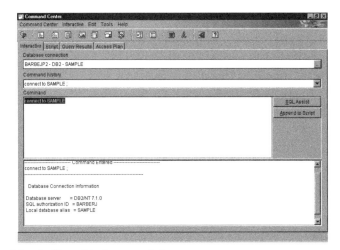

Fig. 2–19 *DB2 Command Center*

Fig. 2–19 shows the DB2 Command Center window. To execute commands or statements, the Script tab must be selected. The Result window is automatically brought to the foreground once the execution of statements entered in the Script window is started. By clicking on the Result tab, you can go to this window at any time.

Additional important and useful features of the DB2 Command Center include:

- The ability to import previously created scripts
- The ability to save entered text as a script for later execution and scheduling
- The ability to schedule a script created (via the DB2 Journal)
- Viewing the explain information for a statement through the Access Plan window

The Command Center is a useful place to experiment with queries and Stored Procedure calls before including them in your programs.

Microsoft Programming Tools

Microsoft supplies several programming tools and utilities to build applications for the 32 bit Windows environment. They have bundled these into a product which they have called Visual Studio. There are two versions of Visual Studio, Professional and Enterprise. It is important to understand that all the programming tools are common to both versions of Visual Studio. You may therefore use either version, in conjunction with the example programs described in this book. The additional components in the Enterprise package are versions of Microsoft's Back Office suite, for example, SQLServer and Exchange Server plus the Windows NT Option Pack. These components are not required for this book, apart from the Option Pack, which is separately downloadable from Microsoft's Web site. The Enterprise version also contains the Source Safe versioning tool for team programming. The Microsoft tools which are illustrated in this book are :

- Visual Basic
- Visual C++
- Interdev

The most popular of these tools is Visual Basic. This is designed to be a Rapid Application Development environment, and a compatible version of this language is also present in the Microsoft Office components, Access, Excel, and Word. A script version of this language is also available in other products; most notable is its use in Active Server Pages, which is currently Microsoft's method of producing dynamic Web pages in their Web server, IIS Server. The tool for creating and debugging Web applications, based on Active Server Pages, is Interdev.

Database access for the tools in both Visual Studio and Visual Basic for Applications in the Office suite, is provided by the Microsoft Data Access Components which are described below. To use the ActiveX Data Objects from MDAC requires the addition of Microsoft ActiveX Data Objects 2.X library to the project references. Please note that the References option is not available on the Office suite menu bar unless you are in the programming environment, for the particular application that you are using.

Microsoft Data Access Components

The operation of ODBC, OLE DB, and ADO is provided by a set of DLLs and other support files, which Microsoft has collected together as an entity called Microsoft Data Access Components. This is freely distributable, and many databases and database access software packages incorporate it in their installations. This includes Microsoft products, such as Visual Studio, MS Office, SQLServer, and Internet Explorer. It also includes third-party products such as IBM AS/400 Client Access.

Set Up Application
Development
Environment

This proliferation of products can result in compatibility problems. Different software packages are issued at different times, and consequently can contain different versions of MDAC. Although Service Packs for these products will probably contain updates for MDAC, it still does not guarantee that you will get the latest version.

If you have installed different software packages which contain MDAC (and with many users installing both Microsoft Office and Internet Explorer, this will probably be the case), then the order in which the packages are installed could affect the behavior of data access.

Microsoft has attempted to deal with such problems by making the latest version of MDAC available on their Universal Data Access site:

http://www.microsoft.com/data/

They have also released a tool that is available from the same site. This tool, called Component Checker, will analyze the MDAC installation and permit you to replace a back-level or faulty installation.

The MDAC downloaded file is a self-extracting installation file called MDAC_TYP.EXE. When run, it will install and register all of the components. However, this can produce another problem. If installing over a previous version, it will not overwrite files which are in use. This will also be the case if you install a software package which contains MDAC. You will therefore have an inconsistent and consequently faulty installation. This may not be immediately obvious, but you will probably get some odd results when running or developing data applications. The component checker is designed to reveal and deal with such problems.

The component checker file will download as CC.EXE. When run on your machine it will create a directory called COMCHECK on the C: drive and install the COMCHECK.EXE program and support files. The directory contains a ReadMe.txt file, and the program has built-in help. This information will detail how to use the program to solve any problems that you may have.

Essentially, the program allows you to analyze your MDAC installation and determine the most probable release that you have installed, by comparison with its built-in list of file versions and sizes for the releases that it knows about. Consequently, you should always download the latest version of ComCheck before use.

Running the program from the command line, with the appropriate switches, will enable the program to remove your current MDAC installation and re-install the latest version from the location you give the program. Note that the Component Checker still will not be able to overwrite files in use. However, it does refuse to install, and it will report that files are in use.

The problem of files in use will occur mostly on NT Servers and Workstations which are running services, such as database servers and Web servers. These must be stopped before running the re-install. It is usually best to disable such services and then reboot the machine, to remove any spurious file locks. Remember to make a note of which services you have disabled, so that you can reinstate them.

After a successful re-install of MDAC, run the Component Checker again to ensure that it reports no errors in the files and registry entries.

Setting Up Connections

DB2 UDB databases can be accessed by applications that run on the same machine as the database, or from a remote machine by using a client/server connection (Fig. 2–20). In addition to providing client access to a centralized database running on a server, client/server connections can also be used to perform administrative tasks on the database server by a Database Administrator using a client workstation. If the application development environment has a DB2 UDB database locally, and your application will not access remote DB2 UDB databases, you can skip this section.

There are many methods for setting up connections using the command line, the Control Center, or the Client Configuration Assistant. As developers will normally only require access to a local or remote instance of the current database for which they are developing, we will only demonstrate one of these methods, using the Client Configuration Assistant.

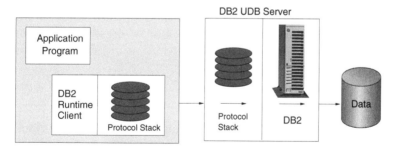

Fig. 2–20 *Remote Client Flow to DB2 UDB Server*

Automated Configuration Using Discovery

DB2 UDB provides a function called *discovery* which is used to gather information from DB2 UDB servers located on the network. This information is then used by the DB2 client to enable it to establish a connection to the DB2 UDB server.

If you use this type of *automated configuration*, you do not need to provide any detailed communications information to enable the DB2 client to contact the DB2 UDB server.

Discovery works in one of two ways:

- *Search discovery* - The DB2 client searches for DB2 UDB servers on the network.
- *Known discovery* - One particular server is queried for information about the instances and databases defined there.

You can use either the Client Configuration Assistant or the Control Center to exploit discovery-based configuration, and this method is normally used to configure small numbers of clients.

Note: The DAS instance must be configured and running on each DB2 UDB server you wish to locate in this manner.

DB2 Discovery

DB2 discovery allows you to automate the configuration of remote clients connecting to DB2 UDB Version 7.1 databases. You can easily catalog a remote database from a client workstation without having to know any detailed communication-specific information. From the client, DB2 discovery requests information from DB2 UDB servers to return to the client issuing the discovery request. A discovery message is sent to the DB2 UDB servers, and if the servers are configured to support the discovery process, data is returned to the client.

The returned data includes:

- A list of instances on the DB2 UDB server that have discovery enabled and information about the protocols that each instance supports for client connection.
- The databases that are defined within the instances and have discovery enabled, including name and description for each available database.

Both the database server and the client have control over DB2 discovery. Using the configuration parameters, the user can control:

- Whether discovery is disabled or enabled, as well as the discovery method that will be used, if it is enabled.
- The protocols that DB2 discovery uses.

- If an instance can be discovered.
- If a database can be discovered.

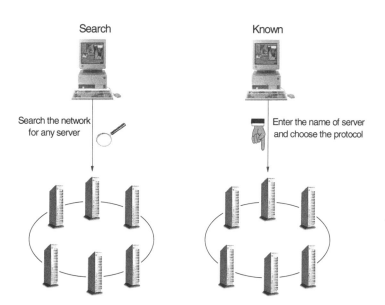

Fig. 2–21 *Discovery Methods*

There are two methods of DB2 discovery, Search and Known (Fig. 2–21).

The Search method searches the network for valid DB2 UDB database servers that a client workstation can access. You do not need to provide specific communication information. The remote client, using the Client Configuration Assistant, searches the network to obtain a list of valid servers.

In the Known discovery method, you must provide some communication-specific information about the server that you want to access. You need to supply:

- A protocol that is configured and running on the Administration Server instance on the server.
- The protocol to be used to connect to the DB2 Administration Server.
- A server name.

Configuring DB2 Clients

DB2 UDB provides several different methods for configuring a remote client that needs to access a DB2 UDB database server. In this section we will go into more details and show some examples of using these methods.

Automated Configuration Using Discovery

You can use the discovery function of DB2 UDB to automate the addition of remote databases. This can be done in one of two ways:

* Enter the name of the machine on the network (for example, the hostname if using TCP/IP) and then use discovery to automatically return the instances and databases on that machine (*Known discovery*).
* Search the network for machines, and then use discovery to automatically return the instances and databases on each machine (*Search discovery*).

You can use either the Client Configuration Assistant (CCA) or the Control Center to perform automated configuration. Let's start with an example of using the CCA to perform known discovery.

Known Discovery Using the CCA

You can access the CCA from the desktop, or from the command line using the db2cca command.

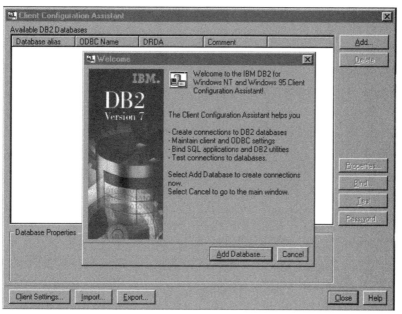

Fig. 2–22 *CCA Welcome Screen*

If no databases are yet cataloged on the client, the Welcome panel is displayed (Fig. 2–22). Otherwise, the databases that are cataloged on your client workstation are displayed under Available DB2 Databases in the main CCA panel. To add another database, click on the **Add** button (or the **Add Database** button from the Welcome panel). The Add Database SmartGuide panel will appear to guide you through the adding of the new database.

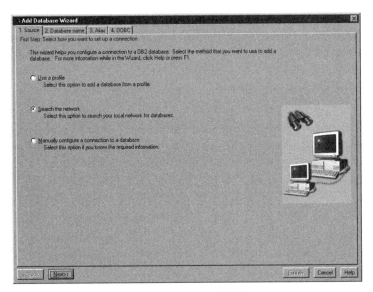

Fig. 2–23 *CCA - Add Database SmartGuide*

Select the **Search the network** radio button (Fig. 2–23). Click on the **Next** push button.

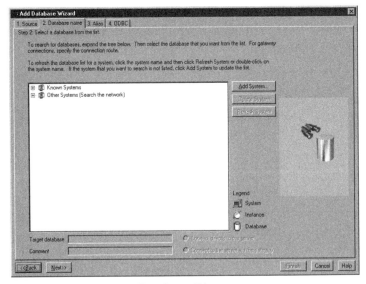

Fig. 2–24 *CCA - Target Database (1)*

You can check if the database server is already known to the client by clicking on the **[+]** next to Known Systems in Fig. 2–24. If it is not, then click on the **Add System** push button. If it is already known, then expand the system until you see the desired database, as shown in Fig. 2–26.

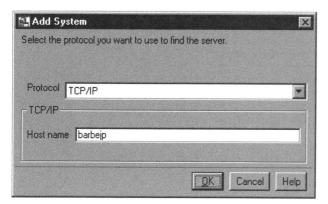

Fig. 2–25 *CCA - Add System*

Choose the protocol in the Add System panel. The contents of the rest of the panel will change according to the protocol you select. Fig. 2–25 shows the panel for TCP/IP. Here are the all the supported protocols together with the parameters for each protocol:

- TCP/IP - Server hostname/IP address, port number
- NetBIOS - Server workstation name, adapter number
- Named Pipe - Server computer name, instance
- IPX/SPX - Server internetwork address, socket number. If using file server addressing, file server name and object name.

You should check that the machine is properly configured on the network before clicking on OK. For example, if using TCP/IP, ping the hostname to check it is available.

  Note: You cannot use Known discovery with the APPC protocol.

If the system is located, then it is displayed under Known Systems, together with all its instances and databases (Fig. 2–26):

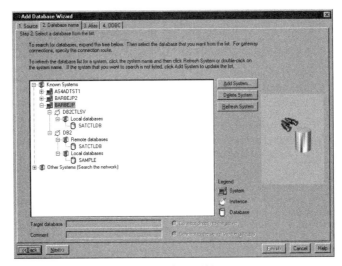

Fig. 2–26 *CCA - Target Database (2)*

Select the database that you wish to connect to. You can select the **Alias** and **ODBC** tabs at the top of the panel (or use the **Next** push button) to specify a database alias name for the database, and/or to select CLI/ODBC options for the database.

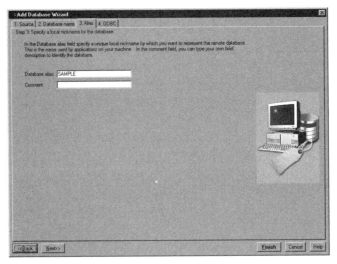

Fig. 2–27 *CCA - Alias for Remote Database*

Choose an alias for the database and optionally add a description (Fig. 2–27).
Click **Next**.

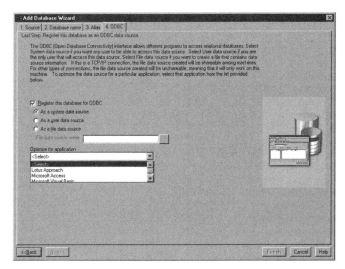

Fig. 2–28 *CCA - ODBC Settings*

You can register the database as an ODBC data source. By default the 'Register this
database for ODBC' check box is checked (Fig. 2–28). You can choose an
application from the 'Optimize for Application' selection box to optimize the
ODBC settings for that application. Click **Done** when finished.

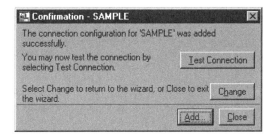

Fig. 2–29 *CCA - Connection Added Successfully*

You can test the connection that has been added by clicking on **Test Connection**
(Fig. 2–29).

Fig. 2–30 *CCA - Test Connection*

Enter the user ID and password to be used when connecting to the remote database (Fig. 2–30). On this panel you can also change the password for the user ID defined at the database server machine. If the connection is successful, you will see a pop-up message similar to this (Fig. 2–31):

Fig. 2–31 *CCA - Test Connection Successful*

Modeling Your Production Database

When you develop application programs, you may wish to have your test system contain a set of your production system's data.

A productivity tool, db2look, is provided that can be run against the production database to generate DDL statements for database data objects, including tables, views, indexes, triggers, and other objects in a database.

When you want to generate DDL statements, the db2look utility should be executed in the extract mode (-e option). The following command generates DDL statements for all database object in the Sample database, and puts them into the `ddlfile.txt` file:

```
db2look -d sample -e -a -o ddlfile.txt
```

Then you can run the command processor script created from the db2look against another database to recreate the database:

```
db2 -tvf ddlfile.txt
```

You can also generate an authorization statement (`GRANT`, `REVOKE`) using the following command:

```
db2look -d sample -e -x -a -o ddlfile.txt
```

Once you have created a test database and loaded a set of your production system's data, you can develop your application programs in that environment; however, if you want to analyze how each SQL statement in your application would be processed (which join strategies, whether indexes are used or not, and so on), you should make the catalog statistics of the test database match those in the production database. This is because if the catalog statistics (such as number of rows, cardinality) are different, different approaches would be taken to process SQL statements.

You can use the db2look utility in the mimic mode (-m option) to meet this requirement. When the db2look utility is executed in the mimic mode, it generates the update statements required to make the catalog statistics of the test database match those in production. You can run the command processor script created from the db2look against another database to update the catalog statistics. The following command generates the update statements for the catalog statistics and saves into the `updatestat.txt` file:

```
db2look -d sample -a -m -o updatestat.txt
```

Set Up Application Development Environment

Note: You can use the -e option with the -m option.

Since the configuration parameters and a series of environment variables also affect how SQL statements would be processed, you should also make the configuration parameters and environment variables for the test system match those of the production system. You can generate the update command and db2set command to update the configuration parameters and environment variables using the following command:

```
db2look -d sample -a -m -f -o updatestat.txt
```

After running the update statements produced by db2look against the test system, the test system can be used to validate the access plans to be generated in production.

For more information on how to use this productivity tool, type the following on a command line:

```
db2look -h
```

The Control Center also provides an interface to the db2look utility called "Generate SQL - Object Name". Using the Control Center allows for the results file from the utility to be integrated into the Script Center. You can also schedule the db2look command from the Control Center.

Summary

In this chapter we have covered the installation of DB2 UDB Version 7 on a developer's workstation. We then created the Sample database to enable access to the application example code. Following the installation and Sample database creation, we explained Microsoft's Data Access Components and the importance of keeping them consistent.

Next, we considered methods of obtaining a connection to a local or remote database. This was discussed at the simplest level, assuming that communications and binding were set up during the database installation phase, and therefore do not need to be taken into account. However, if any problems should occur with getting the connections working, it will become necessary to delve more deeply into the database administration area, which is beyond the scope of this book.

Lastly, the db2look utility was introduced. The db2look utility can be used to model the production database in your development or test environment.

CHAPTER 3

Introducing Programming Interfaces

- ◆ DB2 UDB APPLICATION OVERVIEW
- ◆ EMBEDDED SQL PROGRAMS
- ◆ CLI / ODBC APPLICATIONS
- ◆ JAVA APPLICATIONS
- ◆ DAO, RDO, ADO APPLICATIONS

*T*his chapter introduces the programming methods and features that are available to DB2 UDB. Some of the methods described contain simple examples, and some of the examples provided are not specific to the Microsoft programming environment. The intention is to give you an overview of the interfaces and features available to you for use in developing your application.

In this chapter, we are describing the client-side programming methods, including:

- Embedded SQL - Static, Dynamic
- Call Level Interface (CLI), Open Database Connectivity (ODBC)
- Java Interfaces - JDBC, SQLJ
- Native DB2 Application Programming Interfaces (APIs)
- Microsoft Data Objects - ADO, RDO, DAO

The server-side features including constraints, User-Defined Types (UDTs), Large Objects (LOBs), Stored Procedures, User-Defined Functions and Triggers are described in Chapter 4.

Each programming method has its benefits and drawbacks. The method you choose is usually a function of the application's requirements. This chapter will introduce you to each of the methods. The manual *DB2 UDB Application Development Guide* and *DB2 UDB Application Building Guide* are the good references for each of the methods.

DB2 UDB Application Overview

A generalized overview of the various parts of a DB2 UDB application is given in this section. These parts are the same, but the actual coding to implement these general principles varies among the different programming interfaces, languages, and tools. These details are examined more closely in the following sections. A DB2 UDB application contains code that accomplishes several key tasks:

- Declaration and initialization of variables
- Connection to the database
- Execution of database transactions
- Disconnection from the database
- Termination of the program

These parts are described in more detail in the *DB2 UDB Application Development Guide*.

Fig. 3–1 summarizes the general framework for a DB2 UDB application program in pseudocode format. You must, of course, tailor this framework to suit your own needs and specifications.

```
Start program

Include/load application and database modules
   (e.g. Include dbmodule1)
Declare variables and structures
   (e.g. Declare database1, userid1, password1)

CONNECT to <database1> USER <userid1> USING <password1>

SELECT ...              /* Start first transaction */
Retrieve results
      ...(program logic e.g. process results)
DELETE ...
ROLLBACK or COMMIT      /* End the transaction */

    ... (program logic)

SELECT ...              /* Start second transaction */
INSERT ...
      ...(more SQL statements and/or program logic)
COMMIT                  /* End the transaction */

    ...(program logic)

CONNECT to <database2> USER <userid2> USING <password2>

UPDATE ...              /* Start another transaction */
SELECT ...
COMMIT or ROLLABCK      /* End the transaction */

    ...(more database transactions and application logic)

Disconnect from databases
Clean-up resources

End program
```

Fig. 3–1 *Application Overview Pseudocode*

The sections that follow describe how the actual coding to implement these general principles varies among the different programming interfaces using the Microsoft development tools.

Embedded SQL

Structured Query Language (SQL) is the database interface language used to access and manipulate data in DB2 UDB databases. You can embed SQL statements in your applications, enabling them to perform any task supported by SQL, such as retrieving or storing data.

Introducing Programming Interfaces

An application in which you embed SQL statements is called a host program. A programming language that you compile, and in which you embed SQL statements, is called a host language. The program and language are defined this way because they host or accommodate SQL statements. Using DB2 UDB, you can code your embedded SQL applications in the C/C++, COBOL, FORTRAN, Java (SQLJ), and REXX programming languages.

There are two types of embedded SQL statements: static and dynamic.

Static SQL

Static SQL statements are ones where the SQL statement type and the database objects accessed by the statement, such as column names, are known prior to running the application. The only unknowns are the data values the statement is searching for or modifying. The database objects being accessed must exist when a static embedded application module is bound to the database unless the bind option SQLERROR CONTINUE is specified.

 Note: The bind options SQLERROR CONTINUE and VALIDATE are available in DB2 UDB Version 7.1. The bind option SQLERROR CONTINUE indicates that the package will be created even when one or more SQL errors occur during the bind. The bind option VALIDATE RUN indicates that the rebind process will be performed at execution time for the SQL statements which had errors during the bind time. This type of binding process is called incremental bind.

The development process involves the combination of SQL with a third generation programming language. When the embedded SQL program is executed, it uses pre-defined SQL statements that have been bound to the database as application packages. Thus, the access plan to data is retained in the database in a ready-to-execute package.

There are many performance benefits to having ready-to-execute database logic stored within the database. Static embedded SQL programs have the least run-time overhead of all the DB2 UDB programming methods, and execute faster. The package is in a form that is understood by the database server. However, as you might have guessed already, this method of developing applications is not the most flexible, since every SQL statement that the end user executes needs to be known and understood during the development process.

The transactions are grouped into packages and stored in the database. The SQL statements are embedded within programming modules. The programming modules, which contain embedded SQL statements, must be precompiled. The modified programming modules, created by the precompiler, are then compiled and linked to create the application. During the precompile phase, the SQL statements are analyzed and packages are created. We will examine all of the steps to create static embedded DB2 UDB applications later in this chapter.

Static applications for DB2 UDB can be coded using C/C++, Java, COBOL, or FORTRAN. DB2 UDB provides support for static SQL statements in Java programs using the SQLJ (Embedded SQL for Java) standard. REXX cannot be used for static SQL. See Fig. 3–2 for an example of a static SQL application.

Generally, static statements are well-suited for high-performance applications with predefined transactions. A reservation system is a good example of such an application.

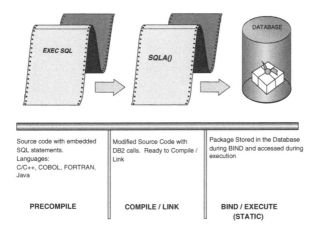

Fig. 3–2 *SQL Statements Prepared during Application Development*

Steps in a Sample Static SQL Application

These steps describe the sample Static SQL application listing that follows. This is a simple example that is included as part of the DB2 UDB product and is installed in the *DB2PATH*\samples directory (*DB2PATH* is the directory where you install the DB2 UDB).

1. Include the SQLCA. The SQLCA is a host language data structure defined by DB2 UDB. It contains data elements which are populated by DB2 UDB during SQL processing. The INCLUDE SQLCA statement defines and declares the SQLCA structure, and defines SQLCODE and SQLSTATE as elements within the structure. The SQLCODE field of the SQLCA structure is updated with diagnostic information by the database manager after every execution of SQL statements or database manager API calls.

2. Declare host variables. The SQL BEGIN DECLARE SECTION and END DECLARE SECTION statements delimit the host variable declarations.These are variables that can be referenced in SQL statements. Host variables are used to pass data to the database manager or to hold data returned by it. They are prefixed with a colon (:) when referenced in an SQL statement.

3. Connect to database. The program connects to the sample database, and requests shared access to it. (It is assumed that a START DATABASE MANAGER API call or db2start command has been issued.) Other programs that connect to the same database using shared access are also granted access.

4. Retrieve data. The SELECT INTO statement retrieves a single value based upon a query. This example retrieves the FIRSTNME column from the EMPLOYEE table where the value of the LASTNAME column is JOHNSON. The value SYBIL is returned and placed in the host variable firstname.

5. Process errors. The CHECKERR macro/function is an error checking utility which is external to the program. The location of this error checking utility depends upon the programming language used. For C the check_error is redefined as CHECKERR and is located in the util.c file.

6. Disconnect from database. The program disconnects from the database by executing the CONNECT RESET statement.

```
#include <iostream.h>
#include <stdlib.h>
#include <string.h>
#include "util.h"

EXEC SQL INCLUDE SQLCA;

#define CHECKERR(CE_STR)    if (check_error (CE_STR, &sqlca) != 0)

class Static {
   public:
      Static ();
      Static (char *, char *);
      Select ();
      ~Static ();
   private:
      EXEC SQL BEGIN DECLARE SECTION;
         char firstname[13];
         char userid[9];
         char passwd[19];
```

```
        EXEC SQL END DECLARE SECTION;
};

Static::Static () {
   cout << "Connect to default database with default userid and
password\n";
   EXEC SQL CONNECT TO sample;
   CHECKERR ("CONNECT TO sample") exit(1);
}

Static::Static (char *userid, char *passwd) {
   cout << "Connect to sample database with inputted userid and
password\n";
   EXEC SQL CONNECT TO sample USER :userid USING :passwd;
   CHECKERR ("CONNECT TO SAMPLE USING...") exit(1);
}

Static::Select () {
   EXEC SQL SELECT FIRSTNME INTO :firstname
            FROM employee
            WHERE LASTNAME = 'JOHNSON';
   CHECKERR ("SELECT statement") return 1;

   cout << "First name = " << firstname << '\n';
   return 0;
}


Static::~Static () {
   EXEC SQL CONNECT RESET;
   CHECKERR ("CONNECT RESET") exit(1);
}

int main(int argc, char *argv[]) {
   cout << "Sample C program: STATIC\n";

   if (argc == 3) {
      Static sampleStatic (argv[1], argv[2]);
      sampleStatic.Select();
   } else if (argc == 1) {
      Static sampleStatic;
      sampleStatic.Select();
   } else {
      cout << "\nUSAGE: static userid passwd\n\n";
   } // end if

   return 0;
}
// end of program : static.sqC
```

Building the Sample Embedded Static SQL Application

Sample batch files are included with DB2 UDB to build the Static SQL applications. The batch file bldmsemb.bat builds a sample C or C++ program containing embedded SQL using the Microsoft Visual C++ compiler. The following points describe the steps performed in the batch file.

To build an embedded Static SQL application, the following steps are necessary:

1. Write your application in source files that contain programs with embedded SQL statements. In our example the source is contained in the static.sqx file.

2. Connect to a database, then precompile each source file.

   The precompiler converts the SQL statements in each source file into DB2 UDB run-time API calls to the database manager. The precompiler creates the following files:

   - Modified source files that can be compiled and linked by the host language compiler.
   - An access package in the database. A package is a database object that contains optimized SQL statements. Each package contains a number of sections that correspond to embedded SQL statements. A section is the compiled form of an SQL statement. The package can be stored directly in the database, or the data needed to create a package can be stored in a bind file.
   - A bind file is created optionally, if specified. A bind file will contain the data needed to create a package. This can be bound in a later separate step known as deferred binding.

   To precompile the static.sqx file using the sample database, issue the following commands. In this example, the userid testid, and the password testpwd is used to connect to the database:

   ```
   connect to sample user testid using testpwd
   precompile static.sqx
   connect reset
   ```

3. If the application is going to connect to another database during execution, you will need to create a bind file. The bind file is bound to create the access package; see step 6. To create a bind file, add the bindfile parameter to the precompile command. For example:

   ```
   precompile static.sqx bindfile
   ```

   The following files are created:

   static.cxx - The modified source files

   static.bnd - The bind file, if the bindfile parameter was specified

4. Compile the modified source files (and other files without SQL statements using the host language compiler. To compile the static.cxx and util.cxx source files using Microsoft Visual C++, use the following command:

```
cl -Z7 -Od -c -W2 -D_X86_=1 -DWIN32 static.cxx util.cxx
```

5. Link the object files with the DB2 UDB and host language libraries to produce an executable program. Use the following command to produce an executable program for the static.cxx source:

```
link -debug:full -debugtype:cv -out:static.exe static.obj
util.obj db2api.lib
```

The static.exe can now be executed against the sample database.

6. If this was not already done at precompile time, or if a different database is going to be accessed, bind the bind file to create the access package. To bind the bind file created for the static.sqx command, issue the following command:

```
bind static.bnd
```

7. Run the application. The application accesses the database using the access plan in the package.

 Note: Our sample programs are packaged with a makefile for easy compilation. Therefore, you can use the `nmake` command to complile sample programs as following:
```
nmake static
```

Dynamic SQL

Dynamic SQL statements are those statements that your application builds and executes at run time. An interactive application that prompts the end user for key parts of an SQL statement, such as the names of the tables and columns to be searched, is a good example of dynamic SQL. The application builds the SQL statement while it is running, and then submits the statement for processing.

Dynamic Embedded SQL still requires the precompile, compile, and link phases of application development. The binding or selection of the most effective data access plan is performed at program execution time, as the SQL statements are *dynamically prepared*. Choosing the access path at program execution time has some advantages and some drawbacks.

The database objects being accessed must exist when a static embedded application module is bound to the database. Dynamic embedded SQL modules do not require that these database objects exist when the application is precompiled. However, the database objects must exist at run time.

An embedded static SQL programming module will have its data access method determined during the static bind phase, using the database statistics available at bind time. An embedded dynamic SQL programming module will have its data access method determined during the statement preparation and will utilize the database statistics available at query execution time.

Therefore, there is no need to rebind dynamic embedded SQL programming modules to the database following a collection of database statistics. The database statistics are collected when the RUNSTATS command is issued. The results are stored in the system catalog tables. There is, of course, a query execution time overhead to choose the access path, since each dynamically prepared SQL statement must be optimized.

In Fig. 3–3, the development steps for embedded dynamic SQL program modules are shown. Using embedding dynamic SQL statements does not remove the precompile phase of development, but it does provide the execution of dynamic SQL statements.

Generally, dynamic SQL statements are well-suited for applications that run against a rapidly changing database where transactions need to be specified at run time. An interactive query interface is a good example of such an application.

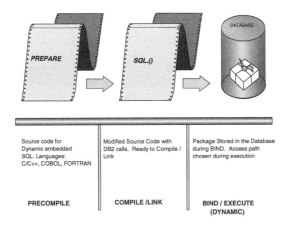

Source code for Dynamic embedded SQL. Languages: C/C++, COBOL, FORTRAN	Modified Source Code with DB2 calls. Ready to Compile / Link	Package Stored in the Database during BIND. Access path chosen during execution
PRECOMPILE	**COMPILE /LINK**	**BIND / EXECUTE (DYNAMIC)**

Fig. 3–3 *SQL Statements Prepared during Application Execution*

Steps in a Sample Dynamic SQL Application

The following steps describe the sample Static SQL application listing that follows. This is a simple example that is included as part of the DB2 UDB product and is installed in the *DB2PATH*\samples directory (*DB2PATH* is the directory where you install the DB2 UDB).

1. Declare host variables. This section includes declarations of three host variables:

   table_name :   Holding the data returned during the FETCH statement.
   st :   Holding the dynamic SQL statement in text form.
   parm_var :   Supplying a data value to replace the parameter marker in st.

2. Prepare the statement. An SQL statement with one parameter marker (indicated by '?') is copied to the host variable. This host variable is passed to the PREPARE statement for validation. The PREPARE statement parses the SQL text and prepares an access section for the package in the same way that the precompiler or binder does, only it happens at run time instead of during preprocessing.

3. Declare the cursor. The DECLARE statement associates a cursor with a dynamically prepared SQL statement. If the prepared SQL statement is a SELECT statement, a cursor is necessary to retrieve the rows from the result table.

Introducing Programming Interfaces

4. Open the cursor. The OPEN statement initializes the cursor declared earlier to point before the first row of the result table. The USING clause specifies a host variable to replace the parameter marker in the prepared SQL statement. The data type and length of the host variable must be compatible with the associated column type and length.

5. Retrieve the data. The FETCH statement is used to move the NAME column from the result table into the table_name host variable. The host variable is printed before the program loops back to fetch another row.

6. Close the cursor. The CLOSE statement closes the cursor and releases the resources associated with it.

```c
#include <stdio.h>
#include <stdlib.h>
#include <string.h>
#include "util.h"
EXEC SQL INCLUDE SQLCA;
#define CHECKERR(CE_STR)    if (check_error (CE_STR, &sqlca) != 0) return 1;
int main(int argc, char *argv[]) {
   EXEC SQL BEGIN DECLARE SECTION;
      char  table_name[19];
      char  st[80];
      char  parm_var[19];
      char  userid[9];
      char passwd[19];
   EXEC SQL END DECLARE SECTION;
   printf( "Sample C program: DYNAMIC\n" );

   if (argc == 1) {
      EXEC SQL CONNECT TO sample;
CHECKERR ("CONNECT TO SAMPLE");
   }
   else if (argc == 3) {
      strcpy (userid, argv[1]);
      strcpy (passwd, argv[2]);
      EXEC SQL CONNECT TO sample USER :userid USING :passwd;
      CHECKERR ("CONNECT TO SAMPLE");
   }
   else {
      printf ("\nUSAGE: dynamic [userid passwd]\n\n");
      return 1;
   } /* endif */

   strcpy( st, "SELECT tabname FROM syscat.tables" );
   strcat( st, " WHERE tabname <> ? ORDER BY 1" );
   EXEC SQL PREPARE s1 FROM :st;
   CHECKERR ("PREPARE");

   EXEC SQL DECLARE c1 CURSOR FOR s1;

   strcpy( parm_var, "STAFF" );
   EXEC SQL OPEN c1 USING :parm_var;
   CHECKERR ("OPEN");
   do {
      EXEC SQL FETCH c1 INTO :table_name;
      if (SQLCODE != 0) break;

      printf( "Table = %s\n", table_name );
   } while ( 1 );
```

```
        EXEC SQL CLOSE c1;
        CHECKERR ("CLOSE");

        EXEC SQL COMMIT;
        CHECKERR ("COMMIT");

        EXEC SQL CONNECT RESET;
        CHECKERR ("CONNECT RESET");
        return 0;
}
```

Building the Sample Embedded Dynamic SQL Application

Sample batch files are included with DB2 UDB to build the Embedded SQL applications. The batch file `bldmsemb.bat` builds a sample C or C++ program containing embedded SQL using the Microsoft Visual C++ compiler. The process for building dynamic SQL application is much the same as it is for Static SQL, except that the preprocessing is not done.

Call Level Interface and ODBC

The DB2 UDB Call Level Interface (CLI) is a programming interface that your C and C++ applications can use to access DB2 UDB databases. DB2 CLI is based on the Microsoft Open Database Connectivity Standard (ODBC) specification, and the X/Open and ISO Call Level Interface standards. Since DB2 CLI is based on industry standards, application programmers who are already familiar with these database interfaces may benefit from a shorter learning curve. Many ODBC applications can be used with DB2 UDB without any modifications. Likewise, a CLI application is easily ported to other database servers.

DB2 CLI is a dynamic SQL application development environment. However, instead of embedding the SQL statements, your application passes dynamic SQL statements as function arguments to the database using C/C++ Application Programming Interfaces (APIs) provided with DB2 UDB. The necessary data structures used to communicate between the database and the application are allocated transparently by DB2 UDB.

Since the SQL statements are issued through direct API calls, CLI programs are not precompiled. Also, CLI applications use common access packages provided with DB2 UDB, hence there is no need to bind the program modules separately. You only need to bind the DB2 UDB CLI packages once to each database you want to access using any DB2 UDB CLI or ODBC applications on a client.

Many differences exist between developing an embedded SQL application module and developing a CLI module. Since an application is usually comprised of a number of program modules, the modules can use different DB2 UDB programming techniques. It can be beneficial to use different DB2 UDB programming interfaces in a single application.

Introducing
Programming
Interfaces

The CLI application development environment is shown in Fig. 3–4.

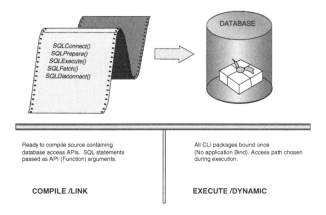

Fig. 3–4 *Application Development Using CLI or ODBC*

A DB2 UDB CLI Application

Coding CLI applications involves writing C/C++ modules that contain DB2 UDB CLI functions (APIs). The fundamental CLI functions are discussed briefly in this section. See the *DB2 UDB Call Level Interface Guide and Reference* for detailed descriptions of the supported CLI functions. You need to be familiar with the purpose, syntax, arguments, and usage of these functions to effectively code CLI applications.

A DB2 UDB CLI application can be broken down into a set of tasks. The basic tasks that apply to all CLI applications are *Initialization*, *Transaction Processing*, and *Termination*.

Handles

All CLI functions take arguments called *handles*. A handle is a variable that refers to a data object controlled by DB2 UDB CLI. There are environment, connection, statement, and descriptor handles (see Table 3–1). Using handles relieves the application from having to allocate and manage global variables or data structures, such as the SQLDA or SQLCA, used in the embedded SQL interfaces. The CLI functions for allocating and freeing handles are SQLAllocHandle() and SQLFreeHandle(). One of the arguments to these functions, HandleType, specifies the type of handle to be allocated or freed.

Table 3–1 *CLI Handles*

HandleType	Used for
SQL_HANDLE_ENV	Environment
SQL_HANDLE_DBC	Connection
SQL_HANDLE_STMT	Statement
SQL_HANDLE_DESC	Descriptor

1. **Initialization.** The initialization task involves allocating and initializing environment and connection handles, as well as connecting to one or more databases. As the first step for an application to interact with DB2 UDB CLI, an environment handle needs to be allocated. An environment handle provides access to global information such as attributes and connections.

   A connection handle refers to a data object that contains information associated with a connection to a particular data source. This includes connection attributes, general status information, transaction status, and diagnostic information. Once a connection handle has been allocated, you can attempt to establish a connection to the data source using that connection handle. The function SQLConnect( ) is used to request a database connection.

2. **Transaction Processing.** The main task of the application is accomplished during the transaction processing phase. SQL statements are passed to DB2 UDB CLI to query and modify the data using a five-step process:

   - Allocating statement handle(s)
   - Preparing and executing SQL statements
   - Processing results
   - Ending the transaction
   - Freeing statement handles

   None of these are described here. See the examples installed with the product and the on-line documentation, which describe each of these steps.

Introducing
Programming
Interfaces

3. **Termination.** The termination phase involves disconnecting your application from the database(s) and freeing allocated resources after the transaction processing has completed. The SQLDisconnect() API closes a connection. The corresponding connection handle can then be freed using SQLFreeHandle() with the argument SQL_HANDLE_DBC. Once all the connection handles have been freed, the SQLFreeHandle() function can be called with argument SQL_HANDLE_ENV to successfully free the environment handle. See Fig. 3–5.

```
int main( ) {
    SQLHANDLE henv;
    SQLHANDLE hdbc;

    /* allocate an environment handle */
    SQLAllocHandle(SQL_HANDLE_ENV, SQL_NULL_HANDLE, &henv );
    /* allocate the connection handle */
    SQLAllocHandle( SQL_HANDLE_DBC, henv, &hdbc );
    /* connect to the db2cert data source */
    SQLConnect( hdbc, "db2cert", SQL_NTS, "userid", SQL_NTS,
                "password", SQL_NTS );

    /********* Start Transaction Processing **********/
    /* allocate statement handle, execute statement, etc.*/
    /********* End Transaction Processing *************/

    /* disconnect from database */
    SQLDisconnect( hdbc ) ;
    /* free the connection handle */
    SQLFreeHandle( SQL_HANDLE_DBC, hdbc ) ;
    /* free environment handle */
    SQLFreeHandle( SQL_HANDLE_ENV, henv ) ;
    return ( SQL_SUCCESS ) ;
}
```

Fig. 3–5 *Sample CLI code for Initialization and Termination*

Java Interfaces (JDBC and SQLJ)

DB2 UDB provides support for many different types of Java programs, including applets, applications, servlets, and advanced DB2 UDB server-side features. Java programs that access and manipulate DB2 UDB databases can use the Java Database Connectivity (JDBC) API, and Embedded SQL for Java (SQLJ) standard. Both of these are vendor-neutral SQL interfaces that provide data access to your application through standardized Java methods. The greatest benefit of using Java, regardless of the database interface, is its *write once, run anywhere* capability, allowing the same Java program to be distributed and executed on various operating platforms in a heterogeneous environment. And since the two Java database interfaces supported by DB2 UDB are industry open standards, you have the added benefit of using your Java program against a variety of database vendors.

DB2 UDB also supports use of the JDBC-ODBC Bridge Driver, which allows Java programs to use JDBC with DB2 ODBC Driver.

Introducing
Programming
Interfaces

For JDBC programs, your Java code passes *dynamic* SQL to a JDBC driver that comes with DB2 UDB. Then, DB2 UDB executes the SQL statements through JDBC APIs which use DB2 CLI, and the results are passed back to your Java code. JDBC is similar to DB2 CLI in that you do not have to precompile or bind a JDBC program, since JDBC uses dynamic SQL.

With DB2 UDB SQLJ support, you can build and run SQLJ programs that contain *static* embedded SQL statements. Since your SQLJ program contains static SQL, you need to perform steps similar to precompiling and binding. Before you can compile an SQLJ source file, you must translate it with the SQLJ translator to create native Java source code. After translation, you can create the DB2 UDB packages using the DB2 for Java profile customizer (`db2profc`). Mechanisms contained within SQLJ rely on JDBC for many tasks, like establishing connections.

 Note: SQLJ can still be used without running DB2 for Java profile customizer (`db2profc`). If you don't run it, then the statement will be prepared and executed dynamically.

Choosing between SQLJ and JDBC for your Java program involves many of the same considerations and trade-offs as for static versus dynamic embedded SQL in other languages (See Table 3–2). SQLJ may be beneficial, since static SQL can be faster. Java programs containing embedded SQL can also be subjected to static analysis of SQL statements for the purposes of syntax checking, type checking, and schema validation. On the other hand, not all data objects to be accessed may be known before execution, requiring JDBC for dynamic SQL. A Java programmer can create a powerful application by including both static and dynamic constructs with ease, since SQLJ shares environment and state information with JDBC.

Table 3–2 *Differences between JDBC and SQLJ*

JDBC	SQLJ
SQL via API calls	SQL is embedded
Dynamic SQL	Static SQL
Precompiling not required	Translate SQLJ and create packages

JDBC Application

Whether you're writing an application or applet, you typically do the following:

1. Import the appropriate Java packages and classes (java.sql.*).

2. Load the appropriate JDBC driver (`COM.ibm.db2.jdbc.app.DB2Driver` is a Type II JDBC driver for applications; `COM.ibm.db2.jdbc.net.DB2Driver` is a Type III JDBC driver for applets).

3. Connect to the database, specifying the location with a URL (as defined in SUN's JDBC specification) and using the db2 subprotocol. For applets, you must also provide the userid, password, hostname, and the portnumber for the applet server; for applications, the DB2 client provides the required values.

4. Pass SQL statements to the database.

5. Receive the results.

6. Close the connection.

After coding your program, compile it as you would any other Java program. You don't need to perform any special precompile or bind steps.

A Sample JDBC Application

The `DB2Appl.java` sample program shows how to write a Java application using the JDBC application driver to access a DB2 database. The sample is installed in the *DB2PATH*/`samples/java` directory (*DB2PATH* is the directory where you install the DB2 UDB). All of the code below is in the order it appears in the application source file.

1. Import the JDBC package. Every JDBC and SQLJ program must import the JDBC package.

2. Declare a Connection object. The Connection object establishes and manages the database connection.

3. Set database URL variable. The DB2 application driver accepts URLs that take the form of `jdbc:db2:`*database name*.

4. Connect to database. The `DriverManager.getConnection()` method is most often used with the following parameters:

   getConnection(String url)
   Establish a connection to the database specified by URL with the default username and password.
   getConnection(String url, **String** userid, **String** password)
   Establish a connection to the database specified by URL with the values for username and password specified by userid and passwd respectively.

5. Create a Statement object. Statement objects send SQL statements to the database.

Introducing Programming Interfaces

6. Execute an SQL SELECT statement. Use the executeQuery() method for SQL statements, like SELECT statements, that return a single result set. Assign the result to a ResultSet object.

7. Retrieve rows from the ResultSet. The ResultSet object allows you to treat a result set like a cursor in host language embedded SQL. The method ResultSet.next() moves the cursor to the next row and returns Boolean false if the final row of the result set has been reached. Restrictions on result set processing depend on the level of the JDBC API that is enabled through the database manager configuration parameters. The JDBC 2.0 API allows you to scroll backwards and forwards through a result set, inserting, updating, and deleting rows.The JDBC 1.2 API restricts you to scrolling forward through a read-only result set with the ResultSet.next() method.

8. Return the value of a column. The ResultSet.getString(*n*) returns the value of the *n* th column as a String object.

9. Execute an SQL UPDATE statement. Use the executeUpdate() method for SQL UPDATE statements. The method returns the number of rows updated as an int value.

```java
//  Source File Name: DB2App1.java  %I%
import java.sql.*;

class DB2App1 {

    static {
        try {
            // register the driver with DriverManager
            // The newInstance() call is needed for the sample to work with
            // JDK 1.1.1 on OS/2, where the Class.forName() method does not
            // run the static initializer. For other JDKs, the newInstance
            // call can be omitted.
            Class.forName("COM.ibm.db2.jdbc.app.DB2Driver").newInstance();
        } catch (Exception e) {
            e.printStackTrace();
        }
    }

    public static void main(String argv[]) {
        Connection con = null;

        // URL is jdbc:db2:dbname
        String url = "jdbc:db2:sample";

        try {
            if (argv.length == 0) {
                // connect with default id/password
                con = DriverManager.getConnection(url);
            }
            else if (argv.length == 2) {
                String userid = argv[0];
                String passwd = argv[1];

                // connect with user-provided username and password
                con = DriverManager.getConnection(url, userid, passwd);
            }
            else {
```

```
            System.out.println("\nUsage: java DB2Appl [username
    password]\n");
            System.exit(0);
    }

    // retrieve data from the database
    System.out.println("Retrieve some data from the database...");
    Statement stmt = con.createStatement();
    ResultSet rs = stmt.executeQuery("SELECT * from employee");

    System.out.println("Received results:");

    // display the result set
    // rs.next() returns false when there are no more rows
    while (rs.next()) {
        String a = rs.getString(1);
        String str = rs.getString(2);

        System.out.print(" empno= " + a);
        System.out.print(" firstname= " + str);
        System.out.print("\n");
    }

    rs.close();
    stmt.close();

    // update the database
    System.out.println("\n\nUpdate the database... ");
    stmt = con.createStatement();
    int rowsUpdated = stmt.executeUpdate("UPDATE employee set firstnme
    = 'SHILI' where empno = '000010'");

    System.out.print("Changed "+rowsUpdated);

    if (1 == rowsUpdated)
        System.out.println(" row.");
    else
        System.out.println(" rows.");

    stmt.close();
    con.close();
    } catch( Exception e ) {
        e.printStackTrace();
    }
    }
}
```

To Build the Application

Before any Java application can be run, it must be compiled. To compile the Java application to bytecode, as with any other Java application, issue the following command:

```
javac DB2Appl.java
```

Running the Application

To run the application within your Java Virtual Machine, issue the following command. Note that `testid` and `testpwd` must be a valid userid and password that have access to the DB2 UDB database used in this example.

```
java DB2Appl testid testpwd
```

SQLJ Applications

Whether you're writing an application or applet, you typically do the following:

1. Import the appropriate SQLJ runtime classes (sqlj.runtime.*).

2. Register the driver.

3. Declare and initialize the iterators; special considerations exist for Positioned Updates and Deletes.

4. Connect to the database, specifying the location with a URL (as defined in SUN's JDBC specification) and using the db2 subprotocol.

5. Issue executable clauses to process data.

6. Process the results.

7. Close the iterators.

With SQLJ, you need to use the SQLJ translator to translate your source into Java source before you do the Java compilation.

DB2 SQLJ support is based on the SQLJ ANSI standard. Refer to the IBM DB2 Java Enablement Home Page at the following URL for a pointer to the ANSI website and other SQLJ resources:

```
http://www-4.ibm.com/software/data/db2/java/
```

Following is an example SQLJ application:

```
import java.sql.*;
import sqlj.runtime.*;
import sqlj.runtime.ref.*;

#sql iterator App_Cursor1 (String empno, String firstnme) ;
#sql iterator App_Cursor2 (String) ;

class App
{

    static
```

```
    {
    try
    {
        Class.forName("COM.ibm.db2.jdbc.app.DB2Driver");
    }
    catch (Exception e)
    {
        e.printStackTrace();
    }
    }

public static void main(String argv[])
{
    try
    {
        App_Cursor1 cursor1;
        App_Cursor2 cursor2;
        String str1 = null;
        String str2 = null;
        int    count1;
        Connection con = null;

        // URL is jdbc:db2:dbname
        String url = "jdbc:db2:sample";
        DefaultContext ctx = DefaultContext.getDefaultContext();
        if (ctx == null) {
            try {
                if (argv.length == 0) {
                    // connect with default id/password
                    con = DriverManager.getConnection(url);
                }
                else if (argv.length == 2) {
                    String userid = argv[0];
                    String passwd = argv[1];

                    // connect with user-provided username and password
                    con = DriverManager.getConnection(url, userid, passwd);
                }
                else {
                    System.out.println("\nUsage: java App [username password]\n");
                    System.exit(0);
                }
                con.setAutoCommit(false);
                ctx = new DefaultContext(con);
            }
            catch (SQLException e) {
                System.out.println("Error: could not get a default context");
                System.err.println(e) ;
                System.exit(1);
            }

            DefaultContext.setDefaultContext(ctx);
        }

        // retrieve data from the database
        System.out.println("Retrieve some data from the database...");
        #sql cursor1 = { SELECT empno, firstnme from employee };

        // display the result set
        // cursor1.next() returns false when there are no more rows
        System.out.println("Received results:");
        while (cursor1.next()) {
            str1 = cursor1.empno();
            str2 = cursor1.firstnme();

            System.out.print (" empno= " + str1);
            System.out.print (" firstname= " + str2);
            System.out.print ("\n");
        }
```

Introducing
Programming
Interfaces

```
        cursor1.close();

        // retrieve number of employee from the database
        System.out.println("\nRetrieve the number of rows in employee
table...");
        #sql { SELECT count(*) into :count1 from employee };
        if (1 == count1)
            System.out.println ("There is " + count1 + " row in employee
table.");
        else
            System.out.println ("There are " + count1 + " rows in employee
table.");

        // update the database
        System.out.println("\n\nUpdate the database... ");
        #sql { UPDATE employee set firstnme = 'SHILI' where empno = '000010'
};

        // retrieve the updated data from the database
        System.out.println("\nRetrieve the updated data from the
database...");
        str1 = "000010";
        #sql cursor2 = { SELECT firstnme from employee where empno = :str1 };

        // display the result set
        // cursor2.next() returns false when there are no more rows
        System.out.println("Received results:");
        while (true) {
            #sql { FETCH :cursor2 INTO :str2 };
            if (cursor2.endFetch()) break;

            System.out.print (" empno= " + str1);
            System.out.print (" firstname= " + str2);
            System.out.print ("\n");
        }
        cursor2.close();

        // rollback the update
        System.out.println("\n\nRollback the update...");
        #sql { ROLLBACK work };
        System.out.println("Rollback done.");
    }
    catch( Exception e )
    {
        e.printStackTrace();
    }
    }
}
```

The previous example SQLJ application, App.sqlj, uses static SQL to retrieve and update data from the EMPLOYEE table of the DB2 sample database.

1. Declare iterators. This section declares two types of iterators:

App_Cursor1
Declares column data types and names, and returns the values of the columns according to column name (Named binding to columns).

App_Cursor2
Declares column data types, and returns the values of the columns by column position (Positional binding to columns).

2. Initialize the iterator. The iterator object cursor1 is initialized using the result of a query. The query stores the result in cursor1.

3. Advance the iterator to the next row. The `cursor1.next()` method returns a Boolean false if there are no more rows to retrieve.

4. Move the data. The named accessor method `empno()` returns the value of the column named empno on the current row. The named accessor method `firstnme()` returns the value of the column named firstnme on the current row.

5. Select data into a host variable. The `SELECT` statement passes the number of rows in the table into the host variable count1.

6. Initialize the iterator. The iterator object `cursor2` is initialized using the result of a query. The query stores the result in `cursor2`.

7. Retrieve the data. The `FETCH` statement returns the current value of the first column declared in the `ByPos` cursor from the result table into the host variable str2.

8. Check the success of a `FETCH..INTO` statement. The `endFetch()` method returns a Boolean true if the iterator is not positioned on a row, that is, if the last attempt to fetch a row failed. The `endFetch()` method returns false if the last attempt to fetch a row was successful. DB2 attempts to fetch a row when the `next()` method is called. A `FETCH...INTO` statement implicitly calls the `next()` method.

9. Close the iterators. The `close()` method releases any resources held by the iterators. You should explicitly close iterators to ensure that system resources are released in a timely fashion.

Compiling and Running SQLJ Programs

To run an SQLJ program with program name `MyClass`, do the following:

1. Translate the Java source code with Embedded SQL to generate the Java source code `MyClass.java` and profiles `MyClass_SJProfile0.ser`, `MyClass_SJProfile1.ser`, ... (one profile for each connection context):

```
sqlj MyClass.sqlj
```

When you use the SQLJ translator without specifying an sqlj.propertiesfile,

Introducing Programming Interfaces

the translator uses the following values:

```
sqlj.url=jdbc:db2:sample
sqlj.driver=COM.ibm.db2.jdbc.app.DB2Driver
sqlj.online=sqlj.semantics.JdbcChecker
sqlj.offline=sqlj.semantics.OfflineChecker
```

If you do specify an sqlj.properties file, make sure the following options are set:

```
sqlj.url=jdbc:db2:dbname
sqlj.driver=COM.ibm.db2.jdbc.app.DB2Driver
sqlj.online=sqlj.semantics.JdbcChecker
sqlj.offline=sqlj.semantics.OfflineChecker
```

In this example, dbname is the name of the database. You can also specify these options on the command line. For example, to specify the database mydata when translating MyClass, you can issue the following command:

```
sqlj -url=jdbc:db2:mydata MyClass.sqlj
```

Note that the SQLJ translator automatically compiles the translated source code into class files, unless you explicitly turn off the compile option with the compile=false clause.

2. Install DB2 SQLJ Customizers on generated profiles and create the DB2 packages in the DB2 database dbname:

```
db2profc -user=user-name -password=user-password -
url=jdbc:db2:dbname
-prepoptions="bindfile using MyClass0.bnd package using
MyClass0"
MyClass_SJProfile0.ser
db2profc -user=user-name -password=user-password -
url=jdbc:db2:dbname
-prepoptions="bindfile using MyClass1.bnd package using
MyClass1"
MyClass_SJProfile1.ser
...
```

3. Execute the SQLJ program:

```
java MyClass
```

The translator generates the SQL syntax for the database for which the SQLJ profile is customized. For example:

```
i = { VALUES ( F(:x) ) };
```

is translated by the SQLJ translator and stored as:

```
? = VALUES (F (?))
```

in the generated profile. When connecting to a DB2 UDB database, DB2 UDB will customize the VALUE statement into:

```
VALUES(F(?)) INTO ?
```

Introducing
Programming
Interfaces

For detailed information on building and running DB2 SQLJ programs, refer to the *DB2 UDB Application Building Guide*.

Native DB2 UDB APIs

DB2 UDB supplies native Application Programming Interfaces (APIs) which can be used to directly manipulate DB2 UDB instances and databases. They are also called administrative or database manager APIs. Some tasks, such as performing a backup of a database, must be coded using these APIs. There is no method of embedding an SQL statement to perform this operation because the BACKUP DATABASE command is not part of SQL.

The DB2 UDB APIs are provided in many programming languages, including C/C++, COBOL and FORTRAN. Information is exchanged between the application and database using special data structures. If the source program module contains only DB2 UDB APIs, there is no need to precompile, and a database package is not created.

The native DB2 UDB APIs are not directly used for coding SQL statements on their own. The native APIs rely on embedded SQL or CLI to perform OLAP/OLTP, and are generally used in conjunction with these interfaces to provide administrative or database management functions. For example, the function sqlaintp() is commonly used to retrieve the complete text for a DB2 UDB error message, so an embedded SQL application can then display the error message to the end user. The DB2 UDB APIs are grouped by functional category (see Table 3–3). For details on using these APIs, see the *DB2 UDB V6 Administrative API Reference*.

Table 3–3 *Types of Native (Administrative) DB2 UDB APIs*

Backup/Recovery	Database Monitoring
Database Control	Operational Utilities
Database Manager Control	Data Utilities
Database Directory Management	General Application Programming
Client/Server Directory Management	Application Preparation
Network Support	Remote Server Utilities
Database Configuration	Table Space Management
Node and Nodegroup management	

Microsoft Data Objects (DAO, RDO, ADO)

The earliest of the tools that are now part of the Microsoft Visual Studio tools collection were Visual Basic and C++. The development of Microsoft's data access technology grew in parallel with that of Visual Basic.

Microsoft Visual Basic is by far the most popular tool today for building application programs for accessing both local and remote databases on the Windows 95/98/NT operating system platforms. It could indeed be said that Visual Basic is used for very little else. Microsoft claims to have figures showing that about 85% of purchasers of the product use it to develop database access programs. It should not be surprising to notice that Microsoft's development of this product has been strongly influenced by these usage figures.

Microsoft considers Visual Basic to be a Rapid Application Development (RAD) tool, and they provide three different data access technologies in the latest version of Visual Basic. These multiple methods can be a little confusing, but the first two are mainly provided to maintain compatibility with earlier versions of the language. Microsoft recommends the use of their latest technology, ADO, for new development projects using their Visual Studio tools. The following subsection explains the background of the three different technologies.

Development of Visual Basic Data Access Methods

Microsoft introduced the Visual Basic programming application in 1991, and it created a marked increase in application development on the Windows 3.x operating system platform. Application development during the beta phase, and early deployment of Microsoft Windows, had required programmers to write their applications in 'C' using the Windows Development Kit to build GUI components. This was a slow and complicated process, as it had been for previous GUI type platforms.

Visual Basic revolutionized Windows programming with its built-in screen objects, which could be dragged and dropped onto a form and readily edited once in place. The decision to base the product on an interpretive language like BASIC, rather than a compiled language such as 'C', produced an easy-to-debug environment which also added to its popularity. Microsoft also created an easy add-in concept which allowed third-party software houses to produce both improvements to the development interface, and additional types of components for users to add to their toolbox.

Introducing
Programming
Interfaces

Data Access Objects

Microsoft had originally intended the language to be a quick and easy system for users to create small local applications on the desktop, and as such, it initially had no built-in tools for database access. This gap was first filled by third-party software houses, but as Microsoft noticed the demand for this functionality, they produced an addition to the language, which they called Data Access Objects, or DAO, as this is commonly called. This technology appeared in Version 3 of Visual Basic Professional in about 1993, and was an immediate success in the market place. One of the reason for this success was that Microsoft added the JET database engine to Visual Basic, which permitted application developers to build an entire database application from Visual Basic.

The JET database engine was originally developed for the Microsoft Access Relational Database product. This combination made development even easier. Microsoft Access could be used for database administration, creating tables and indexes, and administrating user accounts and permissions. User access to the database for reading, inserting and updating data were then provided via a Visual Basic program. One of the benefits of this, for the small system developer, was related to licensing and distribution costs. Only the developer and database administrators needed the Microsoft Access product, and the compiled Visual Basic Program module, for users to access the database could be freely distributed. This approach also lessened the overall programming effort, by removing the complication of database administration from the equation.

Open Database Connectivity (ODBC)

During the 1980s, the SQL language was implemented by all relational database suppliers, such as IBM, Oracle, Informix and Ingress. In order to permit portability among so many different implementations, the American National Standards Institute (ANSI) created a standard specification in 1986. This was also adopted by the International Organization of Standards (ISO) and accepted by the standards bodies of many individual countries. The specification was updated in 1989 and a much larger version produced in 1992, which is often referred to as SQL92.

However, all these standards only covered the SQL language itself. All relational database suppliers had their own methods for accessing their particular database engines and this had proliferated a great number of incompatible 3GL and 4GL languages during the 1980s. A special interest group with representatives from all leading database suppliers met in 1992, and proposed a standard implementation for a Call Level Interface (CLI) to relational databases. This SAG92 (SQL Access Group) recommendation was adopted by the standards authorities (ANSI/ISO) as an Addendum to the SQL Specification in 1995.

It was from the work of the SAG committee, of which they were a member, that Microsoft developed their Open Database Connectivity concept (ODBC). ODBC, and indeed the CLIs from the major database suppliers, provide an Application Programming Interface that permits a programmer in any language to access data in a relational database.

It is not necessary to describe the ODBC interface in any detail in this section. The important fact to remember is that the DAO data access model was based on the non-standard interface to Microsoft's JET database and not the ODBC API. To overcome this problem, Microsoft provided a modification to the JET engine to permit it to pass ODBC requests through JET to the ODBC driver. However, this proved to be very inefficient, and led to ODBC gaining a reputation for poor performance.

Remote Data Objects

The performance problems encountered by users accessing ODBC connections to remote database with DAO, led Microsoft to produce a new database access technology. This was released in the 32 bit version of Visual Basic Version 4. Microsoft called it Remote Data Objects.

Until this time, programmers trying to produce serious data access software had found it necessary to code by directly calling the ODBC APIs. This gave very good performance, but was time-consuming to develop, and very difficult to debug.

Remote Data Objects were designed to replace this concept by providing a set of objects which effectively provided a thin object layer over the ODBC API. This produces comparable performance but much faster development.

The only problem was that Microsoft only released RDO with the Enterprise version of Visual Basic, under the belief that only programmers in large companies would want to program to access midrange computers, and that a larger number would want to program for the JET Engine. This was not a good assessment of the market. The net result was that a large number of programmers, who did not think that they needed the more expensive Enterprise version, were effectively disenfranchised. Thus RDO did not get the market penetration that it deserved. Microsoft did put some of the capabilities of RDO into the Professional version by adding ODBCDirect to DAO, but this probably produced more problems than it solved, because of the large number of exclusive features between the DAO Jet interface and the DAO ODBCDirect interface.

Introducing
Programming
Interfaces

ActiveX Data Objects

The initial success of the Windows operating system was due, undoubtedly, to the fact that the market had been waiting for a standard GUI interface on the standard business PC. However, the concept which cemented its appeal was Microsoft's Object Linking and Embedding technology, OLE. This led to the Office suite concept, which transformed Microsoft into a major force in the application software arena, in addition to their traditional place in the operating system market and programming languages.

During the nineties, Microsoft continued to develop the OLE concept, working towards a network distributed object model, which they now call COM/DCOM, Common Object Model and Distributed Common Object Model, and which is more commonly recognized as ActiveX.

Thus, by the middle of the nineties, Microsoft had a problem. Their technology thrust on the Windows platforms was COM/DCOM, and neither of their existing database object systems, DAO or RDO, supported this technology. These systems were also proprietary and could therefore only be used by Microsoft tools such as Visual Basic and C++. At the same time, Microsoft was becoming aware that the nature of data itself was becoming more fluid. Traditionally, data was held in relational database structures, for which they had developed ODBC. With the tremendous growth of E-mail and groupware products such as Lotus Notes, this was changing the nature of data in respect of both storage and communications.

Microsoft therefore announced OLE DB as the replacement for ODBC and a new Data Access Object technology called ActiveX Data Objects, ADO, to simplify the programming interface to OLE DB.

Structure of Visual Basic Data Access Methods

The three different database access technologies have very different structures. This is due to evolving requirements and changes to accepted methodologies. Visual Basic was first adopted when structured programming methods and procedural languages were commonly in use. Over the last few years there has been a shift towards object oriented programming with code re-use as more of a priority. Although all three technologies are object based, both DAO and RDO fitted more comfortably with the earlier structure, whereas ADO has been developed specifically for Microsoft's Common Object Model, COM/DCOM. The following sections are descriptions of the three types.

These sections are intended to give an overview of the database technologies. More details can be found in Microsoft's on-line help system and the Programmers References for the various Languages in the Visual Studio collection. There is also an extensive collection of books, from various publishers, on specific languages, and elements of use for all the major areas of interest. A good book on data access with Visual Basic is SAMS' *"Database Developer's Guide with Visual Basic 6"* by Roger Jennings, ISBN: 0-672-31063-5. Roger Jennings has written a book on this subject for every version of Visual Basic since version 3. A handy reference to ADO is contained in the Wrox Press book *"ADO 2.1 Programmer's Reference"* by David Sussman and Alex Homer, ISBN: 1-861-00268-8. This pair of authors also collaborated on a similar book for ADO Version 2.0, and David Sussman, with several others, has been involved with one for ADO version 2.5. It should be noted that both of the books recommended only deal with ActiveX Data Objects.

Data Access Objects

Data Access Object technology was originally designed to provide access to the Microsoft Jet Engine, which was used by both Microsoft Access and Visual Basic. Connection to ODBC linked external databases, via the Jet Engine was part of this design, but was not particularly efficient. The introduction of the Remote Data Object technology allowed the modification of DAO to include ODBCDirect. The reason that ODBCDirect had to be added to DAO, was the fact that Microsoft only released the RDO technology in the more expensive Enterprise version of Visual Basic, and not the Professional version, which many developers use.

Hence, after the introduction of ODBCDirect, the DAO technology provided two different environments with some DAO Objects, Methods and Properties, not being applicable, necessarily, to both environments. The following section therefore only deals with those Objects, Methods and Properties which are applicable to ODBCDirect.

The hierarchical diagram in Fig. 3–6 includes plural forms of database object types. These are collections within which one or more of that type of object can be contained. They can be considered as arrays of objects. The difference between a collection and an array is that an array addresses its individual elements by numeric position only, whereas a collection can reference a member of a collection by either ordinal position in the collection, or by the name it was created with. As an example of this, the contents of a specific `Recordset` field could be referenced as `Recordset.Fields(1)` or `Recordset.Fields("Author")`. The diagram also includes the `TableDefs` collection with its associated Indexes collection. This is really part of the JET Engine access structure because the Indexes are JET database indexes. However, this has been included to show the equivalent position in the structure for comparison with the RDO diagram.

Introducing
Programming
Interfaces

Data Access Objects are part of the structure of Visual Basic, and as such, the Help files can be accessed without adding any references to your current program environment. The appropriate section can be found under **Help** -> **Contents** -> **Visual Basic Documentation** -> **Microsoft DAO 3.51**. However, if you wish to use a later version than that supplied in your version of Visual Basic, then you will need to add a reference to the newer version, in **Project** -> **References**, which will then make available its own Help information.

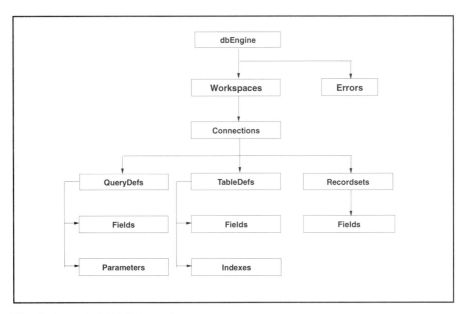

Fig. 3–6 *DAO ODBCDirect Structure*

DBEngine

The DBEngine object is the top level object in the DAO object model and contains and controls the behavior of all other DAO objects. DBEngine directly contains two Collections of Objects, Workspaces and Errors. The whole structure of ODBCDirect using Connections is seen in the above diagram, Fig. 3–6.

The DBEngine is unique in this technology, as there can only be one object of this type and its instance is already available within Visual Basic, and therefore does not require any dimension type statement. This top level object is used mostly to create the type of Workspace object required by the application, JET or ODBCDirect.

The example below creates a new Workspace object for ODBC connections.

```
Set wks = CreateWorkspace(wkODBC, db2admin, db2admin,
dbUseODBC)
```

Nearly all the other methods of the DBEngine refer to its use with the JET database engine.

A complete list of all methods, properties, and collections is available from the Help Summary topic for the DBEngine.

WorkSpace(s)

An ODBCDirect Workspace object defines a session for the user. It handles one or more Connection objects and each Connection must reference its Workspace. It is the Workspace object which handles Transaction Control and it is at the Workspace creation stage that the decision is taken to use ODBCDirect.

A Workspace object can contain four different types of Collections/objects. However, an ODBCDirect type Workspace only uses one of these. This is the Connection type object, which replaces the JET engine Database object.

Similarly, when studying the Methods applicable to the Workspace object, you will find that of the nine available methods, four of them are not applicable to the ODBCDirect type of Workspace. The methods that do apply are:

- OpenConnection
- Close
- BeginTrans, CommitTrans and Rollback.

From this you can see that you would use the Workspace object to manage the current session or to start an additional session. In a session, you can open multiple databases or connections, and manage transactions. The following code shows how to open a connection within a workspace.

Note: In Client/Server work, it is important that any objects that you create are closed, when you have finished using them. The server code needs to be informed that you are releasing a server resource.

Introducing
Programming
Interfaces

```
Dim ws As Workspace
Dim cn As Connection
' Create ODBCDirect Workspace object.
Set ws = CreateWorkspace("ODBCWorkspace", "Admin", "", _
                         dbUseODBC)

' Create connection to DB2 Sample database with default
' user and password.

Set cn = ws.OpenConnection("Con1", dbDriverNoPrompt, , _
            ODBC;DATABASE=Sample;UID=;PWD=;DSN=Sample")

' Do some processing on the Sample database
' Close connection and workspace objects
con.Close
ws.Close
```

Fig. 3–7 *Open a Connection Object*

When you use transactions, all databases in the specified Workspace are affected, even if multiple Database objects are opened in the Workspace. For example, you use a BeginTrans method, update several records in a database, and then delete records in another database. If you then use the Rollback method, both the update and delete operations are canceled and rolled back. If you need to run independent transactions in your application, then you will need to run them in different Workspaces.

Connection(s)

A Connections collection contains the current Connection objects of a Workspace object. This object is specific to the ODBCDirect type of workspace. You can therefore have several connections open within the same workspace (Fig. 3–7). For example, you may wish to transfer data from one database to another, and to achieve this, you will require having a connection to the source database and a separate connection to another.

You may also wish to compile a report from data which is contained in several different databases, perhaps on different computers, and this will also require multiple connection objects to be opened in the workspace.

Within a connection you can create a QueryDef, used for prepared statements and parameter passing, open a Recordset containing returned data to manipulate, or execute an SQL statement directly to the attached database, such as a create or drop table statement.

The following program listing (Fig. 3–8) shows the syntax for creating a QueryDef and opening a Recordset.

```
Dim ws As Workspace
Dim cn As Connection
Dim qd as QueryDef
Dim rs as Recordset

' Create ODBCDirect Workspace object.
Set ws = CreateWorkspace("ODBC", "Admin", "", dbUseODBC)

' Create connection to DB2 Sample database with default
' user and password.
Set cn = ws.OpenConnection("Con1", dbDriverNoPrompt, , _
   "ODBC;DATABASE=Sample;UID=;PWD=;DSN=Sample")

Set qd = cn.CreateQueryDef("", "SELECT * FROM Employee")
Set rs = qd.OpenRecordset( _
   "SELECT * FROM Employee", dbOpenDynaset, dbReadOnly)
```

Fig. 3–8 *Create a QueryDef and Open a Recordset*

QueryDef(s)

A `QueryDefs` collection contains all `QueryDef` objects of a `Connection` object in an ODBCDirect workspace.

The `QueryDef` object, as its name suggests, holds a query definition. The purpose of this is to allow the query to be used more than once, or to contain a query which uses parameters passed to it. This provides the ODBC API concept of prepared statements and parameter binding. As with the ODBC API, the lifetime of a `QueryDef` object is only as long as the existing program runs, or it is closed. When using ODBC to connect to an enterprise type database such as DB2, a permanent query definition will be provided by a Stored Procedure on the server, which can be called in a `QueryDef` statement.

If the query that you have defined in a `QueryDef` returns any records, then you will need to open a `Recordset` which you associate with the `QueryDef`.

The `QueryDef` object has several properties which you can use to define a query and how it should be acted upon. For details, see the Microsoft on-line Help.

Introducing
Programming
Interfaces

Parameter(s)

The Parameters collection contains Parameter objects representing values supplied to a query. If the Prepared property is set on the QueryDef object, then DAO will use the ODBC API's SQLPrepare statement, which requires the query in the QueryDef creation statement to includes parameter markers, which are question marks, for any values in WHERE type clauses, which can be varied, when the query is executed. The values to be used at query execution time are appended to the QueryDef's associated Parameters collection, in the order that they are required by the query. Obviously, this allows the actual values, used by the query, to be supplied by an application's user, without having to build the actual query definition inside the application. DAO uses the ODBC API's SQLBindParams call on the values held in the Parameters collection, prior to using its SQL Execute call.

The Parameter collection is also used to pass parameters to an SQL call to run a Stored Procedure, created on the DB2 UDB Server. The Parameter object has properties which allow you to set the value to be passed, the variable type, and the direction of the parameter.

Recordset(s)

A Recordsets collection contains all open Recordset objects in a Connection object. This is probably the most used object of all for data access. When you use DAO objects, you manipulate data almost entirely using Recordset objects.

A Recordset contains the rows (Records) and columns (Fields) of data returned by a query, either from the QueryDef which opened the Recordset, or the embedded query in an OpenRecordset method. A pointer is maintained against the Recordset, and a request for the value of a particular field in the Recordset, will return the value of the field in the row currently pointed to by the pointer. The pointer is moved using the MoveFirst, MoveLast, MoveNext and MovePrevious methods of the Recordset object.

There are four cursor types for ODBCDirect Recordset objects, and it is important that you select the correct cursor type for the purpose for which you wish to use the Recordset object.

- **Dynaset-type Recordset** (ODBC Keyset Cursor) — the result of a query that can have updatable records. A dynaset-type Recordset object is a dynamic set of records that you can use to add, change, or delete records from an underlying database table or tables. A dynaset-type Recordset object can contain fields from one or more tables in a database.

- **Snapshot-type Recordset** (ODBC Static Cursor) — a static copy of a set of records that you can use to find data or generate reports. A snapshot-type Recordset object can contain fields from one or more tables in a database but cannot be updated.
- **Forward-only-type Recordset** (ODBC Forward-only Cursor) — identical to a snapshot, except that no cursor is provided. You can only scroll forward through records. This improves performance in situations where you only need to make a single pass through a result set.
- **Dynamic-type Recordset** (ODBC Dynamic Cursor) — a query result set from one or more base tables in which you can add, change, or delete records from a row-returning query. Records that other users add, delete, or edit in the underlying database tables will also be appear in your Recordset.

You choose the type of Recordset you want in its creation statement. If you do not specify a Recordset type, then DAO will make its own choices, which are unlikely to be what you want. See the DAO Help topic for the type it will select.

The following code example (Fig. 3–9) opens a Recordset with a simple SELECT statement, which returns three columns from the Employee table, and then scrolls through the rows, printing the values for each row to the Visual Basic immediate window.

Introducing
Programming
Interfaces

```
Private Sub RecordSetExample()
    Dim ws As Workspace
    Dim cn As Connection
    Dim rs As Recordset

    ' Open ODBCDirect workspaces
    Set ws = CreateWorkspace("", "admin", "", dbUseODBC)

    ' Open ODBCDirect connection.
    Set cn = ws.OpenConnection("", , , _
        "ODBC;DATABASE=Sample;UID=;PWD=;DSN=Sample")

    ' Open Recordset with ODBC keyset cursor
    Set rs = cn.OpenRecordset( _
        "SELECT FirstNme,LastName,Salary FROM Employee", dbOpenDynaset)

    ' Loop through recordset printing three field from
    ' each record to the immediate window
    Do While Not rs.EOF
        Debug.Print rs("FirstNme") & "  " & rs("LastName") & _
            " " & rs("Salary")
        rs.MoveNext
    Loop

    ' Close all objects in reverse order to opening
    rs.Close
    cn.Close
    ws.Close
    End
End Sub
```

Fig. 3–9 *Open a Recordset Object*

Fields collection and objects

A Field object represents a column of data with a common data type and a common set of properties. In ODBCDirect Workspaces, you manipulate a field using a Field object and its methods and properties. The field value holds the value of that column in the current record and other properties allow you to determine such things as the type and size of the data in that column. The Visual Basic on-line help for DAO 3.5 describes all the various properties that can be used with a field object.

When you access a Field object as part of a Recordset object, data from the current record is visible in the Field object's Value property. The example in the Recordset section above accesses the Fields collection to print the data in the current record.

Remote Data Objects

Microsoft designed RDO with two basic aims. The first aim was to provide a data access object system, which was directly related to the ODBC API instead of the JET Engine database interface. The second aim was to provide the same look and feel in the new technology, so as to enable users of DAO to move over to RDO with a minimum of retraining.

The significance of ODBC, in this exercise, is that it provides a compatible interface to large scale corporate database engines such as DB2 UDB, ORACLE, INFORMIX, INGRESS, SYBASE, and SQLServer. All these database engine suppliers signed up to the SAG committee's Call Level Interface specification, upon which ODBC is also based. This has made it relatively simple for them to create drivers to interface Microsoft's ODBC API on the PC, to their individual CLIs. Thus Microsoft provides the API calls for applications on the Windows platform to access SQL databases, and the database suppliers provide the specific drivers for their own databases, building in their own preferences for communication methods.

DB2 UDB provides the Client Configuration Assistant to set up driver connections to DB2 UDB databases on all the currently supported platforms, such as OS/390, AS/400, remote and local NT servers and so on (see Chapter 1). The Client Configuration Assistant is also provided separately as DB2Connect, and an ODBC driver is also provided by IBM for the AS/400's database with the AS/400 Client Access product. Many third-party Database Analysis and/or Reporting tools currently utilize these connectivity products.

Introducing
Programming
Interfaces

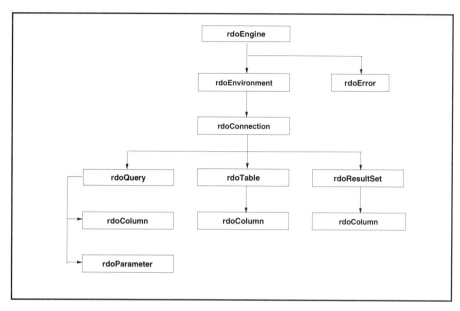

Fig. 3–10 *RDO Structure*

If you compare the diagram in Fig. 3–10 above, with Fig. 3–6 on page 90, you will see that Microsoft appears to have also succeeded in their second aim, as the only difference between the DAO and RDO structures, in these diagrams, are the object names. These have been amended slightly in RDO, so that a programmer can easily detect which method is being used. This comparison does not tell the whole truth, as the DAO diagram only includes the elements used by ODBCDirect, and not those utilized solely by the JET engine interface. The latter has objects which permit the direct administration and use of JET Engine Databases, Indexes, Relations, and so on. However, these elements were not available when using the JET interface to ODBC either, and certainly those elements that are common between DAO and RDO are structurally the same. The administration of ODBC databases is achieved using SQL statements, such as CREATE, ALTER and DROP database objects.

Although the structures of RDO and ODBCDirect look the same, ODBCDirect provides only a subset of RDO's capabilities. This is due to the larger number of methods and properties available with the RDO objects.

rdoEngine

The rdoEngine object is equivalent to DAO's dbEngine. As the top-level object, it contains all other objects in the hierarchy of Remote Data Objects (RDO). It also handles the errors reported by the database and fires InfoMessage events when such errors arise. The rdoEngine has a number of methods and properties to define rdoEnvironment and stand-alone rdoConnection properties.

rdoEnvironment(s)

The rdoEnvironment object is equivalent to the DAO Workspace. The rdoEnvironments collection contains all active rdoEnvironment objects of the rdoEngine object.

An rdoEnvironment object defines a logical set of connections and transaction scope for a particular user name. It contains both open and allocated but unopened connections, provides mechanisms for simultaneous transactions, and provides a security context for data manipulation language (DML) operations on the database.

Generally, an rdoEnvironment object corresponds to an ODBC environment that can be referred to by the rdoEnvironment object's hEnv property.

All rdoEnvironment objects share a common hEnv value that is created on an application basis. You use the rdoEnvironment object to manage the current ODBC environment, or to start an additional connection. In an rdoEnvironment, you can open multiple connections, manage transactions, and establish security based on user names and passwords.

Managing Transactions

The rdoEnvironment also determines transaction scope. Committing an rdoEnvironment transaction commits all open rdoConnection databases and their corresponding open rdoResultset objects. This does not imply a two-phase commit operation — simply that individual rdoConnection objects are instructed to commit any pending operations — one at a time.

Introducing
Programming
Interfaces

When you use transactions, all databases in the specified rdoEnvironment are affected – even if multiple rdoConnection objects are opened in the rdoEnvironment. For example, suppose you use a BeginTrans method against one of the databases visible from the connection, update several rows in the database, and then delete rows in another rdoConnection object's database. When you use the RollbackTrans method, both the update and delete operations are rolled back. To avoid this problem, you can create additional rdoEnvironment objects to manage transactions independently across rdoConnection objects. Note that transactions executed by multiple rdoEnvironment objects are serialized and are not atomic operations. Because of this, their success or failure is not interdependent.

rdoEnvironment Events

This is a significant addition to data objects. The following events are fired as the rdoEnvironment object is manipulated (Table 3–4). These can be used to manage RDO transactions associated with the rdoEnvironment or to synchronize some other process with the transaction.

Table 3–4 *rdo Environment Events*

Event Name	Description
BeginTrans	Fired after the BeginTrans method has completed.
CommitTrans	Fired after the BeginTrans method has completed.
RollbackTrans	Fired after the RollbackTrans method has completed.

rdoConnections

The rdoConnection object manages the connection to a remote database, for the user account defined in the rdoEnvironment, by using an ODBC data source or a connection string to define the database to connect to. Although the connection object needs to belong to an rdoEnvironment in order to connect to a database, the object itself can be defined in a stand-alone configuration. It can then be added and removed from its collection when required.

rdoQuery

The rdoQuery is roughly equivalent to DAO's QueryDef object. In version 1 of RDO, it was called rdoPreparedStatement and was a direct overlay of ODBC's SQLPreparedStatement call. At version 2 of RDO, it was renamed to rdoQuery to better describe its functionality.

As with the `rdoConnection` object, an `rdoQuery` object can be defined before being added to a collection, and can be associated and disassociated from a connection object, and other connection objects, at will.

The `rdoQuery` object is used to manage SQL queries requiring the use of input, output or input/output parameters. Basically, an `rdoQuery` functions as a compiled SQL statement. When working with stored procedures or queries that require use of arguments that change from execution to execution, you can create an `rdoQuery` object to manage the query parameters. If your stored procedure returns output parameters or a return value, or you wish to use `rdoParameter` objects to handle the parameters, you must use an `rdoQuery` object to manage it. For example, if you submit a query that includes information provided by the user such as a date range or part number, RDO can substitute these values automatically into the SQL statement when the query is executed.

The `rdoQuery` object remains similar to the original `rdoPreparedStatement` in its interface. However, the `rdoQuery` objects can be prepared or not, allowing you to choose the most appropriate use of the query.

Stand alone rdoQuery Objects

Stand-alone `rdoQuery` objects are not assigned to a specific `rdoConnection` object, so you must set the `ActiveConnection` property before attempting to execute the query, or to use the `OpenResultset` object against it.

The example code shown below (Fig. 3–11) creates an `rdoQuery` object, associates it with a connection, and executes it. Next, the `rdoQuery` object is associated with a different connection and executed again. The query object becomes more of an encapsulation of any kind of query, and thus can be executed against any kind of connection, provided the SQL statement would be appropriate for the connection.

Introducing
Programming
Interfaces

```
Dim MyQuery As rdoQuery '
MyQuery.SQL = "Update customers " _
   & " Set LastTouched = CURRENT DATE"
MyQuery.Prepared = False     'don't prepare it,
                             'just SQLExecDirect
'assume that cnSomeConnection
'is an rdoConnection or stand-alone object
MyQuery.ActiveConnection = cnSomeConnection
MyQuery.Execute

MyQuery.ActiveConnection = cnOtherConnection
'the cnOtherConnection is over a WAN, so I can increase
'my query timeout to compensate
MYQuery.QueryTimeout = 120
MyQuery.Execute
```

Fig. 3–11 *rdoQuery Object*

rdoQuery object events

The following events are fired as the rdoQuery object is manipulated (Table 3–5). These can be used to assist in managing queries associated with the rdoQuery or coordinate other processes in your application.

Table 3–5 *rdoQuery Events*

Event Name	Description
QueryComplete	Fired when a query has completed.
QueryTimeout	Fired when the QueryTimeout period has elapsed and the query has not begun to return rows.
WillExcute	Fired before the query is executed permitting last-minute changes to the SQL, or to prevent the query from executing.

rdoParameters

An rdoParameters collection contains all the rdoParameter objects of the rdoQuery object that it was created for. It provides information only about marked parameters in an rdoQuery object or stored procedure. An individual rdoParameter object in the collection represents one of the parameters associated with the rdoQuery.

When the `rdoParameters` collection is first referenced, RDO and the ODBC interface parse the query searching for parameter markers – the question mark (?). For each marker found, RDO creates an `rdoParameter` object and places it in the `rdoParameters` collection. However, if the query cannot be compiled or otherwise processed, the `rdoParameters` collection is not created and a trappable error will occur, indicating that the object did not exist.

When working with stored procedures or SQL queries that require use of arguments that change from execution to execution, then an `rdoQuery` object should be created to manage the query and its parameters. For example, if you submit a query that includes information provided by the user, such as a date range, or part number, RDO and the ODBC interface can insert these values automatically into the SQL statement at specific positions in the query.

The following code line shows the question mark (?) being used as parameter placeholders in a stored procedure call that passes parameters. It also uses the first parameter in the rdoParameter collection to hold the return value.

```
"{ ? = Call MySP (?, ?, ?) }"
```

Each query parameter that you want to have RDO manage must be indicated by a question mark (?) in the text of the SQL statement, as shown above, and correspond to an `rdoParameter` object referenced by its ordinal number counting from zero – left to right. For example, to execute a query that takes a single input parameter, your SQL statement would look something like the code shown below.

```
SQL$ = "Select Au_Lname, Au_Fname where Au_ID Like ? "
Dim qd as rdoQuery, rd as rdoResultset
Set qd = CreateQuery ("SeekAUID", SQL$)
qd(0) = "236-66-%"
set rd = qd.OpenResultset(rdOpenForwardOnly)
```

RDO 2.0 supports BLOB data types as parameters, and you also can use the `AppendChunk` method against the `rdoParameter` object to pass `TEXT` or `IMAGE` data types as parameters into a procedure.

Introducing
Programming
Interfaces

rdoTables

The `rdoTables` collection contains all stored `rdoTable` objects in a database. This is equivalent to the DAO tables collection, but Microsoft recommends that Tables should not be used. Instead it is preferable to perform a "`SELECT * FROM <tablename>`" in a create resultset statement.

rdoResultset

The `rdoResultsets` collection contains all open `rdoResultset` objects in an `rdoConnection`.

A new `rdoResultset` is automatically added to the `rdoResultsets` collection when you open the object, and it is automatically removed when you close it. Several `rdoResultset` objects might be active at any one time.

Setting the `ActiveConnection` property to Nothing removes the `rdoResultset` object from the `rdoResultsets` collection and fires events, but does not deallocate the object resources. Setting the `rdoResultset` object's `ActiveConnection` property to a valid `rdoConnection` object causes the `rdoResultset` object to be re-appended to the `rdoResultsets` collection. This behavior is referred to as disconnected `Recordsets`.

Managing the rdoResultsets Collection

An `rdoResultset` object represents the rows that result from running a query.

When you use remote data objects, you interact with data almost entirely by using `rdoResultset` objects. `rdoResultset` objects are created using the RemoteData control, or the `OpenResultset` method of the `rdoQuery`, `rdoTable`, or `rdoConnection` object.

When you execute a query that contains an SQL `SELECT` statement, the data source returns zero or more rows in an `rdoResultset` object. All `rdoResultset` objects are constructed using rows and columns.

A stored procedure (See "Stored Procedures" on page 160) can contain one or more SQL `SELECT` statements and return zero or more result sets. As a result, a single `rdoResultset` can contain zero or any number of result-sets — so-called "multiple" result sets. Once you have completed processing the first result set in an `rdoResultset` object, use the `MoreResults` method to discard the current `rdoResultset` rows and activate the next `rdoResultset`. You can process individual rows of the new result set just as you processed the first `rdoResultset`. You can repeat this until the `MoreResults` method returns `False`.

Processing Multiple Result Sets

When you call a stored procedure that contains more than one SELECT statement, you must use the MoreResults method to discard the current rdoResultset rows and activate each subsequent rdoResultset. Each of the rdoResultset rows must be processed or discarded before you can process subsequent result sets. To process result set rows, use the Move methods to position to individual rows, or the MoveLast method to position to the last row of the rdoResultset. You can use the Cancel or Close methods against rdoResultset objects that have not been fully processed.

Choosing a Cursor Type

You can choose the type of rdoResultset object you want to create using the type argument of the OpenResultset method – the default Type is rdOpenForwardOnly for RDO and rdOpenKeyset for the RemoteData control. If you specify rdUseNone as the CursorDriver property, a forward-only, read-only result set is created. Each type of rdoResultset can contain columns from one or more tables in a database.

There are four types of rdoResultset objects based on the type of cursor that is created to access the data:

- **Forward-only** — type rdoResultset — individual rows in the result set can be accessed and can be updatable (when using server-side cursors), but the current row pointer can only be moved toward the end of the rdoResultset using the MoveNext method — no other method is supported.
- **Static**-type rdoResultset — a static copy of a set of rows that you can use to find data or generate reports. Static cursors might be updatable when using either the ODBC cursor library or server-side cursors, depending on which drivers are supported and whether the source data can be updated.
- **Keyset**-type rdoResultset — the result of a query that can have updatable rows. Movement within the keyset is unrestricted. A keyset-type rdoResultset is a dynamic set of rows that you can use to add, change, or delete rows from an underlying database table or tables. Membership of a keyset rdoResultset is fixed.
- **Dynamic**-type rdoResultset — the result of a query that can have updatable rows. A dynamic-type rdoResultset is a dynamic set of rows that you can use to add, change, or delete rows from an underlying database table or tables. Membership of a dynamic-type rdoResultset is not fixed.

Introducing
Programming
Interfaces

You can also determine where cursor keysets will be created — on the client workstation or on the server using the `CursorDriver` property of the `rdoEnvironment` or `rdoConnection` object. While cursor keysets created on the client workstation (client-side cursors) copy the keyset to the workstation, cursor keysets created on the server (server-side cursors) use the resources of the database server to maintain the cursor keysets. The default location is on the server.

DB2 UDB supports both client-side cursors and server-side cursors. Server-side cursors can eliminate the need to transmit the keyset to the workstation where it consumes needed resources, whereas client-side cursors need more network operations to initially create the keyset. However, if you want to scroll cursors and the size of the result set is small, client-side cursors give you better performance in general.

Some features of the Microsoft Client Cursor Provider (such as disassociated resultset discussing next) cannot be simulated with server-side cursors. You need to use client-side cursors when you want to use such features.

Dissociate rdoResultset Objects

When using the client batch cursor (client-side cursor) library, RDO permits you to disconnect an `rdoResultset` object from the `rdoConnection` object used to populate its rows by setting the `ActiveConnection` property to `Nothing`. While dissociated, the `rdoResultset` object becomes a temporary static snapshot of a local cursor. It can be updated, new rows can be added, and rows can be removed from this `rdoResultset`. You can re-associate the `rdoResultset` by setting the `ActiveConnection` property to another (or the same) `rdoConnection` object. Once reconnected, you can use the `BatchUpdate` method to synchronize the `rdoResultset` with a remote database.

To perform this type of dissociated update operation, you should open the `rdoResultset` using an `rdOpenStatic` cursor, and use the `rdConcurBatch` as the concurrency option.

rdoResultset Events

The following events are fired as the `rdoResultset` object is manipulated (Table 3–6). These can be used to micro-manage result sets or to synchronize other processes with the operations performed on the `rdoResultset` object.

Table 3–6 *rdoResultset events*

Event Name	Description
Associate	Fired after a new connection is associated with the object.

Table 3–6 *rdoResultset events*

Event Name	Description
ResultsChange	Fired after current rowset is changed (multiple result sets).
WillExcute	Fired before the query is executed, permitting last-minute changes to the SQL, or to prevent the query from executing.
Dissociate	Fired after the connection is set to nothing.
QueryComplete	Fired after a query has completed.
RowStatusChange	Fired after the state of the current row has changed (edit, delete, insert).
RowCurrencyChange	Fired after the current row pointer is repositioned.
WillAssociate	Fired before a new connection is associated with the object.
WillDissociate	Fired before the connection is set to nothing.
WillUpdateRows	Fired before an update to the server occurs.

Rdocolumns Collection

An `rdoColumns` collection contains all `rdoColumn` objects of an `rdoResultset`, or an `rdoTable` object. This is equivalent to DAO's `Fields` collection. Columns reflect the terminology used with corporate style databases.

The `rdoTable`, or `rdoResultset` object's `rdoColumns` collection represents the `rdoColumn` objects in a row of data. You use the `rdoColumn` object in an `rdoResultset` to read and set values for the data columns in the current row of the object.

The `rdoColumn` object is created automatically by RDO when a `Resultset` or `Table` object is created.

ActiveX Data Objects

Microsoft refers to their current data access strategy as Universal Data Access (UDA), which they supply with many of their commercial offerings such as Visual Studio and the Windows NT Options Pack. They also maintain a Web site dedicated to Universal Data Access, from which you can download the latest version of the Microsoft Data Access Components product, `MDAC_TYP.EXE`, which currently contains ADO version 2.1.x.xxxx.x. The latest ADO version 2.5, which was released with Windows 2000, is also available for download from the UDA site, to work with Windows 95, Windows 98, and Windows NT 4.0. At the time of writing this book, none of the DB2 UDB samples have been fully tested against ADO 2.5. The UDA Web site URL is:

```
http://www.microsoft.com/data
```

`MDAC_TYPE` contains the latest versions of the ODBC support DLLs and the OLE DB and ADO components. Although OLE DB is intended to supplant ODBC, Microsoft is still supporting this technology, and indeed they do provide a native OLE DB Provider that allows you to use ADO with existing ODBC drivers. The structure of UDA is shown in the following diagram (Fig. 3–12).

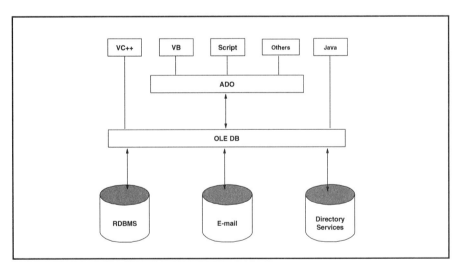

Fig. 3–12 *Universal Data Access*

From this diagram, you can see that far more products can use this data strategy than was the case with DAO and RDO. The Script definition refers to VB Script and Java Script used in Active Server Pages, and Perl. The category "Others" refers to the many tools provided by other suppliers, such as Delphi and Powerbuilder.

ADO Help

This section is intended to discuss the structure of ADO and is not a detailed description. Detailed information on this technology will be found by using the on-line Help in Visual Basic. To enable you to access the ADO help topic, you must include the Reference to "**Microsoft ActiveX Data Objects 2.1 Library**" in your project, by selecting **Project --> References** and checking the entry for that library from the list presented.

If you want to access the section on ADO objects, use the following procedure. Type the name of one of the main objects (`Connection`, `Command`, or `Recordset`), and press the Help key (Function Key 1), when your cursor is on the word. This will usually bring up an applicability list. Select the entry for ADODB. This will list the object description for the item you typed in, which will contain an object hierarchical diagram to indicate the objects' structure within ADO. You can then click on one of the boxes in the Object Diagram to navigate to different objects, or use the Contents list in the left hand pane in the help window.

A good reference book on ADO is the *ADO 2.1 Programmer's Reference* from Wrox Press, ISBN 1-861002-68-8, which is small enough to carry around, but contains most of the information required to write data access programs using ADO. Another good Wrox Press book covering Visual Basic 6 database access with two-and three-tier solutions, and much more, is *Professional Visual Basic 6 Databases* by Charles Williams, ISBN: 1-861002-02-5.

Introducing
Programming
Interfaces

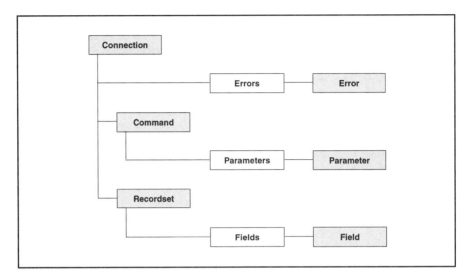

Fig. 3–13 *Structure of ActiveX Data Objects*

OLE DB

OLE DB is the underlying method that ADO uses to access data. OLE DB is based on the concept of Data Providers and Consumers. Providers are COM components which are based on the data format of the data store. This means that they are usually supplied by the database manufacturer. Microsoft has provided a default provider for ODBC drivers. This is called MSDASQL and allows you to use the IBM-supplied ODBC driver with ADO. A native DB2 UDB for NT OLE DB Provider is available since Version 7.1 of the database product. ADO itself can be considered as a data consumer in OLE DB terms, as can a user application.

ADO Object Model

The ADO model is a much flatter structure than DAO or RDO. There are in fact only three major components, with three other subsidiary objects. It is still shown in a hierarchical structure, but this is not really true. Each of the primary objects is a self-contained entity. A Recordset object can be used without using either a Connection object or a Command object, by using its own properties for these functions, and a Command object does not need to refer to a Connection object for its connection details.

The object at the top of the structure is the Connection object and this contains the Command and Recordset objects. All three of these providing the sort of functionality that you would have expected from your use of DAO or RDO, although the Command and Recordset objects have many more methods and properties than the earlier technologies.

The diagram in Fig. 3–13 shows the structure of the ADO objects and how they relate to each other.

The three subsidiary objects are attached below each of the major components. The first of these is the Errors collection, which sits below the Connection object. As both of the other major objects require a Connection object (although sometimes not in an obvious fashion), this is the logical positioning of the collection which lists all errors.

The second collection is the Parameters collection. Again, placing this within the Command object is logical, as this is the object which will use this collection.

The third and last collection is Fields which, as fields exist within Recordsets, sits under the Recordset object.

Connection

The Connection object provides the connection to the data source via the user's selected OLE DB Provider. However, unlike the same object in RDO, it does not necessarily have to be separately defined. This is because both the Command and Recordset objects can define their own connections when they are instantiated. This does not mean that they are connectionless objects. It just means that the Connection object that they use is created under-the-covers, and cannot be re-used by another object, because it has no defined object name.

This method of providing a Connection object can produce easier-to-understand code, but it does have one drawback. Obtaining a connection to a remote host database carries a time penalty and requires resources, both on the client and the host. If you define a connection as a separate object, then this connection can be re-used by all the other Command and Recordset objects in your application, which required a connection to that particular host database. Defining the connection within these separate objects will require a separate connection for each object, with the penalties mentioned above.

The other problem with not defining a specific Connection object is that you cannot set the properties of the object which controls the connection environment. In some cases, this is not a problem, because the Command and Recordset properties mirror some of the Connection properties. However, this does not apply to the Connection Attributes or Isolation Level, which control the behavior of commitment control within the connection.

Introducing
Programming
Interfaces

Opening a Connection

The following short piece of code opens a connection to a data source using a connection object. Notice the use of the NEW keyword in the dimensioning of the connection object. This cannot be used if you include the WithEvents option to enable using events within ADO.

```
Public cnDb2 As New ADODB.Connection
  cnDb2.ConnectionString =
"DSN=Sample;UID=db2admin;PWD=db2admin;"
  cnDb2.Open
```

The above example code dimensions the variable cnDB2 as an object of type connection. Note the prefix ADODB. This is to denote that this is an ADO Connection object and not a RDO connection. This is not essential, but it is considered good programming practice to include it.

The Connection object's Connect String property is then set to use the ODBC data source called Sample. The syntax for the Connect String normally refers to the OLE DB provider first, but in this case we are using the default ODBC bridge provider MSDASQL, and as it is the default Data Provider, it is not necessary to include it.

The Connection object then uses the open method to creates a connection to the database, according to the definition in its ConnectionString.

It is not necessary to define the contents of the ConnectString property, as it can be included in the Open statement.

OpenSchema Method

This returns schema information from the database. The connection must already have been opened. There are 31 defined schema options, but not all will be supported by any particular provider. The sort of data available from the schema options include tables, views, constraints, primary keys, privileges and columns, You will find an example of the use of the OpenSchema method in Chapter 5.

Fig. 3–14 below shows some sample code which returns table names from an Access database.

```
Dim cn As New ADODB.Connection ' Connection for MSACCESS
Dim rs As New ADODB.Recordset ' Read table schema

cn.ConnectionString = _
  "Provider=Microsoft.Jet.OLEDB.3.51;" & _
  "Data Source=c:\Booksale\booksale.mdb;User
Id=admin;Password=;"
cn.Open

Set rs = cn.OpenSchema(adSchemaTables)

Do Until rs.EOF
    debug.print rs!TABLE_NAME
  rs.MoveNext
Loop

rs.Close
Set rs = Nothing
cn.Close
Set cn = Nothing
```

Fig. 3–14 *OpenSchema Method*

Executing a Command in a Connection Object

This method allows you to write code which requires the execution of a query, without defining a `Command` option. This is the reverse of the `Connection` object being defined without a `Connection` object being instantiated.

```
Public Sub ExecuteX()
  Dim cn As ADODB.Connection
  cn.Open "DSN=Sample;UID=db2admin;PWD=db2admin;"
  cn.Execute "UPDATE Employee SET Firstnme = " & _
    "'Fred' WHERE LastName = 'Geyer'"
  cn.Close
End Sub
```

Fig. 3–15 *Executing a Command in a Connection Object*

Fig. 3–15 above gives a simple example of executing a non-record returning query without using a `Command` object. Note that it is also possible for a row returning query to be run in the same way, and for a `Recordset` object to be linked to that query.

Introducing Programming Interfaces

BeginTrans, CommitTrans, and RollbackTrans Methods

If used, these methods affect the operation of transaction control.

Closing a Connection Object

Using the close method on a connection object closes the connection, but it does not destroy the object. The Connection object can be re-used, after this, either against the same connection, or a different connection. To destroy the object and recover the resources consumed, use the command "Set conObj = Nothing"

Connection Events

The following is a list of the Events triggered by the Connection object.

* BeginTransComplete
* CommitTransComplete
* ConnectComplete
* Disconnect
* ExecuteComplete
* InfoMessage
* RollbackTransComplete
* WillConnect
* WillExecute

Error(s)

If a data access error occurs, during an ADO operation, then an Error object is created which contains information about the error. This object is added to the Error collection which is associated with the Connection object being used. Generally when a problem occurs, more than one error is generated and therefore there can be several objects in the collection.

It is good practice to investigate the error collection, after executing any ADO method. The simplest way to see if an error has occurred, is to check the Count property of the error collection. If this is zero then no errors occurred. If Count is greater than 0 then it can be used to reference all the errors in the collection.

Command(s)

This object is used to execute a query, SQL statement, or stored procedure. Where the call will produce a Recordset, this statement is used to set the Recordset object to the results returned by activation of the Command as follows:

```
<RecordsetObject> = <CommandObject>.Execute
```

Functionally, this object fulfills the tasks of the `rdoQuery` object in RDO.

Parameter(s)

This creates a `Parameter` object for the `Command` object. Note that you will need to use the `Append` method to add the parameter to the command's `Parameter` collection, as this does not happen automatically, as it did with RDO. Otherwise it is functionally the same as `rdoParameters`.

Recordset(s)

The `Recordset` is the most important object in ADO, as this is where all data manipulation is carried out. It can define its own connection and query, so it is possible to write code which only uses this one out of the three main objects in ADO. Microsoft actually provides a subset of the ADO library in a library referred to as ADOR, as opposed to ADODB, which is for use where only the `Recordset` is needed.

The `Recordset` object returns data from the database in the form of rows and columns, as you would view data in a spreadsheet. The `Recordset` works on the basis of a current record, and the properties of the `Recordset` refer to the data in the current row. It has a series of `Move` methods to permit you to move a pointer up and down the rows of the record structure. There is also a `Find` method to allow you to move directly to the first row matching a given criteria. After using any of the movement methods, the `Fields` collection then permits you to access the individual column data from the row or record which is the current record at that time.

The ADO `Recordset` retains the RDO object's ability to be disconnected from its connection, allowing off-line editing of the `Recordset`, with batch update, after reconnection. A disconnected `Recordset` can also be physically saved to a disk file, thus allowing it to be reloaded and re-connected at some later point. This would be ideal for staff working remotely from the main database, but given a subset of data in the form of a saved `Recordset`.

Fields Collection

Microsoft has reverted to `Fields`, as opposed to `Columns`, in ADO. This corresponds to the `rdoColumns` collection in RDO, and its contents are manipulated with very similar syntax to that used in RDO.

Introducing
Programming
Interfaces

DAO, RDO, ADO Summary

Data Objects were initially provided by DAO in the 16-bit environment of Windows 3.X with Visual Basic version 3, and it has been maintained in all subsequent versions of Visual Basic and Visual Studio. RDO was introduced in Visual Basic 4 to give better access to ODBC connected databases, and contains a much richer functionality than DAO.

ADO was introduced to deal with a much wider range of data storage types via OLE DB, and has been written to comply with the DCOM specification. This chapter has not dealt with ADO in any great detail, because it is well documented in other sources. Essentially, ADO provides the functionality of RDO, but in a simpler model. Both DAO and RDO have been retained for backward compatibility with existing software developments, but Microsoft expects users to use ADO for future development projects.

All third-party technical books on Data Access with Visual Basic or Visual Studio will be found to discuss only ADO. If you require more detailed usage information on DAO and RDO than that found in the on-line help, you will need to locate older books, which were written to describe earlier versions of the Microsoft tools. All the example code described in Chapter 5 is ADO based.

DB2 Server-Side Features

- ◆ CONSTRAINTS
- ◆ USER-DEFINED DISTINCT DATA TYPES
- ◆ LARGE OBJECTS
- ◆ USER-DEFINED FUNCTIONS
- ◆ TRIGGERS
- ◆ STORED PROCEDURES

As an application designer, you must make the most fundamental design decision: Which DB2 capabilities should I use in the design of my application? In order to make appropriate choices, you need to consider both the database design and target environment for your application. For example, you can choose to enforce some business rules in your database design instead of including the logic in your application, so that you avoid having to write your own client application code to duplicate the same tasks. DB2 UDB also lets you store some parts of your code at the server instead of keeping all of it in your client application. This can have maintenance and performance benefits.

Using DB2 UDB features that run at the database enables you to maintain and change the logic surrounding the data without affecting your application. If you need to make a change to that logic, you only need to change it in one place; at the server, and not in each application that accesses the data.

You can also make your application perform more quickly by storing and running parts of your application on the server. This shifts some processing to generally more powerful server machines, and can reduce network traffic between your client application and the server.

Server-side features may not be useful in certain situations. Your application might have unique logic that other applications do not. For example, if your application processes data entry errors in a particular order that would be inappropriate for other applications, you might want to write your own code to handle this situation.

In some cases, you might decide to use DB2 UDB features that run on the server because they can be used by several applications. In other cases, you might decide to keep logic in your application because it is used by your application only.

The server-side features include *constraints*, *User-defined Distinct Types (UDTs)*, *large objects (LOBs)*, *User-Defined Functions (UDFs)*, *triggers* and *stored procedures*. These features can be used individually or in combination to facilitate more powerful object-oriented paradigms. For example, you can model a complex object in the application domain as a UDT. The UDT may in turn be internally represented as a LOB. The UDT's behavior may be implemented in terms of UDFs, and its integrity rules implemented in terms of constraints and triggers.

This chapter gives you an overview of the DB2 UDB server-side features which can be used to supplement or extend applications.

Constraints

You may define rules to establish relationships between your data or to protect it. These rules can define what data values are valid for a column in a table, or how columns in one or more tables are related to each other. DB2 UDB provides constraints as a way to enforce those rules using the database system, thereby eliminating the need to write code in your application to enforce some of the rules. However, if a rule applies to one application only, you should code it in the application instead of using a global database constraint. DB2 UDB provides support for the following types of constraints:

- **Unique Constraint**
  Ensures the unique values of a key in a table. Any changes to the columns that compose the unique key are checked for uniqueness.
- **Referential Constraint**
  The value of the foreign key is valid if it appears as a value of a parent key, or some component of the foreign key is null. Referential constraints are enforced by the database manager on insert, update, and delete operations. *Referential integrity* is the state of a database in which all values of all foreign keys are valid.

- **Table Check Constraint**
  Verifies that changed or new data does not violate conditions specified when a table was created or altered.

Unique Constraints

A unique constraint is the rule that the values of a key are valid only if they are unique within the table. Each column making up the key in a unique constraint must be defined as NOT NULL. Unique constraints are defined in the CREATE TABLE statement or the ALTER TABLE statement using the PRIMARY KEY clause or the UNIQUE clause. You can issue CREATE TABLE statements or ALTER TABLE statements from the Command Line Processor (CLP), the Command Center, or application programs. You can also define unique constraints when creating or altering tables using the Control Center.

> **Note:** The Command Line Processor (CLP) is a text-based application that is used to execute SQL statements and DB2 commands. The Command Center enables you to issue SQL statements and DB2 commands as well. It also allows recalls of previously executed commands, and scrolling through access plans for SQL queries. The Control Center is the primary DB2 graphical tool for administering your database. From the Control Center, you get a clear overview of all the systems and database objects that exist locally or remotely. These GUI tools are introduced in Chapter 1.

Here is an example of a table whose column has a unique constraint:

```
CREATE TABLE table1 (col0 char(10) NOT NULL PRIMARY KEY,
col1 char(10))
```

In this example, col0 of table1 cannot have any duplicate values. See the *DB2 UDB SQL Reference* for the complete syntax of the CREATE TABLE statement.

A table can have any number of unique constraints; however, a table cannot have more than one unique constraint on the same set of columns.

DB2 Server Side Features

When a unique constraint is defined, the database manager creates a unique index (if needed) and designates it as either a primary or unique system-required index. The enforcement of the constraint is through the unique index. Once a unique constraint has been established on a column, the check for uniqueness during multiple row updates is deferred until the end of the update (deferred unique constraint).

A unique constraint can also be used as the parent key in a referential constraint.

Referential Constraint

A referential constraint allows you to define required relationships between and within tables. The database manager maintains these relationships, which are expressed as referential constraints, and require that all values of a given attribute or table column also exist in some other table column. Fig. 4–1 shows an example of the referential integrity between two tables. This constraint requires that every employee in the EMPLOYEE table must be in a department that exists in the DEPARTMENT table. No employee can be in a department that does not exist.

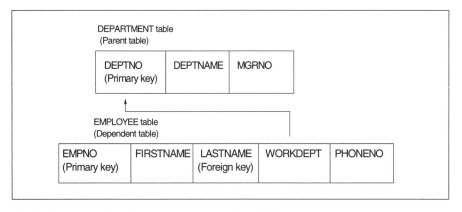

Fig. 4–1 *Referential Constraint between Two Tables*

A *unique key* is a set of columns where no two values are duplicated in any other row. Only one unique key can be defined as a primary key for each table. The unique key may also be known as the *parent key* when referenced by a foreign key.

A *primary key* is a special case of a unique key. Each table can only have one primary key. In this example, DEPTNO and EMPNO are the primary keys of the DEPARTMENT and EMPLOYEE tables.

A *foreign key* is a column or set of columns in a table that refer to a unique key or primary key of the same or another table. A foreign key is used to establish a relationship with a unique key or primary key and enforces referential integrity among tables. The column WORKDEPT in the EMPLOYEE table is a foreign key because it refers to the primary key, column DEPTNO in the DEPARTMENT table.

A parent key is a primary key or unique key of a referential constraint.

A *parent table* is a table containing a parent key that is related to at least one foreign key in the same or another table. A table can be a parent in an arbitrary number of relationships. In this example, the DEPARTMENT table, which has a primary key of DEPTNO, is a parent of the EMPLOYEE table which contains the foreign key WORKDEPT.

A dependent table is a table containing one or more foreign keys. A dependent table can also be a parent table. A table can be a dependent in an arbitrary number of relationships. For example, the EMPLOYEE table contains the foreign key WORKDEPT, which is dependent on the DEPARTMENT table that has a primary key.

A referential constraint is an assertion that non-null values of a designated foreign key are valid only if they also appear as values of a unique key of a designated parent table. The purpose of referential constraints is to guarantee that database relationships are maintained and data entry rules are followed.

Note:
If a column of a foreign key is nullable, you can set a NULL value to the column. Though the parent key cannot have a NULL value as it is a primary key or an unique key, a NULL value can be stored as a value of the foreign key.

Enforcement of referential constraints has special implications for some SQL operations that depend on whether the table is a parent or a dependent. The database manager enforces referential constraints across systems based on the referential integrity rules. The rules are:

- INSERT rule
- DELETE rule
- UPDATE rule

INSERT Rules

The INSERT rule is implicit when a foreign key is specified.

DB2 Server Side Features

You can insert a row at any time into a parent table without any action being taken in the dependent table.

You cannot insert a row into a dependent table unless there is a row in the parent table with a parent key value equal to the foreign key value of the row that is being inserted, unless the foreign key value is null.

If an INSERT operation fails for one row during an attempt to insert more than one row, all rows inserted by the statement are backed out.

DELETE Rules

When you delete a row from a parent table, the database manager checks if there are any dependent rows in the dependent table with matching foreign key values. If any dependent rows are found, several actions can be taken. You determine which action will be taken by specifying a delete rule when you create the dependent table. The following rules can be specified:

- **RESTRICT**
  This rule prevents any row in the parent table from being deleted if any dependent rows are found. If you need to remove both parent and dependent rows, delete the dependent rows first. This rule is enforced before all other constraints, including those referential constraints with modifying rules such as CASCADE or SET NULL.

- **NO ACTION**
  This rule enforces the presence of a parent row for every child after all the referential constraints are applied. This is the default. This rule is enforced after other referential constraints.

- **CASCADE**
  This rule implies that deleting a row in the parent table automatically deletes any related rows in the dependent table.

- **SET NULL**
  This rule ensures that deletion of a row in the parent table sets the values of the foreign key in any dependent row to null. Other parts of the row, and any columns that are not nullable in the foreign key are unchanged. This rule can be specified only if some column of the foreign key allows null values.

There are very few cases where the rules of RESTRICT and NO ACTION can make a difference during a delete. One example where different behavior is evident involves a delete of rows in a view that is defined as a UNION ALL of related tables. Assuming that the table T1 is a parent of table T3 with the delete rule as described below, the table T2 is also a parent of table T3 with the delete rule of CASCADE, and a view is defined as follows:

```
CREATE VIEW V1 AS
   SELECT * FROM T1 UNION ALL SELECT * FROM T2
```

Then, you are deleting rows from the view V1.

If table T1 is a parent of table T3 with delete rule of RESTRICT, a restrict violation will be raised (SQLSTATE 23001) if there are any child rows for parent keys of T1 in T3. This is because the delete rule of RESTRICT is enforced before the delete rule of CASCADE.

If table T1 is a parent of table T3 with delete rule of NO ACTION, the child rows may be deleted by the delete rule of CASCADE when deleting rows from T2 before the NO ACTION delete rule is enforced for the deletes from T1. If deletes from T2 did not result in deleting all child rows for parent keys of T1 in T3, then a constraint violation will be raised (SQLSTATE 23504).

 Note: The SQLSTATE returned is different depending on whether the rule is RESTRICT or NO ACTION.

UPDATE Rules

The database manager prevents the update of a unique key of a parent row. When you update a foreign key in a dependent table, and the foreign key is defined with NOT NULL option, it must match some value of the parent key of the parent table. Two options exist:

- **RESTRICT**
  The update operation for the parent key will be rejected if a row in the dependent table matches the original values of the key.
- **NO ACTION**
  The update operation for the parent key will be rejected if any row in the dependent table does not have a corresponding parent key when the update statement is completed (excluding after triggers). This is the default.

Here is an example of a parent table and dependent table which have a referential integrity constraint:

```
CREATE TABLE department
  (deptno CHAR(3) NOT NULL PRIMARY KEY,
   deptname VARCHAR(29),
   mgrno CHAR(6))

CREATE TABLE employee
  (empno char(6),
   firstname VARCHAR(12),
   lastname VARCHAR(15),
   workdept CHAR(3) REFERENCES department (deptno)
     ON DELETE CASCADE,
   phoneno CHAR(4),
   job CHAR(8))
```

In this example, deptno of the department table is the primary key, workdept of
the employee table is the foreign key. The delete rule of the foreign key is CASCADE.
When you delete a row from the department table, the database manager checks if
there are any dependent rows in the employee table with matching foreign key
values. If any dependent rows are found, they will be deleted as well.

You can define referential constraints using CREATE TABLE statements as in this
example, or ALTER TABLE statements. You can issue CREATE TABLE statements or
ALTER TABLE statements from the command line processor, the Command Center,
or application programs. You can also define referential constraints when creating
or altering tables using the Control Center.

Table-Check Constraints

Table-check constraints will enforce data integrity at the table level. Once a table-
check constraint has been defined for a table, every UPDATE and INSERT statement
will involve a checking of the restriction or constraint. If the constraint is violated,
the data record will not be inserted or updated, and an SQL error will be returned.

A table-check constraint can be defined at table creation time or later using the
ALTER TABLE statement. You can also define table-check constraints when creating
or altering tables using the Control Center.

Here is an example of adding a table-check constraint using the ALTER TABLE
statement:

```
ALTER TABLE employee ADD CHECK
(job IN ('MANAGER','CLERK','SALESREP','OPERATOR'))
```

This newly added table-check constraint ensures that the column job of employee table does not have other values than 'MANAGER', 'CLERK', 'SALESREP', or 'OPERATOR'. If the table contains rows which violate this rule, then on adding this table-check constraint, you will get an error (SQL0544).

The table-check constraints can help implement specific rules for the data values contained in the table by specifying the values allowed in one or more columns in every row of a table. This can save the application developer time, since the validation of each data value can be performed by the database and not by each of the applications accessing the database.

The check constraint's definition is stored in the system catalog tables, specifically the SYSIBM.SYSCHECKS table. In addition, you can use the SYSCAT.CHECKS system catalog view to view the check constraint definitions.

User-defined Distinct Types (UDTs)

DB2 UDB includes a set of built-in data types with defined characteristics and behaviors: character strings, numerics, date/time values, large objects, nulls, graphic strings, binary strings, and datalinks. However, sometimes the built-in data types might not serve the needs of your applications. DB2 UDB provides user-defined distinct types (UDTs) which enable you to define the distinct data types you need for your applications. UDTs are based on the built-in data types.

For example, you might define a KILOGRAM and POUND data type that is based on the DECIMAL data type. If columns are defined using KILOGRAM and POUND, these columns cannot be directly compared. This is known as *strong typing*. DB2 UDB provides this strong data typing to avoid end-user mistakes during the assignment or comparison of different types of real-world data.

UDTs are the foundation for most object-oriented features. You can group similar objects into related data types. These types have a name, an internal representation, and a specific behavior. By using UDTs, you can tell DB2 UDB the name of your new type and how it is represented internally.

You do not lose performance benefits by using UDTs. Distinct types are highly integrated into the database manager and are internally represented the same way as built-in data types. They share the same efficient code used to implement built-in functions, comparison operators, indexes, and so on.

The SYSCAT.DATATYPES catalog view allows you to see the UDTs that have been defined for your database. This catalog view also shows you the data types defined by the database manager when the database was created.

DB2 Server Side Features

Here is an example of defining UDTs based on the DECIMAL data type and used in a CREATE TABLE statement:

```
CREATE DISTINCT TYPE kilogram
     AS DECIMAL (5,2) WITH COMPARISONS
CREATE DISTINCT TYPE pound
     AS DECIMAL (5,2) WITH COMPARISONS
CREATE TABLE product
     (name char(10), weight_k kilogram, weight_p pound)
```

You can issue CREATE DISTINCT TYPE statements from the command line processor, the Command Center, or application programs. You can also define UDTs using the Control Center.

The new data types are used in the table definition just like the DB2 UDB built-in data types. DB2 UDB will not allow you to compare or perform arithmetic operations on the POUND and KILOGRAM typed columns directly. A casting function would need to be used to perform arithmetic operations using the columns defined with these types. In other words, you could not use built-in functions, such as the average function (AVG), for a column defined as POUND or KILOGRAM, unless you use the appropriate casting functions or create a new user-defined function that can use those UDTs as an input parameter.

When you define a UDT, the database manager creates two casting functions using the same name as the based built-in data type and the UDT. The function whose name is same as the base built-in function casts the UDT to the base built-in data type, and the other one whose name is same as the UDT casts the base built-in data type to the UDT.

The following SQL statement would result in an error. The data type for the constant value of 30 is of type INTEGER. An INTEGER data type cannot be directly compared with the POUND data type.

```
SELECT f_name, weight_p
FROM health
WHERE weight_p > 30
```

To resolve the error, a cast of the constant value of 30 is required. By casting, the value of 30 is treated as a POUND data type. In the following example, the POUND(INTEGER) casting function, which was created when the POUND data type was defined, is being used to convert the value of 30 to the POUND data type.

```
SELECT f_name, weight_p
FROM health
WHERE weight_p > POUND(30)
```

Or you can cast the `weight_p` column to integer value using the `INTEGER(POUND)` casting function so that `weight_p` column can be compared with the integer value 30. The `INTEGER(POUND)` function was created when the `POUND` data type was defined.

```
SELECT f_name, weight_p
FROM health
WHERE INTEGER(weight_p) > 30
```

Large Objects (LOBs)

Large objects (LOBs) enable you to store and manipulate large, complex data objects in the database: objects such as audio, video, images, and large documents. DB2 UDB provides three data types to store LOBs: CLOB, DBCLOB, and BLOB.

Character Large Objects (CLOB)

Character large objects are varying-length SBCS or MBCS character strings that are stored in the database (Fig. 4–2). CLOB columns are used to store greater than 32 KB of text. The maximum size for each CLOB column is 2 GB (gigabytes). Since this data type is of varying-length, the amount of disk space allocated is determined by the amount of data in each record. Therefore, you should create the column specifying the length of the longest string.

DB2 Server Side Features

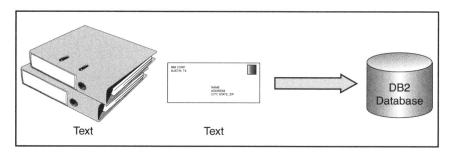

Fig. 4–2 *CLOB Character Strings*

Be aware that 32672 bytes is the maximum length of the VARCHAR column you can define, and you should consider using the VARCHAR type rather than the CLOB type if your data is less than this limit. The VARCHAR type can provide you with better performance, because the buffer pool can be used. The CLOB (and also LONG VARCHAR) data types cannot use the buffer pool, and the data must be read directly from the disk.

This consideration is also applicable for the DBCLOB type that is discussed next. If your data is less than 16336 characters, consider using the VARGRAPHIC type rather than DBCLOB.

> **Note:** To define a 32672 byte VARCHAR column, the table must be created in a table space whose page size is 32 K bytes, because the maximum row length depends on the page size of the table space in which the table is created. In a DB2 UDB database, you can create table spaces with 4 K, 8 K, 16 K and 32 K bytes data page. The maximum row length is 4005, 8101, 16293, and 32677 bytes for each data page size.

Double-byte Character Large Objects (DBCLOB)

Double-byte character large objects are varying-length character strings that are stored in the database using two bytes to represent each character. DBCLOB columns are used for large amounts (>32 KB) of double-byte text data such as Japanese text. The maximum length should be specified during the column definition because each data record will be variable in length.

Binary Large Object (BLOB)

Binary large objects are variable-length binary strings (Fig. 4–3). The data is stored in a binary format in the database. There are restrictions when using this data type, including the inability to sort using this type of column. The BLOB data type is useful for storing non-traditional relational database information, such as video and audio data.

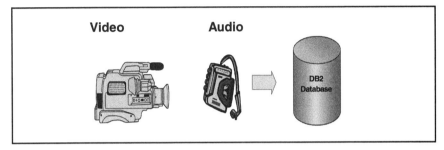

Fig. 4–3 *Binary Large Objects (BLOBs)*

The maximum size of each BLOB column is 2 GB (gigabytes). Since this data type is of varying length, the amount of disk space allocated is determined by the amount of data in each record, not the defined maximum size of the column in the table definition.

Here is an example of a table having a BLOB column:

```
CREATE TABLE emp_photo (
    empno char(6) NOT NULL,
    photo_format varchar(10) NOT NULL,
    picture blob(100k) )
```

In this example, the picture column is a BLOB column.

DB2 Server Side Features

Manipulating Large Objects

To develop applications to handle large objects, a number of options exist. When manipulating large objects, you want to ensure the efficient transfer of data between database and application. Because of the potential size of large objects, DB2 UDB provides several different ways to access the objects: referencing them directly using host variables, referencing them using LOB locators, and referencing them using file reference variables. The following sections detail the various methods of LOB reference and provide examples to show how programs can manipulate and retrieve large objects from DB2 UDB.

Manipulating LOBs Directly Using Host Variables

LOBs can be directly referenced when they are known to be of a small and limited size. This could be the case when dealing with small binary objects such as thumbnail bitmap files. In this scenario, LOBs can be accessed and manipulated directly using host variables like any other data type. The entire LOB value is copied from the server to the client application. Because of their size, small LOBs can be passed to application memory without causing application errors such as a stack overflow or exceeding the capacity of the client memory buffer.

Here is a sample program which retrieves the CLOB field RESUME directly from the EMP_RESUME table and prints the first 15 lines of the CLOB data. Note that a host variable resume is defined for the CLOB field as SQL TYPE IS CLOB(5K) in the declare section. This host variable resume is a structure containing resume.length and resume.data for the length and the content of the retrieved LOB data. The declare section also includes the indicator variable lobind, which indicates if the retrieved LOB data is null. See the DECLARE CURSOR statement and the FETCH statement in our example. The cursor selects two columns from the table, but the FETCH statement retrieves values for three host variables. Two are for the selected data specified in the cursor definition; one is for the indicator variable.

```
#include <stdio.h>
#include <stdlib.h>
#include <string.h>
#include "util.h"

EXEC SQL INCLUDE SQLCA;

#define CHECKERR(CE_STR) if (check_error (CE_STR, &sqlca) != 0)
return 1;

int main(int argc, char *argv[]) {

EXEC SQL BEGIN DECLARE SECTION; /* :rk.1:erk. */
  char number[7];
  SQL TYPE IS CLOB(5K) resume;
  short lobind;
```

```
    char userid[9];
    char passwd[19];
EXEC SQL END DECLARE SECTION;

printf( "Sample C program: LOBVAL\n" );

if (argc == 1) {
  EXEC SQL CONNECT TO sample;
  CHECKERR ("CONNECT TO SAMPLE");
}
else if (argc == 3) {
  strcpy (userid, argv[1]);
  strcpy (passwd, argv[2]);
  EXEC SQL CONNECT TO sample USER :userid USING :passwd;
  CHECKERR ("CONNECT TO SAMPLE");
}
else {
  printf ("\nUSAGE: lobval [userid passwd]\n\n");
  return 1;
} /* endif */

EXEC SQL DECLARE c1 CURSOR FOR
   SELECT empno, resume FROM emp_resume WHERE
resume_format='ascii';

EXEC SQL OPEN c1;
CHECKERR ("OPEN CURSOR");

do {
  char *c;
  unsigned long idx, lines;
  EXEC SQL FETCH c1 INTO :number, :resume :lobind;  /* :rk.2:erk.
*/
  if (SQLCODE != 0) break;
  if (lobind < 0) {
    printf ("NULL LOB indicated\n");
  } else {

/* PRINT OUT THE CONTENTS OF THE LOB */
printf ("Printing the first 15 lines for the resume of empno
%s\n",
number);
for (idx=0, lines=0, c=resume.data; /* :rk.3:erk. */
idx < resume.length, lines < 16; idx++, c++) {
  printf ("%c", *c);
  if (*c == '\n') lines++;
} /* endfor */
printf ("Resume Length (number of characters):%d\n",
resume.length); /* :rk.4:erk. */
printf ("\n\n\n");
} /* endif */
} while ( 1 );

EXEC SQL CLOSE c1;
CHECKERR ("CLOSE CURSOR");
```

```
EXEC SQL CONNECT RESET;
CHECKERR ("CONNECT RESET");
return 0;
}
```

This program is provided by the DB2 product as a sample. The file name is *DB2PATH*\samples\c\lobval.sqc, and *DB2PATH* is the installed directory (C:\Program Files\SQLLIB is the default directory).

LOB Locators

Accessing LOBs directly works well when the LOBs are relatively small. However, the use of large objects is generally concerned with the storage of large amounts of information. Retrieving a 2 GB object into a client application would be inadvisable due to memory constraints. Often, applications may not want to retrieve all of a particular LOB. Perhaps only a certain subset of the LOB is required by the application. It is highly inefficient to retrieve a 1 GB LOB of which only 10 KB is needed. This is where the concept of LOB locators becomes useful. LOB locators are based on the familiar concept of using a small descriptor value to represent a much larger value.

A LOB locator is 4 bytes in size, and can be represented in an embedded SQL program as a host variable. This locator is then associated with a specific LOB in a particular row and a particular column of a table. LOB locators can be allocated to, and freed from, specific LOBs. LOB locators are implicitly freed when the unit of work ends. LOB locators can also be explicitly freed using the FREE LOCATOR statement.

The benefit of a LOB locator is that only the 4 byte value of the LOB locator is passed to the client by a FETCH statement. The actual LOB value itself remains on the server. The use of LOB locators can also eliminate the overhead of large amounts of data transfer between client and server.

In the following program, the LOB locator is first associated with the CLOB value, and then the program retrieves only the department information and education information from the RESUME data using the VALUES statement and then prints it. Notice that the host variable resume is defined as SQL TYPE IS CLOB_LOCATOR.

```
#include <stdio.h>
#include <stdlib.h>
#include <string.h>
#include "util.h"

EXEC SQL INCLUDE SQLCA;

#define  CHECKERR(CE_STR) if (check_error (CE_STR, &sqlca) != 0)
  return 1;
```

```
int main(int argc, char *argv[]) {

EXEC SQL BEGIN DECLARE SECTION; /* :rk.1:erk. */
  char number[7];
  long deptInfoBeginLoc;
  long deptInfoEndLoc;
  SQL TYPE IS CLOB_LOCATOR resume;
  SQL TYPE IS CLOB_LOCATOR deptBuffer;
  short lobind;
  char buffer[1000]="";
  char userid[9];
  char passwd[19];
EXEC SQL END DECLARE SECTION;

printf( "Sample C program: LOBLOC\n" );

if (argc == 1) {
  EXEC SQL CONNECT TO sample;
  CHECKERR ("CONNECT TO SAMPLE");
}
else if (argc == 3) {
  strcpy (userid, argv[1]);
  strcpy (passwd, argv[2]);
  EXEC SQL CONNECT TO sample USER :userid USING :passwd;
  CHECKERR ("CONNECT TO SAMPLE");
}
else {
  printf ("\nUSAGE: lobloc [userid passwd]\n\n");
  return 1;
} /* endif */

/* Employee A10030 is not included in the following select,
because
the lobeval program manipulates the record for A10030 so that it
is
not compatible with lobloc */

EXEC SQL DECLARE c1 CURSOR FOR
  SELECT empno, resume FROM emp_resume WHERE resume_format='ascii'
  AND empno <> 'A00130';

EXEC SQL OPEN c1;
CHECKERR ("OPEN CURSOR");

do {
  EXEC SQL FETCH c1 INTO :number, :resume :lobind;  /* :rk.2:erk.
*/
  if (SQLCODE != 0) break;
  if (lobind < 0) {
    printf ("NULL LOB indicated\n");
  } else {
    /* EVALUATE the LOB LOCATOR */
    /* Locate the beginning of "Department Information" section */
    EXEC SQL VALUES (POSSTR(:resume, 'Department Information'))
```

```
        INTO :deptInfoBeginLoc;
        CHECKERR ("VALUES1");

        /* Locate the beginning of "Education" section (end of
    "Dept.Info" */
        EXEC SQL VALUES (POSSTR(:resume, 'Education')) INTO
    :deptInfoEndLoc;
        CHECKERR ("VALUES2");

        /* Obtain ONLY the "Department Information" section by using
    SUBSTR */
        EXEC SQL VALUES(SUBSTR(:resume,
    :deptInfoBeginLoc,:deptInfoEndLoc
            :deptInfoBeginLoc)) INTO :deptBuffer;
        CHECKERR ("VALUES3");

        /* Append the "Department Information" section to the :buffer
    var. */
        EXEC SQL VALUES(:buffer || :deptBuffer) INTO :buffer;
        CHECKERR ("VALUES4");
      } /* endif */
    } while ( 1 );

    printf ("%s\n",buffer);

    EXEC SQL FREE LOCATOR :resume, :deptBuffer; /* :rk.3:erk. */
    CHECKERR ("FREE LOCATOR");

    EXEC SQL CLOSE c1;
    CHECKERR ("CLOSE CURSOR");

    EXEC SQL CONNECT RESET;
    CHECKERR ("CONNECT RESET");
    return 0;
    }
```

This program is provided by the DB2 product as a sample. The file name is *DB2PATH*\samples\c\lobloc.sqc, and *DB2PATH* is the installed directory (C:\Program Files\SQLLIB is the default directory).

LOB File Reference Variables

LOB File Reference *Variables* are used to avoid the memory constraints of direct LOB reference. The LOB value on the server is copied in its entirety to the client. However, the value is not passed into the application's memory. Instead, it is passed straight into a file at the client, represented by the LOB file reference variable, much as a LOB locator represents a LOB value. File reference variables may be used by applications not only when querying, but also updating a database. In other words, they can act as a source or target data source. LOB file reference variables eliminate the need for routines on the client that read and write to files in order to move LOB data.

The following program provides an example of how a LOB file reference variable would work in an embedded SQL program. This example would make the Direct LOB Reference example redundant, since this is the recommended way to transfer a LOB value to disk by the client application. In this example, the SQL_FILE_OVERWRITE option is set to the file_option field in the file reference variable. This means that a new file is created if none already exists. If the file already exists, the new data overwrites the data in the file.

```c
#include <stdio.h>
#include <stdlib.h>
#include <string.h>
#include <sql.h>
#include "util.h"

EXEC SQL INCLUDE SQLCA;

#define CHECKERR(CE_STR) if (check_error (CE_STR, &sqlca) != 0)
return 1;

int main(int argc, char *argv[]) {

EXEC SQL BEGIN DECLARE SECTION; /* :rk.1:erk. */
SQL TYPE IS CLOB_FILE resume;
short lobind;
char userid[9];
char passwd[19];
EXEC SQL END DECLARE SECTION;

printf( "Sample C program: LOBFILE\n" );

if (argc == 1) {
  EXEC SQL CONNECT TO sample;
  CHECKERR ("CONNECT TO SAMPLE");
}
else if (argc == 3) {
  strcpy (userid, argv[1]);
  strcpy (passwd, argv[2]);
  EXEC SQL CONNECT TO sample USER :userid USING :passwd;
  CHECKERR ("CONNECT TO SAMPLE");
```

DB2 Server Side Features

```
}
else {
  printf ("\nUSAGE: lobfile [userid passwd]\n\n");
  return 1;
} /* endif */

  strcpy (resume.name, "RESUME.TXT");  /* :rk.2:erk. */
  resume.name_length = strlen("RESUME.TXT");
  resume.file_options = SQL_FILE_OVERWRITE;

EXEC SQL SELECT resume INTO :resume :lobind FROM emp_resume /
*:rk.3:erk.*/
  WHERE resume_format='ascii' AND empno='000130';

if (lobind < 0) {
  printf ("NULL LOB indicated \n");
} else {
  printf ("Resume for EMPNO 000130 is in file : RESUME.TXT\n");
  } /* endif */

EXEC SQL CONNECT RESET;
CHECKERR ("CONNECT RESET");
return 0;
}
```

This program is provided by the DB2 product as a sample. The file name is DB2PATH\SQLLIB\samples\c\lobfile.sqc, and DB2PATH is the installed directory (C:\Program Files\SQLLIB is the default directory).

For the file_option field of the file reference variable, you can also specify the following options:

- **SQL_FILE_READ**
  This is used when the application is updating a database. Using this option, the file can be open, read, and closed. DB2 UDB determines the length of the data in the file (in bytes) when opening the file. DB2 UDB then returns the length through the data_length field of the file reference variable structure.

- **SQL_FILE_CREATE**
  This is used when the application is retrieving data from a database. This option creates a new file. If the file already exists, an error will returned.

- **SQL_FILE_APPEND**
  This is used when the application is retrieving data from a database. This option has the output appended to the file, if it exists. Otherwise, it creates a new file.

In this section, we introduced embedded SQL program examples selecting LOB data. In Chapter 5, we will demonstrate how to retrieve LOB data using Visual Basic with ADO.

User-Defined Functions (UDFs)

The built-in functions supplied by DB2 UDB may not satisfy all of your application needs. To allow you to extend those capabilities, DB2 UDB supports user-defined functions (UDFs). Of course, you can implement them as subroutines or functions in your application; however, it is difficult for other users or application developers to re-use those subroutines or functions, because you must inform them and package the functions effectively for their use.

The other benefit is the performance. Invoking a UDF directly from the database engine instead of from your application can have a considerable performance advantage. For example, assume your application retrieves the data by a SELECT statement and then filters it using further processing, or your application calculates any other value using retrieved rows. By using a UDF, only the data of interest can be passed across the interface between the application and the database (Fig. 4–4).

Whether the function is a simple transformation, a trivial calculation, or a complicated multivariate analysis, you can probably use a UDF to do the job.

You can write your own code in C/C++, Java, OLE enabled languages such as Visual C++ and Visual Basic, or SQL to perform operations within any SQL statement that returns a single scalar value or a table. This gives you significant flexibility. Your applications can return single scalar values such as select lists from databases, or they can return whole tables from external data sources such as flat-files, spreadsheets, and OLE DB providers.

UDFs provide a way to standardize your applications. By implementing a common set of user-defined functions, duplication of code is avoided and many applications can process data in the same way, thus ensuring consistent results.

UDFs also support object-oriented programming in your applications. UDFs provide for abstraction, allowing you to define the methods that can be used to perform operations on data objects. Some of these data objects could be represented using user-defined distinct types (UDTs). In addition, UDFs provide for encapsulation, allowing you to control access to the underlying data of an object, protecting it from direct manipulation and possible damage.

DB2 Server Side Features

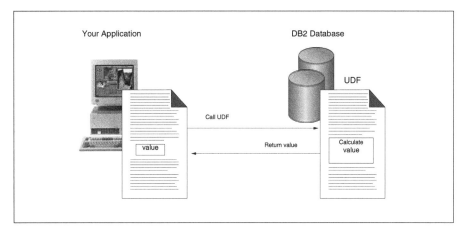

Fig. 4–4 *UDFs Extend SQL Statements in Applications*

Defining UDFs

CREATE FUNCTION statements are used to define UDFs. There are five different types of UDFs that can be created using this statement:

- Source functions
- SQL functions
- External Scalar functions
- External Table functions
- OLE DB External Table functions

Source functions are implemented using the implementation of an existing function. SQL functions are implemented using an SQL statement within the CREATE FUNCTION statement. External functions including external scalar functions and external table functions must be coded in a programming language such as C, and then registered by CREATE FUNCTION statements.

A scalar function returns a single value answer each time it is called. For example, the build-in function SUBSTR() is a scalar function.

A table function returns a table to the SQL statement that references it. A table function can only be referenced in the FROM clause of a SELECT statement. Such a function can be used to apply the SQL language (such as SELECT, GROUP BY, and UNION) to non-DB2 data, or to capture such data and put it into a DB2 table. For example, it could dynamically convert a file consisting of non-DB2 data into a table, or it could retrieve data from the World Wide Web or an operating system and tabulate it. A table function can only be an external function.

An OLE DB external table function is a UDF to access data from an OLE DB provider. As the name implies, an OLE DB external table function returns a table to the SQL statement that references it, as well as an external table function. However, for an OLE DB external table function, you don't need to code the implementation of the function. You only need to register the table function to retrieve data using a generic built-in OLE DB consumer interface with any OLE DB provider.

All UDFs are registered in the system catalog SYSCAT.FUNCTIONS.

Source Functions

Source functions are a type of UDF which are implemented by invoking another function that is already registered in the database. Therefore, you don't need to write any code to implement this type of UDF.

The following example defines a UDT and a table using it:

```
CREATE DISTINCT TYPE kilogram AS DECIMAL (5,2) WITH
COMPARISONS
CREATE TABLE product
    (name char(10), price decimal (5,2), weight_k kilogram)
```

Suppose you want to calculate the average price and weight of all products and execute the following statements:

```
SELECT AVG(price) FROM product
SELECT AVG(weight_k) FROM product
```

The first statement returns the average price of all products; however, the second statement returns an error because the function AVG does not support kilogram, which is the data type of the weight_k column. To get the average value of the weight_k column, you need to define a new function which supports the data type kilogram. Here is an example of a CREATE FUNCTION statement for this UDF:

```
CREATE FUNCTION avg_k (kilogram)
    RETURNS kilogram SOURCE avg(decimal(5,2))
```

DB2 Server Side Features

The function avg_k takes the kilogram type data as the input, calculates the average value using the AVG function specified with the SOURCE option, and then returns that value as the kilogram type. See the *DB2 UDB SQL Reference* for the complete syntax of the CREATE FUNCTION statement. The following example shows how you can use the UDF avg_k:

```
SELECT avg_k(weight_k) FROM product
```

SQL Functions

The SQL function is a type of UDF which is implemented by an SQL statement. There are many occasions where similar expressions or sub-selects are used multiple times within one query or within an application. Using SQL functions can encapsulate this repetitive logic and make SQL statements simpler. SQL functions do not need external languages (such as C, Java) into which their logic gets embedded. Therefore, an SQL language does not have any overhead, such as transforming SQL parameters into parameters of external languages, or mapping the result to the SQL.

 Note: The SQL UDFs are supported from DB2 UDB Version 7.1.

The following is an example defining an SQL function which executes the tangent of a value using the existing sine and cosine function:

```
CREATE FUNCTION tan (x DOUBLE) RETURNS DOUBLE
    LANGUAGE SQL
    CONTAINS SQL
    NO EXTERNAL ACTION
    DETERMINISTIC
    RETURN sin(x)/cos(x)
```

Each clause in this example means the following:

- CREATE FUNCTION tan (x DOUBLE) RETURNS DOUBLE
  This clause specifies that the UDF named tan receives a double value and returns a double value.

- LANGUAGE SQL
  This clause specifies that the function is written using SQL. The supported SQL is currently limited to the `RETURN` statement.
- CONTAINS SQL
  This clause specifies that neither read nor modify are performed to the database. If this function queries or modifies data in the database, specify `READS SQL DATA` instead.
- NO EXTERNAL ACTION
  This optional clause specifies that the function will not take any action that changes the state of an object which is not managed by the database manager. By specifying this option, the system can use certain optimizations that assume functions have no external impacts.
- DETERMINISTIC
  This clause specifies that the UDF always returns the same results for given identical input values.
- RETURN sin (x) / cos (x)
  This is the mandatory clause defining the output of the function. In our example, the output is calculated by `sin (x) / cos (x)`.

You can also define an SQL function which returns a table. Here is an example of an SQL table function which retrieves rows using supplied value and returns them as a table:

```
CREATE FUNCTION deptemployees (deptno CHAR(3))
  RETURNS TABLE
  (empno CHAR(6),lastname VARCHAR(15),firstnme VARCHAR(12))
  LANGUAGE SQL
  READS SQL DATA
  NO EXTERNAL ACTION
  DETERMINISTIC
  RETURN
    SELECT empno,lastname,firstnme FROM employee
      WHERE employee.workdept=deptemployees.deptno
```

And here is an example using the function:

```
SELECT * FROM TABLE (deptemployees(CHAR('A00'))) as t1
```

DB2 Server Side Features

When you use a UDF which returns a table, you must specify the correlation name for the UDF referred as a table. In this example, t1 is the correlation name. When you need to specify a column name of the UDF, such as the case of the join operation, this correlation name should be used like t1.lastname.

External Scalar Functions

As previously described, to implement external scalar functions, you need to code them using programming languages. Here are the steps that should be performed:

- Write the UDF.
- Compile and Link the UDF.
- Register the UDF using the CREATE FUNCTION statement.

These steps are described using a simple example in the following sections.

Write UDFs

DB2 UDB passes the following arguments to the external UDF if it is written in C or C++. You should use this information to implement UDFs. Note that these arguments are pointers.

- **SQL argument**
  This argument is set by DB2 before calling the UDF and repeated n times, where n is specified in the definition of the UDF using a CREATE FUNCTION statement. The value of these arguments is taken from the expression specified in the function invocation.

- **SQL result**
  This argument is set by the UDF before returning to DB2 UDB. Only one SQL result is returned for scalar functions. DB2 UDB allocates the buffer for the SQL result and passes its address to the UDF.

- **SQL argument indicator**
  This argument is set by DB2 before calling the UDF and repeated m times, where m is the number of SQL arguments. The n th SQL argument indicator corresponds to n th SQL argument, and it can be used by the UDF to determine if the corresponding SQL argument is null or not. If the value is 0, it means the corresponding SQL argument is not null. If the value is -1, it is null.

- **SQL result indicator**
  This argument is set by the UDF before returning to DB2 UDB. It indicates if the SQL result is null or not. The value of the SQL result indicator is 0 or positive when the SQL result is not null. It is negative when the SQL result is null.

- **SQL state**
  This argument is set by the UDF before returning to DB2 UDB and used to return the SQL state, which signals warning or error conditions. This argument is a CHAR(5) value. If warning or error conditions are not detected, the value of the SQL state is '00000'.

- **Function name**
  This argument is set by DB2 UDB before calling the UDF and includes the qualified function name, which is specified when defining the UDF using a `CREATE FUNCTION` statement. The form of the function name passed to the UDF is:

  `Schemaname.Function-name`

  The data type of this argument is VARCHAR(27).

- **Specific name**
  This argument is set by DB2 UDB before calling the UDF and includes the specific name, which is a unique name for the instance of the function. The specific name is specified in the `SPECIFIC` clause of the `CREATE FUNCTION` statement for the UDF. The `CREATE FUNCTION` statement will be described in detail in "Register a UDF Using a CREATE FUNCTION Statement" on page 147.

> **Note:** Each UDF in a instance has a unique specific name (if you don't specify it in a `CREATE FUNCTION` statement, DB2 generates a unique name). However, a function name does not need to be unique. Multiple UDFs can use the same function name. It is a good idea to use the same function name for a group of UDFs which have the same functionality. For example, there are four built-in functions corresponding to the function name `SYSFUM.ABS`, which returns the absolute value of the input value. Each of these four functions has a different specific name for the argument of SMALLINT, INTEGER, BIGINT, and DOUBLE data types.

- **Diagnostic message**
  This argument is set by the UDF before returning to DB2 UDB and the UDF can use this argument to include message text in a DB2 message. Its data type is VARCHAR(70). When the UDF returns either an error or a warning, it can include descriptive information here.

DB2 Server Side Features

- **Scratchpad**

  This argument is set by DB2 UDB before calling the UDF. It is only present if the CREATE FUNCTION statement for the UDF has the SCRATCHPAD keyword. If the SCRATCHPAD keyword is specified, at first invocation of the UDF, memory is allocated for a scratchpad to be used by the external function. The allocated memory can be used to save state information from one call of the UDF to the next. In other words, any changes made to the scratchpad by the UDF on one call will be there on the next call and can be referred to.

- **Call type**

  This argument is set by DB2 UDB before calling the UDF. It is only present if the keyword FINAL CALL is specified in the CREATE FUNCTION statement for the UDF. It indicates the call type of the UDF in an integer value: normal call (0), first call (-1), or final call (1). A final call is to enable the UDF to free any system resources (such as a scratchpad) it acquired. A final call occurs at the end-of-statement or the end-of-transaction, and no SQL argument or SQL argument indicator value is passed. A normal call passes all the SQL input. A first call is a normal call, but the scratchpad (if any) is set to binary zeros.

- **DB info**

  This argument is set by DB2 before calling the UDF and only present if the keyword DB2INFO is specified in the CREATE FUNCTION statement for the UDF. This argument is the sqludf_dbinfo structure defined in the header file sqludf.h (see *DB2 UDB Application Development Guide* for the detailed information of the header file sqludf.h). This structure contains database name, application authorization ID, database code page, table name, column name, version/release number, operating platform for the application server, and so on.

The following example is an external scalar function, raisesal. Suppose you have a table including the employee's salary. This UDF receives two double precision floating point number. One is the original salary, the other is the percentage to increase it. Then the UDF returns the raised salary by the percentage factor; 1 is 100%.

```
#include <stdlib.h>
#include <string.h>
#include <stdio.h>
#include <sqludf.h>
#include <sqlca.h>
#include <sqlda.h>
#ifdef __cplusplus
extern "C"
#endif
void SQL_API_FN raisesal (
    SQLUDF_DOUBLE    *salary,
    SQLUDF_DOUBLE    *percentage,
    SQLUDF_DOUBLE    *newSalary,
    SQLUDF_SMALLINT  *salaryNullInd,
```

```
        SQLUDF_SMALLINT  *percentageNullInd,
        SQLUDF_SMALLINT  *newSalaryNullInd,
        SQLUDF_TRAIL_ARGS) {
if (*percentageNullInd == -1) {
        *newSalaryNullInd = -1;
    } else {
        *newSalary = *salary * (1 + *percentage);
        *newSalaryNullInd = 0;
    } /* endif */
}
```

In this example, `salary` and `percentage` are the SQL arguments, `newSalary` is the SQL result, `salaryNullInd` and `percentageNullInd` are the SQL indicator, and `newSalaryNullInd` is the SQL result indicator. Be aware that you don't need to use all arguments which can be passed to UDF from DB2 UDB.

Note: In this example, only a single function called `raisesal` was created. You can, however, create multiple functions in a single source file.

Java UDFs take only SQL argument and SQL result, but they can call extra methods to access the other information. Those methods are available in `COM.ibm.db2.app.UDF` class. For example, if a Java UDF needs to use a scratchpad, it can call `setScratchPad()` method and `getScratchPad()` method without receiving any arguments for the scratchpad. To access the information about the call type, a Java UDF should call `getCallType()` method. For the description of the `COM.ibm.db2.app.UDF` interface, see the manual *DB2 UDB Application Development Guide.*

In a Java UDF, you can use instance variables instead of the scratchpad to achieve continuity between calls of the UDF. The ability to achieve continuity between calls to a UDF by means of a scratchpad is controlled by the `SCRATCHPAD` and `NO SCRATCHPAD` option of `CREATE FUNCTION`, regardless of whether the DB2 scratchpad or instance variables are used.

The Web site `www.software.ibm.com/data/db2/java` and the manual *DB2 UDB Application Development Guide* provides you many useful hints and tips for developing Java UDFs.

The following example is a Java UDF, `ctr`. This UDF increments and returns a counter to number the rows in your SELECT. Observe that an instance variable `counter` is used in this example.

```
import COM.ibm.db2.app.*;
import COM.ibm.db2.jdbc.app.*;
import java.sql.*;
```

DB2 Server Side Features

```
import java.io.*;
import java.net.*;
class DB2Udf extends UDF
{
   int counter = 0; // instance variable
   public void
   ctr (int result) throws Exception
   {
     set (1, ++counter);
   }
}
```

Compile and Link UDFs

To compile and link UDFs written in C/C++ on a machine on which Microsoft Visual C++ was installed, you can simply use the batch file bldmsudf.bat that DB2 UDB provides. The batch file bldmsudf.bat, in *DB2PATH*\samples\c, and in *DB2PATH*\samples\cpp, contains the commands to build a UDF (*DB2PATH* is the directory where you install the DB2 UDB). DB2 UDB also provides bldsqljs.bat for Java UDFs.

The following code is extracted from the bldmsudf.bat file, that compiles, links and copies a UDF program:

```
@echo off
if "%1" == "" goto error
cl -Z7 -Od -c -W2 -D_X86_=1 -DWIN32 %1.c
link -debug:full -debugtype:cv -dll -out:%1.dll %1.obj db2api.lib
db2apie.lib -def:%1.def
copy %1.dll %DB2PATH%\function
goto exit
:error
echo Usage: bldmsudf prog_name
:exit
@echo on
```

The batch file takes one parameter, %1, which specifies the name of your source file. It uses the source file name, %1, for the DLL name. You need to specify a module definition file using -def option in the link command. The module definition file can be as follows:

```
LIBRARY UDF
DESCRIPTION 'Library for DB2 User-Defined Functions'
EXPORTS
   raisesal
```

This example defines only the UDF `raisesal`. If your source file includes more UDFs, put those names in the list.

If you want to build our example shown in the previous section, execute this batch file as follows (assuming the file including our UDF example is udf.c):

```
bldmsudf udf
```

External UDFs cannot contain embedded SQL statements. Therefore, to build an external UDF program, you do not need to connect to a database to pre-compile and bind the program.

Register a UDF Using a CREATE FUNCTION Statement

The next step is registering the UDF using a `CREATE FUNCTION` statement. The following `CREATE FUNCTION` statement registers the UDF `raisesal` which we introduced as an example in "Write UDFs" on page 142.

```
CREATE FUNCTION raisesal (float, float) RETURNS float
EXTERNAL NAME 'udf!raisesal'
NO SQL
PARAMETER STYLE DB2SQL
LANGUAGE C
```

Each clause in this example means the following:

- CREATE FUNCTION raisesal (float, float) RETURNS float
  The UDF named `raisesal` receives two float values and returns one float value.
- EXTERNAL NAME 'udf!raisesal'
  This is used to link to the code written in a programming language. In this example, it is assumed that the DLL file which includes UDF `raisesal` is `udf.dll`, and it is located in *DB2PATH*\function (*DB2PATH* is the directory where you install the DB2 UDB). If you put the DLL file in another directory, you must use the absolute path name as follows:

```
EXTERNAL NAME 'C:\OtherDir\udf!raisesal
```

- NO SQL
  This is a mandatory clause for an external function.

DB2 Server Side Features

- PARAMETER STYLE DB2SQL
  Specifies the convention for passing parameters to and returning the value from UDFs. PARAMETER STYLE DB2SQL must be specified when LANGUAGE C or LANGUAGE OLE is used.
- LANGUAGE C
  The UDF body is written using C language.

Only mandatory clauses are specified in our example; however, a CREATE FUNCTION statement can take more clauses such as:

- FENCED or NOT FENCED
  These clause are used to specify if the UDF is 'fenced' or 'not-fenced'. Fenced functions are insulated from the internal resources on the database manager, whereas not-fenced functions run in the database manager operating environment's process. Therefore, not-fenced functions can provide better performance, but might cause problems to the database manager if they have any bugs. Fenced functions are safe.
- DETERMINISTIC or NOT DETERMINISTIC
  This clause specifies whether the UDF always returns the same results for given identical input values (DETERMINISTIC) or not (NOT DETERMINISTIC). The DB2 Optimizer takes this into account to determine the best access path. An example of a NOT DETERMINISTIC function would be a random number generator.
- SPECIFIC *specific-name*
  As already introduced in "Write UDFs" on page 142, this specifies the specific name, which is a unique name for the instance of the function.

For a UDF written in Java, LANGUAGE JAVA and PARAMETER STYLE DB2GENERAL (for JDBC) or PARAMETER STYLE JAVA (for SQLJ) have to be specified.

There are more clauses which you can use, depending on the required functionality of the UDF. For the complete syntax of the CREATE FUNCTION statement, see the *DB2 UDB SQL Reference*.

External Table Functions

The creation step of external table functions is basically same as that of external scalar functions. You need to write, compile, link, and register the UDF.

Writing UDFs

The arguments introduced in "Write UDFs" on page 142 are passed to the external table functions as well, though some differences and considerations exist.

A table function returns a table to the SQL statement that references it. However, within a reference of the table function per statement, the table function is internally called repeatedly with a different call type from DB2 UDB, and the data is returned from the table function row by row. To implement an external table function, you need to write a procedure for the each call type. The possible call types depend on whether you use the scratchpad to save the state and keep it for the next SQL statement that will reference the table function.

If the function needs to keep the scratchpad for the next SQL statement using the function, the `FINAL CALL` keyword has to be specified in the `CREATE FUNCTION` statement, and the call types for the function are FIRST, OPEN, FETCH, CLOSE and FINAL. If the function does not keep the state, in other words, if the scratchpad must be initialized each time the function is used in an SQL statement, the `NO FINAL CALL` keyword should be specified in the `CREATE FUNCTION` statement. The possible call types in this case are OPEN, FETCH, CLOSE. The argument call-type is always present for table functions. It indicates the call type of the UDF:

- FIRST call (-2)
  This only occurs if the `FINAL CALL` keyword is specified in the `CREATE FUNCTION` statement. The scratchpad of the UDF is initialized by the database manager before this call. The SQL arguments are passed to the UDF, but you should not code the UDF to return any data, since DB2 ignores the returned data.
- OPEN call (-1)
  The scratchpad of the UDF is initialized before this call if `NO FINAL CALL` is specified in the `CREATE FUNCTION` statement. The content of the scratchpad is kept if `FINAL CALL` is specified. So, if you want to control the scratchpad content completely between OPEN calls and don't need to maintain it across OPEN calls, you should set `NO FINAL CALL`.
- FETCH call (0)
  DB2 expects the table function to return either a row comprising the set of return values, or an end-of-table condition indicated by SQLSTATE value '02000'.
- CLOSE call (-1)
  It balances the OPEN call and can be used to perform any external CLOSE processing (for example, closing a source file), and resource release. When `NO FINAL CALL` is specified in the `CREATE FUNCTION` statement, resources should be released on this call as no FINAL call occurs in this case. In cases involving a join or a sub-query, the OPEN/FETCH/CLOSE call sequences can repeat within the execution of an SQL statement, but there is only one FIRST call and only one FINAL call.

- FINAL call (-2)

  It only occurs if the FINAL CALL is specified in the CREATE FUNCTION statement. It balances the FIRST call, and occurs only once per execution of the SQL statement that references the table function. It is intended for the purpose of releasing resources.

DB2 UDB provides a sample external table function, tfweather_u, which is supplied in the source file tblsrv.c in the *DB2PATH*\Samples\c (*DB2PATH* is the directory where you install the DB2 UDB). This UDF returns weather information for various cities in the United States. The weather data for these cities is included in the sample program (or could be read in from an external file as indicated in the comments). The weather information includes a short name for each city and does not include a long name, therefore a matching long name is searched for in the other data source in the program, and then returned as the value of the city column. Fig. 4–5 shows how the external table function is implemented. The entire program code is provided in Appendix A.

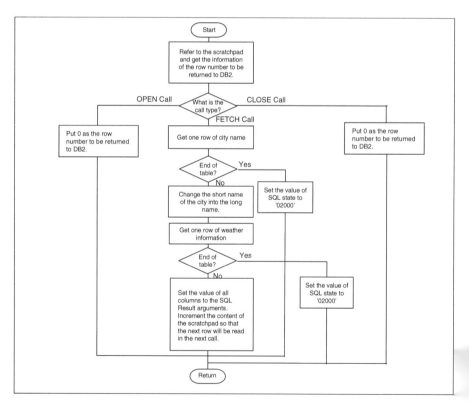

Fig. 4–5 *Sample External Table Function tfweather_u*

This function uses a scratchpad to keep track of the record number of the record to be returned to DB2 (or keep the pointer to the file, including the weather information if the weather information is stored in the external file). This program handles the OPEN call, FETCH call, and CLOSE call only, as the scratchpad content doesn't need to be maintained across OPEN calls, and the function is defined with the NO FINAL CALL keyword.

In our example, shown in Fig. 4–5, the weather information is included in the program. If it is included in an external file, it should be opened and the pointer of the file should be stored in the scratchpad in the procedure of the OPEN call. In the CLOSE call, this opened file should be closed.

Compile and Link UDFs

To compile and link external table functions written in C/C++, you can simply use the batch file bldmsudf.bat as we did for external scalar functions. You can use bldsqlj.bat for Java UDFs. The batch file takes one parameter, which specifies the name of your source file. It uses the source file name for the DLL name. See "Compile and Link UDFs" on page 146 for how to use bldmsudf.bat file.

Register a UDF using a CREATE FUNCTION Statement

The following CREATE FUNCTION statement registers the UDF tfweather_u, which we introduced as an example in "Writing UDFs" on page 148.

```
CREATE FUNCTION tfweather_u()
   RETURNS TABLE (
      CITY VARCHAR(25),
      TEMP_IN_F INTEGER,
      HUMIDITY INTEGER,
      WIND VARCHAR(5),
      WIND_VELOCITY INTEGER,
      BAROMETER FLOAT,
      FORECAST VARCHAR(25))
   EXTERNAL NAME 'tf_dml!weather'
   NO SQL
   PARAMETER STYLE DB2SQL
   LANGUAGE C
   DISALLOW PARALLELISM
   DETERMINISTIC
   SCRATCHPAD
   NO FINAL CALL
   CARDINALITY 20
```

DB2 Server Side Features

Referring to this CREATE FUNCTION statement for the external table function, observe that:

- The RETURNS TABLE clause is used to specify each column name and data type of this table function.
- The DISALLOW PARALLELISM clause is specified so that the UDF cannot be used by multiple users simultaneously. For an external table function, you need to specify this clause, otherwise the state stored in the scratchpad of the UDF may be changed by someone else.
- The NO FINAL CALL clause is specified so that the scratchpad is initialized for each OPEN call. This is the default.
- The optional clause CARDINALITY is specified to tell the DB2 optimizer the total number of rows to be returned from the UDF. This value helps the DB2 optimizer select good access paths.

Once you have registered the external table function, you can use it in a FROM clause as follows:

```
SELECT w.city, w.temp_in_f, w.forecast
  FROM TABLE( tfweather_u() ) AS w
  WHERE w.barometer > 30.0
```

Be aware that you can also use other SQL language constructs such as GROUP BY, JOIN, and UNION with the external table function.

OLE DB External Table Functions

On the Windows platform, Microsoft OLE DB is the emerging standard for data access to non-relational as well as relational data sources. More and more non-relational and relational data sources expose their data through OLE DB interfaces while ODBC is mainly for accessing relational data sources.

The architecture of OLE DB defines OLE DB consumers and OLE DB providers. OLE DB consumers can either access row set data directly, or compose a command text in a language native to the OLE DB provider, and retrieve row set data. OLE DB providers own data and expose the data in tabular format as a row set, or do not own their own data, but encapsulate some services by producing and consuming data through OLE DB interfaces (OLE DB service providers).

Using OLE DB table functions reduces your application development effort by providing build-in access to any OLE DB provider. For C, Java, and OLE automation table functions (external table functions), the developer needs to implement the table function, whereas in the case of OLE DB table functions, a generic built-in OLE DB consumer interfaces with any OLE DB provider to retrieve data. You can just register an OLE DB table function of language type OLE DB, which refers to an OLE DB provider such as the Microsoft Access and the Microsoft SQL Server table as a read-only DB2 table. Once the OLE DB table function is registered, you can move data from OLE tables into DB2 tables, join OLE tables with DB2 tables, use GROUP BY or UNION, and so on.

To use OLE DB table functions with DB2 UDB, you must install OLE DB 2.0 or later, which is included in the Microsoft Data Access Components (MDAC). The OLE DB 2.0 specification defines a number of interfaces, some required, some optional. It also defines levels of OLE DB providers: Minimum, base provider (level 0) and level 1. Each level has a set of required interfaces that have to be supported by the provider. See "Microsoft Data Access Components" on page 41.

The following example registers an OLE DB table function, which retrieves store information from a Microsoft SQL Server database (Version 6.5, 7.0, or later):

```
CREATE FUNCTION sqloledb.authors ()
RETURNS TABLE (
   au_id VARCHAR(11),
   au_lname VARCHAR(40),
   au_fname VARCHAR(20),
   phone CHAR(12),
   address VARCHAR(40),
   city VARCHAR (20),
   state char (2),
   zip char (5),
   contract char (5) )
LANGUAGE OLEDB
EXTERNAL NAME '!authors!Provider=SQLOLEDB;User ID=sa;
Initial Catalog=pubs;Data Source=TETSUYA;'
CARDINALITY 1000
```

The return table clause specifies the table that the OLE DB provider returns. The EXTERNAL NAME clause identifies the OLE DB row set and provides an OLE DB provider connection string. Our sample OLE DB table function returns the table authors defined in the database pubs, which is an SQL Server database. SQLOLEDB is the OLE DB Provider for Microsoft SQL Server. The CARDINALITY clause is optional and provides an estimate of the expected number of rows returned by this UDF for the DB2 Optimizer.

DB2 Server Side Features

For the complete syntax of the `CREATE FUNCTION` statement to define OLE DB table functions, refer to the *DB2 UDB SQL Reference.*

The following example retrieves all rows of the authors table from the SQL Server database using the OLE DB table function:

```
SELECT * FROM TABLE (sqloledb.authors()) AS a
```

When you use a UDF which returns a table, you must specify the correlation name for the UDF referred as a table. In this example, a is the correlation name. When you need to specify a column name of the UDF, such as the case of the join operation, this correlation name should be used like `a.au_id`.

Performance Tips for UDFs

In this section we provide some tips for UDFs to obtain better performance, involving the following features:

* Fenced functions or not-fenced functions
* Statistics for UDFs
* Index scan and table scan

Fenced Functions versus Not-Fenced Functions

The `FENCED` or `NOT FENCED` clause of a `CREATE FUNCTION` statement determines whether the UDF is fenced or not-fenced. Fenced functions are insulated from the internal resources on the database manager, whereas not-fenced functions run in the database manager operating environment's process. Therefore, not-fenced functions can provide better performance, but could cause problems to the database manager if they contain bugs. Fenced functions are safer.

Statistics for UDFs

When the SQL compiler optimizes an SQL query, it estimates the cost of alternative access paths that could resolve the query, and determines the best one. You can update statistics for UDFs so that the SQL compiler can estimates the cost correctly and find the most efficient access path for the query using UDFs.

DB2 UDB provides the updateable catalog view `SYSSTAT.FUNCTIONS` to update statistics for UDFs. When you register a UDF into a database, the entry for the UDF is added to this system catalog view. You can use `UPDATE` statements to update the statistics for each UDF. The view has the following columns (Table 4–1).

Table 4–1 *Columns of SYSSTAT.FUNCTIONS*

Columns	Description
IOS_PER_INVOC	Estimated number of read/write requests executed each time a function is executed.
INSTS_PER_INVOC	Estimated number of machine instructions executed each time a function is executed.
IOS_PER_ARGBYTE	Estimated number of read/write requests executed per input argument byte.
INSTS_PER_ARGBYTES	Estimated number of machine instructions executed per input argument byte.
PERCENT_ARGBYTES	Estimated average percent of input argument bytes that the function will actually process.
INITIAL_IOS	Estimated number of read/write requests executed only the first/last time the function is invoked.
INITIAL_INSTS	Estimated number of machine instructions executed only the first/last time the function is invoked.
CARDINALITY	Estimated number of rows generated by a table function.

When statistics are not available, the statistics column values will be -1.

Index Scan and Table Scan

When a table has an index and a query accessing the table has a predicate specifying the index column in the WHERE clause, the optimizer examines how much the predicate can narrow down the set of qualifying rows by scanning the rows in a certain range of the index before accessing the base table, and then determines if a index scan should be performed or not. For example, the following example may be processed by an index scan if the table has an index on the column col3:

```
SELECT col1,col2 FROM table1 WHERE col3='AAA'
```

Now, let us see what will happen if you use a UDF for the predicate. See the following example:

```
SELECT col1,col2 FROM table1 WHERE UCASE(col3)='AAA'
```

DB2 Server Side Features

The function UCASE(), which is a UDF defined by DB2 UDB when the database is created, converts a character string into upper case. The similar UDF LCASE() converts a character string into lower case.

In our example using UCASE() above, an index scan will not be performed. Each row of the table1 needs to be retrieved and the value of col3 is converted into upper case, and then it is compared with the value 'AAA'. Even if an index is defined on the column col3, all data must be passed to the UDF and converted into upper case first, thus a table scan must be performed. For example, the value 'aaa' or 'AaA' cannot be qualified until the UCASE() function is performed.

If you want to process this query by an index scan, you may rewrite the query as follows:

```
SELECT col1,col2 FROM table1 WHERE col3
    IN ('AAA','aAA','AaA','AAa','Aaa','aAa','aaA','aaa')
```

Triggers

A trigger defines a set of actions executed at, or triggered by, a delete, insert or update operation on a specified table. These actions may cause other changes to the database, perform operations outside DB2 UDB (for example, send an e-mail or write a record in a file), raise an exception to prevent an update operation from taking place, and so on. The trigger can be activated before the SQL operation or after it.

While validation of non-transitional data is usually better handled by check and referential constraints, triggers are appropriate for validation of transitional data (that is, validations which require comparisons between the value before and after an update operation). For example, a trigger can be used for enforcing business rules like checking an account balance and permitting a withdrawal only if the post-withdrawal balance does not fall below the overdraft limit for that account.

Triggers can be used to update data in other tables for maintaining relationships. For instance, if a train reservation is cancelled, that is, if a row from a table is deleted, then a value in another table representing the number of free seats can be incremented using a trigger. Triggers are also beneficial for generating alerts and maintaining audit trail information.

Triggers provide for faster application development. Because triggers are stored in the database, and are available to all applications, they relieve you of the need to code equivalent functions for each application. They also provide for easier maintenance, since any changes need to be made only once in the database instead of in every application.

Fig. 4–6 shows an example of an after trigger which is fired when a row is inserted into the centers table. This trigger updates the totals table and sends an e-mail notification:

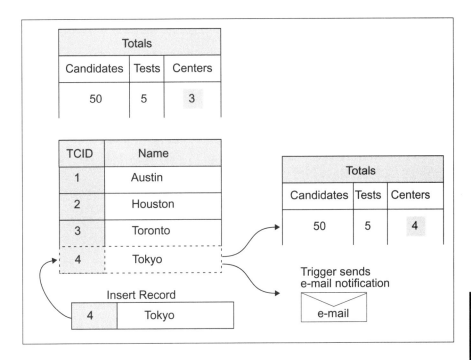

Fig. 4–6 *Inserts Can Activate a Trigger*

Here is the sample definition of the trigger. A trigger is defined using a CREATE TRIGGER statement. This trigger updates the totals table and also executes a UDF sendmail() which sends e-mail notification (assuming this UDF was already defined). Be aware that multiple statements can be included in a trigger definition.

DB2 Server Side Features

```
CREATE TRIGGER new_center AFTER INSERT ON centers
  FOR EACH ROW
  MODE DB2SQL
  BEGIN ATOMIC
   UPDATE totals SET centers=centers+1;
   VALUES(sendmail());
  END
```

Each parameter in this example means following:

- CREATE TRIGGER new_center
  Create a new trigger called new_center.
- AFTER
  The triggered action is performed after the changes of the designated base table are applied. The other option you can specify is NO CASCADE BEFORE.
- INSERT ON centers
  The triggered action is performed when an INSERT operation is performed to the CENTERS table. You can also specify UPDATE or DELETE.
- FOR EACH ROW
  The triggered action is performed once for each row inserted to the base table. If an INSERT statement inserts 10 rows, the trigger is fired 10 times. The other option you can specify is FOR EACH STATEMENT, which means the triggered action is performed once for each INSERT statement.
- MODE DB2SQL
  This is the mandatory option.
- ATOMIC...END
  When you specify multiple statements in a trigger definition, put them between ATOMIC and END.

See the next example that defines a trigger validating transitional data. As discussed before, the validation of transitional data requires comparisons between the value before and after an update operation. To compare the old value and the new value, the REFERENCING clause should be used. In our example, N_ROW is specified to refer the new rows. If any new value of the ON_HAND is less than the 10% of the new MAX_STOCKED, the shipping request of that part will be sent.

```
CREATE TRIGGER reorder
  AFTER UPDATE OF ON_HAND, MAX_STOCKED ON parts
  REFERENCING NEW AS N_ROW
  FOR EACH ROW MODE DB2SQL
  WHEN (N_ROW.ON_HAND < 0.10 * N_ROW.MAX_STOCKED)
  BEGIN ATOMIC
    VALUES( SHIP_REQUEST ( N_ROW.MAX_STOCKED -
                           N_ROW.ON_HAND,
                           N_ROW.PARTNO ));
  END
```

To refer to the old row, the REFERENCING OLD clause should be specified.

You can also create a trigger that refers to the new table state by using the REFERENCING NEW_TABLE clause, as the following example:

```
CREATE TRIGGER reorder
  AFTER UPDATE OF ON_HAND, MAX_STOCKED ON parts
  REFERENCING NEW_TABLE AS N_TABLE NEW AS N_ROW
  FOR EACH ROW MODE DB2SQL
  WHEN ( ( SELECT AVG(ON_HAND) FROM N_TABLE ) > 35)
  BEGIN ATOMIC
    VALUES( INFORM_SUPERVISOR(N_ROW.PARTNO,
                              N_ROW.MAX_STOCKED,
                              N_ROW,ON_HAND ));
  END
```

In this example, the new table is referred as N_TABLE and the new rows are referred as N_ROW. When the parts table is updated, the trigger checks the average value of ON_HAND column and informs the supervisor if the value exceeds 35.

Note: A trigger cannot call a stored procedure. (Stored procedures will be discussed in the following section.)

DB2 Server Side Features

Stored Procedures

A stored procedure resides on a database server, executes, and accesses the database locally to return information to client applications. Using stored procedures allows a client application to pass control to a stored procedure on the database server. This allows the stored procedure to perform intermediate processing on the database server, without transmitting unnecessary data across the network. Only those records that are actually required at the client need to be transmitted. This can result in reduced network traffic and better overall performance.

A stored procedure also saves the overhead of having a remote application pass multiple SQL statements to a database on a server. With a single statement, a client application can call the stored procedure, which then performs the database access work and returns the results to the client application. The more SQL statements that are grouped together for execution in the stored procedure, the larger the savings resulting from avoiding the overhead associated with network flows for each SQL statement when issued from the client.

To create a stored procedure, you must write the application in two separate procedures. The calling procedure is contained in a client application and executes on the client. The stored procedure executes at the location of the database on the database server.

You can write stored procedures in any language supported by DB2 UDB on your operating system. On Windows platform, C/C++, Java, COBOL, and OLE enabled languages (such as Microsoft Visual Basic and Microsoft Visual C++) can be used for writing stored procedures. You do not have to write client applications in the same language as the stored procedure. DB2 UDB transparently passes the values between client application and stored procedure.

You can also write a stored procedure whose procedural logic is contained in the CREATE PROCEDURE statement. This type of stored procedure is called the *SQL procedure*. You don't have to use any external programming language to implement an SQL procedure, although you still need to program calling the procedure in the client application.

If you have more experience writing applications using external program languages such as Java or C/C++, you might choose to create your stored procedures by using those languages rather than SQL. By using external program languages, you can establish a common development environment where you use a common language to create the stored procedures on the database server and the client application that runs on a client workstation or a middle ware server (such as a Web server). Also, there is great potential for code reuse if you have already created many methods that you now want to run as stored procedures.

If you are more comfortable writing SQL statements rather than using any other programming languages, you might choose to create SQL procedures. Using the SQL procedure language allows relational database programmers to support database modules written completely in an SQL language. Also, you can quickly learn to write stored procedures with the SQL procedure language. This ease-of-learning is especially true if you have experience with other database vendor languages.

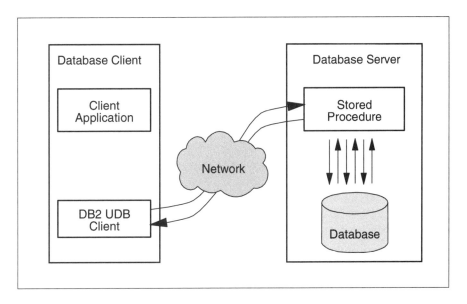

Fig. 4–7 *Application Using a Stored Procedure*

Building Stored Procedures

In this section, we explain the necessary steps in building stored procedures whose procedural logic needs to be written using an external programming language. This type of stored procedure is called an *external procedure*. The SQL procedures will be discussed in the next section ("SQL Procedures" on page 178).

To use an external stored procedure, you must write two programs: the stored procedure itself, which runs on a database server, and a client application, which runs on a client system and invokes the execution of the stored procedure on the server (Fig. 4–7).

DB2 Server Side
Features

The client application performs the following:

1. Declares, allocates, and initializes storage for the optional data structures and host variables.

2. Connects to a database.

3. Invokes the stored procedure through the `CALL` statement.

4. Issues a COMMIT or ROLLBACK to the database.

5. Disconnects from the database.

The application may also issue other SQL statements and transactions before or after calling the stored procedure.

Coding the stored procedure client application is very similar to writing any other DB2 UDB client application. Sometimes there are special considerations for passing parameters to the server procedure and receiving results from it.

How the argument values are sent to the stored procedure varies depending on the programming language and the type of program (embedded, CLI, JDBC or ADO). If your application is written in C/C++, COBOL or Java, the client application sends the argument values to the stored procedure using host variables or parameter markers. These host variables/parameter markers are specified in a `CALL` statement, which, when issued, calls or invokes the stored procedure on the server.

The general syntax of the `CALL` statement is: the keyword `CALL` followed by the qualified or unqualified name of the stored procedure, followed by the host variable or parameter markers. The name can be qualified with a schema name or the location of the stored procedure. For more details on qualifying the stored procedure name, see "Resolving Stored Procedure Location" on page 177.

Here is an example of calling the stored procedure `proc` from an embedded SQL program written in C. This stored procedure takes two arguments.

```
EXEC SQL CALL proc (:arga, :argb)
```

In the above example, `arga` and `argb` are the two host variables, which are declared in the application as any other host variable that is used for an SQL statement. You could have also specified the name of the stored procedure in the `CALL` statement using a host variable.

A CALL statement can pass null values to a stored procedure and also receive null values from it by using null indicators. The host variables may have null indicators if the stored procedure is created with the parameter style GENERAL WITH NULL or DB2SQL (the parameter style will be discussed in "Parameter Style" on page 166). Here is an example of calling the stored procedure proc2 and passing two host variables with null indicators from an embedded SQL program written in C:

```
EXEC SQL CALL proc2 (:arga :nullinda, :argb :nullindb)
```

In this example, the host variable arga has the null indicator nullinda, and argb has nullindb. When the client program or server-side procedure program passes null as the value of a host variable, the null indicators of the host variable must be explicitly set to -1 in the program logic.

For C and COBOL applications, it is also possible to exchange data with the remote procedure using the SQLDA data structure instead of the host variables:

```
EXEC SQL CALL :procname USING DESCRIPTOR :*inout_sqlda;
```

The SQLDA data structure is used to pass data types, length, and values between the application and the database. The SQLDA is more flexible than the host variables, since it can be dynamically configured for different numbers and different types of data. A detailed description of the SQLDA data structure can be found in the appendix of the *DB2 UDB SQL Reference.*

When a stored procedure is called with the SQLDA data structure, the procedure accepts it from the client program, performs the procedure logic, and then returns the SQLCA information and updates the SQLDA structure to the client program if any values are returned. In the client program, before calling the stored procedure, the following steps should be performed:

1. Allocate storage for the SQLDA data structure with the required number of the base SQLVAR element. The number of the base SQLVAR element should be the number of the exchanged data with the database (the number of columns in the case of FETCH).

2. Set the SQLN field to the number of SQLVAR elements allocated.

3. Set the SQLD field to the number of SQLVAR elements actually used.

DB2 Server Side Features

4. Initialize each SQLVAR element used as follows:

- Set the SQLTYPE field to the proper data type.

- Set the SQLLEN field to the size of the data type.

- Allocate storage for the SQLDATA and SQLIND fields based upon the values in SQLTYPE and SQLLEN. SQLDATA is the pointer to the buffer for the data exchange, SQLIND is the pointer to the indicator variable.

See the following client program example of calling a stored procedure with the SQLDA data structure:

```
struct sqlda *inout_sqlda = (struct sqlda *)
malloc(SQLDASIZE(1));
struct sqlca sqlca;
short nullind;

inout_sqlda->sqln = 1;
inout_sqlda->sqld = 1;
inout_sqlda->sqlvar[0].sqltype = SQL_TYP_NFLOAT;
inout_sqlda->sqlvar[0].sqllen  = sizeof( double );
inout_sqlda->sqlvar[0].sqldata = (char *)&rtdata;
inout_sqlda->sqlvar[0].sqlind  = (short *)&nullind;
nullind=-1;

EXEC SQL CALL proc USING DESCRIPTOR :*inout_sqlda;
if (SQLCODE==0)
{printf("Returned value is %.2f\n", rtdata );}
```

In this example, the SQLDA structure inout_sqlda is passed to the stored procedure proc, and then the return value is set to rtdata, which is the sqldata field of the SQLVAR structure. We set the null indicator nullind to -1, as we don't have any input value for this example.

When you want to retrieve and unpack packed decimal (DECIMAL) data from a database or want to know the length of a variable length character string (VARCHAR), you should use the SQLDA data structure. We will discuss this consideration later in this section.

If your client application uses ADO, it can send the argument values using `Parameters` property of a `Command` object. What you need to do is the following:

• Create a `Command` object.

• Set up the `ActiveConnection` property, `CommandText` property (procedure name), and `CommandType` property (`adCmdStoredProc`).

• For the arguments, create `Parameter` objects and set values using `CreateParameter` method, and then append the `Parameter` objects to the `Parameters` collection of the `Command` object.

• Call the `Execute` method of the `Command` object.

Here is a Visual Basic example calling a stored procedure `proc`:

```
Dim SPCall As New ADODB.Command
Dim parm1 As New ADODB.Parameter
Dim parm2 As New ADODB.Parameter
Set SPCall.ActiveConnection = db
SPCall.CommandText = "proc"
SPCall.CommandType = adCmdStoredProc
Set param1 =
SPCall.CreateParameter("Arg1",adInteger,adParamInput, ,1)
SPCall.Parameters.Append param1
Set param2 =
SPCall.CreateParameter("Arg2",adChar,adParamInput,
10,"Textdata")
SPCall.Parameters.Append param2
SPCall.Execute
```

Fig. 4–8 *Calling a stored procedure using ADO*

When invoked, the stored procedure performs the following:

1. Accepts the parameters from the client application.

2. Executes on the database server under the same transaction as the client application.

3. Returns diagnostic (SQLCA) information and optional output data to the client application.

The SQLCA data structure is a collection of variables that is updated at the end of the execution of every SQL statement. The SQLCA contains the information about the previously executed SQL statement such as SQLCODE, SQLSTATE, or diagnostic information. The detailed description of the SQLCA can be found in the appendix of the *DB2 UDB SQL Reference*.

DB2 Server Side Features

Parameter Style

Stored procedures can be categorized based on the parameter style used for receiving and passing variables. The various types of stored procedures are summarized in Table 4–2.

Table 4–2 *Data Returned by the Snapshot Monitor*

Parameter Style	Description
GENERAL	The stored procedure receives parameters as host variables from the CALL statement in the client application. The stored procedure does not directly pass null indicators to the client application. Supported LANGUAGE types: C or COBOL.
GENERAL WITH NULL	In addition to the parameters on the CALL statement as specified in GENERAL, another argument is passed to the stored procedure. This additional argument is a vector of null indicators for each of the parameters on the CALL statement. Supported LANGUAGE types: C or COBOL.
DB2SQL	DB2 passes the following arguments to the stored procedure in addition to the parameters specified on the CALL statement: A NULL indicator for each parameter An SQLSTATE variable to return to DB2 The qualified name of the stored procedure The specific name of the stored procedure An SQL diagnostic string to return to DB2 Supported LANGUAGE types: C or COBOL.
DB2DARI	This uses an older method of passing arguments using SQLDA that conforms with C language calling and linkage conventions. This option is only supported by DB2 Universal Database. Supported LANGUAGE type: C only. To increase portability across the DB2 family, you should write your C stored procedures using the GENERAL or GENERAL WITH NULLS parameter styles.
JAVA	The stored procedure uses a parameter passing convention that conforms to the SQLJ Routines specification. The stored procedure receives IN parameters as host variables, and receives OUT and INOUT parameters as single entry arrays to facilitate returning values. Supported LANGUAGE type: JAVA.
DB2GENERAL	The stored procedure uses a parameter passing convention that is only supported by DB2 Java stored procedures. This is the style supported prior to DB2 UDB V6.1. Supported LANGUAGE type: JAVA. For increased portability, you should write Java stored procedures using the parameter style JAVA.

How each element of the procedure's body is coded depends on the type of stored procedure and the programming language.

We will examine a Java stored procedure in the exercise at the end of this section. Let us start by looking at the general structure of a stored procedure's body.

Initialization

First, you must declare the name of the stored procedure (function/subroutine/ class), all input and output variables (for data to be exchanged with the client application) and data type (int, void, and so on) of the return value.

In this phase, you should also:

- Declare local variables/structures, including those to be used for SQL operations.
- Receive input parameter values into local variables. This may not be always necessary. For DB2DARI procedures, this involves getting the contents of the SQLDA received from the client.

A stored procedure can take arguments that are inputs (IN), outputs (OUT) or both (INOUT). If the data type of an input argument to the stored procedure is the same as the data type of an output, it is better to declare a single INOUT variable and use it both for input and output to cut down on the overhead. You can also have a stored procedure that does not take any arguments, for example to execute a pre-defined delete statement.

For LANGUAGE C stored procedures with a PARAMETER STYLE of GENERAL, GENERAL WITH NULLS, or DB2SQL, you have the option of writing your stored procedure to accept parameters like a main function in a C program (MAIN) or like a subroutine (SUB). For example:

```
MAIN:   int main(int argc, char* argv[])
SUB:    void storproc (int arg1, long arg2, int arg3)
```

Stored Procedure Using Null Indicators

As shown in Table 4–2, null indicators can be used to exchange null values between the client program and the stored procedure if it is defined with the parameter style GENERAL WITH NULL or DB2SQL. The following is a stored procedure example receiving two arguments and null indicators:

```
SQL_API_RC SQL_API_FN proc2 (int        arg1,
                             int        arg2,
                             sqlint16 nullind[2])
```

Compare this example with the CALL statement example on Page 163 and note that the null indicators for two arguments need to be declared as two variables in the client program, whereas they need to be declared as an array in the server-side procedure program.

In our example above, SQL_API_RC and SQL_API_FN are macros defined in the sqlsystm.h file. In a Windows environment, SQL_API_RC expands into int, and SQL_API_FN expands into __stdcall. The data type sqlint16 is also defined in sqlsystm.h file and expands into short.

DB2SQL Stored Procedure

See the next example below, illustrating the case when the stored procedure is defined with the parameter style DB2SQL. In addition to the parameters specified on the CALL statement, the client program can pass other arguments to the stored procedure, such as an SQLSTATE variable, the qualified name and the specified name of the stored procedure, and an SQL diagnostic string.

```
SQL_API_RC SQL_API_FN proc3 (int        arg1,
                             int        arg2,
                             sqlint16 nullind[2],
                             char       sqlst[6],
                             char       qualname[28],
                             char       specname[19],
                             char       diagmsg[71])
```

In our example, the argument sqlst, qualname, specname, and diagmsg are used for an SQLSTATE, the qualified name, the specified name, and an SQL diagnostic string. For example, if you want to return a custom SQLSTATE and diagnostic string to the client program, you can set them into sqlst and diagmsg in the server-side procedure program. They are passed to the client program and set into the SQLCA structure. In the client program they can be retrieved from the sqlstate field and sqlerrmc field of the SQLCA structure. The following is an example C program calling a stored procedure whose parameter style is DB2SQL, and receiving a custom SQLSTATE and diagnostic message:

```
EXEC SQL CALL proc3 (:arga :nullinda, argb :nullindb);
if (strncmp(sqlca.sqlstate, "00000", 5) == 0) {
  printf("Stored procedure returned successfully.\n");
  printf("Returned Value for %hd is %hd\n",arga,argb);
}
else {
  printf("Stored procedure failed with SQLSTATE %s.\n",
         sqlca.sqlstate);
  printf("Diagnostic message:\n");
  printf(" \"%s\"\n", sqlca.sqlerrmc);
```

DB2DARI Stored Procedure

For DB2DARI stored procedures, you do not specify the actual input/output arguments of the stored procedure parameters. Rather, you use the following standard declaration (for C programs), but substitute the name of the stored procedure name (procname):

```
SQL_API_RC SQL_API_FN procname(void *reserved1,
                               void *reserved2,
                               struct sqlda  *inout_sqlda,
                               struct sqlca  *ca)
```

Main Logic

In this phase, the procedure issues SQL statements, performs operations involving local variables, and establishes any values to be passed back to the caller.

The procedure can have a combination of SQL statements and application logic that run on the server. You may even have procedure code that does not access DB2 UDB resources. You should specify the type of SQL statements the stored procedure contains when you register the procedure. That is one of the following:

- **NO SQL**
- **CONTAINS SQL** — the default (SELECT, INSERT, UPDATE, DELETE, DESCRIBE, PREPARE INTO, COMMIT, and ROLLBACK are not permitted)
- **READS SQL DATA** (INSERT, UPDATE, DELETE, COMMIT, and ROLLBACK are not permitted)
- **MODIFIES SQL DATA** (COMMIT and ROLLBACK are not permitted)

DB2 Server Side Features

Note: As a general rule, you should not perform any commits or rollbacks in the stored procedure — the client application should end the transaction.

Your stored procedure also cannot contain any connection related statements or commands such as:

- CONNECT
- CONNECT RESET
- CREATE DATABASE
- BACKUP
- RESTORE
- DROP DATABASE
- ROLLFORWARD DATABASE

CLI, Java, and OLE stored procedures need to issue a null connect to inherit the calling application's connection to the database, but they may not establish any other database connections.

Return to Calling Application

In this phase, the procedure copies outbound values to output (OUT, INOUT) parameters, if there is any data to be passed back to the calling application. Also, you should copy any diagnostic information (such as the SQLCA) if you need it on the client. For DB2DARI procedures, you need to copy the data values into the outbound SQLDA.

You then exit the stored procedure, using a return value if desired.

The return value/code of the stored procedure is not passed back to the calling application. It is used to tell the database manager if the server procedure should be released from memory upon exit. You may have the procedure return the value SQLZ_DISCONNECT_PROC to tell the database manager to release (unload) the library, or SQLZ_HOLD_PROC, to keep the server library in main memory for performance improvement if the stored procedure will be called again.(Stored procedures do not return these values to the database manager)

Considerations for Data Types

If your stored procedure retrieves packed decimal (DECIMAL) data or variable length string (VARCHAR) data, you need to be aware of considerations for each case. We discuss those considerations here.

Packed Decimal Data

C language does not have the packed decimal data type, therefore if you want a stored procedure to retrieve packed decimal (DECIMAL) data and return it to the client program to display it, you have two options:

- Declaring a host variable with the data type float and casting the packed decimal data into float data. The client program receives the float data and displays it.
- Using the SQLDA data structure for the stored procedure. The client program receives the SQLDA structure, including the pointer to the buffer which contains the retrieved packed decimal data, then decodes the packed decimal data and displays it.

The first option is much simpler than the other one; however, you might lose precision by casting decimal type into float type. Depending on what your application wants to do with it, you should choose how to handle the packed decimal data.

When you fetch packed decimal data using the SQLDA structure, the precision and scale is set to the first and second byte of the `sqllen` field of the `sqlvar` entry. The precision and the scale can be retrieved as follows (assuming that `sqldaPoint` points to an SQLDA data structure whose *n* th entry describes a packed decimal value):

```
Precision = ((char *)&(sqldaPoint->sqlvar[n].sqllen))[0];
Scale     = ((char *)&(sqldaPoint->sqlvar[n].sqllen))[1];
```

Using this information, you can decode the retrieved packed decimal data, as shown in Fig. 4–9.

```
/* Calculate the total number of byte */
idx = ( precision + 2 ) / 2 ;
point = precision - scale ;

/* Determine the sign */
bottom = *(ptr + idx -1) & 0x000F ;    /* sign */
if ( (bottom == 0x000D) || (bottom == 0x000B) ) {
   printf("-") ;
} else {
   printf(" ") ;
}

/* Decode and print the decimal number */
for (ind=0; ind < idx; ind++) {
   top = *(ptr + ind) & 0x00F0 ;
   top = (top >> 4 ) ;
   bottom = *(ptr + ind) & 0x000F ;
   if ( point-- == 0 ) printf(".") ;
   printf("%d", top ) ;
   if ( ind < idx - 1 ) { /* sign half byte ? */
      if ( point-- == 0 ) printf(".") ;
      printf("%d", bottom ) ;
   }
}
if ( scale == 0 ) printf(".") ;
```

Fig. 4–9 *Decoding Packed Decimal Data*

In our example, ptr is the pointer corresponding to the sqldata field of the sqlvar entry, precision and scale are the precision and the scale of the packed decimal data, idx is the total number of bytes, and point represents the position of the decimal point. The short type variables top and bottom are used to decode the decimal data.

First, the sign of the decimal data is determined by checking the last byte of the data. If it is 'D' or 'B', the data is determined as a minus value. Then, each byte of the decimal data is decoded and printed. The decimal point is also printed when all of the integer part is decoded and printed.

Variable Length String

When you are fetching a variable length character string data using the SQLDA data structure, the retrieved data is stored in non-null-terminated form into the buffer pointed by the `sqldata` field of the corresponding `sqlvar` entry. Therefore, if you need to handle this data (for example, print it), you need to know the length of the string. Each time when varchar data is fetched, the first 2 bytes of the buffer which is pointed by the `sqldata` field includes the length of the retrieved string. To obtain the length, you can cast the `sqldata` field to the `sqlchar` structure, and then refer to the `length` field of the `sqlchar` structure. The `sqlchar` structure is defined in the `sql.h` header file as follows:

```
struct sqlchar
{short          length;
 char           data[1];};
```

DB2 UDB also provides the `sqlgraphic` structure for the VARGRAPHIC data.

Here is an example to obtain the length of a varchar type data:

```
(struct sqlchar *)(sqldaPoint->sqlvar[n].sqldata)->length
```

This example refers to the varchar data:

```
(struct sqlchar *)(sqldaPoint->sqlvar[n].sqldata)->data
```

DB2 Server Side Features

Example Stored Procedure

Following is a sample program demonstrating the use of an OUT host variable. The client application invokes a stored procedure that determines the median salary for employees in the EMPLOYEE table. (The definition of the median is that half the values lie above it, and half below it.) The median salary is then passed back to the client application using an OUT host variable. Here is the sample program using SQLJ:

```
import java.sql.*;                    // JDBC classes
import sqlj.runtime.*;
import sqlj.runtime.ref.*;

#sql iterator Outsrv_Cursor1 (double salary) ;

///////
// Java stored procedure is in this class
///////
public class Outsrv
{    // (1) stored procedure body
  public static void outputStoredProcedure
  ( /*:rk.2:erk.*/ double[] medianSalary) throws Exception
    {    try
      {
      // Declare Variables
      Outsrv_Cursor1 cursor1;
      short numRecords;
      int counter = 0;

      // Determine the Total Number of Records
      #sql { SELECT COUNT(*) INTO :numRecords FROM STAFF }; /
*:rk.3:erk. */

      // Prepare a Statement to Obtain and Order all Salaries
      #sql cursor1 = { SELECT salary FROM STAFF ORDER BY salary };

      // Fetch Salaries until the Median Salary is Obtained
      while (counter < numRecords/2 + 1)       /* :rk.4:erk. */
      { cursor1.next(); counter++; }
        // set value for the output parameter    /* :rk.5:erk. */
        medianSalary[0] = cursor1.salary();
        cursor1.close();
      }
      catch (Exception e)
      {throw e;}
    }
}
```

Since this stored procedure is written using SQLJ, you should specify the parameter style JAVA in the CREATE PROCEDURE statement.

Returning Result Sets from Stored Procedures

You can code stored procedures that return one or more result sets to a client application. Basically, in the stored procedure, you need to:

- Declare cursors using DECLARE CURSOR statements.
- Open them using OPEN CURSOR statements.
- Exit from the stored procedure without closing the cursors.

Consider the following example:

```
. . . . . . . . . . . . .

SQL_API_RC SQL_API_FN two_result_sets (double *inMedianSalary)
{
  medianSalary = *inMedianSalary;

  EXEC SQL DECLARE r1 CURSOR FOR
    SELECT name, job, CAST(salary AS INTEGER)
    FROM staff
    WHERE salary > :medianSalary
    ORDER BY salary;

  EXEC SQL DECLARE r2 CURSOR FOR
    SELECT name, job, CAST(salary AS INTEGER)
    FROM staff
    WHERE salary < :medianSalary
    ORDER BY salary;

  EXEC SQL OPEN r1;
  EXEC SQL OPEN r2;
  return (SQLZ_DISCONNECT_PROC);
}
```

As you can see, this stored procedure receives the median value of the employee's salary and returns two result sets; one contains the employees whose salary is higher than the median, and the other contains those whose salary is lower. Note that two cursors are declared and left open in the stored procedure.

If a client application accepts result sets from an SQL procedure, it must use the CLI or higher (ODBC, JDBC, SQLJ, or ADO) application programming interface.

For a CLI application, you can call SQLNumResultCols(), SQLDescribeCol() or SQLColAttribute() to know the nature of the result set or the number of columns returned. Then any permitted combination of SQLBindCol(), SQLFetch(), and SQLGetData() can be called to obtain the data in the result set.

Note: We will explain how an ADO application accepts result sets from a stored procedure in Chapter 5.

DB2 Server Side Features

Building and Registering Stored Procedures

The client part of the stored procedure is built like any other client application. The main stored procedure is built as a shared/dynamically loadable library, a Java class file, or a REXX command file, and physically stored on the DB2 UDB server. You can have more than one stored procedure in a library.

To build stored procedures, you can use batch files that DB2 UDB supplies. For an SQLJ stored procedure, `DB2PATH\samples\java\bldsqljs.bat` can be used (`DB2PATH` is the directory where you install the DB2 UDB).

Stored procedures must be registered with each database against which they execute. This is achieved using the `CREATE PROCEDURE` statement. The `CREATE PROCEDURE` statement places an entry for the stored procedure in the `SYSCAT.PROCEDURES` view in the database.

Note: You cannot register two stored procedures with the same name and the same number of parameters. However, you can register a stored procedure with the same name as one already registered, only if the number of parameters are different. This is useful for overloading.

Here is a `CREATE PROCEDURE` statement to register the stored procedure `outsrv` introduced in the previous section. Note that only the OUT host variable is used in our example:

```
CREATE PROCEDURE outsrv (out mediansSalary double)
   LANGUAGE JAVA PARAMETER STYLE JAVA FENCED
   EXTERNAL NAME 'Outsrv.outputStoredProcedure'
   READS SQL DATA
```

Here is an example to register the stored procedure `two_result_sets`. Note that the number of the returning result sets is specified in the `DYNAMIC RESULT SETS` clause.

```
CREATE PROCEDURE two_result_sets (IN salary)
DYNAMIC RESULT SETS 2
LANGUAGE C PARAMETER STYLE GENERAL FENCED
EXTERNAL NAME 'spserver!two_result_sets'@
READS SQL DATA
```

Note: You can also register a stored procedure with no parameters.

Fenced and Not-Fenced Procedure

The CREATE PROCEDURE statements of our examples above use the FENCED parameter, so they are fenced stored procedures. Fenced procedures are insulated from the internal resources on the database manager, whereas not-fenced procedures run in the database manager operating environment's process. Therefore, not-fenced procedures can provide better performance, but could cause problems to the database manager if they contain bugs. To register a stored procedure as a not-fenced procedure, specify the NOT FENCED parameter in the CREATE PROCEDURE statement.

Needed Privilege to Create a Stored Procedure

Each registered stored procedure has a schema name associated with it. Therefore, to use the CREATE PROCEDURE statement you need at least IMPLICIT_SCHEMA privilege to create a schema or CREATEIN privilege on an existing schema. You will also need CREATE_NOT_FENCED authority on the database to register a not-fenced stored procedure.

Resolving Stored Procedure Location

When the stored procedure is invoked, DB2 UDB needs to be able to find the correct routine and execute it. You can specify the stored procedure's location explicitly either in the CALL statement or by using the EXTERNAL NAME clause of the CREATE PROCEDURE statement. It may be easier to register the location of the stored procedure library/class once using the external name during the creation of the procedure, and then use a simpler procedure name to call it repeatedly from one or more of your applications. In the previous CREATE PROCEDURE example, the procedure name is outputStoredProcedure, and the external name is Outsrv!outputStoredProcedure

You can also qualify the stored procedure's procedure name using a schema while registering or calling it. For example, the fully qualified name of the stored procedure could be SCHEMA1.OUTSRV, where SCHEMA1 specifies a schema.

The syntax for specifying the stored procedure's external name depends on its LANGUAGE type:

DB2 Server Side Features

- For C, COBOL, and OLE, specify <path> followed by
  <library_name>!<procname>. For example:
  `c:\mycode\mylib!myproc`
  This directs the database manager to load the shared/dynamic library called
  mylib (.dll) from the `c:\mycode` directory and call the `myproc()` procedure in
  the library.
- For Java, use <jar_filename>:<pkg_fullname>.<class_name>.<method_name>.
  For example:
  `MyJar:MyPackage.MyProcs.MyClass.myMethod`
  Here, the database manager uses the `myMethod` method in the `MyClass` class,
  within the `MyPackage.MyProcs` package in the `MyJar` jar file.

It is optional to specify the path and the jar filename. If the path is not specified,
DB2 UDB will look in the `function` subdirectory or its `unfenced` subdirectory to
locate the stored procedure library. On the Windows operating system, that is
`SQLLIB\function\unfenced` and `SQLLIB\function`, where `SQLLIB` is specified by
the `DB2INSTPROF` registry variable.

Likewise if the Java class containing the stored procedure code is not inside a jar
file, DB2 UDB searches the `function` directory.

SQL Procedures

An SQL procedure is a stored procedure in which the procedural logic is contained
in a `CREATE PROCEDURE` statement.

Though you still need to program calling the procedure in the client application,
you don't have to use any external programming language to implement this type
of stored procedure. Therefore, unlike a `CREATE PROCEDURE` statement for the other
type of stored procedure discussed in the previous section, the `CREATE PROCEDURE`
statement for an SQL procedure does not have the `EXTERNAL` clause. Instead, an
SQL procedure has a *procedure body*, which contains the source statements for the
stored procedure.

The following example shows a `CREATE PROCEDURE` statement to build a simple
SQL procedure. This procedure receives two parameters and updates the table
`table1`. Note that the `LANGUAGE` parameter is set to `SQL`

```
CREATE PROCEDURE updte (IN data1 INT,IN data2 INT)
  LANGUAGE SQL
  BEGIN
   UPDATE table1 SET col1=col+data1 WHERE col2=data2;
  END
```

A client application can call this procedure in the same way as an external procedure, for example, using a `call` statement.

Setting the Environment to Build SQL Procedures

When you execute a `CREATE PROCEDURE` statement to build an SQL procedure, DB2 UDB generates a C program in which the SQL statements of the procedure body are embedded, and then pre-compiles it (compiles it into a DLL file in the background). Therefore, you must install a supported C or C++ compiler on the DB2 UDB server.

Supported Compiler

For the Windows platform, either of the following compilers must be installed:

- Microsoft Visual C++ Version 5.0 or 6.0
- IBM VisualAge C++ for Windows Version 4.2 or Version 5.0

Setting up Environment Variables

You also have to provide the value of `PATH`, `INCLUDE`, and `LIBRARY` environment variables for the compiler. You can create a batch file to set those environment variables and specify it using the `DB2_SQLROUTINE_COMPILER_PATH` DB2 registry variable, as follows:

```
db2set DB2_SQLROUTINE_COMPILER_PATH=Batch_File
```

In this statement, *Batch_File* is the full path name for the batch file setting environment variables.

If you do not set the `DB2_SQLROUTINE_COMPILER_PATH` DB2 registry variable, the default file `DB2PATH\function\routine\sr_cpath.bat` is used (`DB2PATH` is the directory where you install the DB2 UDB). This default file is generated automatically by DB2 UDB.

 Note: On Windows NT and Windows 2000, you can set the necessary environment variables for the compiler as SYSTEM variables without using the `DB2_SQLROUTINE_COMPILER_PATH` DB2 registry variable. Make sure that they are set as SYSTEM variables, not USER variables.

DB2 Server Side Features

Compiler Options

If you installed Microsoft Visual C++ Version 5.0 or Version 6.0, the default compiler command is as follows:

```
cl -Od -W2 /TC -D_X86_=1 -I%DB2PATH%\include
 SQLROUTINE_FILENAME.c
 /link -dll -def:SQLROUTINE_FILENAME.def
 /out:SQLROUTINE_FILENAME.dll %DB2PATH%\lib\db2apillib
```

If you want to change it, specify the new compiler command by using the `DB2_SQLROUTINE_COMPILE_COMMAND` DB2 registry variable.

Precompile and Bind Options

As already described, executing a `CREATE PROCEDURE` statement generates an embedded SQL program and pre-compiles/compiles it. You can provide precompile and bind options to that process using the `DB2_SQLROUTINE_PREPOPTS` DB2 registry variable, as in the following example:

```
db2set DB2_SQLROUTINE_PREPOPTS=BLOCKING ALL ISOLATION UR
```

The following options can be set for the `DB2_SQLROUTINE_PREPOPTS` DB2 registry variable:

- BLOCKING {UNAMIBIG | ALL | NO}
- DATETIME {DEF | USA | EUR | ISO | JIS | LOC }
- DEGREE {1 | degree-parallelism | ANY }
- EXPLAIN { NO | YES | ALL }
- EXPLAINSNAP { NO | YES | ALL }
- INSERT { DEF | BUF }
- ISOLATION { CS | RR | US | RS | NC }
- QUERYOPT optimization-level
- SYNCPOINT { ONEPHASE | TOWPHASE | NONE }

For detailed information about these options, consult the description of the **PRECOMPILE PROGRAM** in the *DB2 UDB Command Reference*.

Keep Intermediate Files

During the execution of a CREATE PROCEDURE statement for an SQL procedure, DB2 UDB generate a number of intermediate files such as sqc, c, and log file in the *DB2PATH*\function\routine\sqlproc*dbname**schemaname* directory (*DB2PATH* is the directory where you install the DB2 UDB, *dbname* and *schemaname* are the database and schema used to create the SQL procedure). Those intermediate files are deleted if the CREATE PROCEDURE statement is successfully completed. But they may be useful when you need to debug the SQL procedure. When you want to keep those intermediate files, set the DB2_SQLROUTINE_KEEP_FILES DB2 registry to YES. Even if DB2 UDB successfully completes the CREATE PROCEDURE statement, the intermediate files are kept.

```
db2set DB2_SQLROUTINE_KEEP_FILES=YES
```

Writing SQL Procedures

Once your environment is set up, you are ready to build SQL procedures.

Unlike the simple example shown in the section "SQL Procedures" on page 178, you can actually put multiple SQL statements, and other statements to describe the logic between BEGIN and END parameters (called the procedure body). See the next example (Fig. 4–10) containing multiple statements in the procedure body. This procedure receives an employee number and their rating, and performs a different UPDATE statement depending on the rating.

DB2 Server Side Features

```
CREATE PROCEDURE update_salary_if
 (IN employee_num CHAR(6), IN rating SMALLINT)
 LANGUAGE SQL
 BEGIN
  DECLARE not_found CONDITION FOR SQLSTATE '02000';
  DECLARE EXIT HANDLER FOR not_found
    SIGNAL SQLSTATE '20000'
    SET MESSAGE_TEXT = 'Employee not found';
  IF (rating=1)
    THEN UPDATE employee SET salary=salary*1.10,bonus=1000
       WHERE empno=employee_num;
    ELSEIF (rating=2)
    THEN UPDATE employee SET salary=salary*1.05,bonus=500
       WHERE empno=employee_num;
    ELSE UPDATE employee SET salary=salary*1.03,bonus=0
       WHERE empno=employee_num;
  END IF;
 END $
```

Fig. 4–10 *Create an SQL Procedure*

Let us look at the procedure body. The first DECLARE statement defines a condition not_found for the SQL state '02000', which means the number of rows identified in the searched UPDATE statement is zero. The next DECLARE statement defines a condition handler which determines the behavior of the SQL procedure when the condition not_found occurs. In our example, a SIGNAL statement is specified that sets the custom SQL state and message text. Instead of using the user-defined condition not_found, the condition NOT FOUND provided by DB2 UDB can be also used for the condition handler definition. DB2 UDB provides the following conditions:

- NOT FOUND
  Identifies any condition that results in an SQLCODE of +100 or an SQLSTATE of '02000' (no row was found).
- SQLEXCEPTION
  Identifies any condition that results in a negative SQLCODE.
- SQLWARNING
  Identifies any condition that results in a warning condition, or that results in a positive SQL return code other than +100.

The main logic starts from an IF statement in our example. Depending on the received value of the rating, three different UPDATE statements will be executed. See Appendix A for the list of the statements allowed within a procedure body.

Another point you should observe is that the dollar sign ('$') is put at the end of this statement. In this example, we are assuming that this example is used as an input script for the DB2 UDB Command Line Processor (CLP), and therefore you must use a terminating character for the CREATE PROCEDURE statement. The default terminating character for a statement is the semicolon (';'). However, you must use an alternative terminating character, since the semicolon is used as the terminating character for each statement in the procedure body. Here, we use the dollar ('$') sign. To notify an alternative terminating character to the CREATE PROCEDURE statement, use -td option of the command line processor as follows:

```
db2 -td$ -vf Input_File
```

Here, *Input_File* is the file including the CREATE PROCEDURE statement.

Returning Result Sets from SQL Procedures

Like external procedures, SQL procedures can return one or more result sets to the application program (see "Returning Result Sets from Stored Procedures" on page 175). In the procedure body, cursors should be declared, opened, and left open as in the following simple example:

```
CREATE PROCEDURE PROC1(INOUT data1 SMALLINT)
  DYNAMIC RESULT SETS 2 LANGUAGE SQL
  BEGIN
   DECLARE c1 CURSOR WITH RETURN TO CLIENT FOR
     SELECT name, dept FROM staff WHERE salary > data1;
   DECLARE c2 CURSOR WITH RETURN TO CLIENT FOR
     SELECT name, dept FROM staff WHERE salary <= data1;
   OPEN c1;
   OPEN c2;
  END
```

Note that the number of the result set is specified in the DYNAMIC RESULT SETS clause, the RETURN TO CLIENT option is specified for each DECLARE CURSOR statement, and the cursors are left open in the procedure.

If a client application accepts result sets from an SQL procedure, it must use the CLI or higher (ODBC, JDBC, SQLJ, or ADO) application programming interface.

DB2 Server Side Features

For a CLI application, you can call `SQLNumResultCols()`, `SQLDescribeCol()` or `SQLColAttribute()` to know the nature of the result set or the number of columns returned. Then any permitted combination of `SQLBindCol()`, `SQLFetch()`, and `SQLGetData()` can be called to obtain the data in the result set.

We will discuss how an ADO application accepts result sets from a stored procedure in Chapter 5.

Nested Stored Procedures

Nested stored procedures are stored procedures that call another stored procedure. Up to 16 levels of nested stored procedure calls are supported. By using this technique, you can implement more complex procedural logic.

When a stored procedure returns result sets to a client application, the application program must be written using the CLI or higher (ODBC, JDBC, SQLJ, or ADO) application programming interface; however, if the stored procedure is an SQL procedure and the caller is also an SQL procedure, the result sets can be accepted by the caller procedure.

Next, we will discuss nested stored procedures using an example of the nested SQL procedure.

Here is an SQL procedure example returning result sets to another SQL procedure. This `CREATE PROCEDURE` statement is very similar to the example shown in the previous section. The only difference is that the `DECLARE CURSOR` statements have the `RETURN TO CALLER` option.

```
CREATE PROCEDURE PROC1(INOUT data1 SMALLINT)
 DYNAMIC RESULT SETS 2 LANGUAGE SQL
 BEGIN
  DECLARE c1 CURSOR WITH RETURN TO CALLER FOR
    SELECT name, dept FROM staff WHERE salary > data1;
  DECLARE c2 CURSOR WITH RETURN TO CALLER FOR
    SELECT name, dept FROM staff WHERE salary <= data1;
  OPEN c1;
  OPEN c2;
 END
```

To call another stored procedure from a stored procedure, simply issue a `CALL` statement. When both of them are SQL procedures, and the target procedure returns result sets to the caller procedure, you can set the result set locator variables and allocate cursors using `ASSOCIATE RESULT SET LOCATOR` statements and `ALLOCATE CURSOR` statements to manipulate each of the returned result sets.

> **Note:** ASSOCIATE RESULT SET LOCATOR statements and ALLOCATE CURSOR statements can be used in the procedure body of SQL procedures only. You cannot use them for embedded SQL programs, CLI programs, and so on.

In the procedure body, you first declare variables as result set locator variables. Next, you associate result sets with them using the ASSOCIATE RESULT SET statement, and specify the locator variables in ALLOCATE CURSOR statements to allocate cursors for the result sets, as in the following example:

```
DECLARE result1 RESULT_SET_LOCATOR VARYING;
DECLARE result2 RESULT_SET_LOCATOR VARYING;
CALL proc1(data1);
ASSOCIATE RESULT SET LOCATORS(result1, result2)
    WITH PROCEDURE proc1;
ALLOCATE callC1 CURSOR FOR RESULT SET result1;
ALLOCATE callC2 CURSOR FOR RESULT SET result2;
```

Once cursors are allocated, you can manipulate result sets using the cursors.

Here is an example of the caller SQL procedure (Fig. 4–11). This SQL procedure receives two result sets and stores the first result set into the result table with the current time stamp.

```
CREATE PROCEDURE caller (INOUT data1 SMALLINT)
LANGUAGE SQL
 BEGIN
  DECLARE result1 RESULT_SET_LOCATOR VARYING;
  DECLARE result2 RESULT_SET_LOCATOR VARYING;
  DECLARE name_result VARCHAR(9);
  DECLARE dept_result SMALLINT;
  DECLARE END_OF_RECORD SMALLINT;
  DECLARE CONTINUE HANDLER FOR NOT FOUND
     BEGIN
      SET RESULT_SET_END = 1;
      SET name_result = 'LAST";
      SET dept_result = 999;
     END;
  SET RESULT_SET_END=0;
  CALL proc1(data1);
  ASSOCIATE RESULT SET LOCATORS(result1, result2)
     WITH PROCEDURE proc1;
  ALLOCATE callC1 CURSOR FOR RESULT SET result1;
  WHILE (RESULT_SET_END=0) DO
     FETCH FROM callC1 INTO name_result,dept_result;
     IF (RESULT_SET_END=0) THEN
      BEGIN
      INSERT INTO result
       VALUES (name_result,dept_result,current timestamp);
      END;
     END IF;
   END WHILE;
   CLOSE RES1;
 END
```

Fig. 4-11 *Nested SQL Procedure*

Since the target SQL procedure returns two result sets, two result set locator variables, result1 and result2, are declared. Note that the variable END_OF_RECORD is declared to control the end-of-record condition. The condition handler switches the value of END_OF_RECORD when all records in the result set have been fetched, and the procedure exits the loop.

Keep Stored Procedure Processes

In an environment in which the number of stored procedure requests is large and the stored procedures are fenced, you should consider keeping a stored procedure process alive after a stored procedure call is completed. This consumes additional system resources; however, the performance of a stored procedure can be improved, because the overhead of creating a stored procedure process is avoided.

To keep stored procedure processes alive, set the database manager configuration parameter KEEPDARI to YES. This is the default value. You can set this configuration parameter by using the Control Center, or by executing the following command from the Command Line Processor in the DB2 UDB Server:

```
db2 UPDATE DBM CFG USING keepdari yes
```

If you are developing a stored procedure, you may want to modify and test loading the same stored procedure library a number of times. This default setting may interfere with reloading the library. It is best to change the value of this keyword to no while developing stored procedures, and then change it back to yes when you are ready to load the final version of your stored procedure.

You can also use the database manager configuration parameter MAXDARI to control the maximum number of the stored procedure process that can be started at the DB2 UDB server, and NUM_INITDARIS to specify the number of the idle stored procedure processes that are started when the database manager is started.

Stored Procedure Builder

DB2 UDB comes with the Stored Procedure Builder (SPB), a graphical application to aid in rapid development of stored procedures. SPB can provide a single development environment of the stored procedure, which means SPB can be used to build stored procedures for the entire DB2 family ranging from the Windows workstation to System/390 whether those procedures are created on local or remote server.

SPB comes with design assistants that guide you through basic design patterns, help you create SQL queries, and estimate the performance cost of invoking a stored procedure. SPB also help you to registering and testing stored procedures. Therefore, you can focus on creating your stored procedure logic rather than the details of registering, building, and installing stored procedures on a DB2 server.

Note: The DB2 UDB Stored Procedure Builder assists you with creating the part of the stored procedure that runs on the database server. Though you can test it using SPB, you must write the client application separately.

DB2 Server Side Features

Stored procedures created with SPB are implemented with Java or SQL procedure language. If you select to use Java, SPB generates a Java stored procedure code whose database connections are managed using Java Database Connectivity (JDBC). SQL statements for the Java stored procedure can be specified using either JDBC or SQLJ. If you select to use SQL procedure language, SPB can generate the procedure body for you.

Once SPB generates a Java stored procedure code or an SQL procedure body, you can modify it and build the stored procedure. You can also modify and rebuild existing stored procedures. If the procedure is successfully built, you can test it using SPB without writing a client application program.

 Note: You can also test stored procedures that were not developed using SPB even if they are not Java or SQL stored procedures.

Building Procedures using SPB

SPB can be started by clicking on **Start** and selecting **Programs** -> **IBM DB2** -> **Stored Procedure Builder**, clicking the SPB icon from the Control Center, or entering the db2spb at a command prompt. SPB can be also started as an add-in tool from Microsoft Visual Basic or Microsoft Visual C++.

When you start SPB, you are prompted to specify the characteristics of a new project or open an old project. A project stores the database name to which the stored procedures connect to, user id and password, and so on. Stored procedures are created in the project.

Once you open a project, you are ready to build a new stored procedure. Right-click on the **Stored Procedures** folder which can be seen under a database folder, and select **Insert**. You can specify whether the language of the procedure is Java or SQL, as shown in Fig. 4–12.

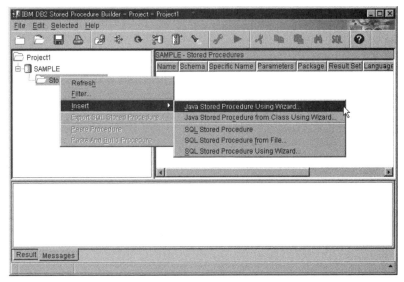

Fig. 4–12 *Stored Procedure Builder: Inserting a New Procedure*

In our example, we are creating a Java stored procedure using the wizard. You should just enter the prompted information. SPB requests you to enter the procedure name, SQL statements, input/output parameters, whether static SQL by SQLJ or dynamic SQL by JDBC is used, and so on. Fig. 4–13 shows the page specifying SQL statements. You can directly enter the SQL statements, or use the SQL Assistant, which is a wizard to create SQL statements.

DB2 Server Side
Features

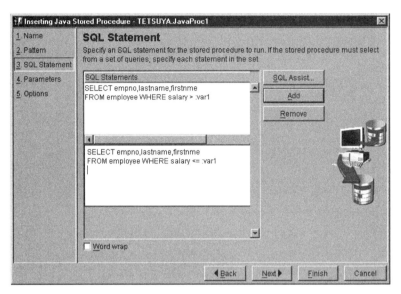

Fig. 4–13 *Stored Procedure Builder: Using the Wizard*

When you have entered all prompted information, click the **Finish** button, and SPB generates the stored procedure code. Fig. 4–14 shows the generated Java stored procedure.

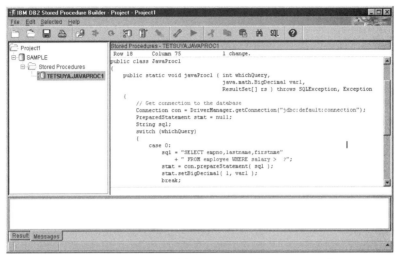

Fig. 4–14 *Stored Procedure Builder: Generated Java Procedure*

The generated procedure code can be modified as you like before building the stored procedure. If you prefer the key behavior as either the `vi` or `emacs` editor, open the **Environment Properties** windows from the **File** menu and set the **editor** option.

To build the stored procedure and register to the database, click the build icon from the icon bar.

If the building phase is completed successfully, you can test the stored procedure. Click the Run icon from the icon bar, and enter the input parameter values if necessary. You will see the test results as in the following example (Fig. 4–15):

DB2 Server Side Features

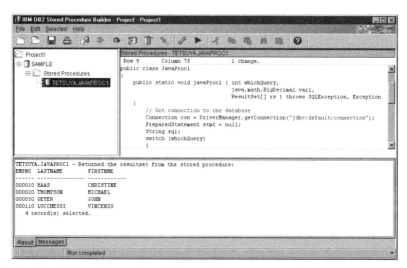

Fig. 4–15 *Stored Procedure Builder: Testing a Procedure*

If you specify to use SQL for the stored procedure in the selection shown in Fig. 4–12 on page 189, the SQL procedure is generated by SPB, as in Fig. 4–16.

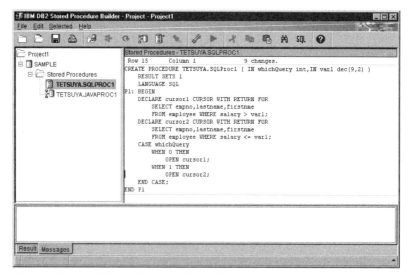

Fig. 4–16 *Stored Procedure Builder: Generated SQL Procedure*

Building Applications Using Visual Basic

- ◆ DATA ENTRY FORMS
- ◆ OPENSCHEMA RECORDSETS
- ◆ DB2 UDB SAMPLE APPLICATION
- ◆ CALLING DB2 STORED PROCEDURES
- ◆ USING COMMITMENT CONTROL

*T*he purpose of this chapter is to describe some sample programs which use Visual Basic to interface with the DB2 UDB for Windows NT database. The samples cover many different aspects of database work, such as building tables and indexes, providing forms for data entry/update, and using ADO specific features such as OpenSchema and Data Shaping. Although there are three different data object technologies available to use with Visual Basic, the choice recommended by Microsoft for new developments is ADO. Consequently, all of the examples used in this chapter utilize ADO. The exception to this is in the first subsection, where the VisData add-in is used to produce a DAO Control entry form.

Some of the sample programs, discussed in this chapter, are available on the DB2 UDB Install CDROM, but this chapter also includes additional samples which were specifically produced for this book. The code listings for these additional samples are included in Appendix B.

Data Entry Forms

The first sample programs show how to produce a simple data entry form, using the Data Form Wizard and the VisData add-in. The first method creates both ADO Data Control and ADO Data Object based forms, whereas the second produces DAO Data Control based forms.

The entry form is based on the Employee table, in the DB2 UDB Sample database. You are asked to create this database in the First Steps application, after installing DB2 UDB.

An ODBC data source must be set up in order to provide a connection between the Visual Basic application and the Sample database. To simplify matters, it is assumed that both Visual Basic and DB2 UDB have been installed on the same computer. However, if they are on different computers, then all the applications will work by simply changing the ODBC Data Source.

The first form will be created using the Visual Basic Form Wizard, which will use the ADO Data Control. The second form duplicates this approach but uses Data Objects instead of the Data Control. A third form is then produced using the old VisData add-in which generates a DAO Data Control based form.

There are three simple steps required before starting the development of the form. The first is to create the ODBC Data Source. The second step is to open the correct type of project in Visual Basic. Finally, the necessary Object Library resources have to be added to the project in order to use ADO with Visual Basic.

ODBC Data Source for Accessing Sample Database

DB2 UDB for Windows NT versions, up until Version 6.1, only provide an ODBC driver for connecting to the database from the Windows environment. This involves using the MSDASQL ODBC Bridge provider in the ADO environment. A native OLE DB provider is available for the Version 7.1 release.

The ODBC data source is created using the Microsoft ODBC Administrator. An icon for this exists in the Windows Control Panel. Open the Control Panel and double click on this icon, which is labeled ODBC Data Sources. This will open a form which has a caption **ODBC Data Source Administrator** as shown below in Fig. 5–1.

This form has several tabbed pages, the first three of which display the three types of Data Sources, User, System and File. Ensure that the selected Tab is User DSN and then click on the Add button; this will open a new window, which is shown in Fig. 5–2.

This window is entitled Create New Data Source and allows you to select the ODBC driver to use.

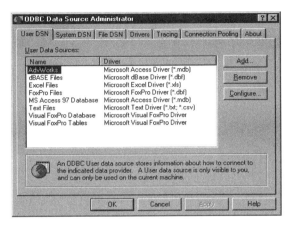

Fig. 5–1 *ODBC Data Source Administrator*

Select the IBM DB2 ODBC Driver and then click on the Finish button at the bottom of the screen.

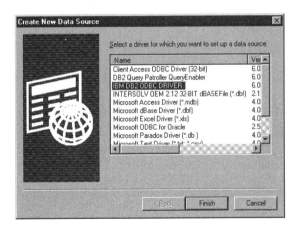

Fig. 5–2 *Create New Data Source*

This will then display a screen to enable you to select the required database alias from the drop-down list, and enter a data source name, which will be used to access this DSN (Fig. 5–3).

This form is provided by the DB2 ODBC Driver and will therefore be different from that provided by other ODBC drivers. The default data source name is the same as the database alias, but this can be amended if you wish to create another ODBC connection to a remote server, which also has a Sample database.

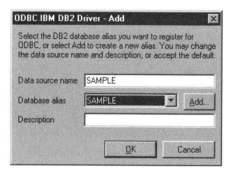

Fig. 5–3 *ODBC IBM DB2 Driver - Add*

If you click on the OK button, and then OK again, to close the ODBC Data Source Administrator form, you will have created a simple ODBC Data Source to connect to the local copy of the Sample database. If you select the Add button, then this will start the connection wizard, which will allow you to set up a connection to a database on a remote machine. This latter step is described in more detail in Chapter 2.

Opening the Visual Basic Project

Opening Visual Basic from the **Start** menu presents you with the Visual Basic IDE, overlaid with a form for selecting the type of project. This Project Type overlay window is shown in Fig. 5–4.

Select a Standard EXE project from the icon in this window. This will create a project in the **Project** Window containing a form called Form1. Rename the project to DataForms and remove Form1 via the **Projects -> Remove** menu option.

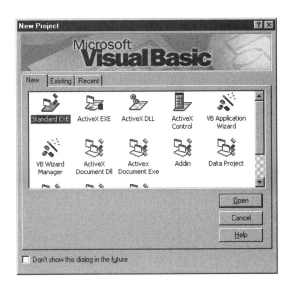

Fig. 5–4 *Visual Basic Project Types*

Setting Project References

Visual Basic has been designed to use external object libraries. This is a very powerful system for extending the programming environment and it is used to add the data access components that are used in this project. However, Visual Basic needs to know which libraries you wish to use in your project. This information is provided by the libraries that you select in **Project -> References**. This selection will display the form in Fig. 5–5.

Scroll down the list and check the entry labelled **Microsoft ActiveX Data Objects 2.1 Library**. This will give Visual Basic access to the basic ADO components.

Note: The Data Form Wizard will automatically add a Reference to the Microsoft ActiveX Data Object 2.0 library if a reference is not found. This is because 2.0 was the version of the library when Visual Basic 6.0 was released. Adding a reference to the latest version of the library before running the wizard prevents this automatic addition to References.

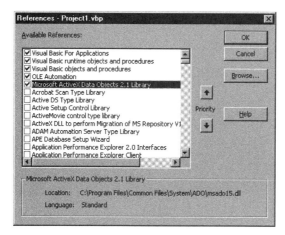

Fig. 5–5 *References*

It is instructive to study the list of References available on your machine. This list will vary, depending on what products you have installed. For instance, if you have IBM Client Access Express for AS/400 installed on your machine, you will find three References to this product, and if using IBM Personal Communications you will find several References to that product's automation objects. You will also find a Reference for the DB2 Stored Procedure Builder.

References point to a type library. An ActiveX component's type library contains definitions of all the objects the component provides, including definitions for all available methods, properties, and events. If an ActiveX component provides a type library, you need to add it to the type library in your Visual Basic project before you can use the library's objects.

Note: Visual Basic's syntax checker automatically reformats lines as you enter them. If commands that you enter do not capitalize, then a Reference to the library containing that command has possibly not been added.

Creating Forms Using the Data Form Wizard

The Data Form Wizard is designed to automatically generate the basic layout of Visual Basic forms that are used for database access. The forms can be produced using either data controls with bound form objects, such as text boxes or grids, or procedures using data objects. The forms can manage information derived from a local Jet Engine database or remote data sources with ODBC. You can use the Data Form Wizard to create single query forms to manage the data from a single table or query, Master/Detail type forms to manage more complex one-to-many data relationships, or grid (datasheet) forms to manage data from a data control.

 Note: The Data Form Wizard will only produce forms using ADO. You cannot use it for DAO or RDO.

Starting the Wizard

To use the VB Data Form Wizard select **Project -> Add Form** from the Visual Basic menu bar. This will open the **Add Form** window shown in Fig. 5–6.

The **Add Form** screen allows you to select from several types of form. The first option is a standard form, and all of the different types displayed could be built from this option by modifying the properties of the standard form. However, selecting from the options given is not only quicker, but also helps to maintain a standard appearance to your projects.

The VB Data Form is more complicated than the other types of form. It will require either a data control, data object coding, or a combination of these to bring back data from a database. It will also need text boxes or grids to display the returned recordset. Consequently, Microsoft has provided a wizard to prompt you for the information that is required to build your form.

Double clicking on the icon labelled **VB Data Form Wizard** will start the normal series of wizard screens which will allow you to set the various properties for your form.

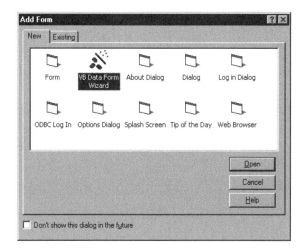

Fig. 5–6 *Add Form to Project*

The first screen is labelled Introduction and allows you to choose a wizard profile from the list of previously saved profiles. A wizard profile (.rwp) is a file that contains the settings you chose and saved when you previously ran the Data Form Wizard. To run the Data Form Wizard without previously saved settings, choose (None) and select Next.

The next screen allows you to select the database type. This is either **Access** or **Remote (ODBC)**. You should select **Remote** and **Next**.

Connection Details

After selecting Remote, you will be presented with the Connection Information screen, see Fig. 5–7. There are six entry boxes on this screen, but not all of these require data to be entered. The first entry is for DSN (Data Source Name). If you select a Data Source from the drop-down list, then the last two entries, Driver and Server, become unavailable. Going down the list for DSN and selecting Sample from the list will therefore leave three more entries, UID, PWD and Database.

However, DB2 UDB uses Windows NT security by default. If you do not enter a user ID or Password, then the ODBC driver will substitute the current Windows NT logged on user information to DB2 UDB. This leaves the database entry, which takes the value supplied by the DSN if it is left empty.

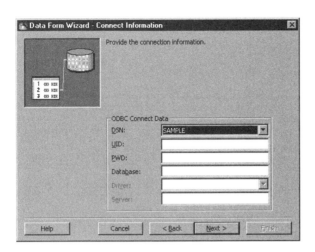

Fig. 5–7 *Connection Information*

Thus it is only necessary to select a DNS name on this screen. If you do enter a user ID and password, then this will replace the current Windows NT user. Select **Next** to continue to the next screen.

Types of Form

Four decisions are required on this form, which is shown in Fig. 5–8. They are listed below:

- Name to be assigned to form
- Form Layout
- Binding Type
- Form Name

The name should be something meaningful within the context of the form's use. The form to be created in this instance will display records from the `Employee` table in the `Sample` database, which is created during the setup of DB2 UDB. Consequently, a sensible name would be `Employee`. If you do not enter a form name, then the wizard will select the name of the table, that you select later, prefixed with `frm`, to denote an object of type form.

Form Layout

The screen gives five choices of layout. The following section describes the choices that are available.

- Single Record

  This is the simplest choice. It allows you to create a form which displays a single record from either a table, or from a simple select query involving either a subset of a single table, or of a join query using one to one relationships. The form uses individual text boxes to display each field in the recordset. Each text box has a matching label box containing the name of the field. The standard text box is data-aware and therefore no additional form controls need to be added to the project's toolbox.

- Grid (Datasheet)

  As the name implies, this will display the same type of data as the Single Record choice but using a scrolling `DataGrid` control to show the recordset in a spreadsheet type view with each row of the grid containing a single record, with a column for each field. The DataGrid control, which will be used to provide the spreadsheet view, is added the project's component toolbox by the wizard.

- Master/Detail

  This option allows you to create a form using two related tables where the relationship is a one to many. An example of this, in the Sample database, would be the relationship between employee and department. The department table would form the master record, displayed as a single record, and the employees, in a given department, would be displayed in a scrolling grid underneath the master record. The relationship uses the primary key, `DeptNo`, in the `Department` table, and the foreign key, `WorkDept`, in the `Employee` table. The wizard will add the `DataGrid` Control to the project's toolbox.

- MSHFlexGrid

  The Microsoft Hierarchical FlexGrid (`MSHFlexGrid`) control displays and operates on tabular data. It allows complete flexibility to sort, merge, and format tables containing strings and pictures. When bound to a data control, `MSHFlexGrid` displays read-only data. As its name suggests, this is a very flexible control and can be used for both simple tables and master/detail type displays, using the Data Shaping provider. Although the wizard allows you to set up a form using this control, its flexibility is best utilized by writing code to specifically use its facilities. The wizard will add the `MSHFlex` control to the project's toolbox.

- MS Chart

  This allows you to create a graph from data in the database. All the standard 2D and 3D chart types are supported as are the normal aggregating type functions, such as max, min, sum and average. The wizard will add the Microsoft Chart Control to the Project's toolbox.

For this exercise, select the Single Record option.

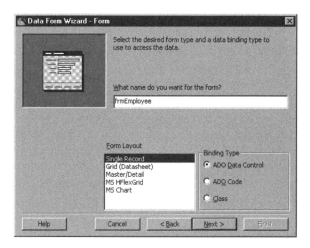

Fig. 5–8 *Form Type*

Binding Type

This selection allows you to determine what form of ADO data access the wizard will use to manage your data. There are three options which you can see in Fig. 5–8. These are the Data Control, Data Objects and Classes. The first is normally used for prototyping applications, as it is quick to create and manipulate. The Data Objects option gives a more controllable application, and the last one is useful for creating multi-tier applications, as it permits the application to be split into two parts, with one part on the server and the physical form on the client, communicating using DCOM.

- ADO Data Control

  The Data control is a form object which provides connection to a database and returns a recordset from that database connection. Its behavior is governed by setting its properties. The most important properties are `ConnectionString` and `RecordSource`, which will connect to the database and select the table or query to return data from.

  The Data control automatically handles a number of contingencies, including empty recordsets, adding new records, editing and updating existing records, and handling some types of errors. However, in more sophisticated applications, you need to trap some error conditions that the Data control can't handle.

  The Data control handles one record at a time, which is normally referred to as the current record, and it incorporates navigation controls to move forward and backwards through the recordset.

If a user makes changes to the current record, and then moves the cursor to the previous or next record, using the navigation controls, then the Data control will attempt to update the changes to the database. The table being edited must have a unique key for the recordset to be updatable. If the table is not updatable, then the Data Control will issue a trappable error, and you will need to write code which prevents the user from changing records.

Most of the standard form display controls are data-aware, which means that they can be bound to one or more fields in the Data control's recordset. There are also many third party controls which can be used in this way. Grid type controls can also manage multiple records when bound to a data control, but only one record will be current and therefore able to be edited. If a user makes changes to the current record, and then moves the cursor to the previous or next record in the grid, then the Data control will update the changes to the database.

- ADO Code

The wizard will produce the standard code to create a `Connection` object and a `Recordset` object. It will also provide buttons to emulate the Data Control's built-in navigation. Essentially, the form produced will functionally act just like the Data Control form, but if it is required to add functionality to the wizard-produced form, then the ADO code is more flexible than the Data Control.

As with the Data Control, data-aware display objects can be bound to the `Recordset` object. It should be noted that the wizard only provides a framework for the forms code, such that although the form will be functional, it will require additional coding to cope with events that the Data Control is designed to handle automatically.

- Class

If this option is selected, then the wizard will produce both a form and a class module. The form will create instances of the classes in the class module to provide its connection to the database and the type of recordset that it needs.

This is related to object oriented programming. A class is a template that defines the characteristics of an object. An object contains methods (procedures) which can be called, and properties which can be set. The class for the object defines these methods and the parameters which are passed between the calling code and the object, and also the properties which govern the appearance and behavior of the object.

Visual Basic allows users to define their own classes or object definitions. The purpose of this is code re-use and consistency. By creating a class for this form, it is possible to compile this class into a type library, and then create instances of this form in different applications. With multiple classes defined in this way for different aspects of a project, it is possible to create a new project merely by plugging together instances of the required components.

Record Source

Pressing the Next button, after making all the selections on the Form Type screen, will open a new screen for Record Source; see Fig. 5–9.

Using the drop-down button on the Record Source list box will reveal all the tables in the `Sample` database. Select the `Employee` table.

The **Available Fields** list will now fill up with the names of all the fields in the `Employee` table. Pressing the top button of the four, positioned between the two list boxes, will transfer the currently highlighted field name from the **Available Fields** list to the **Selected Fields** list. The second button will transfer all the entries in the **Available Fields** List to the **Selected Fields** list. The third and fourth buttons replicate the actions of the top two buttons in the reverse direction so that you can correct any errors. Select the all fields option.

The two buttons to the right of the **Selected Fields** list allow you to re-order the list. This will effect the order that fields appear on the form. Leave the fields in their original order.

The **Column to Sort By** drop-down list box allows you to change the order that the recordset is returned in. Leave this blank. The recordset will be returned, ordered by the table's primary key.

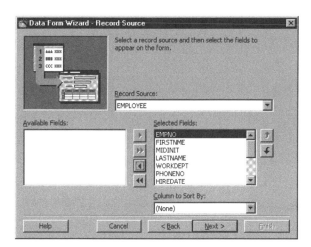

Fig. 5–9 *Record Source*

Press the **Next** key to move on to the next screen.

Control Selection

This screen allows you to select which command buttons you wish to add to the form, from the following options:

- **Add** button — to add a record to the recordset
- **Update** button — to insert a newly created or amended record
- **Delete** button — delete current record in recordset
- **Refresh** button — return a new recordset from the database
- **Close** button — close the form

The wizard will place the selected command buttons on the form and insert code in the click event of each command to perform the required function. For this exercise, select all buttons (Fig. 5–10).

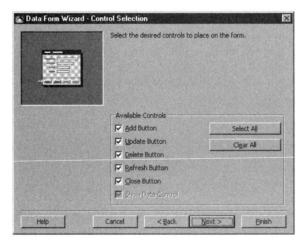

Fig. 5–10 *Form Controls*

Completed Form

After pressing the **Finish** button, the form will be created by the wizard according to the selections that you have made.

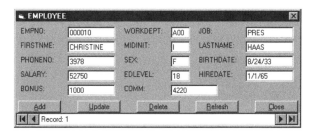

Fig. 5–11 *Resultant Form*

The form will provide a single column of associated label and text boxes, with all label and text boxes of the same width. It is therefore advisable to rearrange the positions and sizes of the individual text boxes and label boxes, in order to produce a more functional form. The figure in Fig. 5–11 shows the rearranged form.

Code Produced by Wizard for ADO Data Control Option

The wizard has very little code to produce when using the ADO Data control. The connection string and record source are embedded as properties of the Data control, and the recordset scrolling is also done by the control. The wizard produces nine sub-programs, but most of these are very small. The code is functional but requires additions for proper error trapping. The sub-programs produced are listed below:

Form Unload Event

This simply returns the mouse cursor to Default.

```
Private Sub Form_Unload(Cancel As Integer)
   Screen.MousePointer = vbDefault
End Sub
```

Data Control Error Event

This is provided as a skeleton procedure giving the parameters which should be passed. The wizard produced code simply displays a message box with any errors received.

```
Private Sub datPrimaryRS_Error(ByVal ErrorNumber As Long,
Description As String, ByVal Scode As Long, ByVal Source As String,
ByVal HelpFile As String, ByVal HelpContext As Long, fCancelDisplay
As Boolean)
    'This is where you would put error handling code
    'If you want to ignore errors, comment out the next line
    'If you want to trap them, add code here to handle them
    MsgBox "Data error event hit err:" & Description
End Sub
```

Data Control MoveComplete Event

This event is used to calculate the record number to insert in the caption property of the Data Control.

```
Private Sub datPrimaryRS_MoveComplete(ByVal adReason As
ADODB.EventReasonEnum, ByVal pError As ADODB.Error, adStatus As
ADODB.EventStatusEnum, ByVal pRecordset As ADODB.Recordset)
    'This will display the current record position for this recordset
    datPrimaryRS.Caption = "Record: " &
CStr(datPrimaryRS.Recordset.AbsolutePosition)
End Sub
```

Data Control WillChangeRecord Event

This is the longest procedure written by the wizard but again it is merely a skeleton to be filled in. As the name of the event suggests, this is the place to put data validation routines, to ensure that the record change can be cancelled, if the validation rules for any of the specified actions, fail.

Building
Applications
Using Visual Basic

```
Private Sub datPrimaryRS_WillChangeRecord(ByVal adReason As
ADODB.EventReasonEnum, ByVal cRecords As Long, adStatus As
ADODB.EventStatusEnum, ByVal pRecordset As ADODB.Recordset)
    'This is where you put validation code
    'This event gets called when the following actions occur
    Dim bCancel As Boolean

    Select Case adReason
    Case adRsnAddNew
    Case adRsnClose
    Case adRsnDelete
    Case adRsnFirstChange
    Case adRsnMove
    Case adRsnRequery
    Case adRsnResynch
    Case adRsnUndoAddNew
    Case adRsnUndoDelete
    Case adRsnUndoUpdate
    Case adRsnUpdate
    End Select

    If bCancel Then adStatus = adStatusCancel
End Sub
```

Add Button Click Event

This uses the command <Data Control>.Recordset.AddNew to prepare the
recordset for a new record to be entered. This will provide a blank record buffer
and all data bound text boxes will be cleared. The procedure contains an error
routine to display any error messages received.

```
Private Sub cmdAdd_Click()
    On Error GoTo AddErr
    datPrimaryRS.Recordset.AddNew
    Exit Sub
AddErr:
    MsgBox Err.Description
End Sub
```

Delete Button Click Event

This uses the command <Data Control>.Recordset.Delete to delete the current
record from the recordset. It then moves next to the next valid record. If the move
next puts it on end of file, then it executes a move last in order to be on a valid
record. The procedure contains an error routine to display any error messages
received.

```
Private Sub cmdDelete_Click()
  On Error GoTo DeleteErr
  With datPrimaryRS.Recordset
    .Delete
    .MoveNext
    If .EOF Then .MoveLast
  End With
  Exit Sub
DeleteErr:
  MsgBox Err.Description
End Sub
```

Refresh Button Click Event

This issues the command <Data Control>.Refresh. The purpose of this is to make the Data control re-query the database to obtain a more recent copy of the recordset. This is required to see if another user has changed the data. This procedure has the same simple error handling mentioned before.

```
Private Sub cmdRefresh_Click()
  'This is only needed for multi user apps
  On Error GoTo RefreshErr
  datPrimaryRS.Refresh
  Exit Sub
RefreshErr:
  MsgBox Err.Description
End Sub
```

Update Button Click Event

This issues the command <Data Control>.UpdateBatch adAffectAll. This will cause any changes in the current record buffer to be updated to the database.

```
Private Sub cmdUpdate_Click()
  On Error GoTo UpdateErr

  datPrimaryRS.Recordset.UpdateBatch adAffectAll
  Exit Sub
UpdateErr:
  MsgBox Err.Description
End Sub
```

Close Button Click Event

This simply unloads the current form. The ADO Data control will destroy its recordset and close its connection automatically when the form ends.

```
Private Sub cmdClose_Click()
   Unload Me
End Sub
```

Additional Code Produced by Wizard from ADO Code Option

If you run the wizard again, but this time select ADO code instead of ADO Data Control, the wizard will produce a form which looks very similar. The Data control is replaced on the form by a picture box, label and four small buttons, which are arranged to look like a Data control. The wizard also adds code to replace the functionality of the ADO Data control. The additions to the code are described below:

General

The General area of the form module now has dimension statements for the Recordset object and various flag variables to be used in the program for tracking events that were handled automatically by the Data control. The code is shown below:

```
Option Explicit
Dim WithEvents adoPrimaryRS As Recordset
Dim mbChangedByCode As Boolean
Dim mvBookMark As Variant
Dim mbEditFlag As Boolean
Dim mbAddNewFlag As Boolean
Dim mbDataChanged As Boolean
```

Form Load Event

This uses the following code to create a connection object, open the Recordset object and bind the recordset fields to the text boxes on the form. With the ADO control, these activities are automatically set up when the form is loaded.

```
Private Sub Form_Load()
  Dim db As Connection
  Set db = New Connection
  db.CursorLocation = adUseClient
  db.Open "PROVIDER=MSDASQL;dsn=SAMPLE;uid=;pwd=;"

  Set adoPrimaryRS = New Recordset
  adoPrimaryRS.Open "select
EMPNO,FIRSTNME,MIDINIT,LASTNAME,WORKDEPT,PHONENO,HIREDATE,JOB,EDLE
VEL,SEX,BIRTHDATE,SALARY,BONUS,COMM from EMPLOYEE", db,
adOpenStatic, adLockOptimistic

  Dim oText As TextBox
  'Bind the text boxes to the data provider
  For Each oText In Me.txtFields
    Set oText.DataSource = adoPrimaryRS
  Next

  mbDataChanged = False
End Sub
```

Form Resize Event

As the simulated Data control is made up of several components, this code is necessary in order to reposition the label and the two buttons that follow it when the form is resized.

```
Private Sub Form_Resize()
  On Error Resume Next
  lblStatus.Width = Me.Width - 1500
  cmdNext.Left = lblStatus.Width + 700
  cmdLast.Left = cmdNext.Left + 340
End Sub
```

Form Keydown Event

This procedure is used to permit the keyboard to be used to navigate through the recordset. This functionality is also built into the ADO Data Control.

```
Private Sub Form_KeyDown(KeyCode As Integer, Shift As Integer)
  If mbEditFlag Or mbAddNewFlag Then Exit Sub
  Select Case KeyCode
    Case vbKeyEscape
      cmdClose_Click
    Case vbKeyEnd
      cmdLast_Click
    Case vbKeyHome
      cmdFirst_Click
    Case vbKeyUp, vbKeyPageUp
      If Shift = vbCtrlMask Then cmdFirst_Click
      Else          cmdPrevious_Click
      End If
    Case vbKeyDown, vbKeyPageDown
      If Shift = vbCtrlMask Then cmdLast_Click
      Else          cmdNext_Click
      End If
  End Select
End Sub
```

Add Button Click Event

The code in this event is slightly more complicated than the ADO Data control. Adding a new record involves moving away from the current record. Consequently the procedure bookmarks the current record so that the `Cancel` event can return to the original record. The procedure also sets a flag to indicate the fact that a new record is being added. This information is required by the Update procedure so that it can move to the last record, after the update command is issued. This is because the last record will be the one that has just been added. The flag is also used to disable record movement using the keyboard. Lastly, the procedure sets the command buttons to a state which will only permit the user to update the changes made or to cancel them. All the record movement keys are disabled and the other keys apart from **Update** and **Cancel** are made invisible.

```
Private Sub cmdAdd_Click()
  On Error GoTo AddErr
  With adoPrimaryRS
    If Not (.BOF And .EOF) Then
      mvBookMark = .Bookmark
    End If
    .AddNew
    lblStatus.Caption = "Add record"
    mbAddNewFlag = True
    SetButtons False
  End With

  Exit Sub
AddErr:
  MsgBox Err.Description
End Sub
```

Edit Button Click Event

As with the `AddNew` procedure, this sets a flag which is used by the `Keyboard` procedure to disable record movement. The `SetButtons` procedure is also used to disable the record movement buttons and to disable the keys other than **Cancel** and **Update**.

```
Private Sub cmdEdit_Click()
  On Error GoTo EditErr

  lblStatus.Caption = "Edit record"
  mbEditFlag = True
  SetButtons False
  Exit Sub

EditErr:
  MsgBox Err.Description
End Sub
```

Cancel Button Click Event

The `Cancel` procedure clears the `AddNew` and `Edit` flags and moves the current record to the previous bookmark, or to the first record if there is no bookmark.

```
Private Sub cmdCancel_Click()
  On Error Resume Next

  SetButtons True
  mbEditFlag = False
  mbAddNewFlag = False
  adoPrimaryRS.CancelUpdate
  If mvBookMark > Ø Then
    adoPrimaryRS.Bookmark = mvBookMark
  Else
    adoPrimaryRS.MoveFirst
  End If
  mbDataChanged = False

End Sub
```

Update Button Click Event

This procedure updates the changes made to the record. It then moves the cursor to the last record if the previous event was an `AddNew`. It then clears the `AddNew` and `Edit` flags and resets the other command buttons to visible and enabled.

```
Private Sub cmdUpdate_Click()
  On Error GoTo UpdateErr

  adoPrimaryRS.UpdateBatch adAffectAll

  If mbAddNewFlag Then
    adoPrimaryRS.MoveLast              'move to the new record
  End If

  mbEditFlag = False
  mbAddNewFlag = False
  SetButtons True
  mbDataChanged = False

  Exit Sub
UpdateErr:
  MsgBox Err.Description
End Sub

Private Sub cmdClose_Click()
  Unload Me
End Sub
```

First Button Click Event

This moves the current record to the first record in the recordset. The Data control has its own built-in button for this function which requires no code.

```
Private Sub cmdFirst_Click()
  On Error GoTo GoFirstError

  adoPrimaryRS.MoveFirst
  mbDataChanged = False

  Exit Sub

GoFirstError:
  MsgBox Err.Description
End Sub
```

Last Button Click Event

This moves the current record to the last record in the recordset. The Data control has its own built-in button for this function which requires no code.

```
Private Sub cmdLast_Click()
  On Error GoTo GoLastError

  adoPrimaryRS.MoveLast
  mbDataChanged = False

  Exit Sub

GoLastError:
  MsgBox Err.Description
End Sub
```

Next Button Click Event

This moves the current record to the next record in the recordset. The Data control has its own built-in button for this function which requires no code.

```
Private Sub cmdNext_Click()
  On Error GoTo GoNextError

  If Not adoPrimaryRS.EOF Then adoPrimaryRS.MoveNext
  If adoPrimaryRS.EOF And adoPrimaryRS.RecordCount > 0 Then
    Beep
      'moved off the end so go back
    adoPrimaryRS.MoveLast
  End If
  'show the current record
  mbDataChanged = False

  Exit Sub
GoNextError:
  MsgBox Err.Description
End Sub
```

Previous Button Click Event

This moves the current record to the previous record in the recordset. The Data control has its own built-in button for this function which requires no code.

```
Private Sub cmdPrevious_Click()
  On Error GoTo GoPrevError

  If Not adoPrimaryRS.BOF Then adoPrimaryRS.MovePrevious
  If adoPrimaryRS.BOF And adoPrimaryRS.RecordCount > 0 Then
    Beep
    'moved off the end so go back
    adoPrimaryRS.MoveFirst
  End If
  'show the current record
  mbDataChanged = False

  Exit Sub

GoPrevError:
  MsgBox Err.Description
End Sub
```

Set Button Sub-Program

This procedure controls the state of the command buttons. At program start, the
Update and **Cancel** buttons are made invisible, while the **AddNew**, **Edit**, **Delete**,
Refresh and **Close** buttons are made visible. The record movement buttons are also
enabled.

If the **AddNew** or **Edit** button is pressed, then the **AddNew**, **Edit**, **Delete**, **Refresh**
and **Close** buttons are made invisible, and the **Update** and **Cancel** buttons are made
visible. At the same time, the record movement buttons are disabled. This ensures
that changes to the new or edited record can only be terminated by an Update or
Cancel action.

```
Private Sub SetButtons(bVal As Boolean)
  cmdAdd.Visible = bVal
  cmdEdit.Visible = bVal
  cmdUpdate.Visible = Not bVal
  cmdCancel.Visible = Not bVal
  cmdDelete.Visible = bVal
  cmdClose.Visible = bVal
  cmdRefresh.Visible = bVal
  cmdNext.Enabled = bVal
  cmdFirst.Enabled = bVal
  cmdLast.Enabled = bVal
  cmdPrevious.Enabled = bVal
End Sub
```

Visual Data Manager Add-In

The DAO Data Control is a form object whose property values permit it to connect to a database and return a recordset, based either on the contents of a table or an SQL query. A data-aware form object can then be bound to a field or several fields in the Data Control's recordset. Data-aware form objects include labels, text boxes, combo boxes, list boxes and the DBGrid. This basically has the same functionality of the ADO Data Control which was described previously.

The simplest way of creating a form, using the DAO control, is to use the Data Form Designer feature of the Visual Data Manager Add-In. This add-in was produced initially as a sample program in an earlier version of Visual Basic, hence it only uses DAO and not ADO. This enables the developer to select a database to access, and decide on a table or query to use. The Add-In will create a complete form, displaying the required fields, with field name labels. The form will also include option buttons for Add, Delete, Refresh, Update and Close, together with the Data Control and its buttons for navigating through the table or recordset.

The following example uses the same Employee table in the Sample database as was used in the ADO example. Start Visual Basic with a New.EXE type project. Open the Visual Data Manager by clicking **Add-Ins --> Visual Data Manager,** on the Visual Basic Menu Bar. This will open a separate window labelled VisData. Select the Sample database by clicking **File --> Open Database --> ODBC** on the VisData menu bar. This will open the ODBC Logon dialog box. Use the drop-down option in the top box to select the DSN (Data Source Name), if the required one is not displayed. Type in the UID and Password, if necessary, and click **OK**. Two windows will appear inside the VisData window. The first is labelled Database Window, and will contain a list of the application and system tables in the database. The second window is labelled SQL Statement and will initially be empty. It is only at this stage that the **Utility** item on the menu becomes enabled.

Start the form create process by clicking on **Utility --> Data Form Designer**. This will open a form labelled Data Form Designer. Type **Employee** in the Form Name box and select <NAME>.EMPLOYEE from the Record Source drop-down list. The form will fill in the Available Fields in the left hand list box. Click on **>>** to include all fields on the form and then click on the **Build the Form** button.

After some flashing activity within the Visual Basic window, the Data Form Designer form will be cleared and the form will have been built. Click on **Close** in the Data Form Designer window and click **Form --> Exit** on the VisData menu bar. Fig. 5–12 shows the form that was created, after manually repositioning the text boxes and labels on the form to give a neater layout.

Note: This should look identical to the form provided by the Data Form Wizard. The only difference is in the Data controls used, which visually look the same.

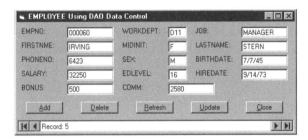

Fig. 5–12 *Visual Basic DAO Control Version of Employee Form*

This add-in is very similar to the Data Form Wizard, but produces forms based on DAO, whereas the Data Form Wizard only produces forms based on ADO code.

There is no equivalent to either of these options to produce forms based on RDO. The basic reason for this is that Microsoft considers the ADO technology to be the replacement for RDO, and in fact it is really an extension of the RDO technology, but now accessible from both the Professional and Enterprise versions of Visual Studio, whereas RDO was only available for the Enterprise Version.

DAO is completely different from the other two technologies. It was designed to provide an efficient interface to the Access database, and evidence from programmers using Visual Basic in this environment, suggests that it is still more efficient than ADO in this environment.

Microsoft would still prefer that programmers move to ADO for all new projects, but as long as a performance difference exists, they have to continue to support DAO, where performance is paramount — hence the maintenance of the VisData add-in. It is obviously uncertain just how much longer DAO will be supported, but probably not for long. Many of the features promised for the next version of Visual Studio are heavily object oriented, and DAO will not fit readily into such an environment.

OpenSchema Recordsets

The purpose of this example is to demonstrate how you can use ADO to obtain information from a connected database. This allows you to write more general purpose type applications, where decisions can be made at run time, rather than design time. It permits you to create such facilities as a query builder, providing the user with selection options for tables and fields in any database requested by the user.

You can also use these facilities to create general purpose programs for managing your databases. Any database can be copied to a database on the same machine or a different machine, or individual tables can be re-built to a different specification and the contents transferred from the original table to the new one. The example that is shown below will build and populate a DB2 UDB database from data in a Microsoft Access database.

Microsoft provides various programming samples on the MSDN Library disks, which are part of the Visual Studio product install set. You are given the option to install these onto your local hard drive when you install the MSDN Library. The default directory structure for these samples is in the following directory.

```
C:\Program Files\Microsoft Visual Studio\MSDN98\98Vsa\1033\Samples
```

The `Booksale` sample program is under `Samples\VB98\Misc\Booksale`, within the above file structure.

The sample has two parts, a client program and a server program, and is described in the MSDN Library. This description can be located as follows:

1. Click on Windows Start button.

2. Select Programs --> Microsoft Developer Network --> MSDN Library Visual Studio 6.0a.

3. Select Contents tab in left-hand window.

4. Open MSDN Library Visual Studio 6.0.

5. Open Visual Basic Documentation.

6. Open Samples.

7. Open Enterprise Edition.

8. Select BookSale Sample.

You will find that Microsoft has supplied an Access database for this sample. Our first programming task will be to create a DB2 UDB database to the same specification, and to transfer the sample data from the original Microsoft Access database to the new DB2 UDB database. We will achieve this by utilizing the OpenSchema property of he ADO Recordset object, to determine the tables and their columns in the Access database. We will then use this information to create these tables in the DB2 UDB BOOKSALES database. Finally, we will transfer the records from the Access database to the DB2 UDB database. An exact copy of the Access database will make the example program too large, and the description repetitive, but it can be enhanced, to add foreign keys for example, quite easily.

It will be necessary to modify the Microsoft example slightly to enable you to use the DB2 UDB database created below. The first requirement is to change the connection string from using the Microsoft Access data provider, to use either the MSDASQL ODBC Bridge provider and ODBC DSN, or the new DB2 OLE DB data provider in DB2 UDB Version 7.1.

The second change relates to the way that Access and DB2 UDB deal with Table and Field names which contain embedded spaces, in SQL statements. Access delimits such fields with square brackets, whereas DB2 UDB uses quotes. There were two ways to deal with this problem. The first way is to create the tables and change the queries to include quotes in place of brackets. The second is to remove the spaces from the names and remove the brackets from the queries. It was decided to use the second method, as you will seldom find such definitions in professional data bases. You will need to find the queries in the application that contain such Table and Field names. Searching for "[" is probably the easiest method, and then remove the brackets.

BookSale Schema

The application requires no screen output and therefore uses a Basic module and no form modules.We have called the application Schema as one of its main purposes is to demonstrate this functionality of the ADO model. ODBC performed similar functions using the GetInfo API calls.

The application utilizes three main procedures, which cover the following tasks:

1. Determine the table names in the Access database

2. Use the table names from (1) to determine the column names for each table, and then create an equivalent table in the DB2 UDB database

3. Transfer all the records from the Access table to the newly created table in DB2 UDB.

The first procedure calls the second procedure for each table name that it finds. The second procedure creates a DB2 UDB table and then calls the third procedure to populate it from the original Access table.

The DB2 ODBC/CLI interface does not support the CREATE DATABASE command. It will therefore be necessary to create a new database called BOOKSALE in DB2 UDB, using the DB2 Control Center, before running this program.

Public Declarations in Schema Module

The first requirements of the Main procedure is to create connections to the two databases. We have dimensioned two connection objects called "cnAccess" and "cnDb2". These objects are dimensioned and instantiated in the Declarations area of the Schema module. Both objects are dimensioned as Public, in order that they can be seen by all procedures. It is good practice in Visual Basic to restrict global variables. Consequently only variables used by more than one procedure are declared here.

```
Option Explicit

Public cnAccess As New ADODB.Connection ' Connection for Access
Public cnDb2 As New ADODB.Connection ' Connection for DB2 UDB
```

Main Procedure in Schema Module

The following screens may be cut and pasted sequentially into the Schema module in the Visual Basic project to produce the Main procedure.

Connections

The first section of the procedure below, dimensions a Recordset object which will be used to return the Table Schema information from the Access database.

The first statement, following the dimension statement, sets up the connection to the Access database, booksale.mdb. This connection uses the Microsoft native OLE DB provider, Microsoft.Jet.OLEDB.3.51. As the database has not been set up for security, you can use the default "admin" user with no password, in the connection string.

The program sets up the ConnectionString property of the connection object first, and then opens the connection. It is equally acceptable to use:
cnAccess.Open ConnectionString.

The following is a listing of the Main procedure:

```
Private Sub Main()

  Dim rstTables As New ADODB.Recordset ' Read table schema

  cnAccess.ConnectionString = _
    "Provider=Microsoft.Jet.OLEDB.3.51;" & _
    "Data Source=c:\Booksale\booksale.mdb;User Id=admin;Password=;"
  cnAccess.Open

  cnDb2.ConnectionString = _
    "DSN=Booksale"
  cnDb2.Open

  Set rstTables = cnAccess.OpenSchema(adSchemaTables, _
    Array(Empty, Empty, Empty, "Table"))

  Do Until rstTables.EOF
    If InStr(rstTables!TABLE_NAME, "MSys") = 0 Then
      Call CreateTable(rstTables!TABLE_NAME)
    End If
    rstTables.MoveNext
  Loop

  rstTables.Close
  Set rstTables = Nothing
  cnAccess.Close
  Set cnAccess = Nothing
  cnDb2.Close
  Set cnDb2 = Nothing
End Sub
```

The next step is to open the connection to the DB2 UDB database. DB2 UDB Version 6 did not supply an OLE DB provider; however, one is available in Version 7. The program uses the Microsoft provider for ODBC, MSDASQL. As this is the default ADO provider, it is not necessary to specify it in the Connection string. The connection string specifies a Data Source Name of Booksale and it will be necessary for you to create this DSN using the ODBC Administrator module, accessible via the Windows Control Panel.

The normal connection string for the DB2 ODBC driver would be:

```
DSN=<data source name>;UID=<user name>;PWD=<password>;DBALIAS=<database
alias>
```

DB2 UDB for NT uses Windows NT security by default, and therefore, when the UID and PWD elements are omitted, as in this program, the driver uses the current logged-on NT user. As this program is going to build tables in the BOOKSALE database, it would be sensible to use the same userid and password as was used when the BOOKSALE database was created. This is because the owner of a database has full privileges to that database.

If you want to use the OLE DB provider which is available in DB2 UDB Version 7.1, the connection string would be as following:

```
cnDb2.ConnectionString = _
   "Provider=ibmdadb2; Data Source=Booksale;"
```

Note that UID and PWD elements are omitted in this example, therefore the driver uses the current logged-on Windows NT user.

Find Table Names

Having connected to the databases, the next section of code opens the rstTable recordset against the Microsoft Access database using the OpenSchema method of the connection object. The syntax for the OpenSchema method is:

```
Recordset = Connection.OpenSchema(QueryType, Criteria, SchemaID)
```

If you search for OpenSchema in the MSDN Library, or select function key F1, when the cursor rests on OpenSchema in the Visual Basic editor, you will find a listing of the QueryTypes and associated Criteria.

There are 31 QueryTypes supported by ADO, of which 11 are supported under ODBC SQL. The QueryType used here is adSchemaTable, which returns several items of information related to each table in the connected database, including the Table Name and Table Type. All of the items, which make up the columns within the returned recordset, are listed in the Visual Basic on-line help.

The only table names that are required for this program are the user defined tables which are to be built into the DB2 UDB database. The Criteria parameter in the OpenSchema method allows the program to restrict the rows returned in the recordset, and this is used to restrict the rows returned to only those of type Table. Each of the QueryTypes use a subset of the returned information, as Criteria, to restrict the data returned. This argument to the call is passed as an array, containing all the criteria used. The criteria are positional in the array, which is the reason for the use of Empty in the first three array entries, so that the method is aware that "TABLE" in the fourth array element refers to TABLE_TYPE.

The recordset now contains the information required for Tables in the Access database. The program now loops through the recordset and calls the CreateTable procedure for each user defined table that is found in the recordset. There is one slight problem with this step. If you examine the contents of the recordset returned, you will find that the Microsoft Access database contains two tables, which are defined as type TABLE, but are prefixed msys as with Access System Tables. It has therefore been necessary to add an IF clause to ignore these tables.

Reclaim Resources

The final part of the Main procedure cleans up the resources used, by first closing each of the objects opened in this procedure, and then setting the object variables to Nothing. This returns the memory allocated to these objects, when they were instantiated, back to the pool of available memory.

CreateTable Procedure in Schema Module

This procedure is called by the Main procedure for each user defined table found in the Access database. The basic requirements are to determine the column names and types for each table and create an equivalent table in DB2 UDB. The database was created in DB2 UDB using the New Table Wizard in DB2's Control Center.

Following is a listing of the CreateTable procedure:

Building
Applications
Using Visual Basic

```
Private Sub CreateTable(strTable)

  Dim cmdDb2 As New ADODB.Command
  Dim rstCols As New ADODB.Recordset ' Recordset to read Column
schema
  Dim strCreate As String
  Dim strCol As String

  Set cmdDb2.ActiveConnection = cnDb2
  Set rstCols = cnAccess.OpenSchema(adSchemaColumns)
  rstCols.MoveFirst
  strCreate = "CREATE TABLE " & Chr$(34) & UCase(strTable) &
Chr$(34) & " ("

  Do Until rstCols.EOF
    If rstCols!TABLE_NAME = strTable Then
      strCol = rstCols!COLUMN_NAME
      strCreate = strCreate & Chr$(34) & UCase(rstCols!COLUMN_NAME)
& Chr$(34) & " "
      Select Case Trim$(rstCols!DATA_TYPE)
        Case "129"
          strCreate = strCreate & "VARCHAR("
          If rstCols!CHARACTER_MAXIMUM_LENGTH = 0 Then
            strCreate = strCreate & "2000)"
          Else
            strCreate = strCreate &
Trim(CStr(rstCols!CHARACTER_MAXIMUM_LENGTH)) & ")"
          End If
        Case "2"
          strCreate = strCreate & "SmallInt"
        Case "3"
          strCreate = strCreate & "Integer"
        Case "6"
          strCreate = strCreate & "Double"
      End Select
      If CheckIfPrimary(strTable, strCol) = True Then
        strCreate = strCreate & " NOT NULL"
      End If
      strCreate = strCreate & ","
    End If
    rstCols.MoveNext
  Loop

  strCreate = Left$(strCreate, Len(strCreate) - 1)
  PrimaryKey strTable, strCreate
  strCreate = strCreate & ");"
  ' Debug.Print strCreate
  cmdDb2.CommandText = strCreate
  cmdDb2.Execute

  rstCols.Close
  Set rstCols = Nothing
  Set cmdDb2 = Nothing

  CreateIndexes strTable
  DataFill strTable
End Sub
```

Declare Variables for the Procedure

The declarations are for those data objects which are only used within this procedure, and two local variables which are also only used within this procedure.

This procedure is called by the Main procedure, passing the name of the table to be processed by the procedure. We dimension two data objects to be used within the procedure. These are a Command object which will be used to pass the SQL create table string to DB2 UDB, and a Recordset object which is used to collect column information from the specified table within the Access database.

The strCreate string is used to build the SQL statement as each column definition is retrieved from the Access database Columns Schema.

Create Columns Schema Recordset

This section of code first sets up the active connection property of the Command object, to the Connection Object cnDb2, which was connected to the DB2 UDB database in the Main procedure.

The procedure uses the OpenSchema method of the Access connection object, cnAccess, to return a recordset of information regarding the columns in the table. It then executes a MoveFirst method on the recordset object to ensure that it is positioned at the beginning of the recordset, and then the procedure starts to compile the CREATE TABLE string with the only information that is currently held, which is the name of the table to be created. As an example, if the table name is "Author" then the strCreate string will contain, at this point in the program:

```
CREATE TABLE "Author" (
```

Note the use of Chr$(34) and Ucase to ensure that the table name is in upper case and that the name is surrounded by quotes. The quotes are necessary in DB2 UDB to permit the use of table names which contain spaces.

According to the ADO specification, the recordset pointer always starts on the first record, when the recordset is opened. The MoveFirst method is not therefore required, but it is good programming practice to make your code more readable by not relying on such default characteristics.

It had originally been intended to produce a recordset restricted to only the table being dealt with, by using the Criteria for TABLE_NAME in the OpenSchema method. However an error was received indicating that the provider does not support this. The procedure therefore uses the unrestricted call, which returns all columns in the database, and selected which columns relate to the required table in the next section of code.

This last point is very important when using OLE DB and ADO. OLE DB covers various types of data, and the requirements may well be different for different type of data and environments. Microsoft has covered a variety of different options in their specifications, but do not insist that all of these must be supported. This flexibility means that not all providers will give the same options. It is important when developing in this environment, that you check the actual facilities provided by your OLE DB provider, or if working with several, that you have error handling mechanisms that will cope with the possible variations. When developing general purpose routines which could involve different providers, it is best to select concepts which are likely to work in most situations, even if the code to do this appears to be larger and less efficient than other options.

The following is an example of the variations that you can find. The adSchemaPrimaryKeys Query Type, of the OpenSchema method, can return eight parameters. The OLE DB provider for Microsoft Access only returns three of these parameters, Table_NAME, COLUMN_NAME and ORDINAL.

Collecting Column Information

Having created a recordset of all the columns in the source database, the procedure now moves through this recordset to collect information from each relevant column.

As it was not possible to restrict the columns to the required table at the recordset create stage, the procedure applies an If statement, within the loop, to apply that restriction.

The procedure adds the column name to the Table Create string. Thus, if the first column in this table is Au_Id, then the contents of the strCreate string will be:

```
CREATE "AUTHOR" ("AU_ID"
```

Please note that there is a space at the end of the above string.

Determine Column Data Types

The Column Schema Data Type returns a numeric value to represent the type of data in that column. One of the ways to determine the meaning of these values is to use the Object Browser to list all the data types. Open the Object Browser within the Visual Basic IDE by pressing function key F2. Search for DataTypeEnum and select ADODB from the resulting two options in the library window.

The lower part of the Object Browser windows contains two panes labelled Classes and Members of 'DataTypeEnum'. The latter will display a list of data type constants, and as you click on each entry, you will see a value statement appear in the bottom grey panel. For example, if you click on adChar, which is obviously character data, you will see a value of 129 appear in the grey panel.

To determine the syntax required in the Create Table string for each type of data, we use a Select statement with a Case for each type of data we expect. Each case statement allows us to vary the format of the text that we add to strCreate for each column definition that we get from the schema information.

The first case statement deals with the CHAR data type, which we have already determined returns a value of 129 decimal from an Access database. Here we meet our first data compatibility problems. Access returns a CHAR type definition for two types of field, the Text field and the Memo field. Access also sets the default length of a Text field to 255 characters, which is the length it will remain at unless the system administrator changes it. However, the maximum length of a CHAR field in DB2 UDB is 254. The Access Memo field is equivalent to a CLOB field in standard SQL databases such as DB2 UDB, but does not need to define a maximum length, as this is fixed at 1.2 GB.

When returning the definition for a Memo field, Access returns a CHARACTER_MAXIMUM_LENGTH of zero, which permits us to differentiate between a Text field and a Memo field.

If the CHARACTER_MAXIMUM_LENGTH column of the recordset has a value of zero, then we define the field as of type VARCHAR with a length of 2000. This is not really correct, as we should define it as a CLOB with length 1.2GB, but from examination of the Booksale database, it is clear that this size is adequate for the memo fields in use. For any other value of this recordset column, we will define the field as VARCHAR with the length as defined by CHARACTER_MAXIMUM_LENGTH.

The next two Data Type Cases are much simpler, as we have direct equivalence for both SmallInt and Integer.

The last type we deal with is the currency type. This is a Decimal type of data, and the schema returns values for both NUMERIC_PRECISION and NUMERIC_SCALE. However Microsoft Access does not return a NUMERIC_SCALE value, and therefore we have used the DOUBLE variable type as the DB2 equivalent to Currency.

Building
Applications
Using Visual Basic

Having determined the data type for the column, it is necessary to determine if the column can contain nulls. This should be obtainable from the IS_NULLABLE column in the recordset. However, it was found that Microsoft Access returns True for all columns in the table. This answer is indeterminate and it was necessary to use another method. The main reason for needing this information is to ensure that any column used to provide a Primary Key cannot contain any null data. Therefore it was decided to determine which columns were used for Primary Keys and to create them as NOT NULL columns. The program therefore calls a procedure, called CheckIfPrimary, at this point, and if the answer is True, then NOT NULL is added to the column definition within strCreate string.

The CheckIfPrimary function creates an OpenSchema type recordset of type PrimaryKeys. It then loops through this recordset to determine if an entry matches the current column and table. If it does, then the function returns a value of True and exits the function. If the loop exits without finding a match, then the function returns a value of False before returning to the calling procedure. The listing for this procedure is given below:

```
Public Function CheckIfPrimary(strTable, strCol)
    Dim rstPrimary As New ADODB.Recordset
    Set rstPrimary = cnAccess.OpenSchema(adSchemaPrimaryKeys)
    Do Until rstPrimary.EOF
        If rstPrimary!TABLE_NAME = strTable Then
            If rstPrimary!COLUMN_NAME = strCol Then
                CheckIfPrimary = True
                Exit Function
            End If
        End If
        rstPrimary.MoveNext
    Loop
    CheckIfPrimary = False
End Function
```

The last few lines of code in the Create Table procedure, increment the array pointer, end the If condition for the required table, move the recordset pointer to the next column and then loops back to deal with the other column definitions in the same way.

Add Primary Keys to Table Definition

The final step of creating the Create Table statement is to add the primary keys to strCreate string. This is achieved by the PrimaryKey procedure, which is listed below:

```
Public Sub PrimaryKey(strTable, strCreate)
  Dim rstPrimary As New ADODB.Recordset
  Dim strCol As String
  Dim Pkey As Boolean
  Pkey = False
  Set rstPrimary = cnAccess.OpenSchema(adSchemaPrimaryKeys)
  Do Until rstPrimary.EOF
    If rstPrimary!TABLE_NAME = strTable Then
      If InStr(strCreate, "PRIMARY KEY") = 0 Then
        Pkey = True
        strCreate = strCreate & ", PRIMARY KEY ("
      Else
        strCreate = strCreate & ", "
      End If
      strCol = rstPrimary!COLUMN_NAME
      spstrip strCol
      strCreate = strCreate & strCol
    End If
    rstPrimary.MoveNext
  Loop
  If Pkey = True Then strCreate = strCreate & ")"
  rstPrimary.Close
  Set rstPrimary = Nothing
End Sub
```

Send Create Table Statement to DB2 UDB and Call TableFill Procedure

The last part of this procedure is to take the strCreate string, which has been built
by the procedure, and use the cmdDb2 command object to issue this SQL statement
to the DB2 ODBC interface. This will result in the table being created in the DB2
UDB BOOKSALE database.

The text section built for each column in the strCreate string has a terminating
comma, as this is required as a separator between column definitions in the SQL
Create Table statement. However, this means that there is a spurious comma
following the last column definition. Hence, this extra comma is stripped from the
final string value, and then a closing bracket and a semi-colon are added to
complete the command syntax. This string is then assigned to the CommandText
property of the cmdDb2 command object and its Execute method called. This
executes the SQL call on the DB2 UDB database which results in the table being
built.

If you un-comment the line containing the statement Debug.Print strCreate,
then you will get a printout, in Visual Basic's Immediate window, of the Create
statements that the program has produced for each of the tables in the Booksale
database. The expected output in the Immediate window from this command is
shown in Fig. 5–13.

```
CREATE TABLE "AUTHORS" ("AU_ID" Integer,"AUTHOR" VarChar(255),"YEAR
BORN" SmallInt);

CREATE TABLE "COGS" ("BLACKWHITE" Decimal(19,0),"COLOR"
Decimal(19,0),"GRADE1" Decimal(19,0),"GRADE2" Decimal(19,0),"GRADE3"
Decimal(19,0),"GRADE4" Decimal(19,0),"HARDCOVER"
Decimal(19,0),"PAPERBACK" Decimal(19,0));

CREATE TABLE "PUBLISHERS" ("ADDRESS" VarChar(50),"CITY"
VarChar(20),"COMMENTS" VarChar(2000),"COMPANY NAME"
VarChar(255),"FAX" VarChar(15),"NAME" VarChar(50),"PUBID"
Integer,"STATE" VarChar(10),"TELEPHONE" VarChar(15),"ZIP"
VarChar(15));

CREATE TABLE "TITLE AUTHOR" ("AU_ID" Integer,"ISBN" VarChar(20));

CREATE TABLE "TITLES" ("COMMENTS" VarChar(2000),"DESCRIPTION"
VarChar(50),"ISBN" VarChar(20),"NOTES" VarChar(50),"PAGES"
Integer,"PRICE" Decimal(19,0),"PUBID" Integer,"SUBJECT"
VarChar(50),"TITLE" VarChar(255),"YEAR PUBLISHED" SmallInt);
```

Fig. 5–13 *Expected Output from Create Table Procedure*

 Note: The table names and column names have been enclosed in quotes. This is because some of the names in the Access database contain spaces.

Schema DataFill Procedure

This procedure is run after the previous routines have created the necessary tables and indexes in DB2 UDB. The procedure is very simple. It opens two recordsets, one for the Microsoft Access database, and one for the DB2 UDB database which has just been created. It then loops through the Microsoft Access recordset and transfers the data from each record into the DB2 UDB recordset's record.

```
Public Sub DataFill(strTable, strTab)
  Dim rstAccess As New ADODB.Recordset
  Dim rstDb2 As New ADODB.Recordset
  Dim destfld As String
  Dim fld As Variant
  Dim n As Integer

  rstAccess.Open "select * from [" & strTable & "]", cnAccess
  With rstDb2
    .CursorLocation = adUseClient
    .CursorType = adOpenKeyset
    .LockType = adLockOptimistic
    .Open UCase(strTab), cnDb2, , , adCmdTable
  End With

  Do While Not rstAccess.EOF
    rstDb2.AddNew

    For Each fld In rstAccess.Fields
      destfld = fld.Name
      spstrip destfld
      rstDb2.Fields(destfld) = rstAccess.Fields(fld.Name)
    Next fld
    rstDb2.Update
    rstAccess.MoveNext
  Loop

  rstAccess.Close
  rstDb2.Close
  Set rstAccess = Nothing
  Set rstDb2 = Nothing
End Sub
```

Building Applications Using Visual Basic

Declare Variables for the Procedure

There are only three variables defined in this procedure. The two recordset objects for the source and destination records, and a variant which is used in the For Each loop which handles the data transfer for the individual fields in each record.

Open Recordsets

Opening the recordset to retrieve data from the Microsoft Access database is very simple. The only thing to note is that Access does not support the Table type recordset, and it is therefore necessary to use the select all option in an SQL select statement.

Setting up to open the DB2 UDB destination recordset is slightly more complicated as this needs to action inserts into the database. The parameters for the CursorLocation, CursorType and LockType need to be set to values which will permit insert and update statements. The requirements vary for different database types for example, SQLServer, Oracle, DB2 UDB and so on. Visual Basic help includes a small example of a program which loops around these parameters, and uses the Recordset's Supports method to confirms that AddNew will work. The values set in this program have been found to permit updates in DB2 UDB. Recordset properties must be set before the recordset is opened.

The DB2 UDB recordset uses a table type recordset as indicated by the adCmdTable option.

Transfer Records

The records are transferred using a While loop, which includes a MoveNext method to deal with each record at a time from the Microsoft Access source database.

The loop starts with an AddNew method for the DB2 UDB database. It then uses a For Each loop to go through each field (column) in the source recordset and transfer its contents into the equivalent field in the DB2 UDB destination recordset. After completing the loop though each field, the program does an Update on the DB2 UDB recordset which inserts the current record buffer contents into the destination table.

Cleanup

After transferring all the records, the procedure closes both recordsets and then destroys them by setting them to Nothing.

Creating Indexes

The following code uses the OpenSchema method to determine the Indexes used in the Microsoft Access database and creates these indexes in the DB2 UDB database. The SchemaIndexes method returns relationship information which could be used to create the relationships required for referential integrity, but these have been ignored in this simple application.

Building
Applications
Using Visual Basic

```
Public Sub CreateIndexes(strTable)
  Dim rstIndexes As New ADODB.Recordset
  Dim cmdIndex As New ADODB.Command
  Dim strT As String
  Dim strIndName As String
  Dim strInd As String
  Dim strTemp As String
  Static n
  cmdIndex.ActiveConnection = cnDb2
  Set rstIndexes = cnAccess.OpenSchema(adSchemaIndexes)
  Do Until rstIndexes.EOF
    If rstIndexes!TABLE_NAME = strTable Then
      If rstIndexes!INDEX_NAME <> "PrimaryKey" Then
        If InStr(rstIndexes!INDEX_NAME, "Reference") = Ø Then
          strInd = "CREATE INDEX "
          strIndName = rstIndexes!INDEX_NAME
          spstrip strIndName
          strInd = strInd & strIndName & " ON "
          strT = strTable
          spstrip strT
          strInd = strInd & strT & "("
          strTemp = rstIndexes!COLUMN_NAME
          spstrip strTemp
          strInd = strInd & strTemp & ")"
          cmdIndex.CommandText = strInd
          cmdIndex.Execute
        End If
      End If
    End If
    rstIndexes.MoveNext
  Loop
  rstIndexes.Close
  Set rstIndexes = Nothing
End Sub
```

Check If Primary Function

The create table routine has to define whether or not any of the fields can contain nulls. The program has been designed to permit all fields to be null unless they form part of a primary Key which must have unique values and not contain nulls.

The following code describes the function which is called by the create table procedure to determine if a given column is part of a primary Key.

```
Public Function CheckIfPrimary(strTable, strCol)
  Dim rstPrimary As New ADODB.Recordset
  Set rstPrimary = cnAccess.OpenSchema(adSchemaPrimaryKeys)
  Do Until rstPrimary.EOF
    If rstPrimary!TABLE_NAME = strTable Then
      If rstPrimary!COLUMN_NAME = strCol Then
        CheckIfPrimary = True
        Exit Function
      End If
    End If
    rstPrimary.MoveNext
  Loop
  CheckIfPrimary = False
End Function
```

Strip Spaces

This simple procedure removes embedded spaces from Table and Column names.

```
Public Sub spstrip(dummy)
  Dim p As Integer
  Dim n As Integer
  n = 1
  Do
    p = InStr(n, dummy, " ")
    If p <> 0 Then
      n = p
      dummy = Left$(dummy, p - 1) & Mid$(dummy, p + 1, Len(dummy))
    End If
  Loop Until p = 0
End Sub
```

Run Booksales Sample Application on DB2 UDB

To make the Booksales sample application run on DB2 UDB, what you need to do is just changing the Connection object's ConnectionString property to the DB2 UDB database. In our case, the DB2 UDB Booksales database has already been registered as an ODBC data source with a Data Source Name of Booksales, you should specify Booksales for the ConnectionString as the Main procedure of our Schema module did (see "Connections" on page 222). The class file sales.cls of the Booksales sample application has the ConnectionString specifying the Access database. Change this to 'Booksales', and execute both the server code and the client code of the Booksales sample application. You would see that it works fine on the DB2 UDB database.

DB2 UDB Sample Application

This example program is available with the installation of DB2 UDB for NT. The Visual Basic project can be located in %DB2PATH%\SAMPLES\ADO\VB, %DB2PATH% is the directory where DB2 UDB product was installed (C:\Program Files\SQLLIB is the default directory). The project file is SAMPLE.VBP. The Sample program demonstrates different types of forms and form objects to display and edit data in a database.

The project uses a Menu form with buttons to navigate to the various forms. This Menu remains open so that the user can call up multiple forms to display, and the exit button routine on the main form will close all open forms before ending the application.

One of the forms uses a grid display to edit individual tables in the database. Two of the other forms use a master/detail type form layout to show one to many type relationships. The master/detail forms use Microsoft's Data Shaping Data provider, which is a feature of ADO. Subsidiary forms, which are called from the Employee form, demonstrate how to handle data from Character Large Object and Binary Large Object data types, using Resumes displayed in a multiline text box, and photos displayed in a picture box.

As its name explains, this application is only a sample. It can be used to display the various forms that it contains, but it would require a number of program additions, notably in error handling, to produce a stable and workable program.

Common Procedures in Main Display Forms

All of the main forms listed below have common features. These will be described in this section, to prevent repetition in the following individual form descriptions. The forms which use these features are:

- ViewTable
- InfoByDept
- Employee
- ProjByEmp

Action Buttons

Each of these forms contain a common set of action buttons which permit the user to add records, edit existing records, execute the update of new and edited records, cancel outstanding edits and to delete records. There are also buttons to refresh the recordset and to close the form. The procedures behind the click events of these buttons are described below, the examples are taken from the ViewTable form, but the code in the other forms is essentially the same.

Add Button Click Event

This calls the Add_Record function in the RecSet module, passing the current recordset to that function. This will move to the last record and execute an AddNew on the recordset, which provides a clear record buffer. This is reflected by the current row on the grid becoming empty because it is bound to the recordset. The procedure then calls the DisplayButtons procedure to ensure that only the right buttons are visible and that the navigation buttons are disabled. The DisplayButtons function is described in "DisplayButtons Procedure" on page 241. Lastly, the procedure sets focus to the grid on the empty row, so that the user can begin adding data to the new record.

```
Private Sub cmdAdd_Click()
  Add_Record adoTableRS
  DisplayButtons False
  DataGrid.SetFocus
End Sub
```

Edit Button Click Event

This adds text to the Status text box which fits between the navigation buttons as part of the ADO Data Control emulation. It also passes False to the DisplayButtons procedure to ensure that the buttons are in the same state as for the Add button above.

```
Private Sub cmdEdit_Click()
  On Error GoTo EditErr
  lblStatus.Caption = "Edit record"
  DisplayButtons False
  Exit Sub

EditErr:
  MsgBox Err.Description
End Sub
```

Delete Button Click Event

This calls the Delete_Record function in the RecSet module which will delete the current record in the recordset passed to it.

```
Private Sub cmdDelete_Click()
    Delete_Record adoTableRS
End Sub
```

Refresh Button Click Event

This refreshes the data in the recordset to reflect the latest state in the database. It achieves this by issuing a Requery method on the recordset. Note that the DataSource property of the DataGrid is divorced from the recordset before the Requery event and then re-attached after it. This ensures that the grid contents are also refreshed.

```
Private Sub cmdRefresh_Click()
    On Error GoTo RefreshErr
    Set DataGrid.DataSource = Nothing
    adoTableRS.Requery
    Set DataGrid.DataSource = adoTableRS
    Exit Sub

RefreshErr:
    MsgBox Err.Description
End Sub
```

Close Button Click Event

This closes the form by executing the `Unload` method on the current form.

```
Private Sub cmdClose_Click()
    Unload Me
End Sub
```

Update Button Click Event

This calls the `Update_Record` function in the `RecSet` module, which updates any pending `AddNew` or `Edit` records. This should also call the `DisplayButtons` procedure with a parameter of True in order to reset the buttons to the Record Navigation state. This seems to have been missed out of the `Sample` program on the CD. To work correctly, add the line `DisplayButtons True` in this procedure.

```
Private Sub cmdUpdate_Click()
    Update_Record adoTableRS
End Sub
```

Cancel Button Click Event

This uses the `CancelUpdate` method of the recordset to cancel changes in the current record. It also uses the `DisplayButtons` procedure to rest the buttons to the Record Navigation state.

```
Private Sub cmdCancel_Click()
    On Error Resume Next
    DisplayButtons True
    adoTableRS.CancelUpdate
End Sub
```

Recordset navigation buttons

<< - Move to First Record

This calls the Move_First function in the RecSet module. This moves the current record pointer to the first record in the recordset, which is passed to the function.

```
Private Sub cmdFirst_Click()
    Move_First adoTableRS
End Sub
```

< - Move to Previous Record

This calls the Previous_Record function in the RecSet module. This moves the current record pointer to the previous record in the recordset, which is passed to the function.

```
Private Sub cmdPrevious_Click()
    Previous_Record adoTableRS
End Sub
```

> - Move to Next Record

This calls the Next_Record function in the RecSet module. This moves the current record pointer to the next record in the recordset, which is passed to the function.

```
Private Sub cmdNext_Click()
    Next_Record adoTableRS
End Sub
```

>> - Move to Last Record

This calls the Move_Last function in the RecSet module. This moves the current record pointer to the last record in the recordset, which is passed to the function.

```
Private Sub cmdLast_Click()
    Move_Last adoTableRS
End Sub
```

DisplayButtons Procedure

This procedure sets the Visible property of the action buttons and the Enabled property of the record navigation buttons. The values set are based on the parameter which is passed into the procedure.

When the user is browsing through the recordset, then the Record navigation buttons should be enabled. The Add, Edit, Delete, Refresh and Close buttons should also be available, that is, visible. The Update and Cancel buttons should not be available as there are no current edits pending.

After the user selects Add or Edit, then he should be prevented from moving the current record pointer away from the New or Edited record, and therefore the navigation buttons are disabled. Any action button which allows the user to change the data in the current record, or to close the form without completing the edit should also not be available, whereas the button to complete or cancel the update should be available. Rather than use the Enable property, the procedure uses the Visible property of the buttons to only reveal those buttons which are valid. This has another advantage, which is that there are more buttons than can fit in the space allocated. By overlaying two buttons in a position where only one is visible at any given time, this allows more buttons to fit into the same space.

```
Private Sub DisplayButtons(Navigate As Boolean)

    cmdAdd.Visible = Navigate
    cmdEdit.Visible = Navigate
    cmdUpdate.Visible = Not Navigate
    cmdCancel.Visible = Not Navigate
    cmdDelete.Visible = Navigate
    cmdClose.Visible = Navigate
    cmdRefresh.Visible = Navigate
    cmdNext.Enabled = Navigate
    cmdFirst.Enabled = Navigate
    cmdLast.Enabled = Navigate
    cmdPrevious.Enabled = Navigate
End Sub
```

RecSet Module

The Sample application has a module which contains record manipulation functions which are used globally by all of the main forms which are listed in "Common Procedures in Main Display Forms" on page 237.

All of the following functions have a simple error routine, which display the error messages returned. The functions are described below.

Building
Applications
Using Visual Basic

Global Declarations

This contains the declarations of certain objects which are used by many different forms. The first variable, DepartmentForm, is not used anywhere, and should be ignored.

Two of the tables, ViewTable and InfoByDept, are used for more than one function. The variable, CurrentTableName, is used to inform these forms as to which function is required.

The application only uses one connection and this is therefore declared globally. The variable name given to the connection object is dbSample.

The last global declaration is a constant, dbName, and holds the name of the ODBC DSN, that is, "SAMPLE".

```
Global DepartmentForm As Integer
Global CurrentTableName As String
Global dbSample As Connection
Public Const DBName = "SAMPLE"
```

Add Record Function

The function moves the current record pointer to the last record in the recordset, which will be the new record, and executes an AddNew statement.

```
Function Add_Record(RecSet As Recordset)

  On Error GoTo AddErr
  RecSet.MoveLast
  RecSet.AddNew
  Exit Function

AddErr:
  MsgBox Err.Description
End Function
```

Delete Record Function

This executes a delete method on the recordset and then executes a move next to place the current record pointer onto a valid record. If the delete action is against the last record in the recordset, then the pointer will move to EOF. Having determined that this has happened, the function will execute a MoveLast method to place the pointer on the new last record.

```
Function Delete_Record(RecSet As Recordset)
On Error GoTo DeleteErr
  With RecSet
    .Delete
    .MoveNext
    If .EOF Then .MoveLast
  End With
  Exit Function

DeleteErr:
  MsgBox Err.Description
End Function
```

Move to First Record Function

This executes a `MoveFirst` method to place the current record pointer onto the first record in the recordset.

```
Function Move_First(RecSet As Recordset)
  On Error GoTo FirstError

  RecSet.MoveFirst
  Exit Function

FirstError:
  MsgBox Err.Description
End Function
```

Move to Last Record Function

This executes a `MoveLast` method to place the current record pointer onto the last record in the recordset.

```
Function Move_Last(RecSet As Recordset)
  On Error GoTo LastError

  RecSet.MoveLast
  Exit Function

LastError:
  MsgBox Err.Description
End Function
```

Move to Next Record Function

This function first checks that the current record pointer is not on the end of file. If it is not, then it executes a `MoveNext` method, to move the current record pointer to the next record in the recordset.

If, after executing the move next action, the pointer is on end of file, and the recordset is not empty, the pointer is moved to the last record in the recordset.

```
Function Next_Record(RecSet As Recordset)
  On Error GoTo NextError
  If Not RecSet.EOF Then
    RecSet.MoveNext
  End If
  If RecSet.EOF And RecSet.RecordCount > Ø Then
    RecSet.MoveLast
  End If
  Exit Function

NextError:
  MsgBox Err.Description
End Function
```

Move to Previous Record Function

This function first checks that the current record pointer is not on the beginning of file. If it is not, then it executes a `MovePrevious` method, to move the current record pointer to the previous record in the recordset.

If, after executing the move previous action, the pointer is at the beginning of file, and the recordset is not empty, the pointer is moved to the first record in the recordset.

```
Function Previous_Record(RecSet As Recordset)
On Error GoTo PrevError

  If Not RecSet.BOF Then
    RecSet.MovePrevious
  End If
  If RecSet.BOF And RecSet.RecordCount > Ø Then
    RecSet.MoveFirst
  End If
  Exit Function

PrevError:
  MsgBox Err.Description
End Function
```

Update Record Function

This executes an update on the current record. The calling form procedure ensures that an `AddNew` or `Edit` procedure has been invoked before calling the update procedure.

```
Function Update_Record(RecSet As Recordset)
   On Error GoTo UpdateError

   RecSet.UpdateBatch adAffectAll
   Exit Function

UpdateError:
   MsgBox Err.Description
End Function
```

Logon Form

The Logon form allows the user to provide a valid user name and password which is then used to provide a connection string to open a connection to the database. An error routine will return a message to the user and reposition the cursor on the form, to enable the user to re-enter or cancel. If the connection is successful, then the `Menu` form will be loaded and the `Logon` form unloaded. Fig. 5–14 shows the `Logon` form.

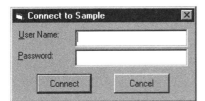

Fig. 5–14 *ODBC Logon Screen*

Cancel Button Click Event of Logon Form

Pressing this button causes an unload of the form. As no other forms have been loaded, this action will close the application.

```
Private Sub cmdCancel_Click()
        Unload Me
End Sub
```

Connect Button Click Event of Logon Form

If the user presses this button on the form, then this procedure will build a connection string for the globally declared connection object. It will then use the connection string to open the dbSample connection. Note that if the user omits to enter a user name or password, then the connection string will not include these parameters. In this event, the connection will be opened using the current Windows NT logged on account.

```
Private Sub cmdOK_Click()
    On Error GoTo LogonError
    Dim ConnectStr As String
    Set dbSample = New Connection
    ConnectStr = "PROVIDER=MSDataShape;dsn=" & DBName & ";"
      If txtUserName <> "" Then
        ConnectStr = ConnectStr & "uid=" & txtUserName & ";"
    End If
    If txtPassword <> "" Then
       ConnectStr = ConnectStr & "pwd=" & txtPassword & ";"
    End If

    dbSample.Open ConnectStr
    Menu.Show
  Unload Me
    Exit Sub

LogonError:
   ' Error On Connect to DB
   ' Display Error Descirption
   MsgBox Err.Description
   txtPassword.SetFocus
    SendKeys "{Home}+{End}"
End Sub
```

Menu Form

This form provides the launching platform for all the facilities which are available in this application. There are four types of forms which can be accessed from this form (Fig. 5–15).

The group of nine buttons on the right hand side of the form loads the table entry form. This allows the user, using the ViewTable form, to edit all the individual tables which exist in the database.

The top two buttons on the left hand side of the form both use the InfoByDept form, which is a Master/Detail type form which uses the ADO DataShape provider to provide interlinked data from a selection in the Department table. One gives Employees by Department and the other Projects by Department.

The bottom left hand button on the menu form presents a form containing the Employee details, together with three buttons that permit the user to overlay the Employee form with a photograph of the employee, the employee's resume, and the projects the Employee is involved in. Note that not all records include data for these three areas.

The button to the right of the Employee button provides another master/detail type form showing projects per employee.

Note: The menu form remains on the screen when the other forms, described above, are loaded. It is only closed when either the exit button on the menu form, or the menu form close button are actioned. Thus you can cycle quite easily through all the forms that are called from the menu form.

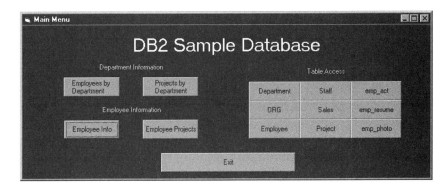

Fig. 5–15 *Sample Menu*

Menu Form — Table Access Buttons Click Events

There is a group of nine buttons under the label Table Access on the Menu form. These buttons refer to the different tables in the `Sample` database. The application uses the same form to display all the different tables. This is achieved by calling the sub-procedure `ShowViewTable`, passing the table name as a parameter. An example for one of the button click events is shown below.

```
Private Sub Dept_Click()
  ShowViewTable ("DEPARTMENT")
End Sub
```

Menu Form — Show View Table Click Event

This is started by one of the Table Access buttons being pressed as described above. The procedure creates an instance of the `ViewTable` form, sets the global variable `CurrentTableName` to the value passed by the calling button click procedure, and then shows the new form.

```
Private Sub ShowViewTable(TTable As String)
   Dim NForm As New ViewTable
   CurrentTableName = TTable
   NForm.Show
End Sub
```

Menu Form — Employee Projects Button Click Event

This loads the form `ProjByEmp` as shown below.

```
Private Sub EmpProj_Click()
   ProjByEmp.Show
End Sub
```

Menu Form — Exit Button Click Event

This unloads the `Menu` form.

```
Private Sub Exit_Click()
   Unload Me
End Sub
```

Menu Form — Department Information Buttons Click Events

There are two buttons in this group, Employee by Department and Project by Department. Both of these buttons run the same form, `InfoByDept`, after setting the global variable `CurrentTableName` to the appropriate table name. The `Employee` event code is shown below.

```
Private Sub EmpByDept_Click()
   CurrentTableName = "EMPLOYEE"
   InfoByDept.Show
End Sub
```

Menu Form — Employee Info Button Click Event

Pressing this button causes the Employee form to be loaded and displayed.

```
Private Sub EmpInfo_Click()
   EMPLOYEE.Show
End Sub
```

Menu Form Unload Event

This is called when the user presses the **Exit** key or the close button on the Menu form. The code loops through the forms collection, closing any of the application's forms which are still open. Its final action is to close the database connection.

```
Private Sub Form_Unload(Cancel As Integer)
   Dim i As Integer
   For i = Forms.Count - 1 To 0 Step -1
      Unload Forms(i)
   Next
   ' When Application is closing close db Connection
   dbSample.Close
End Sub
```

Table Access Form

This form, `ViewTable`, is used to access all of the tables in the `Sample` database. The table to connect to is determined by the choice made on the `Menu` form, from the setting of the global variable, `CurrentTableName`, by that selection. The form is similar to the form generated by the Data Form wizard earlier in this chapter, but uses a grid to display the recordset, rather than individual text boxes (Fig. 5–16).

The form uses ADO code rather than an ADO Data control, and therefore uses an emulation of the control with four small record navigation buttons and a separating text box, which is used to display a record number or status information. All of these components are fitted into a picture box whose `Align` property is set to Align Bottom to put the emulated control along the bottom of the form.

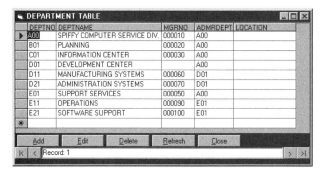

Fig. 5–16 *Table Recordset View*

Table Form — General Code Area

An ADO recordset is dimensioned in the general part of the form. The `WithEvents` keyword is important in this statement if you wish to write code to monitor the recordset's events. These events are listed under **ADO events** which is a sub-section of the **Microsoft ADO Programmer's Reference.** This is only available on-line if you have added ActiveX Data Objects to your project's References.

The easiest way to open the on-line documentation for ADO is to place the editing cursor on an ADO object in your code, such as Recordset, and then press the F1 function key. If another window pops up with more than one instance of the keyword showing, then select the one marked ADODB.

```
Dim WithEvents adoTableRS As Recordset
```

Table Form Load Event

The form is called by the Menu form after it has set a global variable called `CurrentTableName`. As the name indicates, this value tells this form which table the user wishes to display. It uses a SELECT/CASE statement against this variable's value, to determine the recordset to open, and the query to use to return the correct data.

The Resume table cannot return the CLOB (Character Large OBject) field that it contains because the grid could not display it. Consequently the query to return data from this table is restricted to the Employee Number and the Resume Format. This is also true of the BLOB (Binary Large OBject) field which contains the employees picture in the Photo table. This returns the Employee Number and Photo Format fields. The query for all other tables returns all fields from the specified table.

After creating the recordset, the grid's `RecordSource` is bound to the recordset object. The form's caption is also set to reflect the table being displayed.

```
' Form_Load()
' This subroutine is executed when the form is loaded.
' It creates the recordset for the form and binds the data to the
form.
Private Sub Form_Load()

   On Error GoTo Form_Load_Error
   Set adoTableRS = New Recordset
   Select Case CurrentTableName
      Case "EMP_RESUME"
         adoTableRS.Open "select EMPNO, RESUME_FORMAT from " _
                  & CurrentTableName, dbSample, adOpenStatic, _
                     adLockOptimistic
      Case "EMP_PHOTO"
         adoTableRS.Open "select EMPNO, PHOTO_FORMAT from " _
                  & CurrentTableName, dbSample, adOpenStatic, _
                     adLockOptimistic
      Case Else
         adoTableRS.Open "select * from " & CurrentTableName, _
                  dbSample, adOpenStatic, adLockOptimistic
   End Select
   ' Bind the textboxes to the data
   Set DataGrid.DataSource = adoTableRS
   ' Set the Caption on the form
   Me.Caption = CurrentTableName & " TABLE"
Exit Sub

Form_Load_Error:
   MsgBox Err.Description
End Sub
```

Table Form Resize Event

This event is used to ensure that if the user resizes the form, then the grid will be resized to match.

```
Private Sub Form_Resize()
  On Error Resume Next
    DataGrid.Height = Me.ScaleHeight - 30 - picButtons.Height -
picStatBox.Height
    lblStatus.Width = Me.Width - 1500
    cmdNext.Left = lblStatus.Width + 700
    cmdLast.Left = cmdNext.Left + 340
End Sub
```

Table Form — Recordset Move Complete Event

This procedure is used to determine the record number after a current record move event, by using the `AbsolutePosition` property of the recordset object.

```
Private Sub adoTableRS_MoveComplete(ByVal adReason As _
                ADODB.EventReasonEnum, ByVal pError As _
                ADODB.Error, adStatus As _
                ADODB.EventStatusEnum, ByVal pRecordset _
                As ADODB.Recordset)

  lblStatus.Caption = "Record: " &
CStr(adoTableRS.AbsolutePosition)
End Sub
```

Table Form — Action and Navigation Buttons

This form contains a set of action and navigation buttons. It also contains a procedure to enable and disable appropriate combinations of these buttons, related to the current edit status. The click events and `DisplayButton` procedure are described in "Common Procedures in Main Display Forms" on page 237.

Department Information

This form is a Master/Detail display which displays the `Department` form in the top half of the screen and a choice of either the employees who work in the currently displayed department, or the projects that are being worked on in that department, in the bottom half of the screen (Fig. 5–17).

The `Department` display uses a single record form which means that only one department can be displayed at a time. The lower form is in the form of a scrollable grid which displays the associated information for that department. The grid is read-only, which means that a user cannot change any of the records in this display.

The record editing and navigation buttons on the form refer to the department area only.

This form uses a hierarchical recordset provided by the Microsoft Data Shaping provider, MSDataShape. You will remember that this was used in the ADO connection that was set up in the Logon Form. This provider translates the SHAPE commands to provide the hierarchical data used by a Master/Detail display. The SHAPE language is a superset of SQL and is defined in Formal Shape Grammar in the MSDN on-line help. However, the simplest way to set up a SHAPE statement is to start with a data project and define the recordset parameters with the Data Environment Designer. The SHAPE statement used in this example will be explained in the Form Load event below.

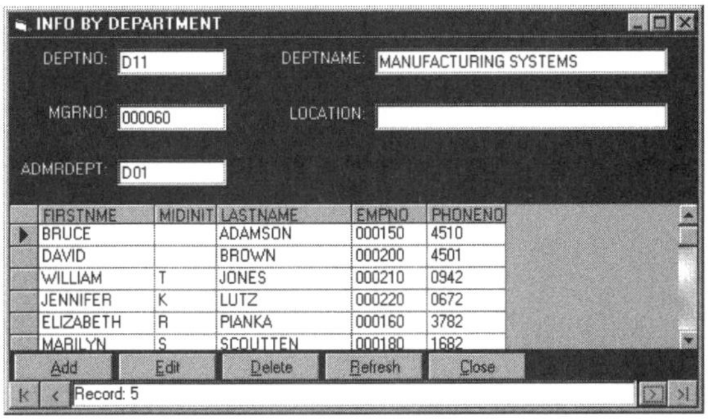

Fig. 5–17 *Master/Detail Form Example*

Department Form — General Code Area

An ADO recordset is dimensioned in the general part of the form. The meaning of the WithEvents keyword can be found in "Table Form — General Code Area" on page 250.

```
Dim WithEvents adoInfobyDeptRS As Recordset
```

Department Form Load Event

The two possible hierarchical recordsets are created here — one for the employees in the department, and one for the projects worked on in the department. They both take the same form, and which recordset definition is used depends on the value of the CurrentTableName. The recordset is opened using a SHAPE statement in place of the normal SQL statement. The SHAPE statement starts with defining a normal select statement for the master table and assigns the alias Stmt1 to it. The statement then appends a second select statement for the child table and assigns an alias of Stmt2 for it. The final part of the statement uses the SHAPE keyword RELATE to specify the primary key in the master table and the foreign key in the detail table which form the join relationship.

Having opened the recordset, the procedure uses a For Each statement to bind all of the text boxes in the Master form to the recordset. The DataSource property of the DataGrid, which forms the display object fro the detail set, is then set to Stmt2, that is, the child section of the hierarchical recordset. The first column of the grid displays the join field, WorkDept, which is already displayed on the master set as field DeptNo, and will appear in every row in the grid. The procedure makes the first column invisible to remove this unnecessary data. from the screen display.

```
Private Sub Form_Load()
  On Error GoTo Form_Load_Error
  Set adoInfobyDeptRS = New Recordset
  If (CurrentTableName = "EMPLOYEE") Then
    adoInfobyDeptRS.Open "SHAPE {select DEPTNO,DEPTNAME,MGRNO," _
                    & "ADMRDEPT,LOCATION from DEPARTMENT} AS " _
                    & "Stmt1 APPEND ({select WORKDEPT,FIRSTNME," _
                    & "MIDINIT,LASTNAME,EMPNO,PHONENO from EMPLOYEE" _
"  _
                    & "Order by LASTNAME } AS Stmt2 RELATE " _
                    & "DEPTNO TO WORKDEPT) AS Stmt2", dbSample, _
                    adOpenStatic, adLockOptimistic
  ElseIf (CurrentTableName = "PROJECT") Then
    adoInfobyDeptRS.Open "SHAPE {select DEPTNO,DEPTNAME,MGRNO," _
                    & "ADMRDEPT,LOCATION from DEPARTMENT} AS " _
                    & "Stmt1 APPEND ({select DEPTNO,PROJNO," _
                    & "PROJNAME,RESPEMP,PRSTAFF,PRSTDATE," _
                    & "PRENDATE,MAJPROJ from PROJECT } AS " _
                    & "Stmt2 RELATE DEPTNO TO DEPTNO) AS " _
                    & "Stmt2", dbSample, adOpenStatic, _
                    adLockOptimistic
  End If

  Dim oText As TextBox
  For Each oText In Me.Data
    Set oText.DataSource = adoInfobyDeptRS
  Next

  Set DataGrid.DataSource =
adoInfobyDeptRS("Stmt2").UnderlyingValue
  DataGrid.Columns.Item(0).Visible = False
  Exit Sub

Form_Load_Error:
  MsgBox Err.Description
End Sub
```

Department Form Resize Event

This procedure resizes the datagrid and record status text box, and repositions the two rightmost record movement buttons, when the form is resized.

```
Private Sub Form_Resize()
  On Error Resume Next
  DataGrid.Width = Me.ScaleWidth
  DataGrid.Height = Me.ScaleHeight - DataGrid.Top - 30 -
picButtons.Height - picStatBox.Height
  lblStatus.Width = Me.Width - 1500
  cmdNext.Left = lblStatus.Width + 700
  cmdLast.Left = cmdNext.Left + 340
End Sub
```

Department Form Record Move Complete Event

This procedure adds in the new record number into the status text box after the current record pointer is moved to a different record.

```
Private Sub adoInfoByDeptRS_MoveComplete(ByVal adReason As _
                    ADODB.EventReasonEnum, ByVal pError As _
                    ADODB.Error, adStatus As _
                    ADODB.EventStatusEnum, ByVal pRecordset _
                    As ADODB.Recordset)

  lblStatus.Caption = "Record: " &
CStr(adoInfobyDeptRS.AbsolutePosition)
End Sub
```

Department Form — Action and Navigation Buttons

This form contains a set of action and navigation buttons. It also contains a procedure to enable and disable appropriate combinations of these buttons, related to the current edit status. The click events and DisplayButton procedure are described in "Common Procedures in Main Display Forms" on page 237.

Employee Information

This form is a standard text box type form, designed to show the employee data, and also includes three buttons, whose click actions are designed to load forms with additional data, related to the currently displayed employee. The form displays all the fields from the employee table and has the usual record navigation and record editing keys, but its key usage is to load the three additional forms, Photo, Resume and Activities (Fig. 5–18).

The Photo form uses a Binary Large Object field in the database to hold the employees photo. The Resume form uses a Character Large Object field to hold the Employee's Resume and the Activities form shows a small test box type form to permit the user to scroll through all the project's that the currently displayed employee is involved with.

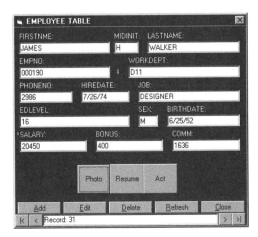

Fig. 5–18 *Employee Information Form*

Employee Form — General Code Area

This dimensions the recordset used by the main area of the form to return the data from the Employee. The meaning of the WithEvents keyword can be found in "Table Form — General Code Area" on page 250.

```
Dim WithEvents adoEmployeeRS As Recordset
```

Employee Form Load Event

This creates a new instance of the adoEmployeeRS recordset, and opens it with an SQL statement, to select the contents of the Employee table, ordered by the LastName field. Hence the use of a select statement, rather than a table for the Recordset. The New keyword could not be used in the dimensioning statement for the recordset, in the General code area of the form, because of the use of WithEvents in the dimension statement.

After opening the recordset, the procedure uses a WithEvents loop to bind each of the text boxes on the form to the recordset.

```
Private Sub Form_Load()
On Error GoTo Form_Load_Error
    Set adoEmployeeRS = New Recordset
    ' Open the recordset of all employees in the EMPLOYEE table
    adoEmployeeRS.Open "select EMPNO,FIRSTNME,MIDINIT,LASTNAME," _
                    & "WORKDEPT,PHONENO,HIREDATE,JOB,EDLEVEL,SEX," _
                    & "BIRTHDATE,SALARY,BONUS,COMM from EMPLOYEE " _
                    & "Order by LASTNAME", dbSample, adOpenStatic, _
                    adLockOptimistic

    Dim oText As TextBox
    'Bind the text boxes to the data provider
    For Each oText In Me.Data
        Set oText.DataSource = adoEmployeeRS
    Next
    Exit Sub
```

Employee Form — Resume Button Click Event

This loads the Resume form while maintaining the Employee form on screen.

```
Private Sub Resume_Click()
  EMP_RESUME.Show
End Sub
```

Employee Form — Photo Button Click Event

This loads the Photo form while maintaining the Employee form on screen. If the Emp_Photo form loads but is not visible, then the employee did not have a bitmap image to display. This procedure therefore unloads the form, if the Photo form's Visible property is False.

```
Private Sub Photo_Click()
  Load Emp_Photo
  If Not Emp_Photo.Visible Then
   Unload Emp_Photo
  End If
End Sub
```

Employee form — Activities Button Click Event

This loads the Employee Activities form while maintaining the Employee form on screen.

```
Private Sub Act_Click()
  Emp_Act.Show
End Sub
```

Employee Form Resize Event

This procedure resizes the status text box and repositions the rightmost two record movement buttons to maintain the appearance of the pseudo data control when the form is resized by the user.

```
Private Sub Form_Resize()
  On Error Resume Next
  lblStatus.Width = Me.Width - 1500
  cmdNext.Left = lblStatus.Width + 700
  cmdLast.Left = cmdNext.Left + 340
End Sub
```

Employee Form — Recordset Move Complete Event

This procedure adds in the new record number into the status text box after the current record pointer is moved to a different record.

```
Private Sub adoEmployeeRS_MoveComplete(ByVal adReason As _
                ADODB.EventReasonEnum, ByVal pError As _
                ADODB.Error, adStatus As _
                ADODB.EventStatusEnum, ByVal pRecordset _
                As ADODB.Recordset)

  lblStatus.Caption = "Record: " &
CStr(adoEmployeeRS.AbsolutePosition)
End Sub
```

Employee Form — Action and Navigation Buttons

This form contains a set of action and navigation buttons. It also contains a procedure to enable and disable appropriate combinations of these buttons, related to the current edit status. The click events and `DisplayButton` procedure are described in "Common Procedures in Main Display Forms" on page 237.

Employee Photo

This Project provides a GUI interface to access the Sample database provided with DB2 UDB. This form is used to display a bitmap photo from the EMP_PHOTO table (Fig. 5–19). It is loaded from the EMPLOYEE form and uses the EMP_NO from that form to find the corresponding photo. It will only show photos of type bitmap because the screen object used to display the photo is a simple picture box. More capable ActiveX display objects are available from third party suppliers if you store pictures in other formats such as JPEG, TIFF etc.

Fig. 5–19 *Employee Photo*

Photo Form — General Code Area

This dimensions the recordset that will be used to return photos that match the employee. The meaning of the WithEvents keyword can be found in "Table Form — General Code Area" on page 250

```
Dim WithEvents adoEmpPhotoRS As Recordset
```

Photo Form Load Event

This subroutine is executed when the form is loaded. It creates the recordset for the form and displays the photo in the PictureBox of the form. The query, used by the recordset open statement, obtains the Employee number from the text box on the Employee form which was left open when this form was loaded. If there is no photo available for the employee, it will display a message indicating this.

```
Private Sub Form_Load()
  Set adoEmpPhotoRS = New Recordset
  adoEmpPhotoRS.Open "select PICTURE from EMP_PHOTO where
PHOTO_FORMAT='bitmap' and EMPNO = '" & EMPLOYEE.Data(0) & "'",
dbSample

  If Not adoEmpPhotoRS.EOF Then
    Dim oPic As PictureBox
    'Bind the ole controls to the data provider
    For Each oPic In Me.Photo
      Set oPic.DataSource = adoEmpPhotoRS
    Next
    Me.Show
  Else
    MsgBox "No Bitmap photo available for Employee"
  End If
End Sub
```

Photo Form — Close Button Click Event

Clicking on this button will close the Photo form, leaving the Menu form and employee for still displayed.

```
Private Sub cmdClose_Click()
  Unload Me
End Sub
```

Employee Resume

This form is used to display the resume of an employee that is stored in the database as a CLOB.

Since the data type CLOB is not recognized, we cast the RESUME column to a LONG_VARCHAR. Since we know that the RESUME column is defined to a maximum size of 5120 bytes, which is less than the maximum LONG_VARCHAR size. If we do not do this cast, the data is determined to be binary data and is not known to be ASCII text. Therefore, a conversion back to character from binary would be necessary for the entire CLOB.

Large object fields can be extracted by using the ADO GetChunk method which is described in the ActiveX Data Object's on-line help. Repetitive calls to this method will extract sequential blocks of data into a variant variable, whose contents can be appended, block by block, to a file. Opening this file to read into a string variable will automatically treat the data as characters which can be added to a text box or other ASCII object. The GetChunk method has a corresponding AppendChunk method for adding data into a large object field, and this would be used to input data into a BLOB or CLOB type field. Thus a large picture bitmap file could be read in blocks with each block using the AppendChunk method to add that block to BLOB field in a database.

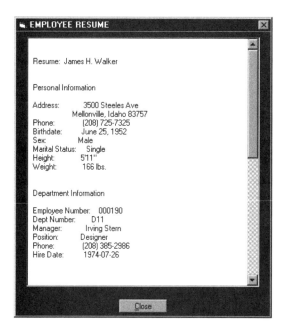

Fig. 5–20 *Employee Resume*

Resume Form — General Code Area

This dimensions the recordset that will be used to return the CLOB field containing the employee's resume (Fig. 5–20). The meaning of the WithEvents keyword can be found in "Table Form — General Code Area" on page 250.

```
Dim WithEvents adoResumeRS As Recordset
```

Resume Form Load Event

The load event creates a instance of the recordset and then populates it from a query which returns any resume from `Emp_Resume`, which matches the employee number from the underlying `Employee` form's text box, and has a format of ASCII. This latter requirement is due purely to the limitations of the multi-line text box, used to display the data. The select statement includes the cast to LONG_VARCHAR mentioned in the overview section above.

```
Private Sub Form_Load()
  Set adoPrimaryRS = New Recordset
  adoPrimaryRS.Open "select LONG_VARCHAR(RESUME) from EMP_RESUME " _
                    & "where RESUME_FORMAT='ascii' and EMPNO = '" _
                    & EMPLOYEE.Data(0) & "'", dbSample

  If Not adoPrimaryRS.EOF Then
  ' If the Employee has a resume in the table, display on the form
    Me.ResumeText = adoPrimaryRS.Fields(0)
  Else
  ' No resume available
    Me.ResumeText.Text = "No RESUME"
  End If
End Sub
```

Resume Form — Close Button Click Event

The close button on the form unloads the form, returning the user to the `Employee` form where another employee can be selected.

```
Private Sub cmdClose_Click()
  Unload Me
End Sub
```

Employee Activities

This form is used to display the info for an employee from the `EMP_ACT` table, which holds information relating to projects being worked on for each employee. It uses the `EMPNO` from the `EMPLOYEE` form to select the employee data (Fig. 5–21).

Building
Applications
Using Visual Basic

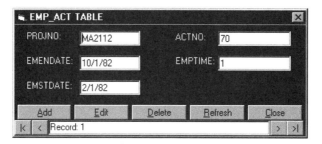

Fig. 5–21 *Employee Activity*

Activities Form — General Code Area

This dimensions the recordset which will be used to return the projects by employee information.

```
Dim WithEvents adoEMPACTRS As Recordset
```

Activities Form Load Event

This creates an instance of the recordset and then populates it from the Emp_Act table. The select query used to populate the recordset does not bring back the employee number field, EmpNo, but does use it to restrict the data to that matching the employee number in the text box on the open Employee form. Having returned the recordset, each of the text boxes on the form are bound to it.

```
Private Sub Form_Load()
On Error GoTo Form_Load_Error
  Set adoEMPACTRS = New Recordset
  adoEMPACTRS.Open "select PROJNO,ACTNO,EMPTIME,EMSTDATE,EMENDATE "
_
                & "from EMP_ACT WHERE EMPNO = '" & _
                EMPLOYEE.Data(0) & " '", dbSample, adOpenStatic, _
                adLockOptimistic

  Dim oText As TextBox
  'Bind the text boxes to the data
  For Each oText In Me.Data
    Set oText.DataSource = adoEMPACTRS
  Next
Exit Sub

Form_Load_Error:
    MsgBox Err.Description
End Sub
```

Activities Form Resize Event

As on the other forms, this event changes the length of the status label on the form, and the position of the two rightmost record navigation buttons, as the form width is varied by the user.

```
Private Sub Form_Resize()
  On Error Resume Next
  lblStatus.Width = Me.Width - 1500
  cmdNext.Left = lblStatus.Width + 700
  cmdLast.Left = cmdNext.Left + 340
End Sub
End Sub
```

Record Move Complete Event for Activities Form

Again, this places the current record number into the status label when the current recorder pointer moves to another record.

```
Private Sub adoEMPACTRS_MoveComplete(ByVal adReason As _
                   ADODB.EventReasonEnum, ByVal pError As _
                   ADODB.Error, adStatus As _
                   ADODB.EventStatusEnum, ByVal pRecordset _
                   As ADODB.Recordset)

  lblStatus.Caption = "Record: " &
CStr(adoEMPACTRS.AbsolutePosition)
End Sub
```

Projects by Employee

This form is used to display all the projects that each employee is responsible for. It uses the same master/detail type of form, and its structure is identical to the Department form. The only difference is that the master section of the form displays the Employee table information, instead of that from the Department table. Please refer to "Department Information" on page 252, for a description of this type of form. This form uses the same form of SHAPE statement to return a hierarchical recordset (Fig. 5–22).

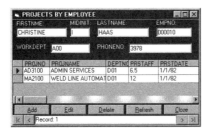

Fig. 5–22 *Projects by Employee*

Calling DB2 UDB Stored Procedures

As described in Chapter 4, a stored procedure is one that is stored on the database server and called by the client application, with the capability of passing parameters between the client application and the database server's stored procedure. The stored procedure is also capable of returning a recordset to the client application. This concept is most useful when the client would otherwise be sending multiple SQL commands to the database server. The client can now send a simple call statement to the stored procedure, and the stored procedure will perform the multiple jobs locally on the server, only sending the final result back to the client application. This can greatly reduce the amount of network traffic required to perform complex tasks.

There are two sample programs related to the calling of stored procedures in %DB2PATH%\SAMPLES\ADO, %DB2PATH% is the installed directory (C:\Program Files\SQLLIB is the default directory). One calls two stored procedures and the other calls only one. Before calling these three stored procedures from the sample programs described below, it necessary to create the stored procedures on the server.

The source code for the stored procedures are provided in the directory: %DB2PATH%\SAMPLES\CLI, if you selected the option to install samples with your DB2 UDB installation. This is achieved by using the provided MAKEFILE in that directory. There is a README file also in this directory which gives full instructions for carrying out this task.

You will need to have installed C++ with your Visual Studio installation, and ensured that you checked the box that sets up the Environmental Path variable to allow you to use the compiler from the command line. Otherwise you will have to add the relevant path statements to that variable manually. The compiler error messages will guide you in this task.

You should use the following NMAKE command from the DB2 Command window, and not a DOS Window, because the MAKEFILE uses a DB2 environmental variable which is not visible in a DOS Window. Start this from **Start Menu -> Programs ->DB2 for Windows NT -> Command Window**.

Move to the CLI samples directory, using CD, and issue the command NMAKE ALL to compile all the CLI examples into the correct directory structure on the server to be usable by DB2 UDB. You can use the command NMAKE <filename> to restrict the compiler to only deal with a single program.

CallSP

This program demonstrates how to call two different types of stored procedures in a DB2 UDB, using ADO. The program allows the user to select calls to stored procedures inpsrv2 and outsrv2. These stored procedures can be found with the CLI examples in %DB2PATH%\SAMPLES\CLI, but the source code for these must be compiled and the compiled procedures copied to the %DB2PATH%\function directory before this sample can be executed. The procedure for this is in the summary statement above.

CallSP — General Code Area of Form

This declares a form level variable for the connection object.

```
Dim db As ADODB.Connection
```

CallSP Form Load Event

When the form loads this procedure, it creates an instance of the connection object, enables the connection button, and disables the two buttons which call the stored procedures and the close button.

```
Private Sub Form_Load()
    Set db = New ADODB.Connection
    ConnectBtn.Enabled = True
    SP1Btn.Enabled = False
    SP2Btn.Enabled = False
    CloseBtn = False
End Sub
```

CallSP — Open Connection Button Click Event

This procedure opens the connection, set up in the form load event, to the Sample database. This will require an ODBC data source "SAMPLE" to be created or catalogued on the machine, if this was not done for the previous examples.

The general format for the connect statement is:

```
db.Open "dsn=SAMPLE;uid=;pwd=;database=SAMPLE;"
```

If your uid and pwd are omitted as this example, the Windows logged on user ID and password are used.

The procedure checks the state of the connection object before attempting to open the connection. If the connection is already open, then it calls the Close Button Click event procedure to close the connection. Having opened the connection, the procedure then re-enables the buttons to allow the user to call the two stored procedures and to close the connection.

```
Private Sub ConnectBtn_Click()
  On Error GoTo ConnectBtnErr
  If db.State = adStateOpen Then
     MsgBox "The database connection is already open. " & _
        vbOKOnly, "SAMPLE Connect Error"
        Call CloseBtn_Click
  End If
  db.Open "SAMPLE"
  ConnectBtn.Enabled = False
  SP1Btn.Enabled = True
  SP2Btn.Enabled = True
  CloseBtn.Enabled = True
  MsgBox "Connection Successful! " & _
     "You can now invoke the stored procedures using the form.", _
     vbOKOnly, "SAMPLE Connect"
  Exit Sub

ConnectBtnErr:
  MsgBox "SAMPLE connect error: " & Err.Description
End Sub
```

CallSP — Close Connection Button Click Event

This procedure checks the state of the connection, and if open, closes it. It then disables the three buttons which were disabled in the form load procedure, thus returning the program to its startup state.

```
Private Sub CloseBtn_Click()
  On Error GoTo CloseBtnError
  If db.State = adStateOpen Then
    db.Close
    MsgBox "The connection to SAMPLE is closed.", _
    vbOKOnly, "SAMPLE Connection Closed"
    ConnectBtn.Enabled = True
    SP1Btn.Enabled = False
    SP2Btn.Enabled = False
    CloseBtn.Enabled = False
  End If
  Exit Sub

CloseBtnError:
  MsgBox "SAMPLE close error: " & Err.Description
End Sub
```

Building
Applications
Using Visual Basic

CallSP — Stored Procedure 1 Button Click Event

The stored procedure, which is called `CallSP`, is stored in the `%DB2PATH%\SAMPLES\ADO` directory. The stored procedure accepts four parameters from the calling program. It uses the first parameter to create a single column table of that name. It then takes the following three parameters and inserts them as rows in that column. If the stored procedure is called successfully, then the message "SAMPLE Stored Procedure inpsrv2 was called successfully" will be displayed confirming this fact. If the stored procedure returns an error, then the `On Error` routine will jump the program over this message code, to the routine which displays an error message.

After running this program, load the Control Center and navigate down to the Sample database and study its tables. You will find a new table called `Presidents`, and if you use the **Sample Contents** option to view that table, you will find entries for `Washington`, `Jefferson`, and `Lincoln`.

This procedure first dimensions and instantiates an ADO `Command` object, called `SPCall`, and four `Parameter` objects. It then sets various properties of this `Command` object as follows:

* Active Connection

  This is set to point to the connection which was created by the **Connect** button click procedure, `SPCall`.
* Command Text

  This is given the name of the stored procedure which will be called, `INPSRV2`.
* CommandType

  This is set to `adCmdStoredProc`, that is, a command of type Call Stored Procedure.

Following these Command object settings, the procedure creates each of the four parameters, and appends them to the Command object's Parameter collection.

The CreateParameter call requires five passed parameters for each Parameter property, which are:

- Name
- Type
- Direction
- Size
- Value

All four of the Parameters in this procedure are of type character, and are all input parameters. An input parameter is for data being transferred from the application into the stored procedure, that is, no data is returned to the application by the stored procedure.

```
Private Sub SP1Btn_Click()
  Dim SPCall As New ADODB.Command
  Dim parm1 As New ADODB.Parameter
  Dim parm2 As New ADODB.Parameter
  Dim parm3 As New ADODB.Parameter
  Dim parm4 As New ADODB.Parameter

  On Error GoTo SP1BtnError
  Set SPCall.ActiveConnection = db
  SPCall.CommandText = "inpsrv2"
  SPCall.CommandType = adCmdStoredProc
  Set param1 = SPCall.CreateParameter("TableName", adChar,
adParamInput, 10, "Presidents")
  SPCall.Parameters.Append param1
  Set param2 = SPCall.CreateParameter("Data1", adChar,
adParamInput, 10, "Washington")
  SPCall.Parameters.Append param2
  Set param3 = SPCall.CreateParameter("Data2", adChar,
adParamInput, 9, "Jefferson")
  SPCall.Parameters.Append param3
  Set param4 = SPCall.CreateParameter("Data3", adChar,
adParamInput, 6, "Lincon")
  SPCall.Parameters.Append param4
  SPCall.Execute
  MsgBox "SAMPLE Stored Procedure inpsrv2 was called successfully"
  Exit Sub
SP1BtnError:
  MsgBox "SAMPLE StoredProcedure error: " & Err.Description
End Sub
```

CallSP — Stored Procedure 2 Button Click Event

The second stored procedure described here uses no input parameters. Instead, it uses one output parameter to pass an answer back from the stored procedure to the calling application. The stored parameter does a fixed task, which is to calculate the median salary from the `employee` table.

This procedure dimensions a command object and a single parameter object. It then sets the appropriate properties of the `Command` object as shown below:

- Active Connection

    This is set to point to the connection which was created by the Connect button click procedure, `SPCall`.

- Command Text

    This is given the name of the stored procedure which will be called, `OUTSRV2`.

- CommandType

    This is set to `adCmdStoredProc`, that is, a command of type Call Stored Procedure.

The procedure then creates the single parameter, which will return the answer from the stored procedure, appends it to the `Command` object's `Parameter` collection, and then executes the command.

The procedure then displays the answer returned by the stored procedure or an error message if there was a problem carrying out the task.

```
Private Sub SP2Btn_Click()
  Dim SPCall As New ADODB.Command
  Dim parm1 As New ADODB.Parameter
  On Error GoTo SP2BtnError
  Set SPCall.ActiveConnection = db
  SPCall.CommandText = "outsrv2"
  SPCall.CommandType = adCmdStoredProc
  Set parm1 = SPCall.CreateParameter("Median", adDouble,
adParamOutput, , 0)
  SPCall.Parameters.Append parm1
  SPCall.Execute
  MsgBox "SAMPLE Stored Procedure outsrv2 calculated median was " &
SPCall(0)
  Exit Sub

SP2BtnError:
  MsgBox "SAMPLE StoredProcedure error: " & Err.Description
End Sub
```

Calling a Stored Procedure Returning a Recordset

This example illustrates the third type of stored procedure, which is where the stored procedure returns a recordset to the calling client program. The program is called RSSP and is stored in the %DB2PATH%\SAMPLES\ADO directory. The stored procedure runs a select query to obtain a subset of fields from the Employee table, which it returns to the calling program as a recordset. The stored procedure also returns the median salary in an output parameter.

The single form in the program contains three buttons: one to initiate the connection to the database, one to call the stored procedure, and one to close the connection. It also contains three text boxes, with associated labels, to display a record from the recordset returned by the stored procedure, and it has a button to move the recordset's current record pointer to the next record. Finally, it contains a label to hold the median salary.

RSSP — General Code Area of Form

This procedure has to dimension one of each type of the main ADO object variables, Connection, Recordset and Command.

```
Dim db As ADODB.Connection
Dim WithEvents rs As ADODB.Recordset
Dim SPCall As ADODB.Command
```

RSSP — Form Load Event

This procedure instantiates the Connection and Recordset objects and then sets up the start state of the various form objects. The **Connection** button is enabled, but the **Stored Procedure Call** button and **Close Connection** button are disabled. This is because these functions are not valid until a connection is made.

All the record display text boxes and labels are made invisible because they cannot show any data until the stored procedure is called. The **Medial** label and **Record Movement** button are also set to be invisible.

```
Private Sub Form_Load()
    Set db = New ADODB.Connection
    Set rs = New ADODB.Recordset
    ConnectBtn.Enabled = True
    CallSPBtn.Enabled = False
    CloseBtn.Enabled = False
    Label1.Visible = False
    Median.Visible = False
    Label2(0).Visible = False
    Label2(1).Visible = False
    Label2(2).Visible = False
    Column(0).Visible = False
    Column(1).Visible = False
    Column(2).Visible = False
    NextBtn.Visible = False
    NextBtn.Enabled = False
End Sub
```

RSSP — Open Connection Button Click Event

The procedure first checks that a connection is not already open by testing the state property of the connection object. If the connection is open, then the procedure displays a message to inform the user of this and then calls the Close button's click event to close the connection.

The procedure then proceeds to open the connection using the simple form of the connect string which does not include user ID or password. The connection will therefore be made using the current NT logon information. The sample connection must be catalogued before this program can run.

The procedure disables the **Connect** button and re-enables the **Stored Procedure Call** button and the **Close Connection** Button, and displays a message informing the user that the stored procedure can now be invoked.

```
Private Sub ConnectBtn_Click()
  On Error GoTo ConnectBtnErr
  If db.State = adStateOpen Then
      MsgBox "The database connection is already open. " & _
        "Click OK to reopen the connection.", _
        vbOKOnly, "SAMPLE Connect Error"
      Call CloseBtn_Click
  End If
  db.Open "SAMPLE"
  ConnectBtn.Enabled = False
  CallSPBtn.Enabled = True
  CloseBtn.Enabled = True
  Label1.Visible = False
  Median.Visible = False
  Median.Caption = ""
  MsgBox "Connection Successful! " & _
    "You can now invoke the stored procedure using the form.", _
    vbOKOnly, "SAMPLE Connect"
  Exit Sub

ConnectBtnErr:
  MsgBox "SAMPLE connect error: " & Err.Description
End Sub
```

RSSP — Close Connection Button Click Event

This procedure first checks the state of the recordset object to determine if the stored procedure has been called and a recordset returned. If this is the case, then it closes the recordset and inserts the median value, returned by the stored procedure's output parameter, in the label on the form. The reason for this, is that ADO does not allow access to the output parameters of a Command object, while a recordset associated with it is still open.

The procedure then checks that the connection is open, and if so, closes it. It then resets the state of all the buttons and text boxes back to the starting state set up by the Form Load event. The only exception to this is that the Median label is left visible so that the result can be seen.

```
Private Sub CloseBtn_Click()
  On Error GoTo CloseBtnError
  If rs.State = adStateOpen Then
    rs.Close
    Median.Caption = SPCall(0)
  End If
  If db.State = adStateOpen Then
    db.Close
    MsgBox "The connection to SAMPLE is closed.", _
    vbOKOnly, "SAMPLE Connection Closed"
    ConnectBtn.Enabled = True
    CallSPBtn.Enabled = False
    CloseBtn.Enabled = False
    Median.Visible = True
    Label1.Visible = True
    Label2(0).Visible = False
    Label2(1).Visible = False
    Label2(2).Visible = False
    Column(0).Visible = False
    Column(1).Visible = False
    Column(2).Visible = False
    NextBtn.Visible = False
    NextBtn.Enabled = False
    Column(0).Text = ""
    Column(1).Text = ""
    Column(2).Text = ""
  End If
  Exit Sub
CloseBtnError:
  MsgBox "SAMPLE close error: " & Err.Description
End Sub
```

RSSP — Call Stored Procedure Button Click Event

The procedure dimensions a `Parameter` object and instantiates the `Command` object that was dimensioned in the general code area. The properties of the `Command` object are then set as follows:

- Active Connection

  This is set to point to the connection which was created by the Connect button click procedure, `SPCall`.

- Command Text

  This is given the name of the stored procedure which will be called, `MRSPSRV`.

- CommandType

  This is set to `adCmdStoredProc`, that is, a command of type Call Stored Procedure.

The procedure then creates an output parameter for the stored procedure to return the median salary value that it calculates. It then sets the contents of the recordset to the recordset returned by executing the stored procedure command. If this recordset is not empty, then it calls the `SetFields` procedure which will fill the text boxes with the values in the first record in the recordset.

Lastly, the procedure disables the **Call Stored Procedure** button and makes all the text boxes and associated labels visible, so that the record display will appear on the form.

```
Private Sub CallSPBtn_Click()
  Dim parm1 As New ADODB.Parameter
  Set SPCall = New ADODB.Command
  On Error GoTo CallSPBtnError
  Set SPCall.ActiveConnection = db
  SPCall.CommandText = "mrspsrv"
  SPCall.CommandType = adCmdStoredProc
  Set parm1 = SPCall.CreateParameter("Median", adDouble,
adParamOutput, , 0)
  SPCall.Parameters.Append parm1
  Set rs = SPCall.Execute
  If (Not rs.EOF) Then
      Call SetFields
      CallSPBtn.Enabled = False
      Label2(0).Visible = True
      Label2(1).Visible = True
      Label2(2).Visible = True
      Column(0).Visible = True
      Column(1).Visible = True
      Column(2).Visible = True
      NextBtn.Visible = True
      NextBtn.Enabled = True
  End If
  Exit Sub

CallSPBtnError:
  MsgBox "SAMPLE StoredProcedure error: " & Err.Description
End Sub
```

RSSP — Setfields Procedure

This fills in the values, from the current record in the recordset, to the text boxes on the form. This is an alternative to binding the text boxes directly to the recordset object, as has been done in the earlier example programs.

```
Private Sub SetFields()
  On Error GoTo ErrorProcess
  Column(0).Text = rs!ID
  Column(1).Text = rs!Name
  Column(2).Text = rs!SALARY
  Exit Sub

ErrorProcess:
  MsgBox "SAMPLE SetFields error: " & Err.Description
End Sub
```

RSSP — Next Record Button Click Event

This procedure moves to the next record in the recordset. If there are no more records, then the recordset is closed, and the median value passed back by the stored procedure is inserted in the label on the form. If the end of the recordset has not been reached, then the `SetFields` procedure is called to update the text boxes on the form with the values from the new record.

```
Private Sub NextBtn_Click()
  On Error GoTo NextBtnError
  rs.MoveNext
  If rs.EOF Then
    rs.Close
    Median.Caption = SPCall(0)
    Median.Visible = True
    Label1.Visible = True
    NextBtn.Enabled = False
  Else
    Call SetFields
  End If
  Exit Sub

NextBtnError:
  MsgBox "Next Record error: " & Err.Description
End Sub
```

Using Commitment Control

This application demonstrates the use of the auto-commit and manual-commit features of ADO. The program queries the EMPLOYEE table in the SAMPLE database for the employee number and name. The user has an option of connecting to the database in either auto-commit or manual-commit mode, using a check box on the form.

In the auto-commit mode, all of the changes that a user makes on a record are updated automatically in the database. This update will occur in the normal way when the user moves from an edited record to the next or previous record.

In the manual-commit mode, the user needs to start a transaction before they can make any changes. The user can change as many records as they want, and moving onto the next record and then moving back to a changed record will reveal that the changes appear permanent on the client. However, all the changes made since the beginning of a transaction can be undone by performing a rollback. All the records that were changed will be reverted to their original values. The changes can be saved permanently by committing the transaction. After a commit or rollback, the program will revert to requiring a new transaction, before further editing can take place. Exiting the program automatically rolls back the changes.

Commitment Control — General Code Area of Form

This dimensions Connection, Command, Parameter and Recordset objects for use in all procedures in the form module. However the Parameter object is not used in this program. The procedure also dimensions a string variable to be used to hold the ConnectionString value for the Connection object.

```
Dim cnSample  As ADODB.Connection
Dim cmdSample As ADODB.Command
Dim prmSample As ADODB.Parameter
Dim rstSample As ADODB.Recordset
Dim strCnn As String
```

Commitment Control — Form Load Event

This initializes all the display and action components of the form. The text boxes are cleared and disabled. All buttons, apart from **Connect** and **Exit** are disabled. The **AutoCommit** check box is enabled and initially takes its default value of unchecked. Hence, unless the user checks this box, all transactions will be manual, that is, they will require BeginTrans, CommitTrans and RollbackTrans methods to control commitment.

```
Private Sub Form_Load()
  EmpNoText.Text = ""
  LaNmeText.Text = ""
  FiNmeText.Text = ""
  EmpNoText.Enabled = False
  LaNmeText.Enabled = False
  FiNmeText.Enabled = False
  AutoCommitCheck.Enabled = True
  ConnectButton.Enabled = True
  PrevButton.Enabled = False
  NextButton.Enabled = False
  OpenRecButton.Enabled = False
  CommitButton.Enabled = False
  NewTransButton.Enabled = False
  RollbackButton.Enabled = False
  DisconnectButton.Enabled = False
End Sub
```

Commitment Control — Disconnect Button Click Event

The first action of the disconnect button procedure is to rollback the uncommitted transactions. If there are no uncommitted transactions, then this will generate a runtime error. The On Error routine is designed to ignore this error.

The procedure then closes the recordset if it is open, and also closes the connection if it is open. It then calls the form load event in order to re-initialize the state of all the controls on the form.

```
Private Sub DisconnectButton_Click()
  On Error Resume Next
  cnSample.RollbackTrans
  If rstSample.State = adStateOpen Then
    rstSample.Close
  End If
  If cnSample.State = adStateOpen Then
    cnSample.Close
  End If
  Form_Load
End Sub
```

Commitment Control — Previous Record Button Click Event

When the **Previous Record** button is pressed, this procedure first calls the UpdateLocalRecord procedure, which copies the contents of the form's text boxes to the appropriate fields in the current record buffer. It then executes a MovePrevious method on the recordset object. If the result of the MovePrevious method is to move the current record pointer before the first record in the recordset, then the procedure executes the MoveFirst method in order to reposition the pointer onto the first record in the recordset. Having moved to a different record, the final task is to refresh the text boxes with the values from the new record, by calling the RefreshText procedure.

```
Private Sub PrevButton_Click()
  On Error GoTo ShowError
  UpdateLocalRecord
  rstSample.MovePrevious
  If rstSample.BOF Then
    MsgBox "Already at beginning of recordset!"
    rstSample.MoveFirst
  End If
  RefreshText
  Exit Sub

ShowError:
  MsgBox Err.Description

End Sub
```

Commitment Control — Next Record Button Click Event

This is almost identical to the Previous Button Click event, except that it executes the MoveNext method of the recordset, and does a MoveLast if the current Record Pointer moves past the end of the recordset.

```
Private Sub NextButton_Click()
  On Error GoTo ShowError
  UpdateLocalRecord
  rstSample.MoveNext
  If rstSample.EOF Then
    MsgBox "Already at end of recordset!" '- show message
    rstSample.MoveLast
  End If
  RefreshText
  Exit Sub

ShowError:
  MsgBox Err.Description
End Sub
```

Commitment Control — Open Record Button Click Event

This starts by instantiated the recordset. It then sets the following properties for the recordset object. See the properties section of the ADO On-line Manual for more information on the possible values which can be set for these properties.

- CursorLocation

  This uses either server side or client side cursors for the recordset.
- Cursor Type

  This is set to Dynamic. This is the best choice for updating a recordset which you wish to scroll both backwards and forwards.
- LockType

  This is set to optimistic locking. See the ADO On-line help for the definitions of table locking.

The procedure then instantiates the Command object and sets it's properties as follows:

- Active Connection

  This is set to point to the connection which was created by the Connect button click procedure, cnSample.
- Command Text

  This is given the name of the Employee table.
- CommandType

  This is set to adCmdTable, that is, Table type recordset.

The procedure then opens the recordset using cnSample as its connection and cmdSample as its command.

The procedure enables the **Next** and **Previous** buttons to allow the user to navigate through the recordset, and disables the **Open Record** button which has now completed its task.

If the user has not checked the **Autocommit** check box, then the **New Transaction** button is enabled. If the user has checked the **Autocommit** box, then the **New Transaction** button remains disabled, but the **First Name** and **Last Name** text boxes are enabled so that the user can edit these fields. The procedure then calls the **RefreshText** box to fill the text boxes with the data from the current record in the recordset.

```
Private Sub OpenRecButton_Click()
  On Error GoTo ShowError
  Set rstSample = New ADODB.Recordset
  rstSample.CursorLocation = adUseClient
  rstSample.CursorType = adOpenDynamic
  rstSample.LockType = adLockOptimistic
  Set cmdSample = New ADODB.Command
  Set cmdSample.ActiveConnection = cnSample
  cmdSample.CommandText = "EMPLOYEE"
  cmdSample.CommandType = adCmdTable
  rstSample.Open cmdSample.CommandText, cnSample
  PrevButton.Enabled = True
  NextButton.Enabled = True
  OpenRecButton.Enabled = False
  If AutoCommitCheck.Value = 0 Then
    NewTransButton.Enabled = True
  Else
    FiNmeText.Enabled = True
    LaNmeText.Enabled = True
  End If
  RefreshText
  Exit Sub

ShowError:
  MsgBox Err.Description
End Sub
```

Commitment Control — Commit Button Click Event

If the **Commit** button is pushed, the procedure calls the UpdateLocalRecord to ensure that changes to the current record are inserted in the local copy of the recordset. The CommitTrans method of the connection object is then executed and the text buttons disabled so that no further editing can be done until the **New Transaction** button is pressed again. The procedure also disables the **Commit** and **Rollback** buttons and re-enables the **New Transaction** button.

```
Private Sub CommitButton_Click()

  On Error GoTo ShowError
  UpdateLocalRecord
  cnSample.CommitTrans
  FiNmeText.Enabled = False
  LaNmeText.Enabled = False
  CommitButton.Enabled = False
  RollbackButton.Enabled = False
  NewTransButton.Enabled = True
  Exit Sub

ShowError:
  MsgBox Err.Description
End Sub
```

Commitment Control — Open Connection Button Click Event

This procedure instantiates the Connection object which was dimensioned in the form's General code area. The procedure then builds the connection string from two elements. The first is the normal DSN, UID and PWD entry. However, in this case it also adds the AUTOCOMMIT section with a value of 0 or 1, depending on the setting of the **Autocommit** check box. The Connection object is then opened using this connection string. Having opened the connection, the procedure disables both the **Connect** button and the **Autocommit** checkbox, and enables the **OpenRec** and **Disconnect** buttons.

```
Private Sub ConnectButton_Click()
  On Error GoTo ShowError
  Set cnSample = New ADODB.Connection
  strCnn = "DSN=SAMPLE;UID=;PWD=;"
  If AutoCommitCheck.Value = 0 Then
    ctrcnn = strCnn + "AUTOCOMMIT=0;"
  Else
    ctrcnn = strCnn + "AUTOCOMMIT=1;"
  End If
  cnSample.Open strCnn
  AutoCommitCheck.Enabled = False
  OpenRecButton.Enabled = True
  ConnectButton.Enabled = False
  DisconnectButton.Enabled = True
  Exit Sub

ShowError:
  MsgBox Err.Description

End Sub
```

Commitment Control — New Transaction Button Click Event

This procedure runs the `BeginTrans` method of the `Connection` object. It then enables the text boxes, so that the user can edit the records, and it also enables the **Commit** and **Rollback** buttons so that the user can terminate the transaction, either by committing the changes or rolling back the changes. It also disables the **New Transaction** button because a transaction is already started.

```
Private Sub NewTransButton_Click()
    On Error GoTo ShowError
    cnSample.BeginTrans
    FiNmeText.Enabled = True
    LaNmeText.Enabled = True
    CommitButton.Enabled = True
    RollbackButton.Enabled = True
    NewTransButton.Enabled = False
    Exit Sub

ShowError:
    MsgBox Err.Description

End Sub
```

Commitment Control — Rollback Button Click Event

The first action of this procedure is to rollback the transaction. It then re-queries the recordset to update the local recordset with the original records from the database, and then runs the `RefreshText` procedure which updates the text fields on the form from the current record in the recordset. It follows these actions by disabling the text boxes, so that the user cannot edit the contents, and finally it disables the **Commit** and **Rollback** buttons, and re-enables the **New Transaction** button.

```
Private Sub RollbackButton_Click()
    On Error GoTo ShowError
    cnSample.RollbackTrans
    rstSample.Requery
    RefreshText
    FiNmeText.Enabled = False
    LaNmeText.Enabled = False
    NewTransButton.Enabled = True
    CommitButton.Enabled = False
    RollbackButton.Enabled = False
    Exit Sub
ShowError:
    MsgBox Err.Description
End Sub
```

Commitment Control — Exit Button Click Event

The click event procedure for this button merely unloads the form. However, the form unload event actually executes a rollback before exiting. Putting the rollback routine into the unload event ensures that it will still be executed if the user closes the form, from either the form close gadget or the form menu. Thus the **Exit** button is just another method of closing the form.

```
Private Sub ExitButton_Click()
  Unload Me
End Sub
```

Commitment Control — Refresh Text

This procedure fills the three text boxes on the form with the values in the fields of the current record in the recordset.

```
Private Sub RefreshText()
    EmpNoText.Text = rstSample!EMPNO
    LaNmeText.Text = rstSample!LASTNAME
    FiNmeText.Text = rstSample!FIRSTNME
End Sub
```

Commitment Control — Update Local Record

This updates the local record buffer with the contents of the form's text boxes.

```
Private Sub UpdateLocalRecord()
    rstSample!EMPNO = EmpNoText.Text
    rstSample!LASTNAME = LaNmeText.Text
    rstSample!FIRSTNME = FiNmeText.Text
End Sub
```

Commitment Control — Form Unload Event

Closing the form generates a rollback of the transaction. If there are no uncommitted transactions to rollback, then this will generate an error, but the On Error routine will cause this error to be ignored. If the recordset is open, then it will be closed, as will be the connection if one is detected.

Normally these objects would also be set to NOTHING to remove the instances from memory, but this has not been done in this example.

```
Private Sub Form_Unload(Cancel As Integer)
   On Error Resume Next
   cnSample.RollbackTrans
   If rstSample.State = adStateOpen Then
      rstSample.Close
   End If
   If cnSample.State = adStateOpen Then
      cnSample.Close
   End If
End Sub
```

Building
Applications
Using Visual Basic

C H A P T E R **6**

Building Applications Using Visual C++

- ◆ ACTIVEX DATA OBJECT
- ◆ GETROWS SAMPLE APPLICATION
- ◆ VARCHAR SAMPLE APPLICATION
- ◆ DB2 UDB ADD-INS FOR VISUAL C++

*I*n this chapter, we describe the application development process using Microsoft Visual C++ with the DB2 UDB for Windows NT database. Visual C++ is a popular C++ tool on the Windows operating system platforms. Visual C++ is widely used by Windows application developers, particularly for creating high performance applications, or creating middle-tier applications including business logic.

As we discussed in Chapter 1, DB2 UDB can be accessed through the OLE DB interface or ODBC interface, therefore you can develop ADO applications to access DB2 UDB using Visual C++. What you need to do is just specify a DB2 UDB database as a property of the ADO Connection object in the code. Once you have developed portable applications such as ODBC or ADO applications, they can work well with great performance on DB2 UDB without any DB2 UDB specific clauses.

In this chapter, first we will show that an ADO sample application on the MSDN library disk can work well on DB2 UDB without any special techniques. Then we will look at an ADO sample application which DB2 UDB provides, and see how to handle ADO objects in Visual C++ applications.

We will also describe the DB2 UDB add-ins. These are the DB2 UDB Project and Tools add-ins provided by DB2 UDB to simplify the building and deployment of DB2 UDB applications from the Visual C++ application development environment. Finally, we will demonstrate how to use DB2 UDB Project and Tools add-ins to build, package, and deploy applications in the Visual C++ development environment.

Visual C++ Applications with ADO

DB2 UDB provides the ODBC driver for DB2 UDB, and also the OLE DB Provider for DB2 UDB in the Version 7.1 release. You can develop ODBC applications and OLE-DB applications using Visual C++. But also you can develop applications using the layer on top of OLE DB, which is ADO.

First, we will show that an ADO application written for another database product can run well on a DB2 UDB database. To demonstrate this, we will use the ADO sample application on the MSDN Library disk, which is a part of the Visual Studio product install set.

 Note: Review Chapter 3 for the ADO Object Model.

GetRows Sample

The MSDN Library provides many sample applications, not only ADO samples for Visual C++, but also COM samples, Internet samples, and so on. To get the ADO samples for Visual C++, perform the following:

- Start the MSDN Library.
- Click on the **Contents** tag in the left-hand pane.
- Expand the **Visual C++ documentation**->**Samples**->**Sdk samples**->**Database Samples**->**ADO samples** folder.
- Select the sample application you are interested in; you will see a brief description of the application.
- To copy the sample application's files, click the link saying "Click to open or copy the files" and click **Copy All** button in the Visual C++ Samples dialog.

Here, we are using the GetRows sample program, which is intended to access the Microsoft Access sample database and to retrieve all the rows of a record set. The look-and-feel of the application is shown below in Fig. 6–1:

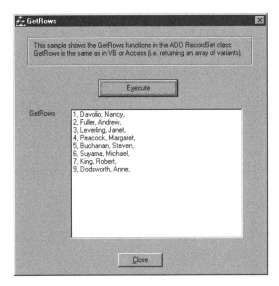

Fig. 6–1 *GetRows Sample Application*

This application creates a Connection object for the Microsoft Access's sample database Northwind, creates a Recordset object to select entire rows of the Employee table, and then retrieves all the rows into a 2-dimensional array with the GetRows method of the Connection object.

Set Up DB2 UDB Database

Before using the GetRows application, you need to create a table similar to the Access's Employee table in a DB2 UDB database. You can write a program to obtain the schema of the table from the Access database using the OpenSchema method of the Connection object and generate a DDL as we did using the Visual Basic program in Chapter 5. Here we are creating a table manually in the DB2 UDB sample database. Fig. 6–2 shows the DDL you can use:

```
CREATE TABLE DB2EMP (
  Employeeid integer generated by default as identity
    (start with 1, increment by 1),
  LastName varchar(20),
  FirstName varchar(10),
  Title varchar(30),
  TitleOfCouresy varchar(25),
  BirthDate date,
  HireDate date,
  Address varchar(60),
  City varchar(15),
  Region varchar(15),
  PostalCode varchar(10),
  Country varchar(15),
  Homephone varchar(24),
  Extension char(4),
  Photo varchar(1024) for bit data,
  Notes varchar(512),
  ReportsTo integer
  );
```

Fig. 6–2 *Create a Table in the DB2 UDB Database*

Note: The Employeeid column of the original Employee table in the Access database is Autonumber data type (data is generated automatically). Therefore, the DDL for DB2 UDB (Fig. 6–2) has a GENERATED clause for the Employeeid column. However, you do not need to specify this clause if you try only the GetRows sample program, because this application does not add any rows. You need to add this clause if you try the other MSDN sample program Employee, which adds records including automatically generated values. The GENERATED clause can be used since DB2 UDB Version 7.1. See the *DB2 UDB SQL Reference* for the complete syntax of the GENERATED clause.

Once you have created the table, you can export data from the Access database and import it. Start Microsoft Access, open the Northwind database, right-click on the Employees table icon, and select Export. Then the Export Table Wizard will be launched. Export the table as a text file with the delimited ASCII format.

The next step is importing the data into DB2 UDB. You can execute the following command. `EMPLOYEE.TXT` is the exported file name:

```
IMPORT FROM employees.txt OF del
  MODIFIED BY DELPRIORITYCHAR IDENTITYIGNORE
  MESSAGES import.msg INSERT INTO db2emp;
```

Note: The keyword `DELPRIORITYCHAR` is specified to revert the delimiter priority to: character delimiter, record delimiter, column delimiter. This is because some records in the `Employees` table have record delimiters within the data.

The keyword `IDENTITYIGNORE` is also specified to ignore the data provided by the input file for the identity column. You don't need to specify this keyword if the `Employeeid` column does not have the `GENERATED` clause in the `CREATE TABLE` statement.

See the *DB2 UDB Command Reference* for a detailed description of each keyword.

Run the GetRows Application on DB2 UDB

To make the GetRows application run on DB2 UDB, what you need to do is just change the `Connection` object's `ConnectionString` property to the DB2 UDB database. Assuming the DB2 UDB sample database has already been registered as an ODBC data source with a Data Source Name (DSN) of `Sample`, you should specify `Sample` for the `ConnectionString`. As the Microsoft OLE DB provider for ODBC, `MSDASQL` is the default OLE DB provider; you do not need to specify anything else.

The source program file `GETRDLG.CPP` has a constant variable specifying 'OLE_DB_NWind_Jet' for the sample Access database. Change this to 'Sample'. This source file also has constant variables for the user name and password used to validate the user before connection to the database is established. If your DB2 UDB database is local, set the user name and password null so that the current logged on Windows NT user will be used. The other constant variable is for the SQL statement used for the `Source` property of the `Recordset` object. Change the table name specified in the `FROM` clause to `DB2EMP`, which is the table in the DB2 UDB sample database (see Fig. 6–2 on page 290).

Simply specify the data source this application will use — that is all you need do before running the sample application. As emphasized, once you develop portable applications such as ODBC or ADO applications, they can work well with great performance on DB2 UDB without any DB2 UDB specific modifications.

Now, compile the GetRows sample application and execute the generated EMP.EXE. You will see that rows are retrieved from the DB2 UDB database and displayed, as shown in Fig. 6–1 on page 289.

More about the GetRows Sample Application

When you run the application, it will launch a form having the **Execute** button, the **Close** button, and a list box. Clicking on the **Execute** button will establish a connection to the database, retrieve data, and display it.

The main logic of this application is written in the GETRDLG.CPP file. Consult the file and see how the Connection object and Recordset object are initialized and opened, and also how the data is retrieved.

In this application, the GetRows method of the Recordset object is used. The GetRows method retrieves multiple rows of a Recordset into a 2-dimensional array. You should observe that the SafeArrayGetElement function is used to access the individual fields of the array after the GetRow method is executed.

VarCHAR Sample

Whether you use Visual C++ or Visual Basic, what you have to code for ADO applications is basically same. If you intend to retrieve data from a database using ADO, your program usually performs the following steps:

- Creating a Connection object
- Opening the Connection object using its Open method
- Creating a Recordset object
- Opening the Recordset object using its Open method
- Navigating data using a series of Move method
- Obtaining field data through the Field object associated with the Recordset object, or getting field data using GetCollect method
- Closing the Recordset object using Close method
- Closing the Connection object using Close method

Note: Actually, ADO is more flexible, and you do not always have to write a program in this way. For example, you can open a Recordset object without creating and opening it explicitly. Instead, the Execute method of the Connection object can be used as introduced later in this chapter.

Clearly, the way you would create those objects, and how you would call methods of the objects, are different than the way you would do these things in Visual Basic programs. To learn these new techniques, we will look at an ADO sample application which DB2 UDB provides. You can find this application in `%DB2PATH%\Samples\ADO\VC` (`%DB2PATH%` is the directory path where the DB2 UDB product is installed).

Here, we are using the `VarCHAR` sample program which views and updates the `Org` table of the `Sample` database. This program's look-and-feel is shown in Fig. 6–3.

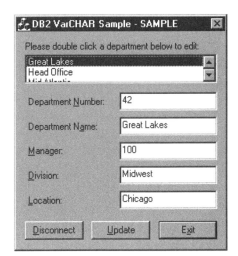

Fig. 6–3 *VarCHAR Sample Application*

This application creates a Connection object for the DB2 UDB Sample database, creates a `Recordset` object to select all department names (`DEPTNAME`) from the `Org` table, retrieves all department names by the `GetCollect` method, and displays it in a list box at the top of the form. Then, double-clicking on a department name in the list box will create another `Recordset` object to select other columns of that department from the `Org` table, retrieve all fields data of the department by the `GetCollect` method, and display it on the dialog box.

This application also performs updates for the Org table. You can modify the strings displayed in the dialog box and make them reflected by clicking the **Update** button.

Now, let us examine this application and see how each ADO object is initialized, how each method for ADO objects is executed, and so on. It might be interesting to compare these things with the way they are handled in Visual Basic programs.

Import ADO Library

The ADO library is included in the Microsoft Data Access Component (MDAC). Once an ADO application program imports the ADO library in itself, it can be compiled in the same way as regular C++ programs.

To have your C++ source program run as an ADO program, you can put the following import pre-compiler directive at the top of your source program file:

```
#import "C:\Program Files\Common
Files\System\ado\msado15.dll" \
no_namespace \
rename( "EOF", "adoEOF")
```

In the example above, msado15.dll may be msado10.dll. It depends on which version of the ADO library you use.

This pre-compiler directive tells the Visual C++ compiler to import the ADO library, therefore, when the program is compiled, the user will need to verify that the ADO library is in the path specified.

An alternative way to use the import directive is to add the path to the environment variable LIBPATH as:

```
PATH=%PATH%;C:\Program Files\Common Files\System\ado
```

And then this shorter import directive can be used in your source file:

```
#import msado15.dll no_namespace rename( "EOF", "adoEOF")
```

With this `import` directive, your DB2 program will have access to the ADO library to get information on ADO objects, and a couple of header files will be created and included in the Visual C++ project. You can now compile your Visual C++ program as you would any other program.

The `VarCHAR` sample application has this `import` directive in the `stdAfx.h` file.

Create Connection Object

When you start the application and click on the **Connect** button, the login dialog will be launched. Clicking the **OK** button will establish a connection to the database and retrieve rows from the `Org` table. The main logic of this application is written in the `VarCHARDlg.cpp` file.

The first step performed to establish a connection to the database is creating a `Connection` object. To create a `Connection` object, you can use the `CreateInstance` function with the `UUID` of the `Connection` as follows:

```
_ConnectionPtr m_pConnection;
HRESULT hr;
hr = m_pConnection.CreateInstance(__uuidof( Connection ));
```

This example is extracted from the `VarCHARDlg.cpp` file of the `VarCHAR` sample program. `HRESULT` is the result handler. You should check the result of the `CreateInstance` function as follows:

```
if (FAILED(hr)) goto ErrorExit;
```

Note that any `Connection` object variables are not declared here. Instead, a `Connection` object pointer `m_pConnection` is initialized by the `CreateInstance` function. All properties and methods of the `Connection` object will be accessed through this pointer.

Open Connection Object

If the Connection object was created successfully, you can call the `Open` method of the `Connection` object to establish the connection to the database. Before calling the `Open` method, you should set the connection string, user ID, and password.

The Open method takes four parameters. The first parameter is the connection string, which specifies the OLE DB data source for the database. This usually contains a series of argument=value statements separated by semicolons, and refers to the OLE DB provider first. But in our case, we are using the ODBC bridge provider MSDASQL and it is the default data provider, thus it is not necessary to include it. Only the Data Source Name (DSN), which is SAMPLE in our case, should be specified.

The second parameter and the third parameter are the user ID and the password for connecting to the database. The logged on Windows NT user ID is used if you don't specify any user ID or password.

The connection string, user ID, and password are passed to the Open method as BSTR type data (length-prefixed unicode strings) using the _bstr_t constructor.

The fourth parameter is the connect option. Supported values are the following (Table 6–1):

Table 6–1 *Connect Option*

Connect option	Description
adConnectUnspecified	Default. The connection will be opened synchronously.
adAsyncConnect	The connection will be opened asynchronously.

The following (Fig. 6–4) is the code extracted from VarCHARDlg.cpp file. Note that the Open method is called through the Connection object pointer m_pConnection.

```
dConnect.m_Database = "SAMPLE";
dConnect.m_UserID = "";
dConnect.m_Password = "";
dsnString = "dsn=" + dConnect.m_Database;
hr = m_pConnection->Open(
            _bstr_t(dsnString),
            _bstr_t(dConnect.m_UserID),
            _bstr_t(dConnect.m_Password),
            adConnectUnspecified);
```

Fig. 6–4 *Open Connection Object*

Retrieve Department Name

Once you have the connection open, you can create a Recordset object for the retrieved data. You can use the CreateInstance function with the UUID of the Recordset to receive the value for the Recordset object pointer, and then open the Recordset object using the Open method with appropriate parameters. However, in this sample application, the Execute method of the Connection object is used to initialize and open a Recordset object alternatively. The Execute method returns a the Recordset object reference. See the following code extracted from the VarCHARDlg.cpp file, and note that a Recordset object pointer m_pRecordset is initialized by the Execute method of the Connection object.

```
_RecordsetPtr m_pRecordSet;
_bstr_t    bstrQuery("SELECT DISTINCT DEPTNAME FROM ORG");
_variant_t vRecsAffected(0L);
m_pRecordSet = \
   m_pConnection->Execute(bstrQuery, \
                      &vRecsAffected, \
                      adCmdUnspecified);
```

Fig. 6–5 *Open Recordset Object using Connection Object's Execute Method*

Using the Execute method of the Connection object accomplishes a task to open a Recordset object with fewer lines of code than creating a Recordset object and then opening it using the Open method (Fig. 6–5). However, if you take this approach, you cannot specify the values for parameters of the Open method or properties of the Recordset object before opening the Recordset object. If you do not want to use the default values for those parameters or properties, you should create a Recordset object, set the property values, and open the Recordset object.

Building Applications Using Visual C++

If you want to create and then open the Recordset object, the code shown in Fig. 6–5 would look like the following code, shown in Fig. 6–6:

```
_RecordsetPtr m_pRecordSet;
_bstr_t    bstrQuery("SELECT DISTINCT DEPTNAME FROM ORG");
hr = m_pConnection.CreateInstance(__uuidof( Recordset ));
hr = m_pRecordSet->put_Source(bstrQuery);
hr = m_pRecordSet->putref_ActiveConnection(m_pConnection);
vNull.vt = VT_ERROR;
vNull.scope = DISP_E_PARAMNOTFOUND;
hr = m_pRecordSet->Open (vNull, \
                         vNull, \
                         adOpenKeyset, \
                         adLockOptimistic, \
                         adCmdUnknown);
```

Fig. 6–6 *Create and Open Recordset Object*

In this example, the Recordset object is created, and then the Source property and the ActiveConnection property is set before opening the Recordset object.

The Source property indicates the source for the data in the Recordset object. This sample application uses an SQL statement for the Source property; however, you can also use a table name, stored procedure name, or a Command object. The Source property is set by the put_Source function.

The ActiveConnection property indicates which connection the Recordset object will use. The Connection object can be set to the ActiveConnection property of the Recordset object by Putref_ActiveConnection. Or if you have not created a Connection object, you can use Put_ActiveConnection to set the ActiveConnection property using a string including the Connection object definition.

Note that the cursor type and the lock type are specified when opening the Recordset in this example. Chapter 3 has a brief description about the properties of the Recordset object including cursor type. For the detailed information, see the MSDN online library.

Let us go back to the Execute method of the Connection object, which is used in our example. The Execute method takes four parameters. The first parameter is a command text containing the SQL statement, table name, or specific text to be executed. The second parameter is an optional parameter indicating the number of records that this operation affected. The third parameter is an options flag indicating how the data provider should evaluate the first parameter. It can be one of the following (Table 6–2):

Table 6–2 *Optional Flag*

Optional flag	Description
adCmdText	Indicates that the provider should evaluate the command text as a textual definition of a command.
adCmdTable	Indicates that ADO should generate an SQL query to return all rows from the table named in the command text.
adCmdStoredProc	Indicates that the provider should evaluate the Source property as a stored procedure.
adCmdTableDirect	Indicates that the provider should return all rows from the table named in the command text.
adCmdUnknown	Indicates that the type of command in the Source property is not known.
adCmdUnspecified	This is the same as adCmdUnknown.

If you set an appropriate value of this parameter, you can optimize performance by eliminating the process to determine which type of command is used. For example, if the command text is an SQL statement, you can optimize performance by passing adCmdText.

A Recordset object returns data from the database in the form of rows and columns. The Recordset works on the basis of a current record, and the properties of the Recordset refer to the data in the current row. Once you open a cursor by the Connect object's Execute method or the Recordset object's Open method, you can scroll the cursor in the record structure by a series of Move methods, and retrieve the data through the Field objects that are associated with the Recordset object. Each Field object represents a column of the Recordset object, and the Value property of the Field object has the value of the field.

The alternative method to obtain the data is using the GetCollect method, which this sample application uses. The GetCollect method of the Recordset object is defined in the msado15.tli file, which will be generated from the imported ADO library when the program is compiled (see "Import ADO Library" on page 294). Thus, GetCollect will expand to code that includes the get_Collect method. The get_Collect method is a short-cut method that you can use to retrieve and set a field value without first obtaining a Field object's reference. In the program code, you can just specify the field name as the parameter for the GetCollect method, and retrieve that field value of the current record.

Whether you use the `get_Collect` method or other approaches to retrieve the field data, you cannot directly add the retrieved data to the list box to display it. When the data is retrieved from the ADO `Recordset` object, the data type is always variant. Though variants work well in Visual Basic programs, most operations in Visual C++ programs require native data types to support the standard library features. Therefore, the retrieved data should be converted into a string data type before being added to the list box.

In the `VarCHAR` sample application, a retrieved department name from the `Org` table is converted into a null-terminated string, and the pointer to the string is passed to the `Addstring` method of the `ListBox` object so that the string can be added to the list box. Then, the cursor is scrolled down to the next row by the `MoveNext` method, and the next data is retrieved and added to the `ListBox` object. This process will continue until the end of the `Recordset` object.

The following code (Fig. 6–7) is extracted from the `VarCHARDlg.cpp` file. Note that a `Recordset` object pointer `m_pRecordset` is initialized by the `Execute` method of the `Connection` object, and each department name is retrieved by the `GetCollect` method and the `MoveNext` method.

```
_RecordsetPtr m_pRecordSet;
_bstr_t    bstrQuery("SELECT DISTINCT DEPTNAME FROM ORG");
_variant_t vRecsAffected(0L);
CListBox   m_cDeptList;
m_pRecordSet = \
    m_pConnection->Execute(bstrQuery, \
                           &vRecsAffected, \
                           adCmdUnspecified);
while (!m_pRecordSet->GetadoEOF())
{
m_cDeptList.AddString( \
 (LPCTSTR) _bstr_t(m_pRecordSet->GetCollect(L"DEPTNAME")));
m_pRecordSet->MoveNext();
}
m_pRecordSet->Close();
```

Fig. 6–7 *Retrieve Department Name*

Retrieve Other Fields by Selected Department Name

At this point, the list of all the department names has been displayed in the list box. Now, double-clicking a department name in the list box will invoke the next step.

The next step is retrieving all fields using the selected department name. This step is similar to the previous one, initializing a Recordset object using an SQL statement, and retrieving the fields data using GetCollect method.

To get the department name that you have double-clicked, the GetText function is used. The GetText function copies an item from the list box into a CString type variable. Then the Format function sets the department name to the SQL statement selecting all fields. The format function writes formatted data to a CString type variable, just as the sprintf function formats data into a character array.

The following code (Fig. 6–8) is extracted from the VarCHARDlg.cpp file. Note that the SQL statement is formed using the Format function first, and then a Recordset object pointer m_pRecordset is initialized by the Execute method of the Connection object. We are executing the GetCollect method once for each field and do not use the MoveNext method this time, because we are interested in only one row.

```
_RecordsetPtr m_pRecordSet;
_ConnectionPtr m_pConnection;
CListBox    m_cDeptList;
CString sQuery;
CString m_sWorkingDept;
CString m_sDeptName;
CString m_sDivision;
CString m_sLocation;
int     m_nDeptNum;
int     m_nManager;
m_cDeptList.GetText( m_cDeptList.GetCurSel(), \
                     m_sWorkingDept);
sQuery.Format("SELECT * FROM ORG WHERE DEPTNAME = '%s'", \
              m_sWorkingDept);
m_pRecordSet = \
   m_pConnection->Execute((LPCTSTR) sQuery, \
                          &vRecsAffected, \
                          adOptionUnspecified);
m_nDeptNum = \
   atoi(_bstr_t(m_pRecordSet->GetCollect(L"DEPTNUMB")));
m_nManager = \
   atoi(_bstr_t(m_pRecordSet->GetCollect(L"MANAGER")));
m_sDeptName = \
   (LPCTSTR)_bstr_t(m_pRecordSet->GetCollect(L"DEPTNAME"));
m_sDivision = \
   (LPCTSTR) _bstr_t(m_pRecordSet->GetCollect(L"DIVISION"));
m_sLocation = \
   (LPCTSTR) _bstr_t(m_pRecordSet->GetCollect(L"LOCATION"));

m_pRecordSet->Close();

UpdateData(FALSE);
```

Fig. 6–8 *Retrieve Other Fields*

Each retrieved data item is set to a Cstring variable or integer variable, depending on the data type of each field. Then it is set to the dialog box by the `UpdateData` function. The parameter `False` indicates that the dialog box is being initialized by those new values.

Update Department Information

This sample application can also update records of the Org table. When you modify the data displayed in the dialog box and click the **Update** button, the data in the dialog box will be retrieved, then the UPDATE statement to reflect it is formed and executed.

First, the UpdateData function is called with the True option to retrieve the data from the dialog box. Then the retrieved data from the dialog box is formatted into the UPDATE statement for the Org table by the Format function.

To execute the UPDATE statement, the Execute method of the Connect object can be used. The Execute method can take the string, including the UPDATE statement, as a parameter.

The following code (Fig. 6–9) is extracted from the VarCHARDlg.cpp file. Note that the SQL statement is formed using the Format function, and then the Execute method of the Connection object is executed.

```
_RecordsetPtr m_pRecordSet;
_ConnectionPtr m_pConnection;
CListBox    m_cDeptList;
CString sQuery;
CString m_sWorkingDept;
CString m_sDeptName;
CString m_sDivision;
CString m_sLocation;
int     m_nDeptNum;
int     m_nManager;
UpdateData(TRUE);
sQuery.Format("UPDATE ORG SET (DEPTNAME, DEPTNUMB, LOCATION,
DIVISION, MANAGER) = ('%s', %d, '%s', '%s', %d) WHERE
DEPTNAME='%s'", m_sDeptName, m_nDeptNum, m_sLocation,
m_sDivision, m_nManager, m_sWorkingDept );

m_pRecordSet = \
  m_pConnection->Execute((LPCTSTR) sQuery, \
                         &vRecsAffected, \
                         adOptionUnspecified);
```

Fig. 6–9 *Update Fields*

Building Applications Using DB2 UDB Add-Ins

Using Microsoft Visual C++, you can create very efficient and lightweight application programs; however, with added efficiency comes greater complexity. As introduced in Chapter 1, DB2 UDB provides a collection of add-ins to simplify the building and deployment of DB2 applications from within the Microsoft Visual C++ component of the Visual Studio integrated development environment (IDE).

These include:

- DB2 UDB Tools add-in for Visual C++
- DB2 UDB Project add-in for Visual C++
- DB2 Stored Procedure Builder

The DB2 UDB Tools add-in for Visual C++ is a tool bar that enables the launch of some of the DB2 administration and development tools, such as the Control Center, from within the Visual C++ component of the Visual Studio integrated development environment (IDE). See Chapter 1 for a description of the supported DB2 graphical tools.

The DB2 Stored Procedure Builder (SPB) is a graphical application that supports the rapid development of DB2 stored procedures. We discussed the DB2 Stored Procedure Builder in Chapter 4.

In this section, we are discussing the application development using the DB2 UDB Project add-in for Visual C++.

The DB2 UDB Project add-in for Visual C++ is a collection of management tools and wizards that plug into the Visual C++ component of the Visual Studio integrated development environment (IDE) to automate and simplify the various tasks of developing applications for DB2 using embedded SQL. The Project add-in may be used to develop, package, and deploy:

- One or more stored procedures written in C/C++ for a DB2 UDB Server on a Windows 32-bit operating system
- Windows 32-bit C/C++ embedded SQL client applications accessing the DB2 family of servers
- Windows 32-bit C/C++ client applications that invoke stored procedures defined in the DB2 family of servers using C/C++ function call wrappers

 Note: A wrapper is a function that provides an interface to another function. The DB2 UDB Project add-in can generate a C source code that includes CALL statements calling specified stored procedures along with the declaration and initialization of the SQLDA data structure.

Some of the DB2 UDB Project add-in development tasks may include:

- Generating skeletal embedded SQL modules
- Generating sample SQL code
- Using the SQL Assistant to generate live insertable SQL statements
- Automatically pre-compiling embedded SQL C/C++ modules to C/C++ modules
- Managing pre-compiler options of embedded SQL modules
- Generating native code function wrappers for imported stored procedures (called from this project)
- Generating skeletal embedded SQL code for exported stored procedures (built in the project)
- Automatically defining the exported stored procedures into the database using generated DDL
- Packaging the DB2 components of the application for deployment
- Deploying the packaged DB2 components of the application to production systems and databases

The goal of the DB2 UDB Project add-in is to allow developers to focus on the design and logic of their DB2 applications rather than the actual building and deployment, while using the Visual C++ component of the Visual Studio integrated development environment.

Activating DB2 UDB Add-Ins

To activate the DB2 UDB add-ins, perform the following steps:

- Register the add-ins by clicking **Start** -> **Programs** -> **IBM DB2** -> **Register Visual C ++ Add-Ins**
- Customize your Visual C++ development environment to enable the Add-In as follows:
    - From the Tools menu, select the Customize menu item.
    - Select the Add-Ins and Macro Files tab.
    - Select the check box for the IBM DB2 Tools Add-In (Fig. 6–10).

Building Applications Using Visual C++

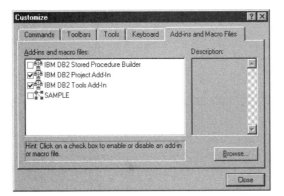

Fig. 6–10 *Customize Visual C++ development environment*

Once you have activated the DB2 UDB add-ins, a floating tool bar will be created containing all the active commands for launching the supported DB2 GUI administration and development tools. The tool bar will have a generated default name, **toolbar-n**, You can rename the tool bar using the standard Visual C++ customization option (Fig. 6–11).

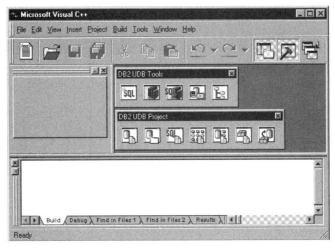

Fig. 6–11 *DB2 UDB add-ins toolbar*

This step is required only if you are using the DB2 UDB Project and Tools Add-In: for the first time. Once you have activated the add-ins, they will stay activated as part of your Visual C++ IDE until they are de-activated. To de-activate the DB2 UDB add-in, simply deselect the check box for the IBM DB2 Tools Add-In.

Note: In order for the registration step to work properly, Visual C++ must have been previously launched by the current user. The reason for this is that the registration step updates the current Visual C++ user profile that is created during the initial launch of Visual C++.

Developing Stored Procedures Using Add-Ins

Now we will demonstrate how exported stored procedures are developed and registered using DB2 UDB Project add-ins. We will develop a stored procedure that retrieves records based on the input parameter value, and returns them to the client program.

Create a New Project

When building DB2 UDB C/C++ stored procedures, you must create a Win32 dynamic-link library that exports one or more C/C++ functions defined as database stored procedures. After launching Visual C++, create a new Visual C++ stored procedure project by performing the following steps:

- Select **New** from the **File** pull down menu. You will be prompted to select which type of project you are creating.
- Select **Win32 Dynamic-Link Library** by clicking it, enter the project name, enter the project location, and then click **OK**.
- You will be prompted to select which type of DLL you are creating. Select an empty DLL project, and then click **Finish**. You will see a new project information screen describing an empty DLL project that will be created. Click **OK**.

Set Up the Project Properties

The DB2 project properties are accessible through the DB2 Project Properties Add-In tool bar button. The default project properties are sufficient for our project; however, you may want to specify the development database. This can be done as follows:

- Click the **DB2 Project Properties** add-in tool bar button (Fig. 6–12), it will bring up the DB2 Project Properties window.

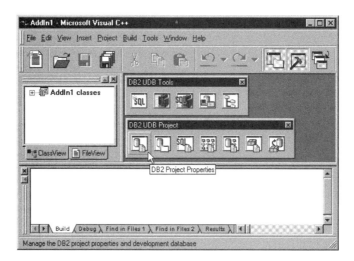

Fig. 6–12 *DB2 Project Properties Button*

- Go to the **Identity** tab, and click the **Database [...]** button. You will see the Select DB2 Database window. Select the instance name and the database name (Fig. 6–13).
- If necessary, enter the user ID and the password. You can test the database connection by clicking the **Test Connection** button. Click **OK**, and **OK** again to dismiss all dialogs.

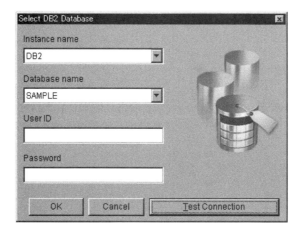

Fig. 6–13 *DB2 Project Properties Window*

Building an Exported Stored Procedure

Now, we are ready to create a new stored procedure. Click the **New DB2 Object**
add-in tool bar button, select the **Exported Stored Procedure** entry, and click **OK**.
The Export New DB2 Stored Procedure Wizard will be launched (Fig. 6–14).

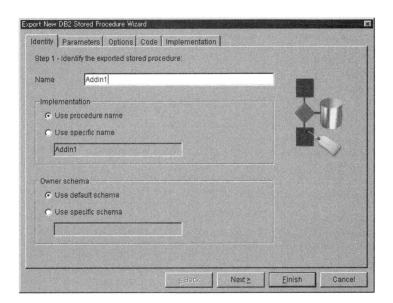

Fig. 6–14 *Export New DB2 Stored Procedure Wizard*

In the **Identity** tab, enter the stored procedure name. In the **Parameters** tab, click
New to launch the Stored Procedure Parameter dialog box. In our example, the
stored procedure uses an input parameter with double type (Fig. 6–15).

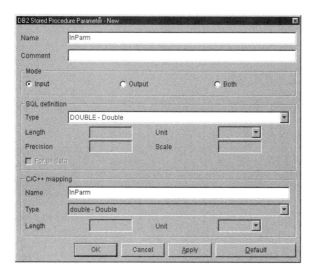

Fig. 6–15 *Stored Procedure Parameter dialog box*

In the **Options** tab, specify 1 for the number of result sets being returned. In the **Code** tab, build the required SQL query. You can type the SQL statements for this stored procedure, or click the **Define SQL** button and use the SQL Assist wizard to graphically generate the SQL statements (Fig. 6–16).

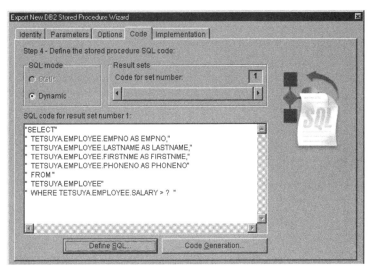

Fig. 6–16 *SQL code for the result set*

Note: Although we are using dynamic SQL, the generated SQL SELECT statement should still contain the host variables. These will be automatically converted to parameter markers when the code is inserted into the implementation module.

In the **Implementation** tab, use the default implementation module name. Clicking **Finish** will generate the embedded SQL program code for the stored procedure and add it to your project. The Visual C++ project should now contain the following two files:

- *.sqx - This is the C/C++ source file containing the embedded SQL code.
- *.cxx - This is the C/C++ source file generated when the corresponding sqx module is precompiled using the DB2 precompiler.

An automatic Visual C++ custom build step is added to your project to precompile every embedded SQL source file to its corresponding plain C/C++ file.

Fig. 6–17 shows the generated embedded SQL code for the stored procedure. Note that the host variable is convered to a parameter marker.

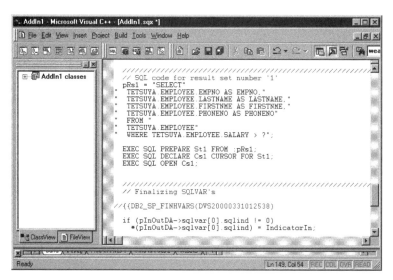

Fig. 6–17 *Generated embedded SQL code*

If you want to create more stored procedures in the project, click the **New DB2 Object** add-in tool bar button again, and repeat the steps described in this section.

To generate the DLL file, select **Rebuild All** from the **Build** menu. The project should build successfully. The custom build step will pre-compile the embedded SQL module and generate its corresponding C/C++ source file. The file is then compiled normally and the project DLL is linked. All messages generated during the compilation will be displayed in the output pane.

Packaging the DB2 Component

Once the Visual C++ project has been built, you should have a binary DLL file, the data definition language file including CREATE PROCEDURE statements for the stored procedures, and a collection of bind files. Some or all of these files can be packaged so that they may be deployed to any number of DB2 UDB database on any number of machines. Keep in mind that the binary generated here is a Win32 DLL and should thus only be deployed to Windows 32-bit operating systems. To create a DB2 project package, do the following:

1. Select the DB2 Visual C++ project, including stored procedures you built in the previous section.

2. Click the **Package DB2 Project** add-in tool bar icon. This will launch the Package DB2 Project dialog (Fig. 6–18).

3. Select the project binary to be included as part of the package. This can be the `debug/AddIn1.dll` or `release/AddIn1.dll`, depending on whether or not you built this project in debug or release mode. Also specify the package name, the directory path where the package will be created, and the bind list file listing the bind files for this project.

4. Click the **OK** button to create the package.

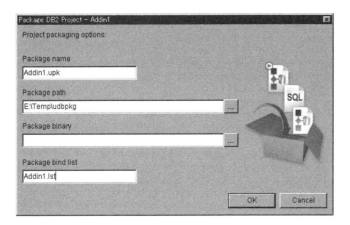

Fig. 6–18 *Packaging DB2 Project*

The package progress dialog box will be displayed, showing the status of the project packaging. Once completed, a message box will be displayed, indicating a successful package creation.

The act of packaging a project involves the following:

- Creating the package directory
- Copying the project binary to the package directory (if specified)
- Copying the embedded SQL module bind files (if any)
- Creating the bind list file enumerating all the bind files (if any)
- Creating the stored procedures definition, DDL, file (if any)
- Creating the package definition file

The package directory may be zipped and copied over to any remote system for later deployment if the remote system is not accessible from the current development machine.

Deploying the Packaged DB2 Component

A packaged DB2 Visual C++ project may be deployed against a DB2 database on the production system which is the same as, or is accessible from, the development system.

To deploy the packaged DB2 Visual C++ project from the Visual C++ integrated development environment, perform the following steps:

1. Select the DB2 Visual C++ project.

2. Make sure that the project is built and packaged.

3. Click the **Deploy DB2 Project** add-in tool bar icon. It will launch the Deploy DB2 Project dialog (Fig. 6–19).

4. Select the target database from the drop-in list, and then click **OK**. The deploy progress dialog box will be displayed showing the status of the project deployment

Once completed, a message box will be displayed, indicating a successful project deployment

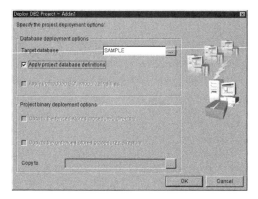

Fig. 6–19 *Deploying DB2 Project*

The act of deploying a project package involves the following:

- Applying the stored procedures DDL file to the deployment database
- Binding the bind list file to the deployment database
- Copying the project binary to the desired file system target location(s)

Deployment is not restricted to one database. It can be done any number of times to any number of databases accessible from the deployment location.

To deploy a project binary, the destination must be a Windows 32-bit operating system. For example, you cannot deploy a list of exported stored procedures to an OS/390 database, because the DLL created by the DB2 UDB Project add-in is compatible only with Windows 32-bit operating systems. However, you can use an OS/390 database as a source for creating Windows 32-bit operating system client applications that access OS/390 stored procedures. You can also create Windows 32-bit operating system client applications that access the OS/390 database using embedded SQL modules.

Once you have built and deployed stored procedure projects against DB2 databases, you can use them from your client applications. Your client applications do not have to use the same language as the stored procedures. Since our example stored procedure returns a result set, the client application program must use the CLI or higher (ODBC, JDBC, SQLJ, or ADO) application programming interface. The method to receive result set from a stored procedure using ADO is described in Chapter 5.

Building
Applications
Using Visual C++

Using Microsoft Transaction Server

- ◆ OVERVIEW
- ◆ MTS ARCHITECTURE
- ◆ MTS CONCEPTS AND PROCEDURES
- ◆ CREATING MTS COMPONENTS
- ◆ USING MTS EXPLORER
- ◆ SECURITY CONSIDERATIONS

*O*ver time, it has become apparent that the two-tier client/server model is simply not flexible or powerful (scalable) enough to handle many larger applications. Maintaining a dialog between each client workstation and the central database server can result in high network traffic and poor performance, for example, when many users try to do simultaneous access to a database.

Three-tier client server applications help address these issues by putting another layer between the users and the database — the application server. This type of central application service can manage network traffic and database server loads more efficiently.

Typically, the application layer handles most of the business services, and may be implemented on its own server computer, separate from the database. One of the main advantages of a three-tier architecture is the ability to extract the business logic from the user and data tiers and into the middle tier, where it is easier to maintain.

Historically, the transition from simple, single-user desktop applications to distributed multi-user, three-tier applications has been a difficult and time-consuming activity. A significant amount of development time must be spent to merely create the application architecture under which distributed multi-user, three-tier applications can run. Microsoft Transaction Server (MTS) eases the transition from single-user to multi-user development by providing the application infrastructure and administrative support for building scalable, robust enterprise applications.

Microsoft Transaction Server (MTS) is a component-based transaction processing system for building, deploying, and administering server applications. MTS defines a programming model, and provides a run-time environment and graphical administration tool for managing enterprise applications.

IBM DB2 Family products can be fully integrated with MTS Version 2.0. In this chapter, we will describe the architecture and concepts of MTS, and then show how to get MTS and DB2 UDB to work together, using an example.

Benefits of Microsoft Transaction Server

MTS provides with the following benefits and services:

- Business object platform

  MTS provides an infrastructure for developing middle-tier business objects.

- Transaction support

  Transactions provide an all-or-nothing simple model for managing work. Either all of the objects succeed and all of the work is committed, or one or more of the objects fail and none of the work is committed.

  MTS automatically support transactions for components. MTS will also automatically handle cleanup and rollback of a failed transaction. No extra transaction management code has to be written for the business components.

- Concurrency model

  In a multi-user environment, a component can receive simultaneous calls from multiple clients. In addition, a distributed application can have its business logic running in multiple processes on more than one computer. Synchronization of object services must be implemented in order to avoid problems such as deadlocks and race conditions.

  MTS provides a simple concurrency model based on activities. An activity is the path of execution that occurs from the time a client calls an MTS object, until that object completes the client request.

- Fault tolerance and isolation

    MTS performs extensive internal integrity and consistency checks. If MTS encounters an unexpected internal error condition, it immediately terminates the process. This policy, called failfast, facilitates fault containment and results in more reliable, robust systems.

    Components can be run in Windows NT server processes separate from Microsoft Internet Information Server (IIS) or the client application. In this manner, if a component catastrophically fails (throws an unhandled exception), it will not cause the client process to terminate as well.

- Resource Management

    As an application scales to a larger number of clients, system resources (such as network connections, database connections, memory, and disk-space) must be utilized effectively. To improve scalability, objects in the application must share resources and use them only when necessary.

    MTS maximizes resources by using a number of techniques such as thread management, just-in-time (JIT) object activation, resource pooling, and in future versions, object pooling.

- Security

    Because more than one client can use an application, a method of authentication and authorization must be used to ensure that only authorized users can access business logic.

    MTS provides declarative security by allowing the developer to define roles. A role defines a logical set of users (Windows NT user accounts) that are allowed to invoke components through their interfaces.

- Distributed computing support

    A transaction typically uses many different server components that may reside on different computers. A transaction can also access multiple databases. Microsoft Transaction Server tracks components on multiple computers, and manages distributed transactions for those components automatically.

Using Microsoft Transaction Server

Transaction Processing Concepts

A transaction is an action that changes a set of data from one state to another. For instance, a customer depositing money in a checking account constitutes a banking transaction.

In Fig. 7–1, three business objects work together to transfer money from one account to another. The Debit object debits an account and the Credit object credits an account. The Transfer object calls the Debit and Credit objects to transfer the money.

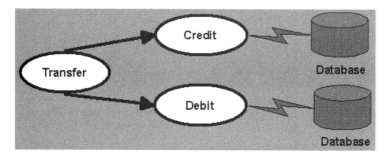

Fig. 7–1 *Transaction Process*

For a transaction to succeed, it must have the following properties, commonly known as the ACID (Atomicity, Consistency, Isolation, and Durability) test.

- **Atomicity** means that a transaction is an indivisible unit of work: all of its actions succeed or they all fail.
- **Consistency** means that after a transaction executes, it must leave the system in a correct state or it must abort. If the transaction cannot achieve a stable end state, it must return the system to its initial state.

  In the transaction described earlier, money can be debited from one account and not yet credited to the other account during the transfer process. When the transaction is finished and able to commit, either both the debit and credit occur, or neither occurs.
- **Isolation** ensures that concurrent transactions are not aware of each other's partial and uncommitted results. Otherwise, they might create inconsistencies in the application state.

  For example, in the transaction of transferring money, if two transfers occur at the same time, neither will know of the partial debit or credit from an incomplete transfer.
- **Durability** ensures that committed updates to managed resources (such as database records) survive communication, process, and server system failures. Transactional logging enables you to recover the durable state after failures.

Together these properties ensure that a transaction does not create problematic changes to data between the time that the transaction begins and the time that it must commit.

This period of a transaction constitutes one part of a two-phase commit process. The second phase occurs when all the business objects used in a transaction process are successful and can proceed with the commitment.

MTS Architecture

Microsoft Transaction Server introduces a new programming and run-time environment model that is an extension of the Microsoft standard Component Object Model (COM). The basic structure of the MTS run-time environment involves several parts working together to handle transaction-based components.

MTS and the Supporting Environment

The MTS architecture comprises one or more clients, application components, and a set of system services. The application components model the activity of a business by implementing business rules and providing the objects that clients request at run-time. Components that share resources can be packaged to enable efficient use of server resources.

The diagram in Fig. 7–2 shows the structure of the MTS run-time environment (including the MTS components) and the system services that support transactions.

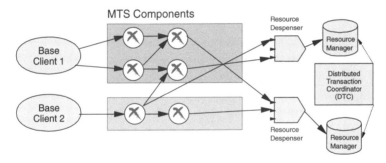

Fig. 7–2 *MTS Run Time Environment*

Base Client

The base client is the application that invokes a COM component running under the MTS environment. The base client could be a Visual Basic executable (EXE) file running on the same Windows NT server computer, or running on a client computer that communicates through a network.

MTS Components

MTS components are COM components that are registered to run in the MTS environment. These COM components must be created as in-process dynamic link libraries (DLLs), although more than one COM component can be placed in a single DLL.

COM components created specifically for the MTS environment commonly contain special code that takes advantage of transactions, security, and other MTS capabilities. The process of creating transaction components is explained in the section "Creating MTS Components" on page 325.

System Services

The diagram above, Fig. 7–2, illustrates several important parts of MTS:

- Resource managers are system services that manage durable data. Resource managers work in cooperation with Microsoft Distributed Transaction Coordinator to guarantee atomicity and isolation of an application. IBM DB2 Family products, including DB2 UDB for Windows NT, can be resource managers in the MTS environment.

- Resource dispensers manage non-durable shared state on behalf of the application components within a process. Resource dispensers are similar to resource managers, but without the guarantee of durability. Resource dispensers are responsible for database connection pooling.

  MTS provides two resource dispensers: the ODBC resource dispenser (for ODBC databases) and the Shared Property Manager for synchronized access to application-defined, process-wide properties (variables).

- Microsoft Distributed Transaction Coordinator is a system service that coordinates transactions among resource managers. Work can be committed as an atomic transaction even if it spans multiple resource managers on separate computers.

MTS Packages

A package is a container for a set of components that perform related application functions. All components in a package run together in the same MTS server process. A package is both a trust boundary that defines when security credentials are verified, and a deployment unit for a set of components.

MTS Explorer is typically used to register COM components as MTS components through a two-step process. First, an MTS package is created. Then the COM components are added to the package. This process is described in the section "Using MTS Explorer" on page 331.

Package Location

Components in a package can be located on the same computer as Microsoft Transaction Server on which they are being registered, or they can be distributed across multiple computers. Components in the same DLL can be registered in different MTS packages. Note the following limitations and recommendations.

- A COM component can only be added to one package per computer.

- Because COM components in the same DLL can share programmatic and operating system resources, place related COM components in the same DLL.

- Because MTS components in the same package share the same MTS security level and resources, place related MTS components in the same package.

Package Rules

The following relationships between the MTS parts are important to note:

- Packages typically define separate process boundaries. Whenever a method call in an activity crosses such a boundary, security checking and fault isolation occur.

- Components can call across package boundaries to components in other packages. Such calls can access existing components or create new components.

- On a single computer, an MTS component may only be installed once. The same component cannot exist in multiple packages in the same machine. However, multiple copies (objects) of the same component can be created and can exist at any time.

MTS Concepts and Processes

Popular tools such as Visual Basic, Visual C++, or Visual J++ to easily build server applications that run within the MTS environment. The MTS architecture utilizes several important concepts and processes to implement the complexity behind transaction processing in a distributed enterprise system.

Activities

All MTS objects run in activities. An activity is a set of objects that run on behalf of a base client application to completely fulfill its request. When an object runs in an activity, it can create additional objects to perform work. All of these objects will run within the same activity and can be viewed as running on a single logical thread. The objects in an activity can be distributed across one or more processes, and can execute on one or more computers.

Every MTS object belongs to one activity. This is an intrinsic property of the object and is recorded in the object's context. The association between an object and an activity cannot be changed. MTS tracks the flow of execution through each activity, preventing inadvertent parallelism from corrupting the application state. This simplifies writing components for Microsoft Transaction Server.

Contexts

A context is an object associated with another object. It is a programmatic and run-time entity that is used to keep track of the state and support processing of its associated object. The MTS run-time environment manages a context for each object.

MTS Context Objects

MTS creates a context object for each MTS server component. As the component runs within the activity, the context object tracks properties of that component, including the activation state, its security information, and transaction state (if any). This frees the object from tracking its own state.

Transaction Context Objects

When multiple objects participate in a single transaction, the associated context objects work together to track the transaction. MTS uses a transaction context object to ensure that the transaction is consistent for all objects. The transaction context object, in conjunction with each of the individual context objects, guarantees that the whole transaction either commits or aborts.

Server Process

A server process is a system process that hosts the execution of one or more MTS components. A server process can service tens, hundreds, or potentially thousands of clients.

Each package has an associated activation property, and the package can be associated with one of the following activation types:

- Library Package

  Components will be activated in the creator's process.
- Server Package

  Components will be activated in a dedicated server process.

Some MTS capabilities, such as security checking and fault tolerance, are only enabled for server package activation.

Automatic Transactions

MTS supports both objects that need transactions and objects that do not.

If an object requires a transaction, MTS creates the transaction when the object is called. When the object returns to the client, the transaction either commits or aborts. When you place components in MTS, all of the infrastructure for processing and managing a transaction is provided for you.

Just-In-Time Activation

Just-in-time activation is the ability for transactional MTS objects to be activated only as needed for executing requests from clients. Objects can be deactivated even while clients hold references to them, allowing otherwise idle server resources to be used more productively. A deactivated object may be completely discarded from memory and created anew when required by another call from the client.

Creating MTS Components

This section describes the requirements of MTS components. It also explains how to add transactional support to your business objects.

You will learn how to obtain access to context objects, and how to indicate that a transaction has been completed or aborted.

Requirements for MTS Components

MTS components are COM components that have been registered in the MTS environment. These components have the following requirements and restrictions:

- MTS components must be implemented as in-process dynamically linked libraries (DLLs). Components that are implemented as executable (EXE) files cannot execute in the MTS run-time environment.

- MTS components should follow proper COM conventions, including a standard class factory, a complete type library, and should use standard marshaling.

- MTS components should be designed as single threaded or apartment-threaded. Apartment-threaded components are more scalable than single-threaded ones.

- MTS components should neither create threads nor terminate threads. This is a strong recommendation, because MTS manages threads and synchronizes MTS activities for you automatically.

- An MTS component should not programmatically alter its process security. The declarative security features of MTS should be used instead.

- MTS components should be stateless; they should not maintain local data between client calls. Stateless objects are more scalable than stateful ones.

Declarative security and package identity are discussed in "Declarative Security: Roles and Identities" on page 338.

Adding Transactional Support

You can easily modify your existing business components so that they become part of a transaction as server-based MTS components.

Support for Transactions

You can use MTS to modify an object so that it supports transactions. In the MTS transaction processing model, each object simply reports to MTS whether it was successful in completing its client's request. MTS handles the complexity of synchronizing activities and transaction processing (committing or aborting the transaction). MTS eliminates the need to call any transaction functions, such as BeginTrans() or EndTrans().

When an object is created, Microsoft Transaction Server creates a corresponding context object. ObjectContext supplies methods through the IObjectContext interface. Commonly used methods include:

- SetComplete

  The SetComplete method informs the context object that it can commit transaction updates, and can release the state of the object along with any resources that are being held. If and only if all other objects involved in the transaction also call SetComplete, the context object will commit the transaction updates of all objects.

- SetAbort

  The SetAbort method signifies that the operation failed. SetAbort informs the ObjectContext object that the transaction updates must be rolled back to their original states. If one or more MTS objects in an activity call SetAbort, the transaction will roll back even if other objects have called the SetComplete method. Typically, SetAbort is called just prior to an MTS object's method exiting.

- CreateInstance

  The CreateInstance method is used by the MTS component to create another object.

Adding Transactions to an MTS Object

To add transactional support to an MTS component, use the following procedure:

1. Using the `GetObjectContext` function, obtain a reference to the component's corresponding context object, as in the following Visual Basic 6.0 example code:

```
Dim ctxObject As ObjectContext
Set ctxObject = GetObjectContext()
```

> **Note:** To call the `GetObjectContext` function in Visual Basic 6, you must set a reference to Microsoft Transaction Server Type Library (mtxas.dll) by selecting References on the Project menu.

2. After the component has executed its logic, determine the outcome of that process.

   If the component was successful, call the context object's `SetComplete` method. The following example code updates `employee` table in the database, and calls `SetComplete` to indicate it has completed work successfully:

```
Dim ctxObject As ObjectContext
Set ctxObject = GetObjectContext()
Set conn = CreateObject("ADODB.connection")
conn.Open "DSN=Sample;UID=db2admin;PWD=db2admin;"
conn.Execute "UPDATE employee SET salary=3000 WHERE empno=20"
ctxObject.SetComplete
```

   If a component was unsuccessful, call the context object's `SetAbort` method as following:

```
ictxObject.SetAbort
```

   For more about `ObjectContext`, refer to the source code of "Server Project — db2com.vbp" on page 350.

Using Microsoft Transaction Server

Handling Errors

MTS performs extensive internal integrity and consistency checks. In this way, MTS automatically provides fault isolation to maximize the robustness of applications. However, as a component developer, you may want to design your components to take a more active role in error handling.

Unhandled Errors in MTS Components

MTS does not allow unhandled errors to propagate outside of an MTS component. If an error occurs while executing within an MTS context and the component doesn't catch the error before returning from the context, MTS catches the error and terminates the process. Using the failfast policy in this case is based on the assumption that the exceptional condition has put the process into an indeterminate state — it is not safe to continue processing.

MTS interprets all aborted processes as exceptional conditions. If the transaction aborts and you do not raise an error to the client, MTS will force an error to be raised. It will set the HRESULT return value to CONTEXT_E_ABORTED informing the client that the call aborted. However, if an MTS object has set an HRESULT error code, MTS never changes this returned value.

Types of Errors

There are three types of errors that can occur in an MTS application: business rule errors, internal errors, and Windows exceptions.

Business Rule Errors

When an activity performs an operation that violates business rules, the activity causes a business rule error. This would be an error such as a client attempting to withdraw money from an empty account. These types of errors must be detected by the MTS objects that you write. They enforce the business rules by checking client actions against existing business rules. For example, a debit object should check an account balance before withdrawing money.

Business rules can also be enforced in the database itself. For example, if a client attempts to withdraw money from an empty account, it may be the database that catches and raises the error (back to the Debit object).

In either cases, abort the current transaction by calling SetAbort and report the error to the MTS client.

Internal Errors

Internal errors are unexpected errors that occur while objects are working on behalf of a client. For example, a file could be missing, network problems could prevent connecting to a database, or creation of a dependent COM component could fail.

In Visual Basic, these errors will be detected and raised by Visual Basic itself. Like business rules errors, you can write code to trap these errors, and then attempt to correct them or abort the transaction.

Optionally, you may want to raise the error to the client using the `Err.Raise` method to pass the same error back. This will inform the client that an error occurred, and that it must display an appropriate error message. The client should take appropriate action, for example by displaying a friendly error message to the user, or by recording the error in an event log.

Windows Exceptions

If for some reason your MTS object causes a Windows exception (a crash), MTS will shut down the process that hosts the object and log an error event in the NT event log. As described above, this process is called failfast. When a failfast occurs, the process hosting the object is terminated. An `HRESULT` indicating the type of error will be returned to the client.

The MTS run time can also raise exceptions that cause your object to fail. In this case, your object automatically aborts.

Description of Standard MTS Error Codes

Table 7–3 shows the standard MTS error code:

Table 7–3 *Standard MTS Error Codes*

MTS error Code	Description
S_OK	The call succeeded.
E_INVALIDARG	One or more of the arguments passed in is invalid.
E_UNEXPECTED	An unexpected error occurred.
CONTEXT_E_NOCONTEXT	The current object doesn't have a context associated with it. This is probably either because its component hasn't been installed in a package or it wasn't created with one of the MTS CreateInstance methods.
CONTEXT_E_ROLENOTFOUND	The role specified in the szRole parameter in the IObjectContext::IsCallerInRole method does not exist.

Table 7–3 *Standard MTS Error Codes*

MTS error Code	Description
E_OUTOFMEMORY	There's not enough memory available to instantiate the object. This error code can be returned by IObjectContext::CreateInstance or ITransactionContext::CreateInstance.
REGDB_E_CLASSNOTREG	There's not enough memory available to instantiate the object. This error code can be returned by IObjectContext::CreateInstance or ITransactionContext::CreateInstance.
DISP_E_ARRAYISLOCKED	One or more of the arguments passed in contains an array that is locked. This error code can be returned by the ISharedProperty::put_Value method.
DISP_E_BADVARTYPE	One or more of the arguments passed in isn't a valid VARIANT type. This error code can be returned by the ISharedProperty::put_Value method.

Creating Efficient Objects

Transaction components place a heavy demand on server resources, but certain programming techniques enable you to gain the maximum efficiency from transaction components. You need to consider the network, database, and processing resources used by the component in the transaction, and how long an object will be active.

Stateless Objects

While an object is active, it maintains data. An object is referred to as "stateful" if data is maintained across multiple client calls. An object is "stateless" if the data is reset with each client call. In general, Microsoft Transaction Server objects should be stateless. Using stateless objects provides the following benefits:

- It helps ensure transaction isolation and database consistency by not introducing data from one transaction to another.
- It reduces the server load by not storing data indefinitely.
- It improves scalability because of the reduced server load and because there are fewer internal data dependencies in the stateless object.

Components built with Visual Basic have Initialize and Terminate events that you can use to create and free resources that the component needs to run. Data created in the Initialize event and maintained across multiple client calls is stateful data and should be avoided. If the component requires localized data to be created during startup, the component should expose the `Activate` and `DeActivate` methods instead.

There are a number of ways in which you can improve the efficiency of the objects you manage using Microsoft Transaction Server.

- Pass arguments by value (`ByVal`) whenever possible. The `ByVal` keyword minimizes trips across networks.
- Use methods that accept all of the property values as arguments. Avoid exposing object properties. Each time a client accesses an object property, it makes at least one round-trip call across the network.
- Avoid passing or returning objects. Passing object references across process and network boundaries wastes time.
- Avoid creating database cursors. Cursors create a large amount of overhead. Whenever you create a Recordset object, ActiveX Data Objects (ADO) creates a cursor. Instead of creating `Recordset` objects, run SQL commands whenever possible.
- When making updates, keep resources locked for as short a time as possible. This will maximize the availability of resources to other objects.
- Enable Microsoft Transaction Server to run simultaneous client requests through objects by making them apartment-threaded. In Visual Basic 6, you make objects apartment-threaded by selecting the Apartment-Threaded option in the Project Properties dialog box.

Using MTS Explorer

Microsoft Transaction Server Explorer is a component of Microsoft Management Console (MMC). It is the graphical interface that you use to create, distribute, install, export, import, maintain, and manage MTS packages and their components.

MTS Explorer does the following to help you work with transactions:

- It creates packages, adds MTS components to packages, creates roles; and helps monitor and debug MTS components.
- It installs, imports, and exports packages; assigns identities to packages; maps roles to NT users; troubleshoots and profiles MTS activities.
- It updates and maintains packages, manages NT users mapped to roles, monitors MTS transactions, and manually resolves transactions under failure conditions.

Using Microsoft Transaction Server

Creating Packages

To run a transaction on MTS, you must first create a new package to hold all components of a transaction.

Perform the following steps to create a new, empty package:

1. In the left pane of the MTS Explorer window, select the computer for which you want to create a new package.

2. Expand the tree under that computer and select the Packages Installed folder.

3. Start the Package Wizard by performing the following:

    On the **Action** menu, click **New**, and then click **Package**. Right-click the **Installed Packages** icon. Click **New**, and then click **Package**. Click on the **Create a new object** button on the MTS toolbar.

4. In the Package Wizard, click the **Create an Empty Package** button.

5. Enter a name for the new package, and then click **Next**.

6. In the **Set Package Identity** dialog box, select either the Interactive User or specify an existing NT user account.

The default selection for package identity is **Interactive User**. The interactive user is the user that logged on to the server computer on which the package is running. Use this setting during the development of MTS components.

For more information about declarative identity and security, see "Declarative Security: Roles and Identities" on page 338.

Fig. 7–3 shows the Package Wizard window:

Fig. 7–3 *Package Wizard*

Setting Package Properties

Once you have created a package, you can set package properties, such as how the package is accessed, how it participates in the security system, and how it ends when the system is shut down.

To set properties for a package, right-click the package in Microsoft Transaction Server Explorer, and then click Properties. The Package Properties dialog boxes will be displayed.

General Package Properties

Table 7–4 describes the basic package properties and lists the tabs under which they can be set:

Table 7–4 *General Package Properties*

Property	Description	Tab
Name	Friendly name of the package (ID number is also listed).	General
Description	Displays a description of the package.	General
Authorization	Enables Microsoft Transaction Server to check the security credentials of any client that calls the package.	Security

Table 7–4 *General Package Properties*

Property	Description	Tab
Process Shutdown	Determines whether the server process associated with a package always runs, or whether it shuts down after a specified period of idle time.	Advanced
Account	Specifies the identity of the package. This is set during package creation.	Identity
Activation Type	Specifies either Library or Server activation for the package.	Activation

Activation Property

You use an activation property of a transaction server package to specify the process where the package's components will run when activated. The activation property determines whether the components in a package will run (as a group) in a separate, new server process (a server package) or will run in their caller's process (a library package). MTS security and fault tolerance are only available for server packages.

Table 7–5 describes the activation property settings for a transaction server component.

Table 7–5 *Activation Property Settings*

Setting	Description	Advantage
Library Package	Will run in the same process as the client that creates it.	Minimum overhead.
Server Package	Will run in its separate process; shared by all the components in the current package.	Fault tolerance, package security enabled.

During development, a component should be generally activated as a server package to prevent any faults that may occur from crashing other processes.

Adding Components to a Package

Once you have created a new package, you can add components to manage related business services. A component can be included only in one package on a single computer, so you must decide how to combine components into packages.

Perform the following steps to add a component to a package:

1. In the left pane of the MTS Explorer window, open the Packages Installed folder, and then expand the package for which you want to install a component.

2. Select the Components folder (under the Packages Installed folder).

3. Start the Component Wizard by performing one of the following:

    On the **Action** menu, click **New**, and then click **Component**. Right-click the **Installed Packages icon**, click New, and then click Package. Click on the **Create a new object** button on the MTS toolbar.

4. Click the **Install New Component(s)** button.

5. In the Install Components dialog box, click **Add Files** to select the component.The component should include all of the files that are used to implement the component. If the component has an external type library or proxy/stub DLL, also add those files.

6. In the **Select Files to Install** dialog box, select the files you want to add, and then click **Open**.

7. In the **Install Components** dialog box, click **Finish**.

Fig. 7–4 shows the Component wizard for adding components to the package.

Using Microsoft Transaction Server

Fig. 7–4 *Component Wizard*

Component Locations and Versioning

Only proper COM in-process components with type library information are recognized by MTS. Other files are ignored.

Adding a component to a package does not physically copy or move the implementation file (usually a DLL) from its original folder location; it simply registers it with MTS. You can force package processes to shut down, which is common when replacing one or more MTS components with a newer version. Shutting down the server processes forces the MTS run time to unload DLLs from memory.

To shut down a package process, right-click **My Computer** in the left pane of the MTS Explorer window and click **Shutdown Server Processes**.

Note: If later you change the name or physical location of the component implementation file, or you replace it with a newer component implementation with a different type library, you must re-register the component in MTS. MTS does not track file changes automatically.

Setting Component Properties

When you set the properties of a component at design time, determine the process in which the component will run and define the component's role with respect to the current transaction.

To set the properties of a component, right-click the component in the MTS Explorer window, and then click **Properties**.

Transaction Property

Each transaction server component has a transaction property. Whenever an instance of a component is created, MTS checks the transaction property of the component to determine whether it needs a transaction to do its work.

Most MTS components are marked as either **Supports Transactions** or **Requires a Transaction**. Fig. 7–5 shows MTS component properties for the Transaction tab:

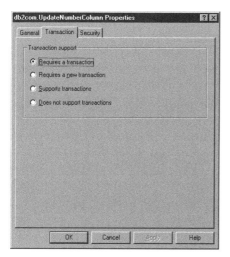

Fig. 7–5 *MTS Component Properties*

Security Considerations

This section describes the declarative security model of MTS. This section also mentions how to use MTS Explorer to set the security properties of packages and components.

Declarative Security: Roles and Identities

The traditional approach to file security in the Windows NT operating system is to define users and user groups (typically with the User Manager for Domains administrative tool), and then set access permissions for a file (typically with Windows Explorer).

Because of security considerations at both the development and distribution phases of a project, MTS extends the traditional approach to security through declarative security. With this approach, security is configured directly with MTS Explorer. In declarative security, MTS introduces the concept of *package roles*.

MTS Roles

A role is a logical group of users that defines security access to the components of a package. Roles are created at development time by the component programmer or Web developer. Roles are subsequently mapped onto actual NT users and user groups during package deployment, by the Web developer or administrator.

The following list describes two important consequences of the role architecture:

- Packages define security boundaries.

  MTS uses roles to determine who can use an MTS component any time a call is made into the package. Method calls from one component to another inside a package are not checked because components in the same package trust each other.

- Security is checked for each method call that crosses packages boundaries.

  MTS checks security on each method call because it is possible for one client (that is authorized) to pass an interface pointer to another client (that may not be authorized). MTS also checks security when a client creates an object from outside of the package.

MTS Package Identity

By default, components take on, or impersonate, the process identity of the calling client. For example, if a process started by the Windows NT guest account calls a component, then that component operates with the security privileges of the guest account. MTS introduces the new concept of package identities to give components a separate, independent security identification.

Rather than impersonate the client, MTS packages typically use declarative identity features of MTS to associate themselves with a Windows NT user account. Therefore, when any component in the package accesses resources such as files or databases, the component's access rights correspond to this identity.

Package identities are set during deployment.

Setting Package Security

Using declarative security to set MTS package roles is a three-step process:

1. During package creation, associate one or more roles with the package. Existing roles can be used or new roles can be created at this time.

2. During deployment time, map Windows NT users and groups to roles.

3. Enable security at the package and component level. If you do not enable security for the package, then roles for the component or interface will not be checked by MTS. In addition, if you do not have security enabled for a component, MTS will not check roles for the component's interface.

Creating and Assigning Security Roles

After you have created a package and added components to it, you can create roles for that package. Roles are defined at the package level and, once created, are mapped to components or interfaces within the package.

Perform the following steps to create a new role:

1. In the left pane of the MTS Explorer window, select the package that will include the role.

2. Double-click the **Roles** folder.

3. On the **Action** menu, click **New**, and then click Role.

4. Type the name of the new role, and then click **OK.**

Fig. 7–6 shows the New Role dialog box:

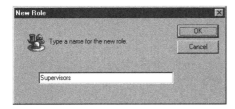

Fig. 7–6 *New Role Window for the Package*

Then, perform the following steps to assign roles to a component or interface:

1. In the left pane of the MTS Explorer, select the component or interface that will include the role.

2. Double-click the Role Membership folder.

3. On the **Action** menu, click **New**, and then click **Role**.

4. In the **Select Roles** dialog box, select the roles you want to add to the component and click **OK**.

Mapping Users to Roles

When you install and deploy your application, you must map Windows NT users and groups to any existing roles. The roles to which you map users determine wha components and interfaces those users can access.

Perform the following steps to assign users to roles:

1. In the left pane of the MTS Explorer window, open the package in which you will assign users to roles.

2. Open the **Roles** folder and double-click the role to which you want to assign users.

3. Open the **Users** folder.

4. On the **Action** menu, click **New**, and then click **Users**.

5. In the **Add Users and Groups** to Role dialog box, add user names or groups t the role.

6. Use the **Show Users** and **Search** buttons to locate a user account and then clic OK.

Enabling Security

There are two levels at which security is enabled: package-level security and component-level security. Package-level security is set once at the package level. Component-level security is set at the component level for each component in the package.

Table 7–6 shows the implications of enabling or disabling authorization checking for packages and components.

Table 7–6 *Authorization Checking for Packages and Components*

Package security	Component security	Result
Enabled	Enabled	Security is enabled for the component.
Enabled	Disabled	Security is disabled for the component, but will be enabled for other components that have security enabled.
Disabled	Enabled or Disabled	Security is disabled for all components.

Perform the following steps to enable or disable authorization checking for packages or components:

1. In the left pane of the MTS Explorer window, click the package or component.

2. Right-click the package or component, and click **Properties**.

3. Click the **Security** property sheet.

4. Select or clear **Enable authorization checking**.

Setting package identity

There are two general identity types a package can assume:

- The interactive user (the default)

  This setting allows the package to assume the identity of the currently logged on user. However, if no user is logged on to the server when a client accesses the package, the package will fail to create a server process. This identity is often used for development testing purposes.

- A specific Windows NT user account

  This setting assigns a specific Windows NT user account to the package. When a client accesses the package, it creates a server process using this account as its identity. All components running in the package share this identity.

Perform the following steps to set package identity:

1. Select the package whose identity you want to change.

2. On the **Action** menu, click **Properties** and select the **Identity** tab.

3. To set the identity to a user account, select **This user** and enter the user domain followed by a backslash (\), user name, and password for the Windows NT user account.

4. Or, to set the identity to **Interactive User**, select the Interactive User option.

Fig. 7–7 shows the Identity tab of the Properties sheet:

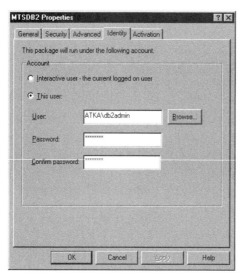

Fig. 7–7 *Package Properties*

Package Identity and Database Access

Package identity is important when your MTS components access databases because database connections can be pooled. Connections are pooled based on userids and passwords, so if a process has many connections using the same userid and password, they can be pooled. If components impersonate clients, each userid is different and the connections cannot be pooled. By using package identity, each component can use the same userid and each connection can be pooled.

Getting DB2 UDB and MTS to Work Together

IBM DB2 Family products can be fully integrated with MTS Version 2.0. Your DB2 applications that are running on Windows 32-bit operating systems can obtain benefits from MTS, such as two-phase commit support. This section describes how to get DB2 UDB and MTS to work together.

Software Prerequisites

MTS support requires DB2 Client Version 5.2 or later, and MTS must be at Version 2.0 with Hotfix 0772 or later releases.

The DB2 Client is a point of contact to DB2 databases for MTS. It is included in the DB2 UDB Server product, or it can be installed as an independent software product ("DB2 UDB Clients" on page 6). You can install the DB2 UDB Server product Version 5.2 or later on the same machine where the MTS application runs, in order to get it to work with MTS. Or, the alternative is installing the DB2 Client Version 5.2 or later on the same machine where the MTS application runs, and configuring the client to access other remote DB2 servers. If you want MTS applications to access host or AS/400 database servers, you need to install DB2 Connect Enterprise Edition on the local or remote machine (see "DB2 UDB Products" on page 5).

The following DB2 servers are supported for MTS-coordinated transactions:

- DB2 UDB Enterprise Edition Version 5.2 or later
- DB2 UDB Enterprise Edition for AIX Version 5.0 with PTF U453782
- DB2 UDB Enterprise Edition for HP-UX Version 5.0 with PTF U453784
- DB2 UDB Enterprise Edition for Solaris Version 5.0 with PTF U453783
- DB2 UDB Enterprise Edition for OS/2 Version 5.0 with PTF WR09033
- DB2 UDB Enterprise Edition for Windows NT Version 5.0 with PTF WR09034
- DB2 for OS/390
- DB2 for MVS
- DB2 for AS/400
- DB2 for VM&VSE
- DB2 Parallel Edition Version 1.2
- DB2 Common Server for SCO, Version 2
- DB2 Universal Database Extended Enterprise Edition for UNIX or Windows NT

Using Microsoft Transaction Server

Installation and Configuration

To get DB2 UDB to work with MTS, perform the following steps:

- Install MTS and the DB2 Client (or DB2 Server) on the same machine where the MTS application runs.
- If host or AS/400 database servers are to be involved in an MTS-coordinated transaction, install a DB2 Connect product on the local or remote machine and configure it.
- Set the TP_MON_NAME database manager configuration parameter to MTS on the machine where the DB2 Client runs with MTS.

To set the TP_MON_NAME database manager configuration parameter to MTS, start a Command Line Processor by selecting **Start -> Programs -> IBM DB2 -> Command Line Processor**, and execute the following command from the window:

```
UPDATE DBM CFG USING TP_MON_NAME MTS
```

CLI/ODBC Configuration Keywords

When running DB2 CLI/ODBC applications, the following configuration keywords (as set in the db2cli.ini file) must not be changed from their default values:

- CONNECTYPE keyword (default value is 1)
- MULTICONNECT keyword (default value is 1)
- DISABLEMULTITHREAD keyword (default value is 1)
- CONNECTIONPOOLING keyword (default value is 0)
- KEEPCONNECT keyword (default value is 0)

DB2 CLI applications written to make use of MTS support must not change the attribute values corresponding to the above keywords. In addition, the applications must not change the default values of the following attributes:

- SQL_ATTR_CONNECT_TYPE attribute (default value is SQL_CONCURRENT_TRANS)
- SQL_ATTR_CONNECTON_POOLING attribute (default value is SQL_CP_OFF)

See the *DB2 UDB Call Level Interface Guide and Reference* for detailed descriptions of these keywords and attributes.

MTS Transaction Time-Out and DB2 Connection Behavior

You can set the transaction time-out value in the MTS Explorer tool. For more information, refer to the online MTS Administrator Guide. If a transaction takes longer than the transaction time-out value (default value is 60 seconds), MTS will asynchronously issue an abort to all Resource Managers involved, and the whole transaction is aborted. For the connection to a DB2 server, the abort is translated into a DB2 rollback request. Like any other database request, the rollback request is serialized on the connection to guarantee the integrity of the data on the database server.

As a result:

- If the connection is idle, the rollback is executed immediately.
- If a long-running SQL statement is processing, the rollback request waits until the SQL statement finishes.

Connection Pooling

Connection pooling enables an application to use a connection from a pool of connections, so that the connection does not need to be re-established for each use. Once a connection has been created and placed in a pool, an application can reuse that connection without performing a complete connection process. The connection is pooled when the application disconnects from the ODBC data source, and will be given to a new connection whose attributes are the same.

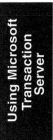

Connection pooling has been a feature of ODBC driver Manager 2.x. With the latest ODBC driver manager (version 3.5) that was shipped with MTS, connection pooling has some configuration changes and new behavior for ODBC connections of transactional MTS COM objects.

ODBC driver Manager 3.5 requires that the ODBC driver register a new keyword in the registry before it allows connection pooling to be activated.

The keyword is:

```
Key Name: SOFTWARE\ODBC\ODBCINST.INI\IBM DB2 ODBC DRIVER
Name: CPTimeout
Type: REG_SZ
Data: 60
```

The DB2 ODBC driver Version 5.0 (with PTF WR09024) or later for 32-bit Windows operating systems fully supports connection pooling; therefore, this keyword is automatically registered when you install the DB2 Client Version 5.0 (with PTF WR09024) or later.

The default value of 60 means that the connection will be pooled for 60 seconds before it is disconnected.

In a busy environment, it is better to increase the `CPTimeout` value to a large number (Microsoft sometimes suggests 10 minutes for certain environments) to prevent too many physical connects and disconnects, because these consume large amounts of system resource, including system memory and communications stack resources.

In addition, to ensure that the same connection is used between objects in the same transaction in a multiple processor machine, you must turn off *multiple pool per processor* support. To do this, copy the following registry setting into a file called `odbcpool.reg`, save it as a plain text file, and issue the command `odbcpool.reg`. The Windows operating system will import these registry settings.

```
REGEDIT4
[HKEY_LOCAL_MACHINE\SOFTWARE\ODBC\ODBCINST.INI\ODBC
Connection Pooling]
"NumberOfPools"="1"
```

Without this keyword set to 1, MTS may pool connections in different pools, and hence will not reuse the same connection.

MTS Connection Pooling using ADO 2.1 and Later

If the MTS COM objects use ADO to access the database, you must turn off the OLEDB resource pooling so that the Microsoft OLEDB provider for ODBC (`MSDASQL`) will not interfere with ODBC connection pooling. This feature was initialized to OFF in ADO 2.0, but is initialized to ON in ADO 2.1. To turn OLEDB resource polling off, copy the following lines into a file called `oledb.reg`, save it as a plain text file, and issue the command `oledb.reg`. The Windows operating system will import this registry setting.

```
REGEDIT4
[HKEY_CLASSES_ROOT\CLSID\{c8b522cb-5cf3-11ce-ade5-
00aa0044773d}]
@="MSDASQL"
"OLEDB_SERVICES"=dword:fffffffc
```

Sample Program — Using ADO with an MTS Component

This sample demonstrates how to use a lightweight Standard executable client program to connect to an MTS hosted dynamic link library.

The code included here demonstrates update operation in the database through MTS using ADO. The DB2MTS table contains one integer attribute and one string attribute. In db2mts (Client Application) Form, a user provides connection information and specifies desired number of updates. Each update will increment the value in the integer attribute by 1, and the string attribute will be updated to contain a new number incremented by 1 as well.

This sample demonstrates using ADO from an MTS hosted dynamic link library to a remote client via DCOM. The source code for client and server projects can be found in the folder %DB2PATH%\samples\mts (%DB2PATH% is the directory where the DB2 UDB product was installed) and is also included in Appendix B.

Steps to Run the Sample Application

The following section explains the steps to run the sample application:

1. The server project (db2com.vbp) contains the ActiveX DLL project for use with Microsoft Transaction Server (MTS) 1.1 or greater. Open the server project file Adomts.vbp.

2. Compile the DLL and then exit the project.

3. Add the DLL to a package in MTS using the MTS Explorer or Microsoft Management Console.

4. Disable the authorization checking for this sample.

5. The client project (db2mts.vbp)folder contains a standard executable (EXE) client project that makes remote calls to the MTS component. Open the client project db2mts.vbp.

6. Add a reference to the server component that was previously created. Run the client project.

7. For DB2 UDB, the database manager configuration parameter TP_MON_NAME has to be set to MTS.

8. In the db2mts (client application) form, the user provides connection information and specifies the desired number of updates. Each update will increment the value in the integer attribute by 1, and the string attribute will be updated to contain a new number incremented by 1 as well. The connection information is the DSN name which you have configured for connecting to the DB2 UDB sample database.

How MTS Handles DCOM

When the client and component reside on different machines, do the following steps to run the sample application:

1. Move the client to another computer.

2. In the MTS Microsoft Management Console, find your package under "Packages Installed", right-click the package name, and then select export.

3. Move the executable (EXE) file that was built by selecting export to the client.

4. Double-click the exported executable (EXE) file. This registers the MTS component.

5. Now, run the client project. If you want to verify that your client is accessing the component on the server, go to the server and open the Microsoft Management Console. Drill down to the components section of the package you just installed. Run the client program again and watch for the ball beside the component name to start spinning.

More About Client and Server Projects

This section provides more information about the client and the server projects for this sample application.

Client Project — db2mts.vbp

In the db2mts (client application) form, the user provides connection information and specifies the desired number of updates. Each update will increment the value in the integer attribute by 1, and the string attribute will be updated to contain a new number incremented by 1 as well for the DB2MTS table of the DB2 UDB sample database. The connection information is the DSN name which you have configured for connecting to the DB2 sample database.

A sample MTS application form is shown in Fig. 7–8:

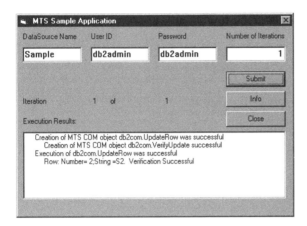

Fig. 7–8 *MTS Sample Application*

The **Submit** Button uses connection information and the number of updates information to update the DB2MTS table of the DB2 sample database. It references directly the two MTS components namely UpdateRow and VerifyUpdate. The MTS component UpdateRow intern uses the other two MTS components namely UpdateNumberColumn and UpdateStringColumn.

The UpdateNumberColumn MTS component provides a function called UpdateNumberColumn which increments the value in the integer attribute by 1 in the DB2MTS table.

The UpdateStringColumn MTS component provides a function called UpdateStringColumn which updates the string attribute to contain a new number incremented by 1 in the DB2MTS table.

Initially, if the DB2MTS table is not found in the sample database, then both UpdateNumberColumn and UpdateStringColumn components create this table with the integer attribute set to 1 and the string attribute set to S1.

The VerifyUpdate component verifies whether the update to DB2MTS table was successful or failed.

The **Info** Button provides the information about the application.

The **Close** Button exits the application.

The following shows the `Submit_Click` event code for `DB2MTS.vbp` project:

```
Private Sub Submit_Click()
    Dim Com1, Com2 As Object
    Dim strResult As String
    Dim rc, nRuns, iRun As Integer

    rc = 0
    iRun = 1
    Iteration.Caption = Str$(1)
    nRuns = Val(NofRunsEdit.Text)
    NofRunsLabel.Caption = NofRunsEdit.Text
    ResultBox.Clear

    On Error GoTo ErrorCreateObject
    Set Com1 = CreateObject("db2com.UpdateRow")
    Call AddItem("Creation of MTS COM object db2com.UpdateRow was successful", 1)
    Set Com2 = CreateObject("db2com.VerifyUpdate")
    Call AddItem("Creation of MTS COM object db2com.VerifyUpdate successful", 2)

    On Error GoTo ErrorHandler
    For iRun = 1 To nRuns

        Iteration.Caption = Str$(iRun)
        strConnect = "DSN=" + DataSource.Text + ";UID=" + UserID.Text + ";PWD=" +
        Password.Text
        rc = Com1.UpdateRow(strConnect, strResult)
        Call AddItem("Execution of db2com.UpdateRow was successful", 1)
        rc = Com2.VerifyUpdate(strConnect, strResult)
        Call AddItem(strResult, 2)
    Next iRun

cleanup:
    Set Com1 = Nothing
    Set Com2 = Nothing
Exit Sub

ErrorCreateObject:
    Call AddItem("Error: Cannot create or execute MTS objects for db2mts package", 1)
    Call AddItem("Please make sure MSDTC service is up and db2mts package has been
installed", 1)
    Resume cleanup
ErrorHandler:
    Call AddItem("Error: (" + Str$(Err.Number) + ")", 2)
    Call AddItem("Source: " + Err.Source, 2)
    Call AddItem("Description: " + Err.Description, 2)
    Resume cleanup
End Sub
```

The complete source code for `db2mts.vbp` project is given in Appendix A.

Server Project — db2com.vbp

The `db2com` server DLL has the following four components:

1. UpdateNumberColumn Component

The `UpdateNumberColumn` component provides a function called `UpdateNumberColumn` which increments the value in the integer attribute by 1 in the `DB2MTS` table.

2. UpdateStringColumn Component

The `UpdateStringColumn` component provides a function called `UpdateStringColumn` which updates the string attribute to contain a new number incremented by 1 in the `DB2MTS` table.

3. UpdateRow Component

The `UpdateRow` component provides a function called `UpdateRow`. This function internally uses the first two components mentioned above; namely, `UpdateNumberColumn` and `UpdateStringColumn`. It uses the `GetObjectContext` function to reference to the components. It makes use of the `CreateInstance` method to create these components. It also makes use of context object's `SetComplete` and `SetAbort` methods. More information about these functions is given in the section "Adding Transactions to an MTS Object" on page 327.

4. VerifyUpdate Component

The `VerifyUpdate` component provides a function called `VerifyUpdate`, which verifies whether the update to `DB2MTS` table was successful or failed.

As shown Fig. 7–9, you can observe that these four components are running in the MTS environment using the Microsoft Management Console:

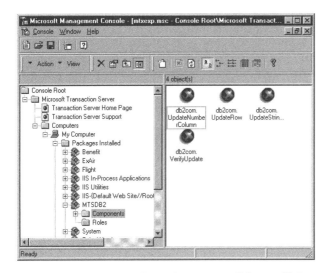

Fig. 7–9 *MTSDB2 Package Containing db2com.dll Server Components*

Here is the source code for the UpdateNumberColumn component. Note that GetObjectContext.Abort or GetObjectContext.SetComplete will be called after checking whether the update is successful or not:

```
Public Function UpdateNumberColumn(ByVal strConnect, ByRef strResult As String) As
Integer
        Dim rc As Integer
        Dim strStmt As String
        Dim adoConn As New ADODB.Connection
        rc = 0

        ' Obtain the ADO environment and connection
        On Error GoTo ErrorReport
        adoConn.Open strConnect

        ' Update Rows
UpdateAgain:
        On Error GoTo ErrorUpdate
        strStmt = "Update db2mts set number = number+1"
        adoConn.Execute strStmt

        ' clean up
cleanup:
        On Error GoTo 0
        If Not adoConn Is Nothing Then
            adoConn.Close
            Set adoConn = Nothing
        End If

        If rc <> 0 Then
            GetObjectContext.SetAbort
            Err.Raise rc, strStmt, strResult
        Else
            GetObjectContext.SetComplete
        End If
        UpdateNumberColumn = rc

Exit Function

CreateTable:
        Dim strCreateTable As String
        On Error GoTo ErrorReport
        ' Create Table
        strStmt = "Create table db2mts (number integer, string varchar(15))"
        adoConn.Execute strStmt
        ' Populate with 1 row
        strStmt = "Insert into db2mts values(1,'S1')"
        adoConn.Execute strStmt
        GoTo UpdateAgain
' End CreateTable

ErrorUpdate:
        ' If error -204 (table not found) then create the table
        ' Otherwise return with failure
        If adoConn.Errors(0).NativeError = -204 Then
            Resume CreateTable
        End If
        Resume ErrorReport

ErrorReport:
        rc = Common.GetError(adoConn, strStmt, strResult)
        Resume cleanup

End Function
```

The complete source code for all the four components or class modules of the db2com.vbp is given in Appendix B.

8

Application Development on IIS

- ◆ CREATING ASP APPLICATIONS
- ◆ CREATING SERVER SCRIPTS
- ◆ ASP BUILT-IN OBJECTS
- ◆ USING ACTIVEX DATA OBJECTS
- ◆ SECURITY CONSIDERATIONS IN ASP
- ◆ SAMPLE PROGRAM

*U*nder Internet Information Server (IIS) 4.0, an application is just a collection of files in a directory whose properties can be set, and that can run in a separate process space. Active Server Page (ASP) applications are just one type of application that can run under IIS 4.0. An Active Server Page is a file with an **.asp** suffix that contains a combination of HTML statements and script logic. When IIS 4.0 receives an HTTP request for an ASP file, the final HTML response is generated dynamically from the static HTML statements, plus the insertion of any HTML generated by the scripting.

This chapter discusses how to use Active Server Pages (ASP) in the Web applications for DB2 UDB. The chapter also highlights how to add server-side script that manipulates objects on a Web server, and how to create a Web application.

Creating ASP Applications

ASP applications are like conventional stand-alone applications. They can retain user information between sessions, or uses, of the application. These types of applications can also retain information while the user moves from one page to another.

ASP applications have two important features:

*   Starting-point directory
*   Global data

Starting-Point Directory

When you create an application, you use Internet Service Manager to designate the application's starting-point directory for your Web site. The Internet Service Manager is a snap-in component of the Microsoft Management Console (MMC). All files and directories under the starting-point directory in your Web site are considered part of the application until another starting-point directory is found. You thus use directory boundaries to define the scope of an application. You can have more than one application per Web site, but each application must be configured differently.

From Microsoft Visual Studio, tools like Visual InterDev will handle all of these tasks for you when you create a new Web project. Under IIS 4.0, Web applications are handled like Visual Basic applications. That is, you can unload them in the same way that you can unload Visual Basic applications. You can also set your application to run in a process space separate from IIS.

Global Data

ASP applications declare global data in the Global.asa file. This optional file is processed by the Web server and can be used to make data available to all pages in the application.

The Global.asa file is processed automatically by the server whenever the following processes occur:

*   The application starts or ends.
*   Individual users start and stop browser sessions that access the application's ASP pages.

You can do the following in the `Global.asa` file:

- Initialize application or session variables.
- Declare COM components with application or session scope.
- Perform other operations that pertain to the application as a whole.

Data Connections

One type of global data for any Web application is a data connection. If you intend your Web application to use data in an ODBC database, you connect to the database by adding a data connection to your Web application. Visual InterDev generates script within the `Global.asa` file to save all of the information for connecting to the database in application variables.

Creating Server Script

Active Server Pages (ASP) are a type of Web application that use **.asp** files. The **.asp** extension tells the Web server that the page contains server script that it should process before returning the page to the browser.

The main difference between ASP and HTML pages is the location where the script is run. DHTML, or client script, is run on the client, in the browser, after the page is sent from the server. ASP, or server script, is run on the server before the page is sent to the browser. The Web server processes the script and generates the HTML pages that are returned to the Web browser.

Coding Active Server Pages

Server script and client script look very similar because they both use the same languages. The main difference is in how script blocks are specified. The following are some of the different kinds of server script:

- The sample server-side code format shown below is the preferred one. It is easy to read and maintain.

```
<SCRIPT LANGAUGE = your choice RUNAT=server>
   - Some Script Code -
</SCRIPT>
```

- The sample code format shown below uses the inline scripting. It makes use of the default scripting language. This can be more difficult to read and maintain.

```
<%  Some Script Code  %>
```

- The following sample shows usage inline scripting to use the value of expression.

```
<% = some results %>
```

The server code sample in Fig. 8–1 gives the date and time of the server.

```
<HTML>
<BODY>
<H3>Welcome to My Server</H3>
The time here is <%=Time()%><BR>
The date is <%=Date()%>.
</BODY>
</HTML>
```

Fig. 8–1 *Server Code Sample*

ASP Processing Directives

Use @ processing directives in your scripts to send information to IIS about how to process **.asp** files. For example, the following script uses the @LANGUAGE processing directive to set the scripting language to VBScript.

```
<% @Language=VBScript
Dim myvar
Application("myvar") = my var
Response.Write(myvar)
%>
```

The following five @ processing directives are supported by ASP in IIS 4.0.

- **@CODEPAGE**

Sets the codepage that will be used for symbol mapping.

- **@LANGUAGE**

  Override the scripting language being used as the server's default language (VBScript) by using the @ language directive.

- **@ENABLESESSIONSTATE**

  Using the Enable Session State directive (set in Internet Services Manager) for your site enables the detailed tracking of user requests.

- **@LCID**

  Sets the Locale identifier.

- **@TRANSACTION**

  Used for the ASP page to be transactional.

Handling Run Time Errors

The most important tools used for handling runtime errors are the `On Error Resume Next` statement and the `Err` object.

- On Error Resume Next

  When a run-time error occurs, control will go to the statement immediately following the statement where the error occurred, and execution will continue.

- Err Object

  To detect run-time errors, check the `Number` property of the `Err` object after each statement that might cause an error. If `Number` is zero, an error has not occurred. If it is not zero, an error has occurred.

  The `Description` property of the `Err` object retrieves the information about the error.

Sample code showing the general syntax of the error handling is given in Fig. 8–2:

Application Development on IIS

```
'Error Handling Code Sample
Sub cmdSubmit_OnClick
On Error Resume Next
'Statement that might cause an error
If Err <> 0 Then
Msgbox "An error occurred. " & Err.Description
Err.Clear
End if
'Statement that might cause an error
If Err <> 0 Then
Msgbox "An error occurred. " & Err.Description
Err.Clear
End if
End Sub
```

Fig. 8–2 *Error Handling*

ASP Built-In Objects

As ASP pages run on the server, it has access to a number of objects available on the server. The following section describes these objects:

- Request

  Retrieves the values that the browser passes to the server during an HTTP request.

- Response

  Controls what information is sent to a browser in the HTTP response message.

- Session

  Used to manage and store information about a particular user session.

- Application

  Used to manage and store information about the Web application.

- Server

  Provides access to resources that reside on a server. More about server objects like ADO Connection, ADO Command, ADO Recordset is given in the section "Using ActiveX Data Objects" on page 365.

- Context Objects

  Used to commit or abort a transaction managed by Microsoft Transaction Server (MTS) for ASP pages that run in a transaction. More about Context Objects is described in the section "Adding Transactional Support" on page 326.

The Request Object

The Request object provides access to any information that is passed to the Web server from the browser. A Web application can use information from an HTTP request when a user requests an HTML document. For instance, when a user submits a form by using the POST method, the values of the controls on the form will be passed in the body of the HTTP request. A Web application can then read these values and use them to return a modified HTML document to the user.

Request Object Collections

The Request object contains five collections that you can use to extract information from an HTTP request. The following section explains about these collections:

1. **Form**

   The values of Form elements posted to the body of the HTTP request message by the form's POST method.

2. **QueryString**

   The values of variables in the HTTP query string, specifically the values following the question mark (?) in an HTTP request.

3. **ServerVariables**

   The values of predetermined Web server environment variables.

4. **Cookies**

   The values of cookies sent in the HTTP request.

5. **ClientCertificate**

   The values of the certification fields in the HTTP request.

Using the Request Object

Each collection of the Request object contains variables that you use to retrieve information from an HTTP request.

In the following example code, the SERVER_NAME variable of the ServerVariables collection retrieves the name of the Web server:

```
Request.ServerVariables("SERVER_NAME")
```

Using QueryString Collection

Use the QueryString collection of the Request object to extract information from the header of an HTTP request message. For example, when a user submits a form with the GET method, or appends parameters to a URL request, you use the QueryString collection to read the submitted information.

The values you read from the request are the parameters that appear after the question mark (?). For example, a user clicks the Submit button on the following form in Fig. 8–3:

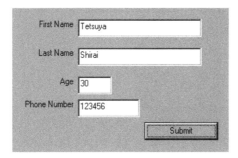

Fig. 8–3 *Employee Details Submission Form*

As a result, the following HTTP request is made:

```
http://Employee.asp?Firstname=Tetsuya&
    Lastname=Shirai&Age=30&Phone=123456
```

You can loop through all of the values in a query string to extract information passed by the user.

The following example code loops through all of the values in an HTTP request:

```
<%For Each Item In Request.QueryString
        'Display the Item
    Next %>
```

Using Form Collection

Use the Form collection of the Request object to extract information from the body of an HTTP request message.

The Form collection contains the values of each standard HTML control that has a NAME attribute. When a user submits a form with the POST method, you can read the values of the controls by using the Form collection.

For example, a user completes and submits a form with the following HTML (see Fig. 8–4):

```
<FORM ACTION="submit.asp" METHOD=POST>
Name: <INPUT TYPE=TEXT NAME="name"><P>
Favorite Sport: <SELECT MULTIPLE NAME="sport">
                <OPTION>BaseBall
                <OPTION>BasketBall
                <OPTION>FootBall
                </SELECT><P>
<INPUT TYPE=SUBMIT NAME="cmdSubmit" VALUE="Submit">
</FORM>
```

Fig. 8–4 *Submitting a Form*

You can read the submitted information by using the following script in the Submit.asp file:

```
Request.Form("name")
Request.Form("sport")
```

You can also loop through all of the values on a form to extract information passed by the user.

The following example code loops through all of the standard HTML controls in an HTTP request:

```
<% For Each Item in Request.Form
    ' Display Item
Next %>
```

The Response Object

The Response object enables you to control the information sent to a user by the HTTP response message.

Properties and Methods of the Response Object

The Response object provides properties and methods that you can use when sending information to the user.

Table 8–1 describes some properties of the Response object:

Table 8–1 *Properties of the Response Object*

Property	Description
Buffer	Shows whether a response is buffered.
Expires	Specifies the length of time before a page cached on a browser expires.
ExpiresAbsolute	Specifies the date and time on which a page cached on a browser will expire.
IsClientConnected	Indicates whether the client has disconnected from the server since the last `Response.Write`.
Status	Specifies the value of the status line returned by the server. Status values are defined in the HTTP specification.

Table 8–2 describes some methods of the Response object:

Table 8–2 *Methods of the Response Object*

Method	Description
Clear	Clears any buffered response.
End	Stops the processing of a Web page and returns whatever information has been processed thus far.
Flush	Sends buffered output immediately.
Redirect	Sends a redirect message to the user, causing the response message to try to connect to a different URL.
Write	Writes a variable to the current HTTP output as a string.

You use the following syntax for the properties and methods of the Response object:

```
Response.property|method
```

The Write Method

The Write method adds text to the HTTP response message, as shown in the following example code:

```
Response.Write variant
```

The Redirect Method

You can use the Redirect method to redirect the user to another URL. When you use the Redirect method of the Response object, you provide the URL as an argument to the method.

```
Response.Redirect newURL
```

The Application Object

The Application object can be used to share information among all users of a Web application. For example, you might store the total number of visitors to a Web site in an application-level variable.

An Application object is created when the user of the application requests an **.asp** file from the starting-point directory of the ASP application. It is destroyed when the application is unloaded.

The example code in Fig. 8–5 makes use of the Application object and its methods Lock and Unlock when changing the value of a hit counter used in a Web application:

Application Development on IIS

```
<% Application.Lock
Application("NumHits") = Application("NumHits") + 1
Application.Unlock
%>
This application has been visited
<%= Application("NumHits") %> times.
```

Fig. 8–5 *Application Object*

NumHits is a variable that contains a count of the number of visits.

The Application Object Events

The Application object has the two events: Application_OnStart and Application_OnEnd. Scripts can be added to these events in the Global.asa file.

Any script you add to the Application_OnStart event will run when the application starts and the script you add to the Application_OnEnd event will run when the application ends.

The following example code shows how to add the Application_OnStart event to the Global.asa file:

```
<SCRIPT LANGUAGE=VBScript RUNAT=Server>
Sub Application_OnStart
  'Your Code Here
End Sub
</SCRIPT>
```

The Session Object

The Session object can be used to store information that is needed for a particular user session. Variables stored in the Session object will not be removed when the user goes between pages in the Web application. Instead, these variables will persist for the entire user session.

The Web server automatically creates a Session object when a session starts. When the session expires or is abandoned, the Web server will destroy the Session object

A session automatically ends if a user has not requested or refreshed a page in an application for a specified period of time. You can change the default for an application by setting the Session Timeout property on the Application Options tab of the Application Configuration property sheet in Internet Service Manager. The Internet Service Manager is a snap-in component of the Microsoft Management Console (MMC). More information about this is given in the section "Setting IIS Permissions" on page 372. The `SessionID` property of the Session object is used to determine the session identification of a user. The Session object has one method, namely the `Abandon` method, which is to destroy a Session object and release its resources.

The following script sets a time-out interval of 10 minutes:

```
<% Session.Timeout = 10 %>
```

Session Object Events

Similar to the Application object, the Session object has the `Session_OnStart` and `Session_OnEnd` events. Script wirtten under `Session_OnStart` event will run when a user without an existing session requests an **.asp** file from your application. Any script you add to the `Session_OnEnd` event will run when a user session ends.

The ample code in Fig. 8–6 shows the usage of `Session_OnStart` event:

```
'when a session starts, redirect the user to a logon page
Sub Session_OnStart
If Session("username") = "" Then
'save the name of the page the user wanted to visit
Session("startpage") =
Request.ServerVariables("SCRIPT_NAME")
'redirect them to a logon page
Response.Redirect "Logon.htm"
End If
End Sub
```

Fig. 8–6 *Submitting a Form*

Using ActiveX Data Objects

Internet Information Server (IIS) 4.0 provides ADO Command, ADO Connection, and ADO Recordset COM components that access information stored in a database or other tabular data structures.

Connecting to the Database

A Connection object represents an open connection to a data source or OLE DB provider. You can use the Connection object to run commands or queries on the data source. When a recordset is retrieved from the database, it is stored in a Recordset object.

The following steps describe how to create an ADO connection.

1. Create a Connection object by calling CreateObject and passing it the ADODB.Connection parameter.

2. Set the ConnectionTimeout property of the Connection object. ConnectionTimeout determines, in seconds, how long the object will wait before timing out when connecting to a data source.

3. Set, in seconds, the CommandTimeout property of the Command object. CommandTimeout determines, in seconds, how long the object will wait for the results of a command or query.

4. Use the Open method to connect to the data source.

The example code in Fig. 8–7 creates a Connection object, and opens a connection to the SAMPLE database of the DB2 UDB:

```
<% Set conn = Server.CreateObject("ADODB.Connection")
conn.ConnectionTimeout = 10
conn.CommandTimeout = 20
conn.Open
"DSN=SAMPLE;UID=db2admin;DBALIAS=SAMPLE;Password=db2admin;"
%>
```

Fig. 8–7 *Connection Object*

The following methods are important features of the Connection object:

• The Execute method runs an SQL query.

• The BeginTrans method initiates a transaction between the client and the database.

• The CommitTrans method ensures a transaction will occur.

• The RollbackTrans method returns a database to its original state if the transaction fails.

The example code in Fig. 8–8 shows how you can use application variables to create a connection:

```
<%
Set conn = Server.CreateObject("ADODB.Connection")
conn.ConnectionTimeout =
Application("Sample_ConnectionTimeout")
conn.CommandTimeout = Application("Sample_CommandTimeout")
conn.Open Application("Sample_ConnectionString"), _
 Application("Sample_RuntimeUserName"), _
 Application("Sample_RuntimePassword")
%>
```

Fig. 8–8 *Creating a Connection*

When you have finished working with the database, you use the `Close` method of the Connection object to free any associated system resources. Using the `Close` method does not remove the object from memory. To completely remove an object from memory, you set the object variable to `Nothing`.

The following example code closes a data connection and sets the object variable to `Nothing`:

```
conn.Close
Set conn = Nothing
```

Creating a Recordset Object

To retrieve records from a database, you create a Recordset object. You use properties and methods of the Recordset object to manipulate the data in the recordset.

The following steps explain how to create a Recordset object.

1. Define a Recordset object variable by passing `ADODB.Recordset` as an argument to `CreateObject`.

2. Call the `Open` method of the Recordset object.

The following example code uses the `CreateObject` function to define a Recordset object variable and then uses the `Open` method to create the Recordset object. The example passes a connection string when invoking the `Open` method of the Recordset object:

```
Set rs = Server.CreateObject ("ADODB.Recordset")
rs.Open "Select * from EMPLOYEE",
"DSN=SAMPLE;UID=db2admin;PWD=db2admin", _
adOpenKeyset, adLockOptimistic
```

You can use `Execute` method of the Connection Object or the Command Object to create the Recordset.

Navigating a Recordset Object

To change to a new record, you use one of the `Move` methods of the Recordset object.

The `BOF` (beginning of file) or `EOF` (end of file) properties are `True` if you are at the beginning or the end of the recordset, respectively. If there are no records in a recordset, both the `BOF` and `EOF` properties are `True`.

The following example code moves through all the records in a recordset:

```
Do Until rs.EOF
    'while not at end of recordset,
    'move to the next record
    rs.MoveNext
Loop
```

To retrieve data from a field in the current record, use the `Fields` collection, and specify the name of the field, as in the following example code:

```
EmpName = rs.Fields("FIRSTNME")
```

Modifying Data

Use the `AddNew` method of the Recordset object to add a record to the database, set values for the record, and then use the `Update` method to save the record.

The example code in Fig. 8–9 retrieves values from the Request object in an **.asp** file and adds a new record to the `EMPLOYEE` table:

```
rsEmployee.Addnew
rsEmployee("EMPNO") = Request("EMPNO")
rsEmployee("FIRSTNME") = Request("FIRSTNME")
        rsEmployee("MIDINIT") = Request("MIDINIT")
        rsEmployee("LASTNAME") = Request("LASTNAME")
        rsEmployee("EDLLEVEL") = Request("EDLLEVEL")
        rsEmployee("SALARY") = Request("SALARY")
rsEmployee.Update
```

Fig. 8–9 *Retrieving Values from a Request Object*

To cancel an update, call the `CancelUpdate` method. To delete the current record, use the `Delete` method of the Recordset object. After you delete a record, invoke a `Move` method to move to the next record. Otherwise the current record pointer points to an empty record.

The following example code deletes the current record in the `rsEmployee` recordset.

```
rsEmployee.Delete
rsEmployee.MoveNext
```

Binary Data

In addition to working with data of various types, it supports the retrieval and manipulation of Binary Large Objects (BLOB) stored in the database.

The example code in Fig. 8–10 retrieves the photograph of the employee from the `EMPLOYEE` table of the database.

Application Development on IIS

```
if Request.Form("cmdPhoto")="Photo" then
    Blocksize=4096
    Response.ContentType="image/JPEG"
    strQuery="select * from EMP_PHOTO where
PHOTO_FORMAT='bitmap' and EMPNO='" _
    & Request.Form("EMPNO") & "'"
    set rs=conn.Execute(strQuery)
    if not rs.EOF then
        rs.MoveFirst
        set Field=rs("PICTURE")
        FileLength=Field.ActualSize
        NumBlocks=FileLength \ Blocksize
        LeftOver=FileLength Mod Blocksize
        Response.BinaryWrite Field.GetChunk(LeftOver)
        for intLoop=1 to NumBlocks
            Response.BinaryWrite Field.GetChunk(Blocksize)
        next
    end if
end if
```

Fig. 8–10 *Retrieving Binary Data*

In the above example, a bitmap image has been stored in a PICTURE field of the EMP_PHOTO table of the DB2 Sample database.

A Blocksize variable is used to determine how much data will be read from the data source at one time. It may seem logical to read the whole image as a single chunk, but we need to move this data from our server to our Web site in a single transaction, a process that can be very resource intensive with large files.

Using the Execute method of the Connection object, we build the Recordset. The object variable Field represents the PICTURE field. It now has a reference to the actual binary data. The variables NumBlocks and LeftOver calculate how much data we need to retrieve in terms of the block size defined earlier.

Using the BinaryWrite method of the Response object, we can read the data from the source with the GetChunk method. GetChunk is designed to read an unstructured binary data stream from an object of a given size.

Security Considerations in ASP

This section describes security considerations that you should consider when building Web applications. The main Web security considerations are:

- User authentication

    Identifies the user requesting files in a Web application. To manage this, we have the options namely Basic Authentication, Anonymous Logon, and Windows NT Challenge/Response at the Web server.

- File permissions

    Controls access to files in the application. To manage this, we can control read, write, script, and execute permissions for files and folders at the Web server.

- Database permissions

    Controls access to objects in the database. DB2 UDB relies on the security mechanism of Windows NT to validate Username / Password.

Web Application Security

Every Web application on a Web server has permission settings that identify authorized users and specify their privileges.

For instance, by default, a new Web application developed using Microsoft Visual Interdev inherits the same permissions as the root Web server. To set unique permissions for a Web application, perform the following steps:

1. In the Microsoft Visual Interdev 6.0 Project Explorer window, select the project for which you want to set permissions.

2. From the **Project** menu, choose **Web Project** and then **Web Permissions**.

3. On the **Settings** tab, select **Use unique permissions for this Web application**. This specifies that the current Web application does not inherit its permissions setting from the root Web application.

4. Click **Apply**.

An illustration of the above is shown in Fig. 8–11:

Application Development on IIS

Fig. 8–11 *Web Project Permissions*

In Microsoft Visual InterDev, you can set one of three levels of user permissions. The following shows which of these are design-time or run-time permissions.

- **Browse** - Design-time and run-time
- **Author** - Design-time only
- **Administer** - Design-time and run-time

In order to set Web application security in Windows NT, the Web application files must be stored on a disk using the NTFS file system, not FAT.

Setting IIS Permissions

You use the Internet Service Manager to set the access permission on the virtual directories of your Web site. The Internet Service Manager is a snap-in component of the Microsoft Management Console (MMC). Perform the following steps to set access permissions on virtual directories:

1. Click Microsoft Internet Information Server.

2. Click Internet Service Manager and this starts Microsoft Management Console

3. Click Properties.

4. Click the Home Directory tab.

5. Set the appropriate access permissions for the virtual directory.

An illustration of the above is shown in Fig. 8–12:

Fig. 8–12 *Web Site Properties*

There are five possible levels of permission that you can grant for a virtual directory. The following describes these settings.

- Read

  Enables Web clients to read or download files stored in a home directory or a virtual directory.

- Write

  Enables Web clients to upload files to the enabled directory, or to change the content in a write-enabled file.

- Script

  Enables applications mapped to a script engine to run in this directory without having Execute permission set. Use Script application permission for directories that contain ASP scripts, Internet Database Connector (IDC) scripts, or other scripts. Script permission is safer than Execute permission because you can limit the applications that can be run in the directory.

- Execute

  Enables any application to run in this directory, including applications mapped to script engines as well as dynamic link libraries and executable files.

- None

  Do not allow any programs or scripts to run in this directory.

Allowing Anonymous Logon

Windows NT requires assigned user accounts and passwords. If you want to allow everybody to access your Web server, you must either provide a valid Windows NT account for every user or allow anonymous logon.

Anonymous logon allows users to access your Web server without providing a user ID and password. When an IIS Web server receives an anonymous request, it maps the user to a special anonymous logon account, referred to as the Internet Guest account. The user receives the access rights that have been granted to this account.

To enable anonymous logon, perform the following steps:

1. Click Microsoft Internet Information Server.

2. Click Internet Service Manager.

3. Within the virtual root, right-click **Default Web Site**.

4. Click **Properties**.

5. Select the **Directory Security** tab.

6. Click **Edit** in the Anonymous Access and Authentication Control group box.

7. Click the Allow Anonymous Access check box.

For setting the Account Used for Anonymous Access, do the following mentioned steps in addition to the above-mentioned steps:

1. Click **Edit.**

2. Disable **Enable Automatic Password Synchronization**.

3. Set the Username and Password text boxes to the values that you want.

4. Click **OK**, and then **OK** again.

An illustration for the Anonymous access is shown in Fig. 8–13:

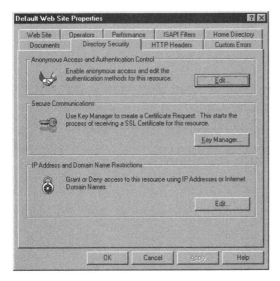

Fig. 8–13 *Default Web Site Properties — Directory Security*

Sample Web Application Using ASP

Now we are demonstrating how Web applications are developed for the DB2 UDB sample database. First section describes the various steps involved in installing Web applications and the second section explains to build a sample Web application using Microsoft Visual Interdev 6.0 with DB2 UDB database.

General Procedure for Installing Web Applications

To install the sample program onto your IIS server, copy the folder containing the Web site to your computer's Web publishing folder. Then test that the site was installed correctly by browsing to the home page.

Check That the Web Publishing Service is Running

The Sample assumes that Microsoft Internet Information Service (IIS) 4.0 and its Web publishing service are running. To check that the Web publishing service is running, perform the following steps:

1. From the desktop's **Start** menu, click **Settings**, and then click **Control Panel**.

2. In the **Control Panel**, start the **Services** applet.

3. In the **Service** list box, locate and select the World Wide Web Publishing Service entry.

4. Verify that its status is Started and its start-up mode is Automatic. If this service is stopped, click the **Start** button. If the start-up mode is not Automatic, click the Startup button and change it to this value.

Check That the ODBC DSN Exists for the DB2 UDB Database

Our sample application assumes the ODBC Data Source Name **Sample** is configured for the DB2 sample database. Perform the following steps to check that the ODBC DSN exists for DB2 UDB database.

1. From the desktop's **Start** menu, click **Settings**, and then click **Control Panel**.

2. In the Control Panel, double click on **ODBC Data sources**. This will display ODBC Data Source Administrator window.

3. Select System DSN tab.Click **Add**. Choose IBM DB2 ODBC DRIVER and press finish.This will open **ODBC IBM DB2 Driver- Add** window.

4. Select Data source name as **Sample** and Database alias as **Sample**. Click **OK**, and then **OK** again.

The DSN name could be anything. Here, for our sample application, we have considered it as **Sample**.

Copy the Sample Web Site Files to the Web Publishing Directory

Because our sample contains only HTML files and Active Server Page (ASP) files, installing it is a relatively straightforward operation. Simply copy the folder containing the sample site to your computer's Web publishing folder.

1. Select the Prototype subfolder and press the CTRL+C key combination to copy it.

2. Navigate to the machine's Web publishing folder. This is the default virtual root folder from which IIS services HTTP requests. By default, this is `C:\InetPub\wwwroot`.

3. Press the CTRL+V key combination to copy the Prototype directory to the Web publishing directory.

Mark the Sample Application Folder as a Web Application

Sub-folders (subdirectories) under the WWWRoot folder are, by default, treated as simple Web sites by Internet Information Server (IIS). If Active Server pages are to be supported, the site folder must be specially marked. Microsoft Visual InterDev automatically does this for you when creating a new site or publishing an existing one through Visual InterDev. To make the application folder:

1. Open the Internet Service Manager by selecting **Start** -> **Programs** -> **Windows NT 4.0 Option Pack** -> **Microsoft Internet Information Server**.

2. In the left-hand pane, expand the node under Internet Information Server until you reach **Default Web Site**, then locate the **Prototype** node. It should have a folder icon associated with it indicating that it is a simple Web site.

3. Right-click the **Prototype** node and choose the **Properties** command. The Prototype Properties dialog box should be displayed.

4. In the Directories tab in the Application Setting group box, click the **Create** button. In the same group box, verify the Permissions are set to Script, which is the default.

5. Click **OK** to close the dialog box. You can also close the Internet Service Manager if you wish.

Test That the Web Site Has Been Installed

To test that the Web site has been properly installed (published), perform the following steps:

1. Open Internet Explorer.

2. In the Address text box, type the following URL and press Enter:
    `<computername>/default.htm`

3. Browse the site and click on the Employee Data Entry link to go to Employee Details page. Check the Resume and Photo buttons.

More Details About the Sample Application

The sample Web site is developed using Microsoft Visual Interdev 6.0 tool. This sample Web application demonstrates mainly the usage of Microsoft IIS, ASP, ADO with DB2 database. The sample application includes `Default.htm`, `Employee.asp`, and `Resume.asp` files and the source code so that these files can be viewed better in the Visual Interdev 6.0 environment.

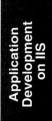

Application Development on IIS

More details about how to build this application using Microsoft Visual Interdev 6.0 are given described in the section "Creating a Web Application: Microsoft Visual Interdev 6.0" on page 386.

Default.html

This is the default/home page of the Sample site application. This page provides the link to the Employee data entry page (`Employee.asp`). The look-and-feel of this page is shown in Fig. 8–14:

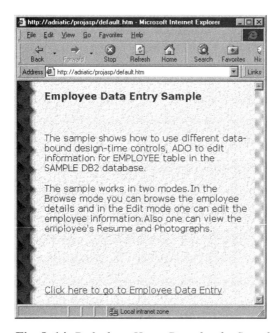

Fig. 8–14 *Default or Home Page for the Sample Site*

Shown below is the source code for Default.htm file:

```
<HTML>
<HEAD>
<META NAME="GENERATOR" Content="Microsoft Visual Studio 6.0">
<TITLE></TITLE>

<LINK REL="stylesheet" TYPE="text/css" HREF="_Themes/redside/THEME.CSS"
VI6.0THEME="Redside">
<LINK REL="stylesheet" TYPE="text/css" HREF="_Themes/redside/GRAPH0.CSS"
VI6.0THEME="Redside">
<LINK REL="stylesheet" TYPE="text/css" HREF="_Themes/redside/COLOR0.CSS"
VI6.0THEME="Redside">
<LINK REL="stylesheet" TYPE="text/css" HREF="_Themes/redside/CUSTOM.CSS"
VI6.0THEME="Redside"></HEAD>
<BODY>
```

```
<P><STRONG><FONT color=mediumblue face="" size=4>Employee
Data Entry Sample </FONT></STRONG>    </P>

<P><STRONG><FONT color=mediumblue face=""
size=4></FONT></STRONG>     </P>

<P>The sample shows how to use different data-bound design-time
controls, ADO to edit information for EMPLOYEE table in the SAMPLE DB2
database.</P>

<P>    The sample works in two modes.In the
Browse mode you can browse the employee details and in the Edit mode one
can edit the employee information.Also one can view the employee's Resume
and
Photographs.</P>

<P>
 </P>

<P>
 </P>

<P><A href="Employee.asp">Click here to go to Employee Data
Entry</A>
</P>


</BODY>
</HTML>
```

Employee.asp

This file uses several different Design-Time Controls (DTC) to browse, edit, and navigate through the records in the database.

- Recordset DTC

    This control connects the page to the EMPLOYEE table of DB2 UDB sample database.

- Textbox DTC

    These controls are used to display and edit the employee number (EMPNO), first name (FIRSTNME), middle name (MIDINIT), last name (LASTNAME), date of birth (BIRTHDATE), phone number (PHONENO), job (JOB), education level (EDLEVEL), and salary (SALARY) fields in the EMPLOYEE table. Each of these controls is bound to a field in the table.

- OptionGroup DTC

    This control is bound to the SEX field in the EMPLOYEE table. Static values of Male and Female are set in the properties of the control. They correspond to a "1" for Male and "0" for Female in the table.

- RecordsetNavBar DTC

    This control is bound to the Recordset DTC to allow the user to step through the records in the EMPLOYEE table.

- FormManager DTC

  This control manages the entire form. When the form is first viewed, it is in the Browse mode. There are two buttons visible at the top of the form that allow you to toggle between Browse and Edit modes. When you switch to Edit mode, three more buttons become visible and the RecordsetNavBar is hidden. The three extra buttons allow you to Insert, Delete or Update information in the EMPLOYEE table.

In the FormManager properties dialog box, the Browse and Edit mode properties are set to enable and disable the controls within the form. The Browse mode is also set to be the default mode when you enter this Web page.

In the Action tab of the FormManager properties dialog box, the properties for the buttons are set. Each button performs a different set of actions:

- The Edit button will enable the controls on the form, will display three buttons for Insert, Delete and Update, and will also hide the RecordsetNavBar.
- The Insert button will call the Recordset.AddRecord method and then call the Recordset.MoveLast method to allow you to edit the newly added record.
- The Delete button will call the Recordset.DeleteRecord method to delete the currently selected record and then call the Recordset.MoveFirst method to display the first record in the recordset.
- The Update button calls the Recordset.UpdateRecord method to save any changes that have been made to the currently selected record. This button needs to be clicked in order to save any changes that have been made to a new record that has been created using the Insert button.
- The Browse button will disable the controls on the form, hide the three editing buttons, and display the RecordsetNavBar.
- The Resume button will display the resume for the employee (retrieves Resume.asp file). Resumes are stored as character large objects (CLOBs) in the DB2 UDB sample database.
- The Photo button displays the Photograph for the Employee. Photographs are stored as binary large objects (BLOBs) in the DB2 UDB sample database.

The look-and-feel of this page is shown in Fig. 8–15:

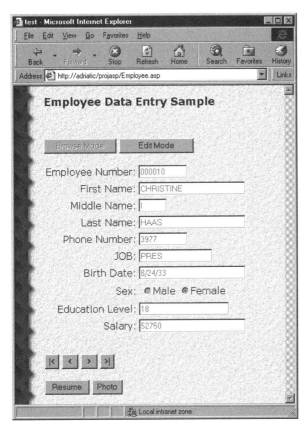

Fig. 8–15 *Employee ASP File of the Sample Site Application*

Since this ASP file uses mostly Design Time Controls, the code can be better viewed in the Visual Interdev 6.0 environment.

Resume.asp

This file retrieves the resume for the submitted employee from EMP_RESUME table of the DB2 UDB sample database. The file uses ADO and Text DTC to display the resume of the employee. A sample section of this page is shown in Fig. 8–16:

Application Development on IIS

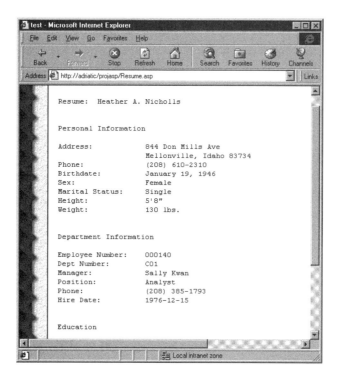

Fig. 8–16 *Sample Resume ASP File of the Sample Site*

Photo of the Employee

The Photo button on the Employee data entry page retrieves the photograph for the submitted employee from EMP_PHOTO table of the DB2 UDB sample database. A sample photo for the Employee Number 000140 is shown in Fig. 8–17:

Fig. 8–17 *A Sample Photo of the Employee*

The source code behind Resume.asp, which does both the retrieval of the resume as well as the photograph for the employee, is shown below. For the resume retrieval part, as the data type CLOB is not recognized, we cast the RESUME column to a LONG_VARCHAR. Since we know that the RESUME column is defined to a maximum size of 5120 bytes, which is less than the maximum LONG_VARCHAR size. If we do not do this cast, the data is determined to be binary data and is not known to be ASCII text. Therefore, a conversion back to character from ASCII would be necessary for the entire CLOB.

For the Resume functionality, we have made use of the Recordset object and its Open method to build the recordset. Here we have also made use of Textbox Design Time Control to display the resume of employee, and it is programatically bound to the recordset's Field object.

The retrieval part for the photograph of the employee was already explained in the section "Binary Data" on page 369.

The ASP page also makes use of the global data declared in the global.asa file.

The following section shows the complete source code for Resume.asp page.

```
<%@ Language=VBScript %>
<SCRIPT id=DebugDirectives runat=server language=javascript>
// Set these to true to enable debugging or tracing
@set @debug=false
@set @trace=false
</SCRIPT>

<%
Set conn = Server.CreateObject("ADODB.Connection")
conn.ConnectionTimeout = Application("ConnSample_ConnectionTimeout")
conn.CommandTimeout = Application("ConnSample_CommandTimeout")
```

Application Development on IIS

```
conn.Open Application("ConnSample_ConnectionString"), _
Application("ConnSample_RuntimeUserName"), _
Application("ConnSample_RuntimePassword")

ifRequest.Form("cmdPhoto")="Photo" then
   Blocksize=4096
   Response.ContentType="image/JPEG"
   strQuery="select * from EMP_PHOTO where PHOTO_FORMAT='bitmap' and
EMPNO='" _
   & Request.Form("EMPNO") & "'"
   set rs=conn.Execute(strQuery)
   if not rs.EOF then
      rs.MoveFirst
      set Field=rs("PICTURE")
      FileLength=Field.ActualSize
      NumBlocks=FileLength \ Blocksize
      LeftOver=FileLength Mod Blocksize
      Response.BinaryWrite Field.GetChunk(LeftOver)
      for intLoop=1 to NumBlocks
         Response.BinaryWrite Field.GetChunk(Blocksize)
      next
   end if
end if
%>


<% ' VI 6.0 Scripting Object Model Enabled %>
<!--#include file="_ScriptLibrary/pm.asp"-->
<% if StartPageProcessing() Then Response.End() %>
<FORM name=thisForm METHOD=post>
<HTML>
<HEAD>
<META NAME="GENERATOR" Content="Microsoft Visual Studio 6.0">
<TITLE>test</TITLE>

<LINK REL="stylesheet" TYPE="text/css" HREF="_Themes/redside/THEME.CSS"
VI6.0THEME="Redside">
<LINK REL="stylesheet" TYPE="text/css" HREF="_Themes/redside/GRAPH0.CSS"
VI6.0THEME="Redside">
<LINK REL="stylesheet" TYPE="text/css" HREF="_Themes/redside/COLOR0.CSS"
VI6.0THEME="Redside">
<LINK REL="stylesheet" TYPE="text/css" HREF="_Themes/redside/CUSTOM.CSS"
VI6.0THEME="Redside"></HEAD>
<BODY bgColor=White>
<!-- Establish the Connection to DB2 Sample Database and displays the
Resume
     of the choosen employee-->

<%
ifRequest.Form("cmdResume")="Resume" then
   Set rs = Server.CreateObject ("ADODB.Recordset")
   rs.Open "Select LONG_VARCHAR(RESUME) from EMP_RESUME where
RESUME_FORMAT='ascii' and EMPNO='" & Request.Form("EMPNO") & "'", conn, _
   adOpenKeyset, adLockOptimistic
   if not rs.EOF then
      Textbox1.value =rs.Fields(0)
   else
      Textbox1.value ="NO RESUME present for the Employee"
   end if
end if

ifRequest.Form("cmdPhoto")="Photo" and rs.EOF then
   Textbox1.value ="NO PHOTOGRAPH present for the Employee"
end if

rs.Close
conn.Close
set conn=nothing
%>
```

```
<!--METADATA TYPE="DesignerControl" startspan
<OBJECT classid="clsid:B5F0E469-DC5F-11D0-9846-0000F8027CA0" height=510
id=Textbox1
style="HEIGHT: 510px; LEFT: 0px; TOP: 0px; WIDTH: 540px" width=540>
<PARAM NAME="_ExtentX" VALUE="14288">
<PARAM NAME="_ExtentY" VALUE="13494">
<PARAM NAME="id" VALUE="Textbox1">
<PARAM NAME="ControlType" VALUE="1">
<PARAM NAME="Lines" VALUE="39">
<PARAM NAME="DataSource" VALUE="">
<PARAM NAME="DataField" VALUE="">
<PARAM NAME="Enabled" VALUE="-1">
<PARAM NAME="Visible" VALUE="-1">
<PARAM NAME="MaxChars" VALUE="256">
<PARAM NAME="DisplayWidth" VALUE="90">
<PARAM NAME="Platform" VALUE="0">
<PARAM NAME="LocalPath" VALUE=""></OBJECT>
-->
<!--#INCLUDE FILE="_ScriptLibrary/TextBox.ASP"-->
<SCRIPT LANGUAGE=JavaScript RUNAT=Server>
function _initTextbox1()
{
Textbox1.setStyle(TXT_TEXTAREA);
Textbox1.setRowCount(39);
Textbox1.setColumnCount(90);
}
function _Textbox1_ctor()
{
CreateTextbox('Textbox1', _initTextbox1, null);
}
</script>
<% Textbox1.display %>

<!--METADATA TYPE="DesignerControl" endspan-->
</BODY>
<% ' VI 6.0 Scripting Object Model Enabled %>
<% EndPageProcessing() %>
</FORM>
</HTML>
```

Global.asa

Here you declare the global data for the application. The source code of the file for the sample site is given below, and is used by the above-mentioned ASP files.

More information about the Global.asa file is provided in the section "Global Data" on page 354.

```
<SCRIPT LANGUAGE=VBScript RUNAT=Server>
Sub Application_OnStart
'==Visual InterDev Generated - startspan==
'--Project Data Connection
Application("ConnSample_ConnectionString") = "Provider=MSDASQL.1;" _
& "Persist Security Info=False;Connect Timeout=15;" _
& "Extended Properties=""DSN=SAMPLE;UID=db2admin; DBALIAS=SAMPLE;" _
& "Passsord=db2admin"";Locale Identifier=1033;"
Application("ConnSample_ConnectionTimeout") = 15
Application("ConnSample_CommandTimeout") = 30
Application("ConnSample_CursorLocation") = 3
Application("ConnSample_RuntimeUserName") = "db2admin"
Application("ConnSample_RuntimePassword") = "db2admin"
'-- Project Data Environment
Set DE = Server.CreateObject("DERuntime.DERuntime")
```

```
Application("DE") = DE.Load(Server.MapPath("Global.ASA"), "_private/
DataEnvironment/DataEnvironment.asa")
'==Visual InterDev Generated - endspan==
End Sub
</SCRIPT>
```

Creating a Web Application: Microsoft Visual Interdev 6.0

Microsoft Visual InterDev 6.0 is used for designing, building, testing, debugging, deploying, and managing component-based, data-intensive Web applications. Here we are explaining how to develop our sample Web application using Microsoft Visual Interdev 6.0. If you are familiar with Microsoft Visual Interdev 6.0, you can skip this section entirely.

Create the Sample Web Application

Perform the following steps to create the sample Web application:

1. From the **Start** button, select **Programs** -> **Microsoft Visual Studio** -> **Microsoft Visual Interdev**.

2. From the **File** menu, click **New Project**.

3. On the **New** tab, click the **New Web Project** icon.

4. Enter the name of project as `SampleASP`, note the physical location for the new project that you are creating, and click Open.

An illustration of steps 1 - 4 is shown in Fig. 8–18:

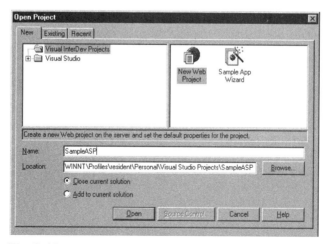

Fig. 8–18 *New Project Window*

5. In the drop-down list box, set the name of the server to the name of the computer you are using. If you do not know the computer name, start the **Control Panel**, click the **Network** icon, and inspect the **Computer Name** field on the Identification tab. Here, in the sample, the name of the computer is ADRIATIC.

6. Leave the working mode check box set to **Master** mode, and click **Next**.

An illustration of steps 5 - 6 is shown in Fig. 8–19:

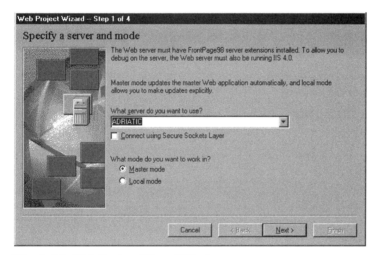

Fig. 8–19 *Web Project Wizard Window*

7. Leave the default value for the name of the Web project that you are creating (which is SampleASP), but notice that you can connect to an existing Web application on this server. Click **Next**.

8. Select several of the layouts that are offered, inspect them for their content, and note the differences between them. Notice that you can browse for other layouts on other computers. For the SampleASP application we will not use any layouts, and hence select **<none>**. Click **Next**.

9. Select several of the themes that are offered, inspect them for their content, and note the differences between them. For the SampleASP application, select the **Redside** theme from the theme list box.Click **Finish**.

An illustration of step 9 is shown in Fig. 8–20:

Application
Development
on IIS

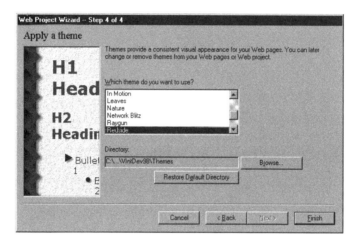

Fig. 8–20 *Selecting a Theme for the Web Project*

By this time, the Web application folder by the name SampleASP would have been created in the Web Publishing folder (by default, this is `C:\InetPub\wwwroot`).

Now, for this blank application, you will add Data Connection. You will also build three files: the `Employee.asp`, `Resume.asp` and `Default.htm` files.

Note: Since Sample application makes use of ADO Objects, you must set a reference to Microsoft ActiveX Data Objects 2.0 Library (msado20.tlb) by clicking **References** on the **Project** menu.

Adding a Data Connection

Steps 1 to 5 describe how to add Data Connection to the `SampleASP` application.

1. In the **Project Explorer** window select the `SampleASP` project.

2. Right-click to open the context menu; then click **Add Data Connection**.

3. Select **Microsoft OLE DB providers for ODBC** in the provider tab. Click **Next**.

4. In the Connection tab, select **Sample** from the Use Data Source names list box. In the 'Enter information to log on to server' section, enter Username as **db2admin** and Password equals to **db2admin**. In the same section, check the **Allow Password saving option**, then click **OK**.

An illustration for step 4 is shown in Fig. 8–21:

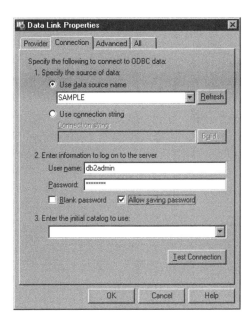

Fig. 8–21 *Data Connection Properties*

For more information about DSNs, see "Check That the ODBC DSN Exists for the DB2 UDB Database" on page 376.

5. In the `Connection1` properties window, set the Connection Name to **ConnSample**, and then click **OK**.

6. Save the project by clicking the **Save All** toolbar button.

By now, you would have gotten the source code generated for the global.asa file. The sample of this source code is available in the section "Global.asa" on page 385.

Adding a Data Command

Steps 1 to 3 describe how to add Data Command to the SampleASP application.

1. In the Project Explorer window, select the `SampleASP` project.

2. Right-click to open the context menu; then click **Add Data Command**. This will show the Command Properties window and set the various properties as shown in Fig. 8–22.

3. Click **OK**.

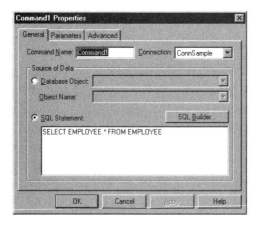

Fig. 8–22 *Data Command Properties*

Adding the Employee.asp File to the Sample Application

1. In the Project Explorer window, select the `SampleASP` project.

2. Right-click to open the context menu; then click Add and select **Active Server Page**.

3. Let the name of ASP page be **Employee.asp** and Click **Open**.

An illustration of step 3 is shown in Fig. 8–23:

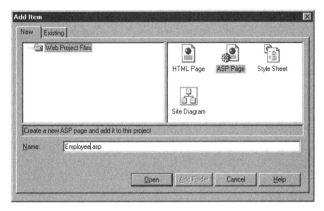

Fig. 8–23 *Add ASP Page Window*

The Employee.asp file uses several different Design-Time Controls (DTC), as explained in the section "Employee.asp" on page 379. The following section describes how you can create this page so that the page will look like the one shown in Fig. 8–15 on page 381.

Adding Required Buttons to the Employee.asp File

To add the Design Time Control (DTC) button to the page, just drag the Button control onto a page. Right-click on the added button to go the properties window to set the appropriate Caption and Name. A section of the buttons added to the Employee.asp page is shown in Fig. 8–24:

Application Development on IIS

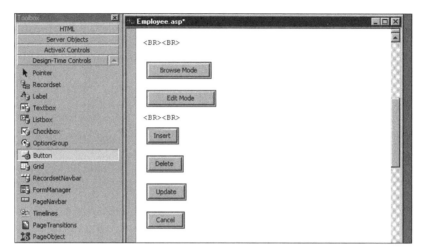

Fig. 8–24 *Source Window of Employee.asp Showing Added Buttons*

Adding the Recordset DTC to the Employee.asp File

To add the Recordset object, drag the Data Command object (Command1) created earlier from Project Explorer onto a page. Visual InterDev automatically creates the control and binds it to the Data Environment (DE) object.

Fig. 8–25 shows the Recordset control on the Employee.asp page.

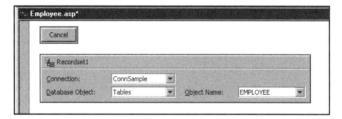

Fig. 8–25 *Recordset Control on the Employee.asp Page*

Thus, the Recordset1 control can now be used to connect EMPLOYEE table attributes to data-bound controls on an ASP page.

Adding the Textbox DTC to the Employee.asp File

These controls are used to display and edit the employee number, first name, middle name, last name, date of birth, phone number, job, education level, and salary fields in the EMPLOYEE table. Each of these controls is bound to a field in the table through Recordset1 Control.

To add a Textbox DTC to the Employee.asp page, drag the Textbox DTC onto the page. Fig. 8–26 shows the employee number, first name and middle name Textbox Controls added to the Employee.asp page.

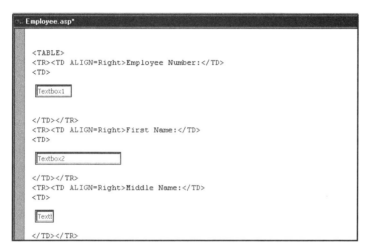

Fig. 8–26 *Source Window of Employee.asp Showing Added Textbox Controls*

Similarly, add the remaining Textbox controls for the last name, date of birth, phone number, job, education level, and salary. To set the Textbox control properties, right-click on the control and select properties. Fig. 8–27 shows properties set for the employee number Textbox control which is bound to the Recordset1 control.

Application
Development
on IIS

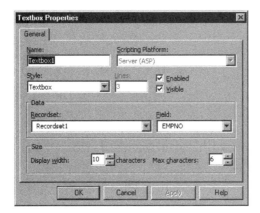

Fig. 8–27 *Textbox1 Property Window*

Similarly, the other Textbox controls are also bound to the `Recordset1` control.

Adding OptionGroup DTC

This control is bound to the `SEX` field in the `EMPLOYEE` table. To add OptionGroup DTC, drag the OptionGroup Control onto the `Employee.asp` page. An illustration of this control is shown in Fig. 8–28:

Fig. 8–28 *OptionGroup Control*

Static values of `Male` and `Female` are set in the properties of the control. They correspond to a "1" for `Male` and "0" for `Female` in the table. To set the properties, right-click on the control and select **Properties**. An Illustration of this is shown in Fig. 8–29:

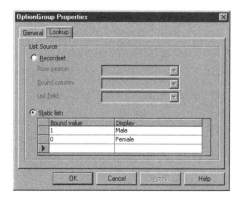

Fig. 8–29 *OptionGroup Control Property Window*

Adding RecordsetNavBar DTC

To add the RecordsetNavBar Control to the page, drag the control onto the page. An illustration of this control added to the `Employee.asp` file is shown in Fig. 8–30:

Fig. 8–30 *RecordsetNavBar Control*

This control is bound to the Recordset1 control to allow the user to step through the records in the `EMPLOYEE` table. You do this by setting the Recordset property of the control to `Recordset1`.

Adding FormManager DTC

More details about this control are in the section "Employee.asp" on page 379. An illustration of this control added to the `Employee.asp` page is shown in Fig. 8–31:

Fig. 8–31 *FormManager Control*

Application
Development
on IIS

In the FormManager properties dialog box, the Browse and Edit mode properties are set to enable and disable the controls within the form. The Browse mode is also set to be the default mode when you enter this Web page. Add the three modes, that is, Edit, Browse, and Insert, as shown in Fig. 8–32:

Fig. 8–32 *FormManager Properties*

Do the settings shown in Table 8–3 for Edit Mode in the 'Action Performed For Mode' grid of the Form Mode tab of the FormManager properties dialog box.

Table 8–3 *Actions Performed for Form Edit Mode*

Object	Member	Value
BrowseBtn	disabled	false
EditBtn	disabled	true
DeleteBtn	show	()
DeleteBtn	disabled	false
InsertBtn	show	()
InsertBtn	disabled	false
UpdateBtn	show	()
CancelBtn	show	()
Textbox1	disabled	false
Textbox2	disabled	false

Table 8–3 *Actions Performed for Form Edit Mode*

Object	Member	Value
Textbox3	disabled	false
Textbox4	disabled	false
Textbox5	disabled	false
Textbox6	disabled	false
Textbox7	disabled	false
RecordsetNavbar1	hide	()
OptionGroup1,getButton(0)	disabled	false
OptionGroup1,getButton(0)	disabled	false
Textbox8	disabled	false
Textbox9	disabled	false

Do the settings shown in Table 8–4 for Insert Mode in the 'Action Performed For Mode' grid of the Form Mode tab of the FormManager properties dialog box.

Table 8–4 *Actions Performed for Form Insert Mode*

Object	Member	Value
DeleteBtn	disabled	true
BrowseBtn	disabled	true
InsertBtn	disabled	true
Textbox1	value	""
Textbox2	value	""
Textbox3	value	""
Textbox4	value	""
Textbox5	value	""
Textbox6	value	""
Textbox7	value	""
Textbox8	value	""
Textbox9	value	""

Application Development on IIS

Do the settings shown in Table 8–5 for Browse Mode in the 'Action Performed For Mode' grid of the Form Mode tab of the FormManager properties dialog box.

Table 8–5 *Actions Performed for Form Browse Mode*

Object	Member	Value
BrowseBtn	disabled	true
EditBtn	disabled	false
DeleteBtn	hide	()
InsertBtn	hide	()
UpdateBtn	hide	()
CancelBtn	hide	()
Textbox1	disabled	true
Textbox2	disabled	true
Textbox3	disabled	true
Textbox4	disabled	true
Textbox5	disabled	true
Textbox6	disabled	true
Textbox7	disabled	true
RecordsetNavbar1	show	()
	disable_opt	(OptionGroup1)
Textbox8	disabled	true
Textbox9	disabled	true

In the Action tab of the FormManager properties dialog box, the properties for the buttons are set. Each button performs a different set of actions. Do the settings for the various buttons on the Employee.asp page as shown in the following seven figures.

Settings for the Update button of Edit Mode are shown in Fig. 8–33:

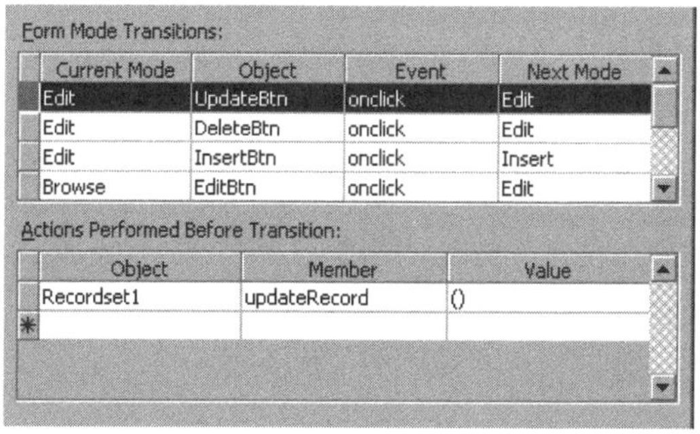

Fig. 8–33 *Action Tab of FormManager Properties Dialog Box (Update Button)*

Settings for the Delete button of Edit mode are shown in Fig. 8–34:

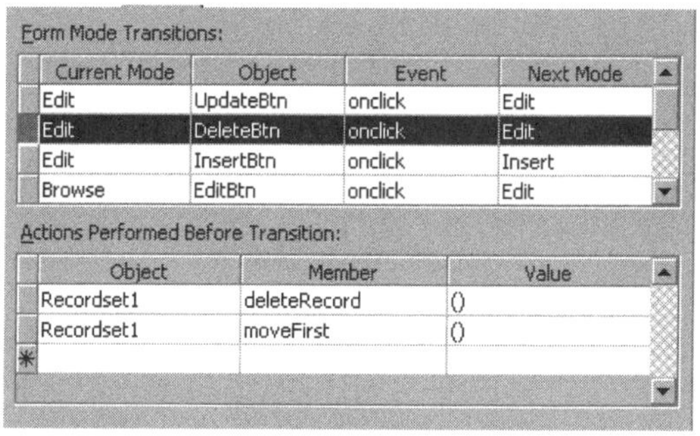

Fig. 8–34 *Action Tab of FormManager Properties Dialog Box (Delete Button)*

Settings for the Insert button of Edit mode are shown in Fig. 8–35:

Application Development on IIS

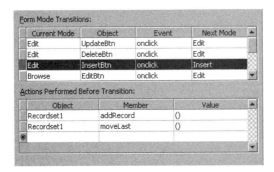

Fig. 8–35 *Action Tab of FormManager Properties Dialog Box (Insert Button)*

Settings for the Edit button of Browse mode are shown in Fig. 8–36:

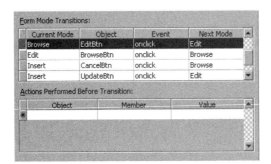

Fig. 8–36 *Action Tab of FormManager Properties Dialog Box (Edit Button)*

Settings for the Browse button of Edit mode are shown in Fig. 8–37:

Fig. 8–37 *Action Tab of FormManager Properties Dialog Box (Browse Button)*

Settings for the Cancel button of Insert mode are shown in Fig. 8–38:

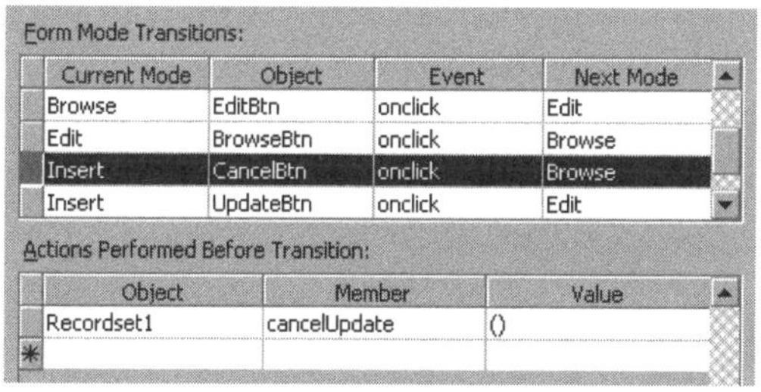

Fig. 8–38 *Action Tab of FormManager Properties Dialog Box (Cancel Button)*

Settings for the Update button of Insert mode are shown in Fig. 8–39:

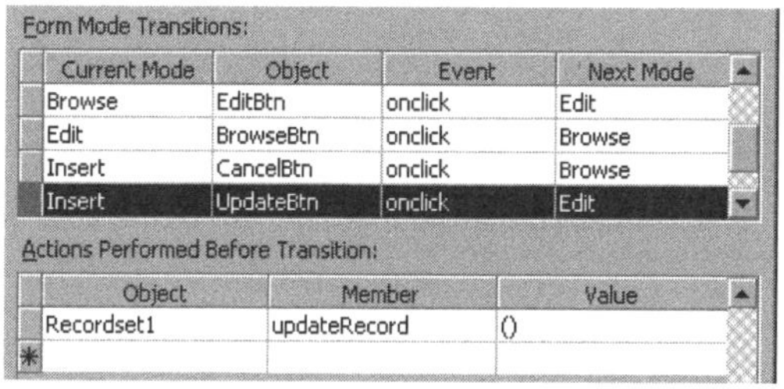

Fig. 8–39 *Action Tab of FormManager Properties Dialog Box (Update Button)*

Adding Resume and Photo Buttons to the Employee.asp File

Add the following code to the `Employee.asp` page. which adds Resume and Photo buttons to the ASP page. It also sends the information required for the `Resume.asp` page.

```
<FORM ACTION="Resume.asp" METHOD=POST id=form1 name=form1>
<INPUT TYPE=hidden NAME="EmpNo"
value="<%=Recordset1.fields.getValue("EMPNO") %>">
<INPUT TYPE=SUBMIT NAME="cmdResume" VALUE="Resume">
<INPUT TYPE=SUBMIT NAME="cmdPhoto" VALUE="Photo">
</FORM>
```

Application Development on IIS

The Form collection contains the values of each standard HTML control that has a NAME attribute. When a form is submitted with the POST method, the values of these controls are also submitted to the Resume.asp page. You can read the values of the controls by using Form collection, as explained in the section "Using Form Collection" on page 361.

By now, you have completed the development of the Employee.asp page. Save the project by clicking the **Save All** toolbar button.

Adding Resume.asp File to the SampleASP Application

Follow the same steps as mentioned in "Adding the Employee.asp File to the Sample Application" on page 390, but now, do these steps for the Resume.asp file. Delete the existing code of the page. Copy all the source code given for Resume.asp in the section "Photo of the Employee" on page 382 to this ASP page.

Save the project by clicking the **Save All** toolbar button. This completes the Resume.asp page.

Adding Default.htm File to the SampleASP Application

Perform the following steps to add the Default.htm file to the Sample application:

1. In the Project Explorer window, select the SampleASP project.

2. Right-click to open the context menu; then click **Add** and select **HTML Page**

3. Let the name of the HTML page be Default.htm, and click Open.

An illustration of step 3 is shown in Fig. 8–40:

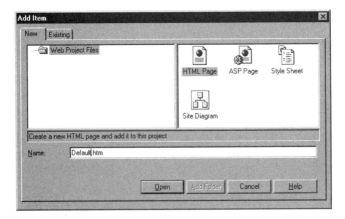

Fig. 8–40 *Add HTML Page Window*

4. Delete the existing code of the page. Copy all the source code given for `Default.htm` in the section "Default.html" on page 378 to this **.htm** page. This automatically will make the HTML page look like the one shown in Fig. 8–14 on page 378.

5. Save the project by clicking **Save All** toolbar button.

6. Exit the application by clicking **File** in the main menu, and then selecting **Exit**.

Test That the Web site Has Been Properly Installed (Published)

Do the following steps to check the Sample Web application.

1. Open Internet Explorer.

2. In the Address text box, type the following URL and press Enter:

   `<computer-name>/SampleASP/default.htm`.

3. Browse the site and click on the Employee Data Entry link to go to the Employee Details page. Check the Browse and Edit modes of operation of this page. Also check the Resume and Photo buttons.

Application
Development
on IIS

Tuning Application Performance

- ◆ CONSIDERATIONS WHEN USING SELECT
- ◆ CONCURRENCY
- ◆ DECLARED TEMPORARY TABLE
- ◆ CONVERT ODBC TO STATIC SQL
- ◆ CONSIDERATIONS IN A PARTITIONED ENVIRONMENT
- ◆ ANALYZING AND IMPROVING PERFORMANCE USING CLI TRACE

*P*erformance is the way a computer system behaves, given a particular workload. Performance is measured through one or more of these system variables: response time, throughput, and availability; and it is affected by the availability of the resources and how well those resources are used and shared.

In general, a database administrator who wants to improve the performance of the database server should undertake performance tuning by updating the database manager or database configuration parameters. Creating appropriate indices, and balancing the demand for disk I/O across several disk storage devices, can also improve the performance. Basically, these are the database administrator's tasks.

On the other hand, the best way for application programmers to get better performance is to write efficient application programs. For example, SQL is a high-level language with much flexibility, and as a result, different SELECT statements can be written to retrieve the same data.

However, the performance can vary for the different forms of select statements. This is because one statement may have a higher processing cost than another. In such a case, you should choose the SQL statement which has the lower processing cost, so that the application will have good performance. In this chapter, we discuss considerations for writing efficient SQL statements in your application programs.

Application programmers also need to consider the concurrency of their applications. Even if SQL statements in an application are good for performance, they may need to wait to retrieve data records until all locks held on them by other applications are released, and this can decrease the application performance. Therefore, we will discuss concurrency in this chapter.

We will explain declared temporary tables and conversion of ODBC applications into static SQL. These functions were introduced in DB2 UDB Version 7.1, and can be used to improve your application performance. We also provide tips to improve application performance in a partitioned database environment.

Finally, we introduce the CLI/ODBC trace facility of DB2 UDB, which is an essential tool for problem determination and general understanding of a CLI/ODBC application.

Using SELECT Statements

DB2 UDB provides the SQL compiler which creates the compiled form of SQL statements. When the SQL compiler compiles SQL statements, it rewrites the SQL statements into a form that can be optimized more easily. This is known as *query rewrite*.

The SQL compiler then generates many alternative execution plans for satisfying the user's request. It estimates the execution cost of each alternative plan using the statistics for tables, indexes, columns, and functions, and chooses the plan with the smallest estimated execution cost. This is known as *query optimization*.

It is important to note that the SQL compiler (including the query rewrite and optimization phases) must choose an access plan that will produce the result set for the query you have coded. Therefore, as noted in many of the following guidelines, you should code your query to obtain only the data that you need. This ensures that the SQL compiler can choose the best access plan for your needs.

The guidelines for using a SELECT statement are:

- Specify only needed columns.
- Limit the number of rows.
- Specify the OPTIMIZED FOR n ROWS clause.
- Specify the FETCH FIRST n ROWS ONLY clause.

- Specify the `FOR FETCH ONLY` clause.
- Avoid numeric data type conversion.

Each of these guidelines are further explored in the next section.

Specify Only Needed Columns in the Select List

Specify only those columns that are needed in the select list. Although it may be simpler to specify all columns with an asterisk (*), needless processing and returning of unwanted columns can result.

Limit the Number of Rows by Using Predicates

Limit the number of rows selected by using predicates to restrict the answer set to only those rows that you require. Also be aware there are four categories of predicates. The category is determined by how and when that predicate is used in the evaluation process. These categories are listed below, ordered in terms of performance, starting with the most favorable:

- Range delimiting predicates
- Index SARGable predicates
- Data SARGable predicates
- Residual predicates

Note: SARGable refers to something that can be used as a search argument.

Range delimiting predicates are those used to bracket an index scan. They provide start and/or stop key values for the index search. Index SARGable predicates are not used to bracket a search, but can be evaluated from the index because the columns involved in the predicate are part of the index key. For example, assume that an index has been defined on the `NAME`, `DEPT`, and `YEARS` columns of the `STAFF` table, and you are executing the following select statement:

```
SELECT name, job, salary FROM staff
    WHERE NAME  = 'John'
          DEPT  = 10
          YEARS > 5
```

The first two predicates (NAME = 'John', DEPT=10) would be range delimiting predicates, while YEARS > 5 would be an index SARGable predicate, as the start key value for the index search cannot be determined by this information only. The start key value may be 6, 10, or even higher. If the predicate for the YEARS column is YEARS => 5, it would be a range delimiting predicate, as the index search can start from the key value 5.

The database manager will make use of the index data in evaluating these predicates, rather than reading the base table. These range delimiting predicates and index SARGable predicates reduce the number of data pages accessed by reducing the set of rows that need to be read from the table. Index SARGable predicates do not affect the number of index pages that are accessed.

Data SARGable Predicates are the predicates that cannot be evaluated by the Index Manager, but can be evaluated by Data Management Services (DMS). Typically, these predicates require the access of individual rows from a base table. If required, Data Management Services will retrieve the columns needed to evaluate the predicate, as well as any others to satisfy the columns in the SELECT list that could not be obtained from the index.

For example, assume that a single index is defined on the PROJNO column of the PROJECT table but not on the DEPTNO column, and you are executing the following query:

```
SELECT projno,projname,repemp FROM project
    WHERE deptno='D11'
    ORDER BY projno
```

The predicate DEPTNO='D11' is considered data SARGable, because there are no indexes on the DEPTNO column, and the base table must be accessed to evaluate the predicate.

Residual predicates, typically, are those that require I/O beyond the simple accessing of a base table. Examples of residual predicates include those using quantified sub-queries (sub-queries with ANY, ALL, SOME, or IN), or reading LONG VARCHAR or large object (LOB) data (they are stored separately from the table). These predicates are evaluated by Relational Data Services (RDS). Residual predicates are the most expensive of the four categories of predicates.

As residual predicates and data SARGable predicates cost more than range delimiting predicates and index SARGable predicates, you should try to limit the number of rows qualified by range delimiting predicates and index SARGable predicates whenever possible.

Let us briefly look at the following DB2 UDB components: Index Manager, Data Management Service, and Relational Data Service. Fig. 9–1 shows each DB2 UDB component and where each category of predicates is processed.

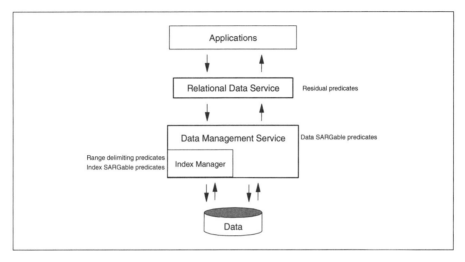

Fig. 9–1 *DB2 UDB Components and Predicates*

 Note: Fig. 9–1 provides a simplified explanation. Actually, DB2 UDB has more components than are shown in this diagram.

Relational Data Service (RDS) receives SQL requests from applications and returns the result set. It sends all predicates to Data Management Service (DMS) except residual predicates. Residual predicates are evaluated by Relational Data Service (RDS).

DMS evaluates data SARGable predicates. Also, if the select list has columns which cannot be evaluated by the index search, DMS scans data pages directly.

Index Manager receives range delimiting predicates and index SARGable predicates from DMS, evaluates them, and then returns row identifiers (RIDs) to the data page to DMS.

Specify the OPTIMIZE FOR n ROWS Clause

Specify the OPTIMIZE FOR n ROWS clause in the SELECT statement when the number of rows you want to retrieve is significantly less than the total number of rows that could be returned. Use of the OPTIMIZE FOR clause influences query optimization based on the assumption that n rows will be retrieved. This clause also determines the number of rows that are blocked in the communication buffer.

```
SELECT projno,projname,repemp FROM project
    WHERE deptno='D11' OPTIMIZE FOR 10 ROWS
```

Row blocking is a technique that reduces database manager overhead by retrieving a block of rows in a single operation. These rows are stored in a cache, and each FETCH request in the application gets the next row from the cache. If you specify OPTIMIZE FOR 10 ROWS, a block of rows is returned to the client every ten rows.

Note: The OPTIMIZE FOR n ROWS clause does not limit the number of rows that can be fetched or affect the result in any way other than performance. Using OPTIMIZE FOR n ROWS can improve the performance if no more than n rows are retrieved, but may degrade performance if more than n rows are retrieved.

Specify the FETCH FIRST n ROWS ONLY Clause

Specify the FETCH FIRST n ROWS ONLY clause if you do not want the application to retrieve more than *n* rows, regardless of how many rows there might be in the result set when this clause is not specified. This clause cannot be specified with the FOR UPDATE clause.

For example, with the following coding, you will not receive more than 5 rows:

```
SELECT projno,projname,repemp FROM project
    WHERE deptno='D11'
    FETCH FIRST 5 ROWS ONLY
```

The FETCH FIRST n ROWS ONLY clause also determines the number of rows that are blocked in the communication buffer. If both the FETCH FIRST n ROWS ONLY and OPTIMIZE FOR n ROWS clause are specified, the lower of the two values is used to determine the communication buffer size.

Specify the FOR FETCH ONLY Clause

If you have no intention of updating rows retrieved by a SELECT statement, specify the FOR FETCH ONLY clause in the SELECT statement. It can improve performance by allowing your query to take advantage of row blocking. It can also improve data concurrency since exclusive locks will never be held on the rows retrieved by a query with this clause specified (see "Concurrency" on page 412).

> **Note:** Instead of the FOR FETCH ONLY clause, you can also use the FOR READ ONLY clause. 'FOR READ ONLY' is a synonym for 'FOR FETCH ONLY'.

Avoid Data Type Conversions

Data type conversions (particularly numeric data type conversions) should be avoided whenever possible. When two values are compared, it may be more efficient to use items that have the same data type. For example, suppose you are joining TableA and TableB using column A1 of TableA and column B1 of TableB as in the example.

```
SELECT * FROM TableA,TableB WHERE A1=B1
```

If columns A1 and B1 are the same data type, no data type conversion is required. But if they are not the same data type, a data type conversion occurs to compare values at run time and it might affect the performance. For example, if A1 is a decimal column and B1 is an integer column and each has a value '123', data type conversion is needed, as TableA stores it as x'123C', whereas TableB stores it as x'7B'.

Also, inaccuracies due to limited precision may result when data type conversions occur.

Other Considerations for Data Types

DB2 UDB allows you to use various data types. You can use SMALLINT, INTEGER, BIGINT, DECIMAL, REAL, and DOUBLE for numeric data; CHAR, VARCHAR, LONG VARCHAR, CLOB for character data; GRAPHIC, VARGRAPHIC, LONG VARGRAPHIC, and DBCLOB for the double byte character data, and so on. As the amount of database storage and the cost to process varies depending on the data type, you should choose the appropriate data type.

The following are guidelines when choosing a data type:

- Use character (CHAR) rather than varying-length character (VARCHAR) for short columns. The varying-length character data type can save database storage when the length of data values varies, but there is a cost to check the length of each data value.
- Use integer (SMALLINT, INTEGER, BIGINT) rather than floating-point number (REAL or DOUBLE) or decimal (DECIMAL) if you don't need to have the fraction part.
- Use date-time (DATE, TIME, TIMESTAMP) rather than character (CHAR).
- Use numeric data types rather than character.

For detailed information about the supported data types, refer the *DB2 UDB SQL Reference*.

Concurrency

When many users access the same database, some rules must be established for the reading, inserting, deleting, and updating of data records to guarantee the integrity of the data. The rules for data access are set by each application connected to a DB2 UDB database and are established using locking mechanisms. DB2 UDB implicitly locks database resources at the row level. You can control record locking behavior by specifying *isolation levels*. Choosing an appropriate isolation level ensures data integrity, and also avoids unnecessary locking. This can improve your application's performance, since unnecessary lock-waits can be eliminated.

Note: Some of the DB2 UDB database resources, databases, table spaces, and tables can be explicitly controlled using an SQL statement or using a DB2 UDB command for concurrency purposes. Some examples are the CONNECT statement, the QUIESCE TABLESPACE command, and the LOCK TABLE statement.

lifferent levels of protection to isolate the data
ms while it is being accessed.

n as isolation levels, or locking strategies. The
JDB include:

on level, also known as dirty read, is the lowest
UDB. It can be used to access uncommitted
or example, an application using the
ill return all of the matching rows for a query,
being modified, and may not be committed to
ware that two identical queries may get
d within a unit of work, since other concurrent
lose rows that the first query retrieves.

Uncommitted Read transactions. If you are
care about getting uncommitted data updated
tion level.

vel locks any row on which the cursor is
lock on the row is held until the next row is
ted. If a row has been updated, the lock is held
unit of work is terminated when either a
cuted.

cannot read uncommitted data. In addition,
been currently fetched, and no other
f the current row. As the application locks
ositioned, two identical queries may still get
d within a unit of work.

Read Stability

The Read Stability (RS) isolation level locks those rows that are part of a result set. If you have a table containing 10,000 rows and the query returns 10 rows, then only 10 rows are locked until the end of the unit of work.

An application using Read Stability cannot read uncommitted data. Instead of locking a single row, it locks all rows that are part of the result set. No other application can change or modify these rows. This means that if you issue a query twice within a unit of work, the second run can retrieve the same answer set as the first. However, you may get additional rows, as another concurrent application can insert rows that match to the query.

Repeatable Read

The Repeatable Read (RR) isolation level is the highest isolation level available in DB2 UDB. It locks all rows that an application references within a unit of work. Locks are held on all rows processed to build the result set, no matter how large the result set. In some cases, the optimizer decides during plan generation that it may get a table level lock instead of locking individual rows.

Each database has a lock list which is allocated from the memory and contains all locks held by all applications concurrently connected to the database. As an application using Repeatable Read may acquire and hold a considerable number of locks, a table level lock may be obtained instead. This depends on the number of rows that need to be locked, the size of the lock list (specified by the LOCKLIST database configuration parameter), and the value of the MAXLOCKS database configuration parameter which defines the percentage of the lock list which can be held by an application.

An application using Repeatable Read cannot read uncommitted data of a concurrent application. As the name implies, this isolation level ensures the Repeatable Read to applications, meaning that a repeated query will get the same record set as long as it is executed in the same unit of work.

Choosing an Isolation Level

Choosing the proper isolation level is very important, because the isolation level influences not only the concurrency, but also the performance of the application. The more protection you have, the less concurrency is available.

Decide which concurrency problems are unacceptable for your application and then choose the isolation level which prevents these problems:

- Use the Uncommitted Read isolation level only if you use queries on read-only tables, or if you are using only SELECT statements and do not care whether you get uncommitted data from concurrent applications.
- Use the Cursor Stability isolation level when you want the maximum concurrency while seeing only committed data from concurrent applications.
- Use the Read Stability isolation level when your application operates in a concurrent environment. This means that qualified rows have to remain stable for the duration of the unit of work.
- Use the Repeatable Read isolation level if changes to your result set are unacceptable.

Setting an Isolation Level

The isolation level is defined for embedded SQL statements during the binding of a package to a database using the ISOLATION option of the PREP or the BIND command. The following PREP and BIND examples specify the isolation level as the Uncommitted Read (UR).

```
PREP program1.sqc ISOLATION UR
```

```
BIND program1.bnd ISOLATION UR
```

If no isolation level is specified, the default level of Cursor Stability is used.

If you are using the command line processor, you may change the isolation level of the current session using the CHANGE ISOLATION command.

```
CHANGE ISOLATION TO rr
```

For DB2 Call Level Interface (DB2 CLI), you can use the SQLSetConnectAttr function with the SQL_ATTR_TXN_ISOLATION attribute at run time. This will set the transaction isolation level for the current connection referenced by the ConnectionHandle. The accepted values are:

- SQL_TXN_READ_UNCOMMITTED : Uncommitted Read
- SQL_TXN_READ_COMMITTED   : Cursor Stability

- SQL_TXN_REPEATABLE_READ : Read Stability
- SQL_TXN_SERIALIZABLE : Repeatable Read

You can also set the isolation level using the TXNISOLATION keyword of the DB2 CLI configuration (db2cli.ini file) as follows:

```
[SAMPLE]
TXNISOLATION=1
DBALIAS=SAMPLE
```

The following values can be specified for the TXNISOLATION keyword: 1, 2, 4, 8, or 32. Here are their meanings:

- 1 = Uncommitted Read
- 2 = Cursor Stability (default)
- 4 = Read Stability
- 8 = Repeatable Read

On a Windows NT machine, if a database is registered as a system data source, the DB2 CLI configuration file is under the directory where DB2 UDB is installed (the default path is C:\SQLLIB). If a database is registered as a user data source, it is under C:\WINNT\Profiles\User (assuming the user name is User).

The isolation level for DB2 CLI programs can also be set using the Client Configuration Assistant (CCA). From the main window of the Client Configuration Assistant (CCA), select a database entry and click on **Properties** and the database properties window will appear. Clicking **Setting** on that window will bring up the ODBC/CLI settings window. Then, clicking the **Advanced** button on the ODBC/CLI settings window will bring up the ODBC/CLI Settings-Advanced Settings window, as shown in Fig. 9–2. You can change the isolation level through this window.

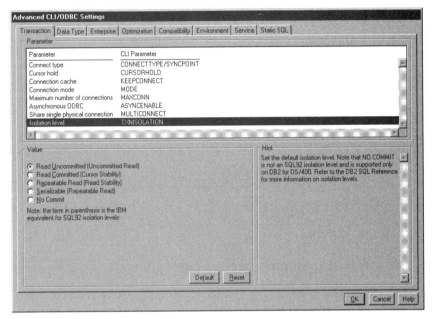

Fig. 9–2 *ODBC/CLI Settings — Advanced Settings Window*

Note: For JDBC and SQLJ applications, you can also use the db2cli.ini file to set the isolation level. This is because JDBC and SQLJ are implemented with CLI on DB2 UDB.

For ADO applications, you can set the isolation level using the `IsolationLevel` property of the `ADODB.Connection` object. The following values can be specified:

- `adXactReadUncommitted` : Uncommitted Read
- `adXactCursorStability` : Cursor Stability
- `adXactRepeatableRead` : Read Stability
- `adXactSerializable`   : Repeatable Read

You can also specify the value `adXactBrowse` for Uncommitted Read, `adXactReadCommitted` for Cursor Stability, and `adXactIsolated` for Repeatable Read.

The following is a Visual Basic example to set the isolation level to Uncommitted Read for a new connection:

```
Dim cnn1 As ADODB.Connection
Dim strCnn1 As String
strCnn1 = "DSN=SAMPLE;UID=;PWD=;"
Set cnn1 = New ADODB.Connection
cnn1.IsolationLevel = adXactReadUncommitted
cnn1.Open strCnn1
.....
```

LOCK TABLE Statement

You can use the LOCK TABLE statement to override the rules for acquiring initial locks. It locks the specified table until the unit of work is committed or rolled back. A table can be locked either in SHARE MODE or in EXCLUSIVE MODE as following:

```
LOCK TABLE TableA IN SHARE MODE
```

When using the LOCK TABLE statement in SHARE MODE, no other user's application can update, delete, or insert data in the locked table. If you need a snapshot of a table that is frequently changed by concurrent applications, you can use this statement to lock the table for changes without using the Repeatable Read isolation level for your application.

The EXCLUSIVE MODE is more restrictive than SHARE MODE. It prevents other users' concurrent applications from accessing the table for read, update, delete, and insert. If you want to update a large part of the table, you can use the LOCK TABLE statement in EXCLUSIVE MODE rather than locking each row.

LOCKSIZE Parameter of ALTER TABLE Statement

The default locking method for tables in DB2 UDB is row locking. DB2 UDB provides you with the ability to override this default for a table by using the ALTER TABLE statement and the LOCKSIZE parameter.

The LOCKSIZE parameter allows you to specify the granularity of locking you wish DB2 UDB to do for you for a particular table; either row or table level locking. For example, to change the default locking method for TableA table from row locking to table locking, you would issue the following SQL statement:

```
ALTER TABLE TableA LOCKSIZE TABLE
```

Whenever an application requires a lock to access data in the table an appropriate table level lock will be issued. It is important to realize that since all locks on the table are at the table level, and not at the row level, it reduces the concurrency of applications accessing this table.

Declared Temporary Table

In some cases, particularly when you need to process large amounts of data with a complex query, you need to implement solutions that involve the creation of intermediate tables that are used to process the data. Often such intermediate tables do not need to be recovered, or even they can be dropped after the query is completed, but high performance is required. To meet this requirement, DB2 UDB supports *declared temporary tables*.

Before discussing what a declared temporary table is, let us see what type of tables are supported by DB2 UDB.

DB2 UDB supports two general physical implementations of a table.

The first type is the regular table, which:

- Exists as an entry in the system catalog tables
- Is accessible to any application process (with appropriate privileges)
- Resides in a regular table space

The second type is the temporary table, which:

- Does not exist as an entry in the system catalog tables
- Only used on behalf of a single application
- Changes are not logged
- Uses only minimal locking

A temporary table is created automatically by the database manager in a system temporary table space when it is necessary to process a statement (for example, sorting rows). This temporary table is called a system temporary table. You cannot manipulate it directly and the system temporary table does not persist beyond the current statement.

You can create a temporary table using the DECLARE GLOBAL TEMPORARY TABLE statement when you need it as an intermediate table. This temporary table is called a declared temporary table. A declared temporary table persists within the current application's connection and is dropped implicitly at the termination of the connection. During the connection period, the application can select rows from the declared temporary table, perform INSERT/UPDATE/DELETE statements without logging, and even drop the table explicitly. Declared temporary tables can be used from the standard SQL interfaces such as ODBC, CLI, and static/dynamic SQL.

Defining a Declared Temporary Table

Here is an example of creating a declared temporary table (assuming the application is connected to a database):

```
DECLARE GLOBAL TEMPORARY TABLE tt1
   (empno CHAR(10),salary DECIMAL (9,2))
   ON COMMIT RESERVE ROWS NOT LOGGED;
```

This example creates a declared temporary table tt1. The schema SESSION is assigned when a declared temporary table is created. If you want rows to persistent beyond a commit, you must specify the ON COMMIT RESERVE ROWS clause. The other clause you can specify is the ON COMMIT DELETE ROWS clause (it is the default value). You are also required to specify the NOT LOGGED clause. Note that other applications can create their own session.tt1 table at the same time. These are different tables; however can use the same table name because a temporary table does not have any entries in the system catalog tables.

 Note: For declared temporary tables, you must create a user temporary table space in advance using CREATE USER TEMPORARY TABLESPACE statement, and also you need to use DB2 UDB Version 7.1 or later to use declared temporary tables.

Here is an example of manipulating this table:

```
INSERT INTO session.tt1
  SELECT empno,salary FROM employee WHERE salary>30000;

SELECT count(*) FROM session.tt1;

COMMIT;

SELECT count(*) FROM session.tt1;

CONNECT RESET;

CONNECT TO sample;

SELECT count(*) FROM session.tt1;
```

First, a subset of the employee table is retrieved and inserted into the declared temporary table tt1. Notice that the schema name of the declared temporary table is SESSION and the inserted rows are not logged. Then two SELECT statements are performed for tt1 before and after a COMMIT statement. Both of them get the same result. The third SELECT statement after reconnecting to the sample database would get an error (SQL0204), as the declared temporary table tt1 is dropped when the first connection was terminated.

Since any changes to a declared temporary table are not logged, when a ROLLBACK statement is executed, the temporary table cannot go back to the state of the last commit point. Instead, all rows of the temporary table are deleted if the table was changed during this unit of work. If the temporary table was created in this unit of work, the table will be dropped. However, if the temporary table was dropped in this unit of work, the table will be restored without any rows.

Create Table with NOT LOGGED INITIALLY Option

DB2 UDB provides another feature that allows you to avoid the logging for a table, which is the NOT LOGGED INITIALLY option of the CREATE TABLE statement. A table created with the NOT LOGGED INITIALLY option (we will call it a 'not-logged' table) is a regular table which has an entry in the catalog table. It can be used from the standard SQL interfaces such as ODBC, CLI, static/dynamic SQL, and you can perform any operation on it. Any changes to a not-logged table are not logged if they are done in the same unit of work as the CREATE TABLE statement for the table. After a COMMIT statement is issued, changes to the table are logged.

If you want to reactivate the 'not-logged' state, issue an ALTER TABLE statement with ACTIVATE NOT LOGGED INITIALLY option. Any changes in the same unit of work as the ALTER TABLE statement are not logged.

Since the 'not-logged' state is active within the unit of work in which the CREATE TABLE or the ALTER TABLE statement was issued, a Z lock is held at that time. In other words, only the application that issued the CREATE TABLE or ALTER TABLE statement can access the table and change it without logging.

The locking on the catalog tables is different between the CREATE TABLE statement and ALTER TABLE statement. The CREATE TABLE statement takes W locks on the rows of several catalog table that are associated with the table. Whereas the ALTER TABLE statement takes an NS lock on its entry (row) of the SYSTABLE table. Therefore, when there are concurrent applications scanning the catalog tables (such as the LIST TABLE statement), you should consider to use the ALTER TABLE statement to set the 'not-logged' state.

For example, if an application creates a not-logged table, the other applications executing the LIST TABLES statement, which takes S locks on each rows of the SYSTABLES catalog table, must wait until the first application issues COMMIT or ROLLBACK. This is because an S lock cannot be obtained when a W lock is held on the resource by the other application. If an application creates a not-logged table, issues COMMIT, and then activates the 'not-logged' state using the ALTER TABLE statement, the other application can execute the LIST TABLES statement without any lock wait. This is because an S lock can be obtained even if an NS lock is held on the resource.

See the *DB2 UDB Administration Guide: Performance* for the detailed information about the lock types of DB2 UDB.

Table 9–1 is a comparison between a not-logged table and a declared temporary table.

Table 9–1 *Not-Logged Table versus Declared Temporary Table*

	Not Logged Table	**Declared Temporary Table**
How is it created?	CREATE TABLE...NOT LOGGED INITIALLY	DECLARE GLOBAL TEMPORARY TABLE
Where is it located?	In a regular table space	In a user temporary table space
Are changes logged?	Not logged within the same UOW as the CREATE/ ALTER table statement	No
What is its life span?	Until being explicitly dropped	Until the connection is terminated or the table is explicitly dropped
Are any locks held?	A Z lock is held on the table during the not-logged state	Minimal locks are held

Table 9–1 *Not-Logged Table versus Declared Temporary Table*

	Not Logged Table	Declared Temporary Table
Does it have catalog entries?	Yes	No
Which operations can be performed?	Any operations as a regular table	SELECT, INSERT, UPDATE, DELETE
Which interface can be used?	Any standard interface	Any standard interface
What happens if a ROLLBACK statement is issued?	If it is in the same UOW as the CREATE TABLE, the table will be dropped. If it is in the same UOW as the ALTER TABLE and the table was changed, the table will be inaccessible.	All rows are deleted if the table was changed during the unit of work. If the table was created in this unit of work, the table will be dropped. If the table was dropped in this unit of work, the table will be restored without any rows.

As you can see in Table 9–1, one of the obvious differences is the life span. Since a not-logged table persists until being dropped explicitly, the table can be used by other applications after the first application is disconnected from the database. You should consider using not-logged tables in cases when the table needs to persist beyond the connection of a single application and does not have to be recovered. For example, when you want to create a summary table, specifying the NOT LOGGED INITIALLY option is a good idea since you can always recover the data from the original.

Note: A summary table is a table whose definition is based on the result of a query. As such, the summary table typically contains pre-computed results based on the data existing in the table or tables on which its definition is based. If the SQL compiler determines that a dynamic query will run more efficiently against a summary table than the base table, the query executes against the summary table, and you should receive the result faster than accessing to the base table directly. See the *DB2 UDB Administration Guide: Performance* for the detailed information.

Convert ODBC into Static SQL

To improve the performance of ODBC/CLI applications, you can convert them into static SQL applications.

As you saw in Chapter 3, ODBC/CLI applications are dynamic SQL applications and the most effective data access plan of each query is generated at program execution time. This process is expensive, since the system catalog tables are accessed and the SQL statement is optimized. Because of this overhead, a dynamic SQL application can be slower than a static SQL application.

To improve the performance of dynamic SQL, the global package cache was introduced in DB2 UDB Version 5.0. The generated access plan for an SQL statement is stored the global package cache, and it can be reused by the same or other applications.

Though the global package cache can improve the performance of dynamic SQL, the statement must be identical to the cached statement or parameter markers must be used in the statement, as shown below, so that the cached statement can be reused.

```
SELECT EMPNO,LASTNAME,FIRSTNME FROM EMPLOYEE
    WHERE LASTNAME = ?
```

 Note: Parameter markers indicate the places in which a host variable is to be substituted inside of an SQL statemnt. Question marks (?) are used to represent parameter markers.

Many ODBC/CLI applications might generate or code SQL statements with literals instead of parameter markers, and the cached statement can only be reused if the incoming statement is identical to the cached statement. In other words, an SQL statement executed twice but with different input values cannot reuse the cached access plan.

To loosen this consideration, you can convert ODBC/CLI applications into static SQL applications. The information of an executed ODBC/CLI application can be captured, and the executable form of statements are stored in the database as a package. Other ODBC/CLI applications can use it like static SQL applications.

Note: You need to use DB2 UDB Version 7.1 or later to convert ODBC/CLI applications to static SQL applications.

ODBC/CLI applications run in the following three different modes:

- **Normal Mode**
  This is the default value and the traditional ODBC/CLI usage.
- **Capture Mode**
  This is the mode used by the database administrator who will run an ODBC/CLI application to capture its connection and statement attributes, SQL statements, and input as well as output SQLDAs. When a connection is terminated, the captured information is saved into an ASCII text file specified by STATICCAPFILE keyword in the db2cli.ini file. This file should be distributed to other clients as well as the application, and also the package should be created using the db2cap bind command, just as you would create a package using the bind command for a static SQL application.
- **Match Mode**
  This is the mode used by the end user to run ODBC/CLI applications that were pre-bound and distributed by the database administrator. When a connection is established, the captured information associated with the DSN will be retrieved from the local capture file specified in the db2cli.ini file. If a matching SQL statement is found in the capture file, the corresponding static SQL statement will be executed. Otherwise, the SQL statement will still be executed as a dynamic SQL statement.

These modes are specified using the STATICMODE keyword of the db2cli.ini file as in the following example:

```
[SAMPLE]
STATICCAPFILE=D:\PKG.TXT
STATICPACKAGE=TETSUYA.ODBCPKG
STATICMODE=Capture
DBALIAS=SAMPLE
```

This example specifies the capture mode. Captured information of the ODBC/CLI application accessed SAMPLE database is saved into the D:\PKG.TXT file. The STATICPACKAGE keyword is used to specify the package name to be later bound by the db2cap bind command.

You can also set these parameters using the ODBC/CLI Settings-Advanced Settings window of the Client Configuration Assistant, as shown in Fig. 9–2 on page 417, and in Fig. 9–3 below:

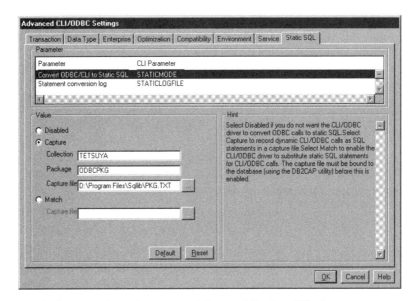

Fig. 9–3 *ODBC/CLI Settings — Advanced Settings Window*

The captured file is a text file, as shown in Fig. 9–4:

```
[COMMON]
CREATOR=
CLIVERSION=06.01.0000
CONTOKENUR=
CONTOKENCS=
CONTOKENRS=
CONTOKENRR=
CONTOKENNC=

[BINDOPTIONS]
COLLECTION=TETSUYA
PACKAGE=ODBCPKG
DEGREE=
FUNCPATH=
GENERIC=
OWNER=TETSUYA
QUALIFIER=TETSUYA
QUERYOPT=
TEXT=

[STATEMENT1]
SECTNO=
ISOLATION=CS
STMTTEXT=select DEPTNO,DEPTNAME,MGRNO,ADMRDEPT,LOCATION
from DEPARTMENT
STMTTYPE=SELECT_CURSOR_WITHHOLD
CURSOR=SQLCURCAPCS1
OUTVAR1=CHAR,3,,FALSE,FALSE,DEPTNO
OUTVAR2=VARCHAR,29,,FALSE,FALSE,DEPTNAME
OUTVAR3=CHAR,6,,FALSE,TRUE,MGRNO
OUTVAR4=CHAR,3,,FALSE,FALSE,ADMRDEPT
OUTVAR5=CHAR,16,,FALSE,TRUE,LOCATION
```

Fig. 9–4 *Captured File*

If necessary, the database administrator can edit the captured file to change the bind options such as QUALIFIER, OWNER, and FUNCPATH.

This example captured only one statement, although you can save more than one statement in the captured file. You can also have more than one captured file to create packages in the same database. In this case, you should execute db2cap bind command several times using each captured file. Be sure that the PACKAGE keyword of each captured file has different value.

If changes to the captured file are done, the db2cap bind command should be executed to create a package. The captured file and the database name must be specified as the following example:

```
D:\> db2cap bind D:\PKG.TXT -d sample
DB2CAP processing completed successfully.
```

The created package name have the suffix number depending on its isolation level.
The suffix for the package is one of the following:

- 0 = Uncommitted Read
- 1 = Cursor Stability
- 2 = Read Stability
- 3 = Repeatable Read

In our example, the package name will be TETSUYA.ODBCPKG1. As our example
shown in Fig. 9–4 on page 427 has only one SQL statement, just one package will
be created; however, if the captured file has more than one statement and their
isolation levels are different, multiple packages will be created with different
suffixes.

Lastly, you should distribute both the captured file and the application to all client
workstations on which you intend to utilize the pre-bound package. On each client
workstation, the STATICMODE keyword of the db2cli.ini file should be set as
MATCH, and the captured file should be specified using the STATICCAPFILE
keyword.

```
[RMTSAMPL]
STATICCAPFILE=D:\PKG.TXT
STATICMODE=Match
DBALIAS=RMTSAMPL
```

Considerations in a Partitioned Environment

As introduced in Chapter 1, DB2 UDB Enterprise-Extended Edition (EEE) allows
you to partition a database across the same or multiple independent machines,
while providing a single logical database interface. DB2 UDB EEE is designed for
applications where the database is simply too large for a single computer to handle
efficiently. SQL operations can operate in parallel on the individual database
partition, thus, increasing the execution speed of a single query.

As an SQL operation is processed in parallel, it is important for performance reasons to make your data distributed uniformly across all database partitions. Otherwise, a database partition which has less data may idle when others are working.

The other key for good performance (particularly for OLTP applications) is making data communications between the database partitions efficient and minimum. Since the database is partitioned, more or less cross-database partition communications may occur to process query requests from applications. If a considerable amount of data communications are needed, it may impact the performance. Thus, you should be aware of the considerations that we discuss in the following sections.

Specify FOR FETCH ONLY

The FOR FETCH ONLY clause of a SELECT statement has already been introduced. It can improve performance of your application by allowing your query to take advantage of row blocking, and it also improves the data concurrency.

When your database is managed by DB2 UDB EEE, the improvement is significant. Assume you have an application retrieving rows from a table partitioned across the multiple database partitions with a simple SELECT statement. The application connects to one of the database partitions (this partition is called the *coordinator partition*) first, and sends the SQL. The coordinator partition broadcasts the SQL to the other database partitions and they process it in parallel; then the answer set is returned to the coordinator partition from each database partition.

The answer set is received through the queue (called *table queue*) which is allocated by DB2 UDB. If you specify the FOR FETCH ONLY clause in a SELECT statement, the coordinator partition can fetch multiple rows from the table queue at a time. This type of table queue is called the *asynchronous table queue*. When you do not explicitly specify the FOR FETCH ONLY clause, the coordinator partition treats it as updatable and retrieves only a single row from the table queue per fetch request. This type of table queue is called the *synchronous table queue*. If you are only fetching rows, the asynchronous table queue is faster.

OLTP Applications in a Partitioned Environment

Roughly speaking, all database systems can be categorized into two groups, Decision Support Systems (DSS), and OnLine Transaction Processing (OLTP). In the case of DSS, each query is complex and runs for relatively a long time. You can measure the performance by the elapsed query time. The key for good performance is that the tables scanned are uniformly distributed across the database partitions, and each query is being executed in parallel across all database partitions.

In the case of OLTP, each query is fairly short, but the frequency of the query requests (transactions) and the number of concurrent users is higher. The performance is typically measured by throughput and response time. In such an environment, executing each transaction in parallel may not be a good idea, as the overhead of the parallel processing can cost more than the benefit you can expect. This overhead occurs since the coordinator partition has to broadcast the query to other related database partitions and receives the results. Therefore, in the case of OLTP, you should make each transaction run on a single database partition rather than on multiple database partitions in parallel so that you can get the best performance. You may also want to perform the load-balancing by distributing each database connection to a different database partition.

Directed Distributed Subsection

In a partitioned database environment, an SQL statement is partitioned into *subsections* by the SQL compiler. Each subsection is executed by a different DB2 sub-agent and can be distributed to the other partitions from the coordinator partition. When the coordinator partition receives a query request, subsections of that query are usually broadcast to all related database partitions. However, if a single database partition that has the requested rows can be determined, DB2 UDB send the subsection to that partition only. Such a subsection is called a Direct Distributed Subsection (Direct DSS). In the case of OLTP, use this type of query in your application to avoid the overhead occurred, as a query is broadcast to all partitions.

Assume you have an `EMPLOYEE` table encompassing all employee information, and it is partitioned using the last name (`LASTNAME`) and the first name (`FIRSTNME`) as the partitioning key. When you retrieve employee information by the last name, you would execute an SQL statement like:

```
SELECT LASTNAME,FIRSTNME,SALARY FROM EMPLOYEE
    WHERE LASTNAME = :hostvar
```

This statement is broadcast to all database partitions on which the `EMPLOYEE` table resides, since any database partition may have a record with the same last name.

Now, let's examine the next example:

```
SELECT EMPNO,LASTNAME,FIRSTNME,SALARY FROM EMPLOYEE
    WHERE LASTNAME = :hostvar1
      AND FIRSTNME = :hostvar2
```

This query searches records by the last name and the first name. Remember that the EMPLOYEE table is partitioned using values of the LASTNAME and the FIRSTNME column. This means that all records having the same full name can be found in only one database partition. In this case, DB2 UDB calculates the database partition number using the value provided in the WHERE clause and then sends the subsection to that database partition only.

Note: When a table is created in a partitioned database, it is assigned a partition key composed of one or more columns. As rows are inserted into the table, the row's partitioning value is hashed into a hash table that consists of 4096 hash buckets. Each hash bucket is assigned to a specific database partition number based on the partitioning map. Therefore, all rows having the same values of the partitioning key are stored in the same partition.

You can see whether each SQL statement uses Direct DSS or not, using the Explain utility of DB2 UDB. A simple way is to use the Dynamic Explain utility. Execute the dynexpln command from the command line. Then you can get the output as following after entering the prompted information (Fig. 9–5).

```
SQL Statement:

  select lastname, firstnme, salary
  from employee
  where lastname='CHRISTINE'
  and firstnme='HAAS'

Estimated Cost       = 26
Estimated Cardinality = 1

Coordinator Subsection:
  Distribute Subsection #1
  |  Directed by Hash
  |  |  #Columns = 2
  |  |  Partition Map ID = 1, Nodegroup =
IBMDEFAULTGROUP,#Nodes = 1
  Access Table Queue  ID = q1  #Columns = 5
  Return Data to Application
  |  #Columns = 3

Subsection #1:
  Access Table Name = SHIRA.EMPLOYEE  ID = 2,6
  |  #Columns = 3
  |  Relation Scan
  |  |  Prefetch: Eligible
  |  Lock Intents
  |  |  Table: Intent Share
  |  |  Row  : Next Key Share
  |  Sargable Predicate(s)
  |  |  #Predicates = 2
  Insert Into Synchronous Table Queue  ID = q1

  |  Broadcast to Coordinator Node
```

Fig. 9–5 *Dynamic Explain Output*

Coordinator Subsection (line 1) shows the part processed by the coordinator
partition. You can see that line 3 says 'Directed by Hash'. This means that the
coordinator partition examines which partition should process the 'Subsection #1'
and sends the subsection to that partition only. When the subsection is broadcast to
all related partitions, line 3 will become 'Broadcast to Node List', and a list of
those partitions will be displayed.

Local Bypass

When your query has a directed DSS and the partition that processes it is the coordinator partition, this query can be completed within only the coordinator partition without any communication with another partition. This special form of the directed DSS is called *local bypass*. It can reduce the coordinator partition overhead even more (see Fig. 9–6).

Local bypass is enabled automatically whenever possible, but you can increase its use by routing transactions to the partition containing the data for that transaction.

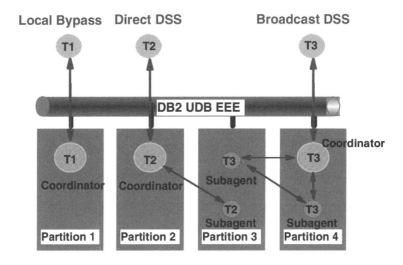

Fig. 9–6 *Local Bypass*

CLI/ODBC Trace Facility

The CLI/ODBC trace facility of DB2 UDB is an essential tool for problem determination and general understanding of your CLI/ODBC applications. All function calls executed are recorded in a text file for later analysis. In addition to functional information, however, the trace file contains elapsed time information which can be extremely useful for application and database tuning. In this section, we provide tips, tools, and techniques for using CLI traces for these tuning tasks.

Note: The traces shown in this section were generated using the DB2 UDB Version 7.1 open beta, as of April, 2000.

Getting Started

Let's review how you can obtain a CLI trace. Full information can be found in Appendix K of the *Call Level Interface Guide and Reference* for DB2 UDB.

First of all, be sure to distinguish CLI tracing from ODBC tracing. An ODBC trace shows the calls from the application to an ODBC Driver Manager. A CLI trace shows the calls made to CLI, either directly from the application or from an ODBC Driver Manager. It is sometimes useful to obtain both traces, but only CLI tracing is discussed in this section.

To obtain a CLI trace, run the application after using one of these means to activate tracing:

- Client Configuration Assistant: Select a database (it must be one registered for ODBC), then Properties, CLI/ODBC Settings, Advanced, and Service.
- Command Line Processor: See the following example:

```
db2 update cli cfg for section common using trace 1
tracepathname <fully qualified pathname>
db2 update cli cfg for section common using tracecomm 1
```

Edit the db2cli.ini file (default location is \Program Files\sqllib), and add the following lines:

```
[COMMON]
TRACE=1
TRACEFILENAME=<fully qualified filename>
TRACECOMM=0
TRACEFLUSH=0
TRACETIMESTAMP=0
TRACEPIDTID=0
```

Setting TRACE=1 turns on the CLI/ODBC trace facility.

The TRACEFILENAME keyword specifies the file used to store the CLI/ODBC trace information. Instead of the TRACEFILENAME keyword, you may use the TRACEPATHNAME keyword, which specifies the directory path name used to store individual trace files. The TRACEPATHNAME is typically used only in multi-user scenarios.

The TRACECOMM keyword specifies whether the network request information is included in the trace file. For the TRACECOMM keyword, you can specify 0 or 1. For the default setting of 0, no network request information is captured. Setting 1 for this keyword significantly changes the trace output, as described later.

The TRACEFLUSH keyword specifies whether a write to disk is forced after each CLI/ODBC entry. For the default setting of 0, a write is not performed after every entry. Setting TRACEFLUSH=1 has a large performance impact; use only if the application may not exit normally.

The TRACETIMESTAMP keyword specifies whether a timestamp is added at the beginning of each line, as described later.

The TRACEPIDTID keyword causes each line to begin with the process ID and thread ID of the application thread issuing the corresponding call.

 Note: The TRACETIMESTAMP and TRACEPIDTID were new keywords added in Version 7.1 (and Version 6.1 FixPak 4).

CLI Trace File Contents

The *Call Level Interface Guide and Reference* contains a full description of the contents of a CLI trace file. The TRACECOMM keyword was introduced in DB2 UDB Version 5.2 and causes information to be generated in addition to what is produced by a "regular" trace. The TRACETIMESTAMP and TRACEPIDTID keywords are new in Version 7.1 and provide additional timing and thread identification information. We will now discuss what each type of trace contains, paying particular attention to TRACECOMM output and the new Version 7.1 keywords.

Regular Trace Contents

The CLI driver writes trace records when it is entered and when it exits, to reflect the activity just completed. Thus, in the following code snippet (Fig. 9–7), the first SQLDisconnect record (2) is written on entry to the CLI driver, as are all records marked by "--->". The "Time elapsed" (+8.430000E-004 seconds = 0.0008 seconds) represents the elapsed time in the application between the last exit from the CLI driver (after the SQLFreeHandle call) and the re-entry to process the SQLDisconnect call. So, if you see long elapsed times in the "--->" records, it could reflect a performance problem or heavy activity in the application, or, conversely, idle time while waiting for user input to be supplied.

```
(1) SQLFreeHandle( )
        <--- SQL_SUCCESS    Time elapsed - +2.758000E-003
seconds

(2) SQLDisconnect( hDbc=0:1 )
        ---> Time elapsed - +8.430000E-004 seconds

(3) SQLDisconnect( )
        <--- SQL_SUCCESS    Time elapsed - +1.001400E-002
seconds
```

Fig. 9–7 *Regular Trace*

The second SQLDisconnect record (3) was written on exit from the CLI driver, and its "Time elapsed" (+1.001400E-002 seconds = 0.01 seconds) represents the elapsed time in DB2 UDB to process the SQLDisconnect call. As do all records marked by "<---" (which is followed by the return code of the call), this time includes time in the CLI driver, the DB2 runtime client (formerly known as the CAE), the entire communication infrastructure between the client and the database server, and the time in the database server itself. (In the remainder of this section, the phrase "in DB2" will refer to these components collectively.)

It should be noted that the granularity of elapsed times has differed on various platforms. On Windows NT prior to DB2 UDB Version 6.1 with FixPak 4, the minimum recorded elapsed time was a relatively large 10 milliseconds. Times that appeared as zero (+0.000000E+000) could in reality have had any duration up to that minimum. As of DB2 UDB Version 6.1 with FixPak 4 and later, microsecond granularity is in effect on all platforms.

As useful as these elapsed times are (and later we'll discuss how to maximize their usefulness), it is often more interesting to obtain the additional information that comes with TRACECOMM.

TRACECOMM Trace Contents

There are three main reasons to use TRACECOMM=1 in db2cli.ini:

- To find out when a client-to-server communication occurs, either locally or over the network. Many CLI functions are processed completely on the client, and it makes sense to pay less attention to them than to the calls involving communication: (a) network requests typically have a cost of at least an order of magnitude higher than requests that are processed on the client only; (b) generally, there is less that can be done to affect the execution time of client-only calls.

- To find out the number of bytes sent and received in each communication.
- To break down CLI call elapsed times into their components: (a) in-CLI and (b) in-communication-and-server.

Let's now look at how the trace records in the above example change if the fetch program is run again, this time with TRACECOMM activated (=1). (Record numbers on the left in Fig. 9–8 below were added to aid in the discussion.)

```
    SQLFreeHandle( )
(1)     <--- SQL_SUCCESS    Time elapsed - +2.894000E-003
seconds

    SQLDisconnect( hDbc=0:1 )
(2)     ---> Time elapsed - +1.587000E-003 seconds
(3)     sqlccsend( ulBytes - 72 )
(4)     sqlccsend( Handle - 539269544 )
(5)     sqlccsend( ) - rc - 0, time elapsed - +1.960000E-004
    sqlccrecv( )
(6)     sqlccrecv( ulBytes - 27 ) - rc - 0, time elapsed -
+4.278810E-001
    SQLDisconnect( )
(7)     <--- SQL_SUCCESS    Time elapsed - +4.296480E-001
seconds
```

Fig. 9–8 *TRACECOMM Trace*

The obvious change is in the additional lines under the SQLDisconnect entry record. The existence of these lines confirms that a server communication occurred to process the SQLDisconnect.

Other points to note about these new lines are as follows:

- Line (2), "---> Time elapsed ..." indicates that approximately 1 millisecond was spent in the application. So, the application time in this line has the same meaning as in a trace file generated without TRACECOMM.
- Line (3), "sqlccsend(ulBytes - 72)" indicates that 72 bytes were sent to the server.
- Line (4), "sqlccsend(Handle - 539269544)" indicates that the send was to be a thread with the handle ID indicated.

- Line (5), "`sqlccsend( ) - rc - 0 ...`" indicates that the send was successful and had an elapsed time of approximately 0.2 milliseconds. Note that these sends are done asynchronously, so they should always have a very small elapsed time. CLI then waits for the response to come back.
- Line (6), "`sqlccrecv( ulBytes - 27 ) ...`" indicates that 27 bytes were received from the server. It also indicates that 0.4296 seconds were spent from the completion of the send to the completion of the receive.

Note that some functions, such as `SQLConnect`, can execute multiple send-receive pairs, and there will be an entry for each send and receive.

To see the derivation of the elapsed times in a different way, refer to the following diagram (Fig. 9–9). It shows the main components involved in executing the calls in the previous trace snippet. The arrows represent the flow of control as time passes (going down the page). The letters (a), (b), etc. represent the points at which the DB2 UDB CLI driver records timestamp information:

- The elapsed time in line (2) above is the difference between times (a) and (b). This is the time spent in the application between the return to the application after the `SQLFreeHandle` call was processed, and the entry to the CLI Driver to process the `SQLDisconnect` call. (Actually, it also includes the communication time from and to the CLI driver, and the time in the driver between when the timestamp was taken and the exit or entry, but those times are generally negligible.)
- The time in line (5) is the difference between (c) and (d), or the Send time.
- The time in line (6) is the difference between (d) and (e), or the Server and Receive time.
- The time in line (7) is the difference between (b) and (f), or the "DB2 time".

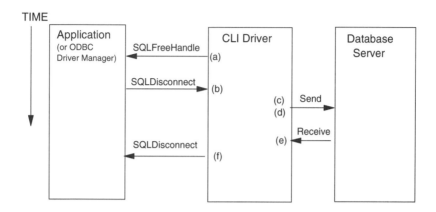

Fig. 9–9 *CLI calls*

Version 7.1 Enhancements: Timestamps and Process/Thread IDs in Trace

In Version 7.1 (and Version 6.1 with FixPak 4) two new trace keywords were added:

- TRACETIMESTAMP. This causes a timestamp to be added at the beginning of each line. There are three formats available, with the default value being 0 (off):
  - =1 [<number of seconds since 01/01/1970>.<microseconds>-<formatted timestamp>]
  - =2 [<number of seconds since 01/01/1970>]
  - =3 [<formatted timestamp>]
- TRACEPIDTID. This causes each line to begin with the process ID and thread ID of the application thread issuing the corresponding call.

Here are sample outputs for the various combinations of values for TRACETIMESTAMP and TRACEPIDTID (Fig. 9–10). Note that the regular trace output is unchanged, but is shifted to the right of the new information.

```
**********************
* TraceTimestamp=1  *
* TracePidTid=1     *
**********************
[ Process: 298, Thread: 317 ]
[ Date & Time:          02-11-2000 09:49:07.000048 ]
(lines omitted here in this and the other examples)

[0000000298 0000000317] [950280547.000306 - 02-11-2000 09:49:07.000306]
SQLSetEnvAttr( )
[0000000298 0000000317] [950280547.000393 - 02-11-2000 09:49:07.000393]
<--- SQL_SUCCESS    Time

[0000000298 0000000317] [950280547.162111 - 02-11-2000 09:49:07.162111]
SQLAllocConnect( hEnv=0:1,
[0000000298 0000000317] [950280547.162256 - 02-11-2000 09:49:07.162256]      -
--> Time elapsed - +1.6343

[0000000298 0000000317] [950280547.336041 - 02-11-2000 09:49:07.336041]
SQLAllocConnect( phDbc=0:1 )
[0000000298 0000000317] [950280547.336164 - 02-11-2000 09:49:07.336164]
<--- SQL_SUCCESS    Time ela

**********************
* TraceTimestamp=1  *
* TracePidTid=0     *
**********************
[ Process: 298, Thread: 317 ]
[ Date & Time:          02-11-2000 09:49:14.000025 ]

[950280554.000182 - 02-11-2000 09:49:14.000182] SQLSetEnvAttr( )
[950280554.000246 - 02-11-2000 09:49:14.000246]      <--- SQL_SUCCESS    Time
elapsed - +6.400000E-005

**********************
* TraceTimestamp=2  *
* TracePidTid=0     *
**********************
[950280554.000183] SQLSetEnvAttr( )
[950280554.000213]      <--- SQL_SUCCESS    Time elapsed - +3.000000E-005
seconds

**********************
* TraceTimestamp=3  *
* TracePidTid=0     *
**********************
[02-11-2000 09:49:15.000184] SQLSetEnvAttr( )
[02-11-2000 09:49:15.000233]      <--- SQL_SUCCESS    Time elapsed -
+4.900000E-005 seconds
```

Fig. 9–10 *TRACETIMESTAMP and TRACEPIDTID keyword*

Analysis Objectives

You may have specific objectives in mind when analyzing a CLI trace, or you ma
just be looking to see if anything interesting appears.   Here are some of the most
common objectives (from a performance point of view), which are discussed
individually in the next section:

• Get a breakdown of time spent in the application versus time spent in DB2 UD

• Find out how long a particular CLI call is taking.

• Focus on those CLI calls which are typically where performance problems lie.

- Find the longest intervals of execution, in either the application or in DB2 UDB.
- Find the number of CLI calls of various types.
- Find out how much data is transferred to or from the server.
- Study the timing relationships between multiple threads in an application.

Some other typical objectives are simply to see which CLI calls are occurring (a third-party tool could be generating them) or to look for execution errors, but these objectives are beyond the scope of this section.

Analyzing the Trace and Finding the Problem

Depending on your objectives, the analysis of the trace file can be attacked in various ways and with various tools to extract interesting information.

Application Time versus DB2 Time

Before embarking on a journey to improve a DB2 UDB application's performance, it is important to know where the majority of time is being spent. For some applications, the vast majority of the elapsed time is spent in the application, not in DB2 UDB. In such cases, spending time on DB2 UDB tuning is essentially a wasted exercise, at least until the application problem is dealt with.

Application and DB2 times can be summarized very easily using a Java tool called `CLITraceParser`, which is available at: `ftp://ftp.software.ibm.com/ps/ products/db2/tools/` in the file `CLITraceParser.zip`. See the `README.TXT` file in that tool subdirectory for information on installation and usage. Note that `CLITraceParser` replaces and improves upon `parseCLITrace`, which is also available at that FTP site.

The `CLITraceParser` parses a CLI trace and produces a summary of it. Here is the output of the tool for a sample CLI trace file:

```
        CLI Trace Report generated by CLITraceParser
==========================================================

CLI Trace file                    : casestudy1_TraceComm_Off
Lines read in file                : 108
Trace build info                  : null

Overall Trace statistics
==========================================================

            14 statements in trace.
        93.110 seconds total trace time.
         0.012 seconds spent for application processing.
        93.098 seconds spent for CLI processing.

Network Specific CLI processing time statistics
==========================================================
             0 network flows sent to transmit
             0 bytes, requiring a total of
         0.000 seconds.
```

```
                0 network flows received, transmitting
                0 bytes, requiring a total of
         0.000 seconds.

End of overall trace statistics report

**************************************************************************

Function specific statistics
==========================================================

                        Timing               Network Send      Network Receive
Function Name   Total Application CLI    Flows Bytes Time  Flows Bytes Time
------------------------------------------------------------------------
SQLSetConnectAttr 1   0.001      0.001   0     0    0.000  0     0    0.000
SQLExecDirect    1    0.000      92.204  0     0    0.000  0     0    0.000
SQLBindCol       1    0.000      0.000   0     0    0.000  0     0    0.000
SQLFetch         2    0.001      0.002   0     0    0.000  0     0    0.000
SQLFreeHandle    3    0.001      0.005   0     0    0.000  0     0    0.000
SQLAllocHandle   3    0.008      0.017   0     0    0.000  0     0    0.000
SQLConnect       1    0.000      0.856   0     0    0.000  0     0    0.000
SQLDisconnect    1    0.001      0.010   0     0    0.000  0     0    0.000
SQLEndTran       1    0.000      0.002   0     0    0.000  0     0    0.000

End of function specific statistics report

**************************************************************************

Report of errors that occurred in this CLI Trace
=================================================
No errors in trace.

End of error report.

=========================================================
                End of CLI Trace Report
```

The output is quite self-explanatory: the first section ("Overall Trace statistics") shows the total trace time and the breakdown of time between application and DB2 UDB; the next section ("Network Specific CLI processing time statistics") summarizes the number of sends and receives and the total bytes transmitted; and the final noteworthy section ("Function specific statistics") shows the number of calls by function, each function's elapsed time in application and DB2, and the related network activity (if TRACECOMM=1 was specified). The output clearly indicates that time in DB2 is the key component of elapsed time to be addressed in this particular example.

Below is the output of CLITraceParser for a trace file from the same application as for the summary above, but this time with TRACECOMM=1. (A different run was made to collect this trace, so there are small differences in elapsed times.)

```
            CLI Trace Report generated by CLITraceParser
==============================================================

CLI Trace file                 : casestudy1_TraceComm_On
Lines read in file             : 133
Trace build info               : null

Overall Trace statistics
==============================================================

        14 statements in trace.
    88.332 seconds total trace time.
     0.014 seconds spent for application processing.
    88.319 seconds spent for CLI processing.

Network Specific CLI processing time statistics
==============================================================
         5 network flows sent to transmit
      2762 bytes, requiring a total of
     0.001 seconds.

         5 network flows received, transmitting
      1935 bytes, requiring a total of
    88.068 seconds.

End of overall trace statistics report

*************************************************************************

Function specific statistics
==============================================================
```

Function Name	Total	Timing Application	CLI	Network Send Flows	Bytes	Time	Network Receive Flows	Bytes	Time
SQLSetConnectAttr	1	0.001	0.001	0	0	0.000	0	0	0.000
SQLExecDirect	1	0.000	87.136	1	324	0.000	1	382	87.130
SQLBindCol	1	0.000	0.000	0	0	0.000	0	0	0.000
SQLFetch	2	0.001	0.001	0	0	0.000	0	0	0.000
SQLFreeHandle	3	0.001	0.005	0	0	0.000	0	0	0.000
SQLAllocHandle	3	0.009	0.017	0	0	0.000	0	0	0.000
SQLConnect	1	0.000	1.150	2	2170	0.000	2	1499	0.933
SQLDisconnect	1	0.001	0.005	1	72	0.000	1	27	0.003
SQLEndTran	1	0.000	0.003	1	196	0.000	1	27	0.002

```
End of function specific statistics report

*************************************************************************

Report of errors that occurred in this CLI Trace
==============================================================
No errors in trace.

End of error report.

==============================================================
                   End of CLI Trace Report
```

Note that the information in the report is the same as with `TRACECOMM=0`, except that the network statistics, which were previously zero, are now supplied.

Finding How Long a Particular CLI Call Took

This task is trivial, requiring only that you can find the trace record of interest. Often this can be done by searching for the CLI call type. Other times you may be interested in a particular SQL statement, and you can search for it using a search string such as `SELECT`, or a table name, or other text that you know occurs within the statement.

Focusing on Typical Problem Calls

In general, most of the performance problems in CLI applications occur in a relatively small subset of calls. Focusing on these functions will allow you to get a sense of what the database requests are and how the data is flowing between the application and the server. A close look at these and other CLI functions comes later. We suggest that you look particularly at this set of calls:

- SQLConnect or SQLDriverConnect — Connect to a database.
- SQLExecDirect — Combined prepare and execute of an SQL statement.
- SQLPrepare and SQLExecute — Prepare and Execute done separately to allow many execute requests for the same statement, using only one prepare.
- SQLFetch — Fetch data either from the local data block or from the server. In the case of a blocking cursor, most fetches are handled locally. Data is either retrieved into bound application variables, or into CLI memory, ready for SQLGetData calls.
- SQLGetData — Copy (and convert if required) data from CLI to the application.
- SQLError — Some applications may continually generate warnings or errors, but you can treat them as 'normal'. Note that the `CLITraceParser` lists all of the errors in its output file for a given trace.

Finding the Longest-Running Events

Finding the longest-running events, particularly in DB2 UDB, is a very common and important task, and the use of appropriate tools can speed up the process significantly. If the trace is small, you can simply page through the file, but usually a better alternative is to edit the file and search for the desired strings. For files that are too large to be edited, you can use findstr (on Windows) or grep (on UNIX, or on NT with the MKS toolkit) to extract occurrences of the desired strings.

Some strings of particular interest to search for are:

- E+   Occurs in all events of 1 second or longer (or zero)

- E+000   Occurs in all events of 1 second to 9.9 seconds (or zero)
- E+001   Occurs in all events of 10 seconds to 99.9 seconds
- E-   Occurs in all events of less than 1 second (except zero)
- <---   Flags times in DB2 UDB
  (does not appear in TRACECOMM-specific entries)
- --->   Flags times in the application

Tuning Application Performance

Search Examples

Here are some examples of commands to do specific searches. In each one, "trace_file" must be replaced by the name of the trace file being analyzed. Note that trace file lines that are specific to TRACECOMM contain "E+" or "E-", but not "<---" or "--->"; so, the first example below will find TRACECOMM-specific entries, but all of the other examples, because they include a search for an "arrow", will not.

- The following can be used on a Windows command line to list all elapsed times, both in DB2 UDB and the application, along with their line numbers in the trace file:

```
findstr /n "E+ E-" trace_file | more
```

- The following can be used on a Windows command line to list elapsed times of 10 to 999.9 seconds in DB2 UDB, with their line numbers in the trace file:

```
findstr /n "E+001 E+002" trace_file | findstr /c:"<---"
```

- The following can be used on a Windows command line to list elapsed times of 0.10 to 0.99 seconds in the application, with their line numbers in the trace file:

```
findstr /n "E-001" trace_file | findstr /c:"--->"
```

- The sort command in Windows is quite limited, compared to sort in UNIX. The following can be used on UNIX, or on Windows with the MKS toolkit (or possibly via other tools from freeware or shareware sources), to list, in descending order and with line numbers within the trace file, the 20 longest elapsed times in DB2 UDB that are one second or longer.

```
grep -n -e "<---" trace_file | grep -e "E+" | sort
   -k 6.12b,6rn -k 6.2b,6.9brn | head -n 20
```

- This slight variation of the previous command gives the 20 longest DB2 times under one second:

```
grep -n -e "<---" trace_file | grep -e "E-" | sort
   -k 6.12b,6n -k 6.2b,6.9brn | head -n 20
```

Note that "E+" is changed to "E-", and "r" is omitted from "-k 7.12b,7rn". The 6's in the commands indicate that the 6th token in each line is to be used as a sort key. If the "-n" option had not been specified in the grep command, there would not be a line number in each grep output line (one less token per line), and so the 6's in the sort commands would have to be changed to 5's. Similar adjustments need to be made if non-zero values of the TRACETIMESTAMP or TRACEPIDTID keywords are specified when generating the trace.

Finding the Numbers of Calls

In some scenarios, it is not the elapsed times of individual CLI calls that is the problem, but the fact that hundreds or even thousands of calls may be occurring for a given application task. Obviously, even very short calls can become a performance burden if executed enough times.

The CLITraceParser tool, discussed in "Application Time versus DB2 Time" on page 441, is tailor-made for addressing this issue. It provides the number of calls to each function and the total time for each.

Finding the Amount of Data Transferred to or from the Server

The amount of data transferred between the application and the server can be a key factor in application response times. Determining the amount of data transferred is easily accomplished by using the TRACECOMM option in db2cli.ini, as discussed in "TRACECOMM Trace Contents" on page 436.

Analyzing timing relationships between multiple threads in an application

It can be difficult to relate the behavior of different threads in an application, but using CLI trace options can make this much easier. First of all, recall that TRACEPATHNAME is used to name the path in which a separate trace file for each thread will be created. Using TRACETIMESTAMP and TRACEPIDTID, you can have timestamp and process/thread information added to each trace entry.

The example below shows how you can use the sort command on UNIX or on Windows with the MKS toolkit (or possibly via other tools from freeware or shareware sources) to merge the trace entries for multiple files, sort them by timestamp, and write them to a new file, allowing you to follow the sequence of events in all of the threads:

Tuning Application Performance

```
Trace for PID = 298, TID = 317, in file 000298.317

[0000000298 0000000317] [950280547.000306 - 02-11-2000 09:49:07.000306]
SQLSetEnvAttr( )
[0000000298 0000000317] [950280547.000393 - 02-11-2000 09:49:07.000393]
<--- SQL_SUCCESS    Time

[0000000298 0000000317] [950280547.162111 - 02-11-2000 09:49:07.162111]
SQLAllocConnect( hEnv=0:1,
[0000000298 0000000317] [950280547.162256 - 02-11-2000 09:49:07.162256]
---> Time elapsed - +1.6343

[0000000298 0000000317] [950280547.536041 - 02-11-2000 09:49:07.536041]
SQLAllocConnect( phDbc=0:1 )
[0000000298 0000000317] [950280547.536164 - 02-11-2000 09:49:07.536164]
<--- SQL_SUCCESS    Time ela

Trace for PID = 298, TID = 318, in file 000298.318

[0000000298 0000000318] [950280547.000612 - 02-11-2000 09:49:07.000612]
SQLSetEnvAttr( )
[0000000298 0000000318] [950280547.001393 - 02-11-2000 09:49:07.001393]
<--- SQL_SUCCESS    Time

[0000000298 0000000318] [950280547.262111 - 02-11-2000 09:49:07.262111]
SQLAllocConnect( hEnv=0:1,
[0000000298 0000000318] [950280547.262256 - 02-11-2000 09:49:07.262256]
---> Time elapsed - +1.6343

[0000000298 0000000318] [950280547.336041 - 02-11-2000 09:49:07.336041]
SQLAllocConnect( phDbc=0:1 )
[0000000298 0000000318] [950280547.336164 - 02-11-2000 09:49:07.336164]
<--- SQL_SUCCESS    Time ela
```

Merged file 000298.mrg, created by "**sort -k 3.2n 000298.* >
000298.mrg**" on Unix

```
[0000000298 0000000317] [950280547.000306 - 02-11-2000 09:49:07.000306]
SQLSetEnvAttr( )
[0000000298 0000000317] [950280547.000393 - 02-11-2000 09:49:07.000393]
<--- SQL_SUCCESS    Time
[0000000298 0000000318] [950280547.000612 - 02-11-2000 09:49:07.000612]
SQLSetEnvAttr( )
[0000000298 0000000318] [950280547.001393 - 02-11-2000 09:49:07.001393]
<--- SQL_SUCCESS    Time
[0000000298 0000000317] [950280547.162111 - 02-11-2000 09:49:07.162111]
SQLAllocConnect( hEnv=0:1,
[0000000298 0000000317] [950280547.162256 - 02-11-2000 09:49:07.162256]
---> Time elapsed - +1.6343
[0000000298 0000000318] [950280547.262111 - 02-11-2000 09:49:07.262111]
SQLAllocConnect( hEnv=0:1,
[0000000298 0000000318] [950280547.262256 - 02-11-2000 09:49:07.262256]
---> Time elapsed - +1.6343
[0000000298 0000000318] [950280547.336041 - 02-11-2000 09:49:07.336041]
SQLAllocConnect( phDbc=0:1 )
[0000000298 0000000318] [950280547.336164 - 02-11-2000 09:49:07.336164]
<--- SQL_SUCCESS    Time ela
[0000000298 0000000317] [950280547.536041 - 02-11-2000 09:49:07.536041]
SQLAllocConnect( phDbc=0:1 )
[0000000298 0000000317] [950280547.536164 - 02-11-2000 09:49:07.536164]
<--- SQL_SUCCESS    Time ela
```

You can also use this approach to merge trace files for different applications, or for different invocations of the same application, but be careful: if multiple clients are involved, each one will have a slightly (or greatly) different system time that will be used for the timestamps, so the merged sequence of events may not reflect the true sequence.

One thing you may see in the merged trace file is one thread not having any entries for a long period. This could simply indicate that a long-running task was being executed, but it could also indicate that the thread is in a lock wait state. Note that an application's multiple threads can have multiple connections to a database, and from the database server's point of view there is no special relationship between those connections. For instance, they can lock each other out, even though they belong to the same application and are executed through the same authorization ID.

Fixing the Performance Problem

After extracting elapsed time information from the CLI trace using the approaches mentioned earlier, you should have a good basis on which to decide where to focus your efforts in improving performance. The bulk of improvements usually come from reducing or speeding up the communication with, and work done by, the database server. This may involve database server tuning and application changes. These areas should almost always be addressed first. After that, if small improvements are still required, they can sometimes be achieved by dealing with those CLI calls that are executed within the client only.

It is well beyond the scope of this section to discuss all possible routes to achieve performance improvement with DB2 UDB. In fact, some of the most important techniques are completely independent of CLI/ODBC usage and so are not closely tied to the intent of this section. However, we'll now cover all of the key ways to improve performance. They are listed generally in order of most important to least important, and communication and server related to client specific, so for a given situation we suggest going through the topics in order, using those that are applicable. Note that many CLI/ODBC specific performance tips are given in Appendix A of the *DB2 UDB Call Level Interface Guide and Reference*.

Confirm That the problem Is Not in the Application Itself

As mentioned earlier (in "Application Time versus DB2 Time" on page 441), before doing anything else, you should confirm via CLITraceParser that the bulk of time is being spent in DB2 UDB. If it is not, none of the suggestions given in this section will solve the fundamental problem.

Improve Query Access Plans

Indicators that this is needed: Running `CLITraceParser` shows that the bulk of time is in DB2 UDB; sorting elapsed times shows a small percentage of calls to the server taking a significant percentage of the total time.

What to do: Making radical improvements in performance on the server, especially for tasks of over a few seconds, is most commonly achieved by causing a change in the access plan for one or more queries. The most common reasons for bad access plans are:

- `RUNSTATS` was not executed to gather statistics on tables and indexes, which means that DB2 UDB is forced to guess such key facts as the number of rows in a table and the number of distinct key values in an index.
- `RUNSTATS` was executed, but at a time when tables which have frequent Inserts and/or Deletes are in an atypical state. An example is a history table that is emptied every day. If `RUNSTATS` is run when the table is empty, the optimizer will usually choose a table scan for retrievals from that table. As a result, retrievals of even single rows will take longer and longer during the day as the table grows in cardinality.
- Lack of appropriate index(es), which might force DB2 UDB to scan entire (large) tables.

- It is very easy to check if `RUNSTATS` has been run. Use the Control Center or issue a Select statement to look for values of -1 ("unknown") in the NPAGES column in `SYSCAT.TABLES` and the `NLEAF` column in `SYSCAT.INDEXES`. Any value of -1 indicates that `RUNSTATS` was not run for the table or index. If it has not been run, that should be done before any further access plan analysis is done. There are various forms of `RUNSTATS`, but a good default to use is:

```
RUNSTATS ON TABLE xxx AND DETAILED INDEXES ALL
```

Adding the `with distribution` clause can be a very effective way to improve access plans where data is not uniformly distributed.

The indexes for a table are most easily checked through the Control Center or by issuing a query against SYCAT.INDEXES.   There should normally be an index on columns against which there are predicates used to significantly restrict the rows qualifying for the answer set, and on join columns, among others.

- The access plan for a query can be examined through the various forms of the Explain tool. The simplest approach is to extract the query from the CLI trace file, store it with a terminating semi-colon in another file, and execute the dynexpln command (shipped in \Program Files\sqllib\bin):

```
dynexpln -d <database> -f <query input file>
    -o <output file> -e
```

An alternative approach to using Explain is to capture access plans during application execution. To do this, create the Explain tables in the database, set the DB2EXPLAIN keyword to a value of 3 in the db2cli.ini file, execute the application, and run the db2exfmt command or use Visual Explain to exhibit the access plan.

For much more information on statistics, indexes, Explain, and access plans, see the *DB2 UDB Administration Guide*.

Perform Database Server Tuning

Indicators that this is needed: The same symptoms are occurring as for bad access plans, or else database access is generally unexpectedly slow, but access plans have been checked and appear to be okay.

What to do: If server elapsed times are unexpectedly long, it could be a result of the database not being configured optimally. The steps to take to investigate are:

Use operating system tools to check for memory over-consumption (paging) or disk I/O contention, and reduce or eliminate these. In the case of disk contention, you may need to spread the database over more disks, or, if there is a high rate of updates on the database, place the log on separate disk(s) from the data.

If there is a lot of disk I/O occurring, it may be because the total buffer pool size is too small. In general, the buffer pool(s) should be given at least 10% of the memory on the server, and as much as 75%, on servers with "large" memory (approximately 1 GB or more). However, the buffer pool(s) should never be set so large that paging occurs continuously on the system.

Try to have the sort heap size (SORTHEAP database configuration parameter) be as large as the largest sort done by queries (for example, due to ORDER BY), and the sort heap threshold (SHEAPTHRES database manager configuration parameter) be approximately (N+2) times SORTHEAP, where N is a typical number of concurrent sorts done by DB2 UDB as a result of query processing requirements. (The number of sorts done for a query can be found by using the Explain tool to check its access plan.).

The effectiveness of the buffer pool(s) in avoiding disk I/O, and the appropriateness of the sort-related and other configuration parameter settings, should be checked using DB2 UDB's snapshot or event monitoring tools. For more information on monitoring, see the *DB2 UDB System Monitor Guide and Reference*.

- If you would like to monitor the database activity for a set of queries, the db2batch tool (in \Program Files\sqllib\bin) is an excellent vehicle. You can store the queries in a file, then execute the following command:

```
db2batch -d <dbname> -f <infile> -r <outfile>
-o p 5 r -1 f -1 -i complete
```

You can get a comprehensive set of elapsed time and snapshot monitor information for each query using this command.

For much more information on database tuning, see the *DB2 UDB Administration Guide*.

Reduce Network Costs

Indicators that this is needed: Access plans are okay and database server tuning has been done, but CLITraceParser shows many network flows or a large amount of time being spent in DB2 UDB.

What to do: Network costs are often the performance gating factor for applications. A good first step in investigating this is to run the application, or individual queries from it, locally on the server (db2batch is a good vehicle to use, if there is a relatively small set of queries in the application) and see how much faster it runs. That, and the use of network monitoring tools, can indicate if network tuning or a faster network is called for. Note that here "network" includes the local case, since even though local connections have much less overhead than a network protocol, the overhead is still significant.

If the network itself is in good shape, you should focus on reducing the number of calls that flow from the application to the database (even for local applications). The CLI trace TRACECOMM keyword allows you to easily identify those calls.

There are several ways to reduce network costs. Most of the CLI-specific methods involve having multiple actions take place through one call, and we now describe these:

- Array Input: One extremely expensive scenario is where a large number of inserts are performed, and for each row a network crossing occurs. An alternative is array input, with which an array of, perhaps, 100 rows can be inserted or updated in one call; one or more network transmissions of up to 32KB take place to send the data. Use `SQLBindParameter` to bind the parameter markers in an SQL statement to arrays.
- Deferred Prepare (default is On): The traditional prepare and execute flow consists essentially of an `SQLPrepare` call being sent to the database, then an `SQLExecute` call being sent and the first row being returned. With Deferred Prepare, the `SQLPrepare` call is cached and only sent to the server when the subsequent `SQLExecute` call is made. This reduces two network crossings to one.

  Note that the use of `SQLColAttribute`, `SQLDescribeCol`, or `SQLNumResultCols` before `SQLExecute` causes the prepare to flow immediately to the server, thus negating the deferred prepare. These calls should therefore be made only after `SQLExecute`. Deferred Prepare can also be turned off deliberately by setting the CLI keyword `DeferredPrepare` to 0, or by turning off the `SQL_ATTR_DEFERRED_PREPARE` statement attribute.

- Early Close (default is On): With this feature in use, when the last block of data for a cursor is sent from the server to the application, the cursor is closed automatically at the server. Otherwise, an explicit `Close` request would normally be sent across the network as part of an `SQLFreeStmt` call. `Close` is the default CLI behavior, but it can be turned off by setting the CLI keyword `EarlyClose` to 0 or by turning off the `SQL_ATTR_EARLYCLOSE` statement attribute.
- Close with Open (default is Off): When Early Close is in use, the cursor is closed when the entire answer set is fetched. If the entire set is not fetched, however, the cursor will remain open. A way to have the cursor closed without an explicit `Close` is to use `Close` with `Open`, whereby the next `Open` using the same statement handle will cause the previous cursor to be closed automatically.
- Autocommit (default is On): When multiple SQL statements do not need to be combined into an atomic transaction, the Autocommit facility can be used. With Autocommit, a `Commit` request is sent to the database as part of each `SQLExecute` or `SQLClose`, instead of a separate `SQLEndTran` (or `SQLTransact`) call being needed. Autocommit can be turned on or off, when more or less transaction control is needed. ON is the default.

- Stored Procedures: This approach is not restricted to CLI/ODBC. By creating a stored procedure at the database server and invoking it through a CALL statement executed via SQLExecDirect, or via SQLPrepare and SQLExecute, multiple SQL statements can be executed in one communication with the server.
- No Describe Information: By setting the PATCH2=17 keyword, the client indicates to the server (if supported), to not send any information describing parameters or result sets. This only applies to applications that do not need the dynamic describe information. Although primarily only a concern for low bandwidth configurations, it can provide savings in a scenario involving a heavy data flow between the application and server.

More information on all of the above techniques is available in the *DB2 UDB Call Level Interface Guide and Reference*.

Avoid Repeated Prepares — Use SQLPrepare with Parameter Markers

Indicators that this is needed: Trace shows significant number of SQLPrepare or SQLExecDirect calls with non-trivial elapsed times.

What to do: When an SQL statement is prepared it is parsed, optimized, and otherwise made ready to be executed. The cost of preparing can be very significant, especially relative to the cost of executing very simple queries (it can take longer to prepare such queries than to execute them). DB2 UDB caches access plans for statements prepared via CLI (as well as statements in static SQL, and non-CLI dynamic SQL), so if the same exact statement is prepared again, the cost will be minimal. However, if there is any difference in syntax between the old and new statements, the cached plan cannot be used.

For example, suppose an application issues an SQLPrepare for the statement "Select * from employee where empno = '000100' ", then issues another SQLPrepare for "Select * from employee where empno = '000200' " (the same statement but with a different literal value). The cached plan for the first statement cannot be reused for the second, and the latter's SQLPrepare time will be non-trivial.

The solution is to replace the literal '000100' by a question mark (?), SQLPrepare the statement (once), issue an SQLBindParameter call to bind a program variable to each ? parameter, and issue SQLExecute as many times as required (changing the program variable(s) appropriately before each call).

If the application is using SQLExecDirect to execute multiple statements that differ only in the literal values they contain, those SQLExecDirect calls should be replaced by SQLPrepare, SQLBindParameter, and SQLExecute, as above.

Note: Parameter markers can and should be used not just for Select, but also for repeated executions of Insert, Update, or Delete statements. If a statement is being executed via SQLPrepare and SQLExecute and is known to be needed only once, it is more efficient to use SQLExecDirect instead.

Sometimes another cause of long prepare times is the use of a query optimization class that is higher than necessary. That is, the DB2 UDB Optimizer can spend more time finding the best access plan for a query than is justified by a reduction in execution time. To set the optimization class to a lower value, use DB2OPTIMIZATION = (integer value such 1) in db2cli.ini, or use SQLExecDirect to issue a SET CURRENT QUERY OPTIMIZATION statement.

Reduce the Amount of Data Returned

Indicators that this is needed: All server tuning has been performed and there are no unnecessary calls to the server, but the use of TRACECOMM and CLITraceParser shows a large amount of data being transferred between the client and the server.

What to do: You should be sure to only return the rows and columns that are absolutely required. As simple as this sounds, it is quite common to see the entire contents of tables being requested by an application, instead of only the required subset. If it is absolutely necessary to return large answer sets for the application or the user to sift through, the data should be cached on the client if it will be reused, so that at least it is not requested multiple times.

Some ways to limit the number of rows returned are as follows:

- Use the FETCH FIRST n ROWS ONLY clause in a Select statement (see "Specify the FETCH FIRST n ROWS ONLY Clause" on page 410).
- Use CLI keyword TableType to limit the results of catalog function calls (for example, SQLTables) to only the specified types of tables; for example, you may want base tables only, not views or synonyms.
- Use CLI keyword SchemaList to limit catalog function results to only those tables with the specified schema(s).
- Use CLI keyword DBNAME to limit catalog function results to a specific DB2 for OS/390 database.

Use an Optimized Copy of Catalog (db2ocat tool)

Indicators that this is needed: This is the same as for "Reduce the Amount of Data Returned" on page 455, but a significant amount of time is spent in catalog accesses, such as SQLTables calls.

What to do: Many applications written using ODBC or DB2 CLI interfaces make heavy use of the system catalog. While this does not usually present a problem for databases with a small number of database objects (tables, views, synonyms etc.), it can lead to performance problems when using these applications with larger DB2 UDB databases. This performance degradation can be attributed to 2 main factors: the amount of information that has to be returned to the calling application and the length of time that locks are held on the catalog tables.

The db2ocat tool solves both problems by creating a separate system catalog that is optimized for ODBC access by a particular application. This utility helps database administrators to identify a subset of tables that are needed for a particular application and creates an ODBC-optimized catalog that is used to access data about those tables. That catalog is pointed to by the CLISCHEMA keyword, and through the use of that catalog, no locks are placed on the real system catalog tables, and catalog query times and amount of data returned as a result of these queries are substantially reduced. db2ocat is a 32-bit Windows program that can be used on Windows workstations running the DB2 Version 6.1 (or later) Client. It is available at: ftp://ftp.software.ibm.com/ps/products/db2/tools/ in the file db2ocat.zip.

Minimize Data Conversion

Indicators that this is needed: Significant elapsed CLI times are occurring in SQLFetch or SQLGetData calls, or in SQLExecute calls with parameter markers.

What to do: The CLI driver will automatically perform data conversion when transferring data between the application and the DBMS, based on the SQL and C datatypes involved. As convenient as this is, it does consume CPU processing. As much as possible, you should use the natural datatypes; for example, for a DB2 UDB INTEGER column, use a C LONG field, not a character field.

Reduce the Number of Local Client Calls

Indicators that this is needed: Other tuning actions have been taken, but performance still needs improvement; CLITraceParser shows a large number of calls that do not flow to the server.

What to do: Until you analyze a trace it may not be apparent just how many CLI calls are executed. Tasks such as allocating and freeing resources are sometimes done repetitively through generic routines in applications, instead of the resources being reused. The CLITraceParser tool is an excellent way to summarize the numbers and types of calls made.

The most common calls to be avoided are:

- SQLGetData, instead of using SQLBindParameter or SQLBindCol. With the latter two calls, data is moved automatically into the bound variables without explicit SQLGetData calls.
- SQLBindParameter, when executed for each row of the answer set, instead of to bind to an array of variables. The optimal way to use both SQLBindParameter and SQLBindCol is to call them once after Prepare, and reuse the application buffers for each Execute request.

Tuning Application Performance

Supported Statements for SQL Procedures

This appendix provides the supported statements for SQL procedures. You can use the following SQL statements in the procedure body of SQL procedures:

- **ALLOCATE CURSOR**

  Allocates a cursor for the result set identified by the result set locator variable.

- **ASSOCIATE LOCATOR**

  Gets the result set locator value for each result set returned by a stored procedure.

- **CALL**

  Invokes a procedure stored at the location of a database.

- **CLOSE**

  Closes a cursor. If a result table was created when the cursor was opened, that table is destroyed.

- **COMMENT ON**

  Adds or replaces comments in the catalog descriptions of various objects.

- **COMMIT**

  Terminates a unit of work and commits the database changes that were made by that unit of work.

- **CREATE TABLE / VIEW / INDEX**

  Defines a table / a view / an index.

- **DECLARE CURSOR**

  Defines a cursor.

- **DECLARE GLOBAL TEMPORARY TABLE**

  Defines a temporary table for the current session.

- **DELETE**

  Deletes rows from a table or view.

- **DROP TABLE / VIEW / INDEX**

  Deletes a table / a view / an index.

- **EXECUTE**

  Executes a prepared SQL statement.

- **EXECUTE IMMEDIATE**

  Prepares an executable form of an SQL statement from a character string form of the statement, and then executes the prepared SQL statement.

- **EXPLAIN**

  Captures information about the access plan chosen for the supplied explainable statement and places this information into the Explain tables.

- **FETCH**

  Positions a cursor on the next row of its result table and assigns the values of that row to host variables.

- **FREE LOCATOR**

  Removes the association between a locator variable and its value.

- **GRANT**

  Grants privilege or authorities.

- **INSERT**

  Insert rows into a table or a view.

- **LOCK TABLE**

  Prevents concurrent application processes from changing a table (share option) or prevents concurrent application processes from using a table (exclusive option).

- **OPEN**

  Opens a cursor so that it can be used to fetch rows from its result table.

- **PREPARE**

  Used by application programs to dynamically prepare an SQL statement for execution.

- **RELEASE**

  Places one or more connections in the release-pending state.

- **RELEASE SAVEPOINT**

  Indicates that the application no longer wishes to have the named save point maintained.

- **REVOKE**

  Revokes privileges or authorities.

- **ROLLBACK**

  Backs out of the database changes that were made within a unit of work or a save point.

- **SAVEPOINT**

  Sets a save point within a transaction.

- **SELECT INTO**

  Produces a result table consisting of at most one row, and assigns the values in that row to host variables.

- **SET CURRENT DEFAULT TRANSFORM GROUP**

  Changes the value of the CURRENT DEFAULT TRANSFORM GOUP special register.

- **SET CURRENT DEGREE**

  Changes the value of the CURRENT DEGREE special register.

- **SET CURRENT EXPLAIN MODE**

  Changes the value of the CURRENT EXPLAIN MODE special register.

- **SET CURRENT EXPLAIN SNAPSHOT**

  Changes the value of the CURRENT EXPLAIN SNAPSHOT special register.

- **SET CURRENT QUERY OPTIMIZATION**

  Changes the value of the CURRENT QUERY OPTIMIZATION special register.

- **SET EVENT MONITOR STATE**

  Activates or deactivates an event monitor.

- **SET PASSTHRU**

  Opens and closes a session for submitting a data source's native SQL directly to that data source.

- **SET PATH**

  Changes the value of the CURRENT PATH special register.

- **SET SCHEMA**

  Changes the value of the CURRENT SCHEMA special register.

- **SET SERVER OPTION**

  Specifies a server option setting that is to remain in effect while a user or application is connected to the federated database.

- **SET transition variable**

  Assigns values to new transition variables.

- **UPDATE**

  Updates the values of specified columns in rows of a table or view.

- **VALUES INTO**

  Produces a result table consisting of at most one row and assigns the values in that row to host variables.

Also, the procedure body can have the following statements:

- **Assignment statements**

  Assign a value to an output parameter, a local variable, or a special register.

- **CASE**

  Selects an execution path based on multiple conditions.

- **Compound statement**

  Groups other statements together in an SQL procedure.

- **FOR**

  Executes a statement or group of statements for each row of a table.

- **GET DIAGNOSTICS**

  Obtains information about the previous SQL statement invoked.

- **GOTO**

  Branches to a user-defined label within an SQL routine.

- **IF**

  Selects an execution path based on the evaluation of a condition.

- **ITERATE**

  Causes the flow of control to return to the beginning of a labelled loop.

- **LEAVE**

  Transfers program control out of a loop or a compound statement.

- **LOOP**

  Repeats the execution of a statement or a group of statements.

- **REPEAT**

  Executes a statement or group of statements until a search condition is true.

- **RESIGNAL**

  Re-signals an error or warning condition.

- **RETURN**

  Returns from the routine.

- **SIGNAL**

  Signals an error or warning condition.

- **WHILE**

  Repeats the execution of a statement or group of statements while a specified condition is true.

For the complete syntax of each statement, consult the manual *DB2 UDB SQL Reference*.

Example DB2 UDB Source Code

This appendix provides the example DB2 UDB source code introduced in each chapter including:

- User defined table function (Chapter 4)
- Visual Basic example using ADO (Chapter 5)
- Visual Basic example for the MTS environment (Chapter 7)

The following code is a user defined table function introduced in Chapter 4:

```
#include <stdlib.h>
#include <string.h>
#include <stdio.h>
#include <sql.h>
#include <sqludf.h> /* for use in compiling User Defined Function */

#define   SQL_NOTNULL   0    /* Nulls Allowed - Value is not Null */
#define   SQL_ISNULL   -1    /* Nulls Allowed - Value is Null */

/* Short and long city name structure */
typedef struct {
  char * city_short ;
  char * city_long ;
} city_area ;

/* Scratchpad data */
/* Preserve information from one function call to the next call */
typedef struct {
  /* FILE * file_ptr; if you use weather data text file */
  int file_pos ;  /* if you use a weather data buffer */
} scratch_area ;

/* Field descriptor structure */
typedef struct {
  char fld_field[31] ;                    /* Field data */
  int  fld_ind ;               /* Field null indicator data */
  int  fld_type ;                         /* Field type */
  int  fld_length ;  /* Field length in the weather data */
  int  fld_offset ;  /* Field offset in the weather data */
} fld_desc ;

/* Short and long city name data */
city_area cities[] = {
    { "alb", "Albany, NY"                 },
    { "atl", "Atlanta, GA"                },
    { "aus", "Austin, TX"                 },
    { "bgm", "Binghamton, NY"             },
    { "btv", "Burlington, VT"             },
    { "chi", "Chicago, IL"                },
    { "clt", "Charlotte, NC"              },
    { "den", "Denver, CO"                 },
    { "ftw", "Dallas - Fort Worth, TX"    },
    { "hou", "Houston, TX"                },
    { "lax", "Los Angeles, CA"            },
    { "lex", "Lexington, KY"              },
    { "mci", "Kansas City, MO"            },
```

```
      { "mem",  "Memphis, TN"                  },
      { "mia",  "Miami - Fort Lauderdale, FL"  },
      { "mke",  "Milwaukee, WI"                },
      { "msp",  "Twin Cities, MN"              },
      { "nyc",  "New York City, NY"            },
      { "pbi",  "Palm Beach, FL"               },
      { "pit",  "Pittsburgh, PA"               },
      { "rdu",  "Raleigh - Durham, NC"         },
      { "ric",  "Richmond, VA"                 },
      { "rst",  "Rochester, MN"                },
      { "sea",  "Seattle, WA"                  },
      { "sfo",  "San Francisco, CA"            },
      { "sjc",  "San Jose, CA"                 },
      { "slc",  "Salt Lake City, UT"           },
      { "stl",  "St. Louis, MO"                },
      { "tus",  "Tuscon, AZ"                   },
      { "wbc",  "Washington DC, DC"            },
      /* You may want to add more cities here */

      /* Do not forget a null termination */
      { ( char * ) 0, ( char * ) 0            }
   } ;

   /* Field descriptor data */
   fld_desc fields[] = {
      { "", SQL_ISNULL, SQL_TYP_VARCHAR, 30,  0 }, /* city          */
      { "", SQL_ISNULL, SQL_TYP_INTEGER,  3,  2 }, /* temp_in_f      */
      { "", SQL_ISNULL, SQL_TYP_INTEGER,  3,  7 }, /* humidity       */
      { "", SQL_ISNULL, SQL_TYP_VARCHAR,  5, 13 }, /* wind           */
      { "", SQL_ISNULL, SQL_TYP_INTEGER,  3, 19 }, /* wind_velocity  */
      { "", SQL_ISNULL, SQL_TYP_FLOAT,    5, 24 }, /* barometer      */
      { "", SQL_ISNULL, SQL_TYP_VARCHAR, 25, 30 }, /* forecast       */
      /* You may want to add more fields here */

      /* Do not forget a null termination */
      { ( char ) 0, 0, 0, 0, 0 }
   } ;

/* Following is the weather data buffer for this example. You */
/* may want to keep the weather data in a separate text file. */
/* Uncomment the following fopen() statement.  Note that you  */
/* have to specify the full path name for this file.          */
char * weather_data[] = {
   "alb.forecast",
   "   34    28%    wnw   3  30.53 clear",
   "atl.forecast",
   "   46    89%   east  11  30.03 fog",
   "aus.forecast",
   "   59    57%  south   5  30.05 clear",
   "bgm.forecast",
   "   36    32%  south  10  30.34 overcast",
   "btv.forecast",
   "   38    30%  south   5  30.36 clear",
   "chi.forecast",
   "   41    55%    nne  12  30.15 partly cloudy",
   "clt.forecast",
   "   37   100%    nne  10  30.18 light rain",
   "den.forecast",
   "   58    24%    nne   8  29.67 clear",
   "ftw.forecast",
   "   49    73%    nne   4  30.05 overcast",
   "hou.forecast",
   "   65    46%   west  10  30.03 clear",
   "lax.forecast",
   "   60    86%   east   6  29.96 light drizzle",
   "lex.forecast",
   "   46    92%   east   8  29.99 fog",
   "mci.forecast",
   "   46    51%     ne   9  30.06 overcast",
   "mem.forecast",
   "   53    96%    wnw   8  29.97 moderate rain",
   "mia.forecast",
   "   82    64%     se  17  30.08 mostly cloudy",
   "mke.forecast",
   "   37    59%     ne  12  30.18 clear",
   "msp.forecast",
   "   41    39%     se   6  30.19 n/a",
   "nyc.forecast",
```

```
    "    37    56%    sse    6  30.44 overcast",
    "pbi.forecast",
    "    81    69% south  17  30.09 partly cloudy",
    "pit.forecast",
    "    39    82%   east  11  30.21 light drizzle",
    "rdu.forecast",
    "    39    96% north   8  30.10 light rain",
    "ric.forecast",
    "    39    75%    ene  12  30.20 light rain",
    "rst.forecast",
    "    40    50%     se  10  30.17 n/a",
    "sea.forecast",
    "    51    37%    ssw   8  29.93 clear",
    "sfo.forecast",
    "    53    54%   west  19  29.98 partly cloudy",
    "sjc.forecast",
    "    62    44%    wnw  17    n/a partly cloudy",
    "slc.forecast",
    "    63    26% south  25  29.45 mostly cloudy",
    "stl.forecast",
    "    43    55% north   9  30.06 overcast",
    "tus.forecast",
    "    73    18% south   8  29.80 clear",
    "wbc.forecast",
    "    38    96%    ene  16  30.31 light rain",
    /* You may want to add more weather data here */

    /* Do not forget a null termination */
    ( char * ) 0
} ;

#ifdef __cplusplus
extern "C"
#endif
/* Find a full city name using a short name */
int get_name( char * short_name, char * long_name ) {

    int name_pos = 0 ;

    while ( cities[name_pos].city_short != ( char * ) 0 ) {
        if (strcmp(short_name, cities[name_pos].city_short) == 0) {
            strcpy( long_name, cities[name_pos].city_long ) ;
            /* A full city name found */
            return( 0 ) ;
        }
        name_pos++ ;
    }
    /* Could not find such city in the city data */
    strcpy( long_name, "Unknown City" ) ;
    return( -1 ) ;

}

#ifdef __cplusplus
extern "C"
#endif
/* Clean all field data and field null indicator data */
int clean_fields( int field_pos ) {

    while ( fields[field_pos].fld_length != 0 ) {
        memset( fields[field_pos].fld_field, '\0', 31 ) ;
        fields[field_pos].fld_ind = SQL_ISNULL ;
        field_pos++ ;
    }
    return( 0 ) ;

}

#ifdef __cplusplus
extern "C"
#endif
/* Fills all field data and field null indicator data ... */
/* ... from text weather data */
int get_value( char * value, int field_pos ) {

    fld_desc * field ;
    char field_buf[31] ;
    double * double_ptr ;
```

```
            int * int_ptr, buf_pos ;
        while ( fields[field_pos].fld_length != 0 ) {
           field = &fields[field_pos] ;
           memset( field_buf, '\0', 31 ) ;
           memcpy( field_buf,
                 ( value + field->fld_offset ),
                 field->fld_length ) ;
           buf_pos = field->fld_length ;
           while ( ( buf_pos > 0 ) &&
                   ( field_buf[buf_pos] == ' ' ) )
              field_buf[buf_pos--] = '\0' ;
           buf_pos = 0 ;
           while ( ( buf_pos < field->fld_length ) &&
                   ( field_buf[buf_pos] == ' ' ) )
              buf_pos++ ;
           if ( strlen( ( char * ) ( field_buf + buf_pos ) ) > 0 ||
                strcmp( ( char * ) ( field_buf + buf_pos ), "n/a") != 0 ) {
              field->fld_ind = SQL_NOTNULL ;

              /* Text to SQL type conversion */
              switch( field->fld_type ) {
                case SQL_TYP_VARCHAR:
                   strcpy( field->fld_field,
                         ( char * ) ( field_buf + buf_pos ) ) ;
                   break ;
                case SQL_TYP_INTEGER:
                   int_ptr = ( int * ) field->fld_field ;
                   *int_ptr = atoi( ( char * ) ( field_buf + buf_pos ) ) ;
                   break ;
                case SQL_TYP_FLOAT:
                   double_ptr = ( double * ) field->fld_field ;
                   *double_ptr = atof( ( char * ) ( field_buf + buf_pos ) ) ;
                   break ;
                /* You may want to add more text to SQL type conversion here */
              }

           }
           field_pos++ ;
        }
        return( 0 ) ;

}

#ifdef __cplusplus
extern "C"
#endif
void SQL_API_FN weather( /* Return row fields */
              SQLUDF_VARCHAR * city,
              SQLUDF_INTEGER * temp_in_f,
              SQLUDF_INTEGER * humidity,
              SQLUDF_VARCHAR * wind,
              SQLUDF_INTEGER * wind_velocity,
              SQLUDF_DOUBLE  * barometer,
              SQLUDF_VARCHAR * forecast,
              /* You may want to add more fields here */

              /* Return row field null indicators */
              SQLUDF_NULLIND * city_ind,
              SQLUDF_NULLIND * temp_in_f_ind,
              SQLUDF_NULLIND * humidity_ind,
              SQLUDF_NULLIND * wind_ind,
              SQLUDF_NULLIND * wind_velocity_ind,
              SQLUDF_NULLIND * barometer_ind,
              SQLUDF_NULLIND * forecast_ind,
              /* You may want to add more field indicators here */

              /* UDF always-present (trailing) input arguments */
              SQLUDF_TRAIL_ARGS_ALL
           ) {

   scratch_area * save_area ;
   char line_buf[81] ;
   int line_buf_pos ;

   /* SQLUDF_SCRAT is part of SQLUDF_TRAIL_ARGS_ALL */
   /* Preserve information from one function call to the next call */
   save_area = ( scratch_area * ) ( SQLUDF_SCRAT->data ) ;
```

```
/* SQLUDF_CALLT is part of SQLUDF_TRAIL_ARGS_ALL */
switch( SQLUDF_CALLT ) {

  /* First call UDF: Open table and fetch first row */
  case SQL_TF_OPEN:
      /* If you use a weather data text file specify full path */
      /* save_area->file_ptr = fopen("/sqllib/samples/c/tblsrv.dat",
                                                     "r"); */
      save_area->file_pos = 0 ;
      break ;

  /* Normal call UDF: Fetch next row */
  case SQL_TF_FETCH:
      /* If you use a weather data text file */
      /* memset(line_buf, '\0', 81); */
      /* if (fgets(line_buf, 80, save_area->file_ptr) == NULL) { */
      if ( weather_data[save_area->file_pos] == ( char * ) 0 ) {

          /* SQLUDF_STATE is part of SQLUDF_TRAIL_ARGS_ALL */
          strcpy( SQLUDF_STATE, "02000" ) ;

          break ;
      }
      memset( line_buf, '\0', 81 ) ;
      strcpy( line_buf, weather_data[save_area->file_pos] ) ;
      line_buf[3] = '\0' ;

      /* Clean all field data and field null indicator data */
      clean_fields( 0 ) ;

      /* Fills city field null indicator data */
      fields[0].fld_ind = SQL_NOTNULL ;

      /* Find a full city name using a short name */
      /* Fills city field data */
      if ( get_name( line_buf, fields[0].fld_field ) == 0 ) {
          save_area->file_pos++ ;
          /* If you use a weather data text file */
          /* memset(line_buf, '\0', 81); */
          /* if (fgets(line_buf, 80, save_area->file_ptr) == NULL) { */
          if ( weather_data[save_area->file_pos] == ( char * ) 0 ) {
              /* SQLUDF_STATE is part of SQLUDF_TRAIL_ARGS_ALL */
              strcpy( SQLUDF_STATE, "02000" ) ;
              break ;
          }
          memset( line_buf, '\0', 81 ) ;
          strcpy( line_buf, weather_data[save_area->file_pos] ) ;
          line_buf_pos = strlen( line_buf ) ;
          while ( line_buf_pos > 0 ) {
              if ( line_buf[line_buf_pos] >= ' ' )
                  line_buf_pos = 0 ;
              else {
                  line_buf[line_buf_pos] = '\0' ;
                  line_buf_pos-- ;
              }
          }
      }

      /* Fills field data and field null indicator data ... */
      /* ... for selected city from text weather data */
      get_value( line_buf, 1 ) ;  /* Skips city field */

      /* Builds return row fields */
      strcpy( city, fields[0].fld_field ) ;
      memcpy( (void *) temp_in_f,
              fields[1].fld_field,
              sizeof( SQLUDF_INTEGER ) ) ;
      memcpy( (void *) humidity,
              fields[2].fld_field,
              sizeof( SQLUDF_INTEGER ) ) ;
      strcpy( wind, fields[3].fld_field ) ;
      memcpy( (void *) wind_velocity,
              fields[4].fld_field,
              sizeof( SQLUDF_INTEGER ) ) ;
      memcpy( (void *) barometer,
              fields[5].fld_field,
              sizeof( SQLUDF_DOUBLE ) ) ;
```

```
            strcpy( forecast, fields[6].fld_field ) ;

            /* Builds return row field null indicators */
            memcpy( (void *) city_ind,
                    &(fields[0].fld_ind),
                    sizeof( SQLUDF_NULLIND ) ) ;
            memcpy( (void *) temp_in_f_ind,
                    &(fields[1].fld_ind),
                    sizeof( SQLUDF_NULLIND ) ) ;
            memcpy( (void *) humidity_ind,
                    &(fields[2].fld_ind),
                    sizeof( SQLUDF_NULLIND ) ) ;
            memcpy( (void *) wind_ind,
                    &(fields[3].fld_ind),
                    sizeof( SQLUDF_NULLIND ) ) ;
            memcpy( (void *) wind_velocity_ind,
                    &(fields[4].fld_ind),
                    sizeof( SQLUDF_NULLIND ) ) ;
            memcpy( (void *) barometer_ind,
                    &(fields[5].fld_ind),
                    sizeof( SQLUDF_NULLIND ) ) ;
            memcpy( (void *) forecast_ind,
                    &(fields[6].fld_ind),
                    sizeof( SQLUDF_NULLIND ) ) ;

            /* Next city weather data */
            save_area->file_pos++ ;

            break ;

        /* Special last call UDF for cleanup (no real args!): Close table */
        case SQL_TF_CLOSE:
            /* If you use a weather data text file */
            /* fclose(save_area->file_ptr); */
            /* save_area->file_ptr = NULL; */
            save_area->file_pos = 0 ;
            break ;

    }

}
```

The following code is the Visual Basic example using ADO. This code extracts the schema of the MS Access database and creates it in the DB2 UDB Sample database.

```
Option Explicit
Public cnAccess As New ADODB.Connection ' Connection for MSACCESS
Public cnDb2 As New ADODB.Connection ' Connection for DB2 UDB

Private Sub Main()

  Dim rstTables As New ADODB.Recordset ' Read table schema

  cnAccess.ConnectionString = _
    "Provider=Microsoft.Jet.OLEDB.3.51;" & _
    "Data Source=c:\Booksale\booksale.mdb;User Id=admin;Password=;"
  cnAccess.Open

  cnDb2.ConnectionString = _
    "DSN=Booksale"
  cnDb2.Open

  Set rstTables = cnAccess.OpenSchema(adSchemaTables, _
    Array(Empty, Empty, Empty, "Table"))

  Do Until rstTables.EOF
    If InStr(rstTables!TABLE_NAME, "MSys") = 0 Then
      Call CreateTable(rstTables!TABLE_NAME)
    End If
    rstTables.MoveNext
  Loop
```

```
      rstTables.Close
      Set rstTables = Nothing
      cnAccess.Close
      Set cnAccess = Nothing
      cnDb2.Close
      Set cnDb2 = Nothing
End Sub


Private Sub CreateTable(strTable)

    Dim cmdDb2 As New ADODB.Command
    Dim rstCols As New ADODB.Recordset ' Recordset to read Column schema
    Dim strCreate As String
    Dim strTab As String
    Dim strCol As String
    Dim strC As String

    Set cmdDb2.ActiveConnection = cnDb2
    Set rstCols = cnAccess.OpenSchema(adSchemaColumns)
    rstCols.MoveFirst

    strTab = strTable
    spstrip strTab
    strCreate = "CREATE TABLE " & strTab & " ("

    Do Until rstCols.EOF
      If rstCols!TABLE_NAME = strTable Then
        strCol = rstCols!COLUMN_NAME
        strC = strCol
        spstrip strC
        strCreate = strCreate & strC & " "
        Select Case Trim$(rstCols!DATA_TYPE)
          Case "129"
            strCreate = strCreate & "VARCHAR("
            If rstCols!CHARACTER_MAXIMUM_LENGTH = 0 Then
              strCreate = strCreate & "2000)"
            Else
             strCreate = strCreate & Trim(CStr(rstCols!CHARACTER_MAXIMUM_LENGTH)) & ")"
            End If
          Case "2"
            strCreate = strCreate & "SmallInt"
          Case "3"
            strCreate = strCreate & "Integer"
          Case "6"
            strCreate = strCreate & "Double"
        End Select
        If CheckIfPrimary(strTable, strCol) = True Then
          strCreate = strCreate & " NOT NULL"
        End If
        strCreate = strCreate & ","
      End If
      rstCols.MoveNext
    Loop

    strCreate = Left$(strCreate, Len(strCreate) - 1)
    PrimaryKey strTable, strCreate
    strCreate = strCreate & ");"
    'Debug.Print strCreate
    cmdDb2.CommandText = strCreate
    cmdDb2.Execute

    rstCols.Close
    Set rstCols = Nothing
    Set cmdDb2 = Nothing

    CreateIndexes strTable
    Call DataFill(strTable, strTab)
End Sub


Public Sub DataFill(strTable, strTab)
    Dim rstAccess As New ADODB.Recordset
    Dim rstDb2 As New ADODB.Recordset
    Dim destfld As String
    Dim fld As Variant
    Dim n As Integer
```

```
rstAccess.Open "select * from [" & strTable & "]", cnAccess
With rstDb2
  .CursorLocation = adUseClient
  .CursorType = adOpenKeyset
  .LockType = adLockOptimistic
  .Open UCase(strTab), cnDb2, , , adCmdTable
End With

Do While Not rstAccess.EOF
  rstDb2.AddNew

  For Each fld In rstAccess.Fields
    destfld = fld.Name
    spstrip destfld
    rstDb2.Fields(destfld) = rstAccess.Fields(fld.Name)
  Next fld
  rstDb2.Update
  rstAccess.MoveNext
Loop

rstAccess.Close
rstDb2.Close
Set rstAccess = Nothing
Set rstDb2 = Nothing
End Sub
```

```
Public Function CheckIfPrimary(strTable, strCol)
  Dim rstPrimary As New ADODB.Recordset
  Set rstPrimary = cnAccess.OpenSchema(adSchemaPrimaryKeys)
  Do Until rstPrimary.EOF
    If rstPrimary!TABLE_NAME = strTable Then
      If rstPrimary!COLUMN_NAME = strCol Then
        CheckIfPrimary = True
        Exit Function
      End If
    End If
    rstPrimary.MoveNext
  Loop
  CheckIfPrimary = False
End Function
```

```
Public Sub PrimaryKey(strTable, strCreate)
  Dim rstPrimary As New ADODB.Recordset
  Dim strCol As String
  Dim Pkey As Boolean
  Pkey = False
  Set rstPrimary = cnAccess.OpenSchema(adSchemaPrimaryKeys)
  Do Until rstPrimary.EOF
    If rstPrimary!TABLE_NAME = strTable Then
      If InStr(strCreate, "PRIMARY KEY") = 0 Then
        Pkey = True
        strCreate = strCreate & ", PRIMARY KEY ("
      Else
        strCreate = strCreate & ", "
      End If
      strCol = rstPrimary!COLUMN_NAME
      spstrip strCol
      strCreate = strCreate & strCol
    End If
    rstPrimary.MoveNext
  Loop
  If Pkey = True Then strCreate = strCreate & ")"
  rstPrimary.Close
  Set rstPrimary = Nothing
End Sub
```

```
Public Sub CreateIndexes(strTable)
  Dim rstIndexes As New ADODB.Recordset
  Dim cmdIndex As New ADODB.Command
  Dim strT As String
  Dim strIndName As String
  Dim strInd As String
  Dim strTemp As String
  Static n
  cmdIndex.ActiveConnection = cnDb2
```

```
    Set rstIndexes = cnAccess.OpenSchema(adSchemaIndexes)
    Do Until rstIndexes.EOF
      If rstIndexes!TABLE_NAME = strTable Then
        If rstIndexes!INDEX_NAME <> "PrimaryKey" Then
          If InStr(rstIndexes!INDEX_NAME, "Reference") = 0 Then
            strInd = "CREATE INDEX "
            strIndName = rstIndexes!INDEX_NAME
            spstrip strIndName
            strInd = strInd & strIndName & " ON "
            strT = strTable
            spstrip strT
            strInd = strInd & strT & "("
            strTemp = rstIndexes!COLUMN_NAME
            spstrip strTemp
            strInd = strInd & strTemp & ")"
            cmdIndex.CommandText = strInd
            cmdIndex.Execute
          End If
        End If
      End If
      rstIndexes.MoveNext
    Loop
    rstIndexes.Close
    Set rstIndexes = Nothing
End Sub
```

```
Public Sub spstrip(dummy)
  Dim p As Integer
  Dim n As Integer
  n = 1
  Do
    p = InStr(n, dummy, " ")
    If p <> 0 Then
      n = p
      dummy = Left$(dummy, p - 1) & Mid$(dummy, p + 1, Len(dummy))
    End If
  Loop Until p = 0
End Sub
```

The following code is the client side project (db2mts.vbp) of the sample MTS application introduced in Chapter 7:

```
'''''''''''''''''''''''''''''''''''''''''''''''''''''''''''''''''''''''''
'   Project DB2MTS.vbp
'   Form db2mts.frm
'''''''''''''''''''''''''''''''''''''''''''''''''''''''''''''''''''''''''
' cancel_Click
'''''''''''''''''''''''''''''''''''''''''''''''''''''''''''''''''''''''''
Private Sub cancel_Click()
    End
End Sub

'''''''''''''''''''''''''''''''''''''''''''''''''''''''''''''''''''''''''
' Form_Activate
'''''''''''''''''''''''''''''''''''''''''''''''''''''''''''''''''''''''''
Private Sub Form_Activate()
    DataSource.SetFocus
End Sub

'''''''''''''''''''''''''''''''''''''''''''''''''''''''''''''''''''''''''
' InfoButton_Click
'''''''''''''''''''''''''''''''''''''''''''''''''''''''''''''''''''''''''
Private Sub InfoButton_Click()
 InfoDialog.Show vbModeless, Me
End Sub

'''''''''''''''''''''''''''''''''''''''''''''''''''''''''''''''''''''''''
' Submit_Click
'''''''''''''''''''''''''''''''''''''''''''''''''''''''''''''''''''''''''
Private Sub Submit_Click()
    Dim Com1, Com2 As Object
```

```
        Dim strResult As String
        Dim rc, nRuns, iRun As Integer

        rc = 0
        iRun = 1
        Iteration.Caption = Str$(1)
        nRuns = Val(NofRunsEdit.Text)
        NofRunsLabel.Caption = NofRunsEdit.Text
        ResultBox.Clear

        On Error GoTo ErrorCreateObject
        Set Com1 = CreateObject("db2com.UpdateRow")
        Call AddItem("Creation of MTS COM object db2com.UpdateRow was successful", 1)
        Set Com2 = CreateObject("db2com.VerifyUpdate")
        Call AddItem("Creation of MTS COM object db2com.VerifyUpdate successful", 2)

        On Error GoTo ErrorHandler
        For iRun = 1 To nRuns

            Iteration.Caption = Str$(iRun)
            strConnect = "DSN=" + DataSource.Text + ";UID=" + UserID.Text + ";PWD=" +
            Password.Text
            rc = Com1.UpdateRow(strConnect, strResult)
            Call AddItem("Execution of db2com.UpdateRow was successful", 1)
            rc = Com2.VerifyUpdate(strConnect, strResult)
            Call AddItem(strResult, 2)
        Next iRun

cleanup:
    Set Com1 = Nothing
    Set Com2 = Nothing
Exit Sub

ErrorCreateObject:
    Call AddItem("Error: Cannot create or execute MTS objects for db2mts package", 1)
    Call AddItem("        Please make sure MSDTC service is up and db2mts package has
been installed", 1)
    Resume cleanup
ErrorHandler:
    Call AddItem("Error: (" + Str$(Err.Number) + ")", 2)
    Call AddItem("Source: " + Err.Source, 2)
    Call AddItem("Description: " + Err.Description, 2)
    Resume cleanup
End Sub
'''''''''''''''''''''''''''''''''''''''''''''''''''''''''''''''''''''''''
' CheckError
'''''''''''''''''''''''''''''''''''''''''''''''''''''''''''''''''''''''''
Private Function CheckError(ByVal rc As Integer, _
                        ByVal strResult As String) As Integer
    Select Case rc
    Case 0
        Call AddItem("Successful", 3)
    Case 1
        Call AddItem("Successful.  " + strResult, 3)
        rc = 0
    Case Else
        Call AddItem("Error:  " + strResult, 3)
    End Select
    CheckError = rc
End Function
'''''''''''''''''''''''''''''''''''''''''''''''''''''''''''''''''''''''''
' AddItem
'''''''''''''''''''''''''''''''''''''''''''''''''''''''''''''''''''''''''
Private Sub AddItem(strText As String, ByVal Level As Integer)
    ResultBox.AddItem (Space(Level * 5) + strText)
End Sub


'''''''''''''''''''''''''''''''''''''''''''''''''''''''''',,,,,,,,,''''''''''''''
'
'  Project DB2MTS.vbp
'  Form InfoDialog.frm
Option Explicit

''''''''''''''''''''''''''''''''''''''''''''''''''''''''''''''''''''''''''
' Form_Load
```

```
''''''''''''''''''''''''''''''''''''''''''''''''''''''''''''''
Private Sub Form_Load()
    InfoText1.Caption = "Sample application is written in Visual Basic v6: " + _
        "client exe: db2mts Project(db2mts.vbp) ( db2mtsform Form(db2mts.frm) ) " + _
        "server dll: db2com Project(db2com.vbp) with 4 class modules: " + _
        "UpdateNumberColumn.Cls  UpdateRow.Cls  UpdateStringColumn.Cls  VerifyUp-
date.Cls " + _
        "Table used in this example is DB2MTS table in SAMPLE database. "
    InfoText2(0) = "The sample demonstrates update operation in the database through
MTS. " + _
        "The DB2MTS table contains one integer and one string attribute. " + _
        "In db2mts form user provides connection information and specifies " + _
        "desired number of updates. Each update will increment value in integer
attribute " + _
        "by 1, and string attribute will be updated to contain new number incremented
by 1 as well."
    InfoText2(1) = " In MTS applications, connections participating in the same trans-
action " + _
        "use loosely coupled transaction ID. " + _
        "2 connections participating in the same transaction can lock one another " + _
        "out if they are accessing the same data (same row as in example below), " + _
        "the reason for that is that DB2 server treats loosely coupled transactions " + _
        "as if they are totally unrelated. " + _
        "The user has to manage their own COM objects to make sure no 2 connections " + _
        "are accessing the data at the same time."

End Sub

''''''''''''''''''''''''''''''''''''''''''''''''''''''''''''''
' OKButton_Click
''''''''''''''''''''''''''''''''''''''''''''''''''''''''''''''
Private Sub OKButton_Click()
    Hide
End Sub
```

The following is the server side project (db2com.vbp) of the MTS sample application:

```
'''''''''''''''''''''''''''''''''''''''''''''''''''''''''''''''
'
'  Project DB2Com.vbp
'  Module Common.bas
''''''''''''''''''''''''''''''''''''''''''''''''''''''''''''''
Private Declare Sub OutputDebugStringA _
        Lib "KERNEL32" (ByVal strError As String)
Private Declare Function MessageBoxA _
        Lib "USER32" (ByVal hwnd As Long, _
        ByVal lpText As String, _
        ByVal lpCaption As String, _
        ByVal uType As Long) As Long
    'API Constants
Private Const API_NULL                 As Long = 0
Private Const MB_ICONERROR             As Long = &H10
Private Const MB_SERVICE_NOTIFICATION As Long = &H200000

''''''''''''''''''''''''''''''''''''''''''''''''''''''''''''''''''''''''''
' GetError
''''''''''''''''''''''''''''''''''''''''''''''''''''''''''''''''''''''''''
Public Function GetError(ByVal adoConn As ADODB.Connection, _
                    ByVal ErrorText As String, _
                    ByRef strResult As String) As Integer

Dim Error998 As String

Error998 = "Explanation for error SQL0998N:" + _
Chr$(15) + "    Reason code = 13: - Make sure the DBM CFG parameter TP_MON_NAME" + _
Chr$(15) + "                               is set to MTS" + _
Chr$(15) + "    Reason code = 14: - Make sure MSDTC service is still up or" + _
Chr$(15) + "                          - Use MTS explorer to Shutdown Server Processes"
+ _
Chr$(15) + "                              and Stop and Start MSDTC service"

    Dim Indent As String
```

```
        Indent = Chr$(15) + "------>"
        NativeErrorCode = Ø
        Call DebugMessage("In Error")

        If adoConn Is Nothing Or adoConn.Errors Is Nothing Or _
           adoConn.Errors.Count = Ø Then
           Call DebugMessage("In error: Table is empty")
        Else
           For i = Ø To adoConn.Errors.Count - 1

                NativeErrorCode = adoConn.Errors(i).NativeError
                If (NativeErrorCode <> Ø) Then
                    strResult = BuildResult(strResult, adoConn.Errors(i).Description)
                End If
                Call DebugMessage(strResult)

                Select Case NativeErrorCode
                Case -998
                    strResult = BuildResult(strResult, Error998)
                End Select

           Next i
        End If

        If (NativeErrorCode = Ø) Then
           strResult = BuildResult(strResult, "VB Message: " + Err.Description)
        End If
        GetError = NativeErrorCode

End Function

'''''''''''''''''''''''''''''''''''''''''''''''''''''''''''''''''''''''''''''
' BuildResult
'''''''''''''''''''''''''''''''''''''''''''''''''''''''''''''''''''''''''''''
Public Function BuildResult(ByVal strResult As String, ErrMsg As String) As String

    BuildResult = strResult + Indent + ErrMsg
End Function

'''''''''''''''''''''''''''''''''''''''''''''''''''''''''''''''''''''''''''''
' DebugPrint
'''''''''''''''''''''''''''''''''''''''''''''''''''''''''''''''''''''''''''''
Public Sub DebugPrint(ByVal strError As String)
    Call OutputDebugStringA(strError)
End Sub

'''''''''''''''''''''''''''''''''''''''''''''''''''''''''''''''''''''''''''''
' DebugMessage
'''''''''''''''''''''''''''''''''''''''''''''''''''''''''''''''''''''''''''''
Public Sub DebugMessage(ByVal strError As String)
    Dim lngReturn As Long
        lngReturn = MessageBoxA(API_NULL, strError, "Error In Component", _
                MB_ICONERROR Or MB_SERVICE_NOTIFICATION)
End Sub


,'''''''''''''''''''''''''''''''''''''''''''''''''''''''''''''''''''''''''''''
'
'   Project DB2Com.vbp
'   Class UpdateNumberColumn.cls
Option Explicit

Private Const ERROR_NUMBER = vbObjectError + Ø
Private Const APP_ERROR = -2147467008

'''''''''''''''''''''''''''''''''''''''''''''''''''''''''''''''''''''''''''''
' UpdateNumberColumn
'''''''''''''''''''''''''''''''''''''''''''''''''''''''''''''''''''''''''''''
Public Function UpdateNumberColumn(ByVal strConnect, ByRef strResult As String) As
Integer
    Dim rc As Integer
    Dim strStmt As String
    Dim adoConn As New ADODB.Connection
    rc = Ø

    ' Obtain the ADO environment and connection
    On Error GoTo ErrorReport
```

```
        adoConn.Open strConnect

        ' Update Rows
UpdateAgain:
        On Error GoTo ErrorUpdate
        strStmt = "Update db2mts set number = number+1"
        adoConn.Execute strStmt

        ' clean up
cleanup:
        On Error GoTo 0
        If Not adoConn Is Nothing Then
          adoConn.Close
          Set adoConn = Nothing
        End If

        If rc <> 0 Then
          GetObjectContext.SetAbort
          Err.Raise rc, strStmt, strResult
        Else
          GetObjectContext.SetComplete
        End If
        UpdateNumberColumn = rc

Exit Function

CreateTable:
        Dim strCreateTable As String
        On Error GoTo ErrorReport
        ' Create Table
        strStmt = "Create table db2mts (number integer, string varchar(15))"
        adoConn.Execute strStmt
        ' Populate with 1 row
        strStmt = "Insert into db2mts values(1,'S1')"
        adoConn.Execute strStmt
        GoTo UpdateAgain
' End CreateTable

ErrorUpdate:
        ' If error -204 (table not found) then create the table
        ' Otherwise return with failure
        If adoConn.Errors(0).NativeError = -204 Then
          Resume CreateTable
        End If
        Resume ErrorReport

ErrorReport:
        rc = Common.GetError(adoConn, strStmt, strResult)
        Resume cleanup

End Function




',,,,,,,,,,,,,,,,,,,,,,,,,,,,,,,,,,,,,,,,,,,,,,,,,,,,,,,,,,,,,,,,,,,,,
'
'   Project DB2COM.vbp
'   Class UpdateRow.cls
Option Explicit

Private Const ERROR_NUMBER = vbObjectError + 0
Private Const APP_ERROR = -2147467008

'..................................................................................
' UpdateRow
'..................................................................................
Public Function UpdateRow(ByVal strConnect, ByRef strResult As String) As Integer
        Dim Com1 As Object
        Dim Com2 As Object
        Dim rc As Integer
        Dim strStmt As String
        rc = 0
        On Error GoTo ErrorCreateInstance
        Set Com1 = GetObjectContext.CreateInstance("db2com.UpdateNumberColumn")
        Set Com2 = GetObjectContext.CreateInstance("db2com.UpdateStringColumn")
        On Error GoTo Abort
        rc = Com1.UpdateNumberColumn(strConnect, strResult)
        rc = Com2.UpdateStringColumn(strConnect, strResult)
```

```
commit:
    Set Com1 = Nothing
    Set Com2 = Nothing
    GetObjectContext.SetComplete
    UpdateRow = rc
Exit Function
Abort:
    Call DebugMessage("Error happened in UpdateRow. I am in Abort")
    Set Com1 = Nothing
    Set Com2 = Nothing
    GetObjectContext.SetAbort
    Err.Raise Err.Number, Err.Source, Err.Description
Exit Function

ErrorCreateInstance:
    Err.Source = "Creating MTS COM object for db2mts package"
    Err.Description = "Please follow the readme and reinstall db2mts package"
    Resume Abort
End Function



'''''''''''''''''''''''''''''''''''''''''''''''''''''''''''''''''''''''
'
'   Project DB2COM.vbp
'   Class UpdateStringColumn.cls
Option Explicit

Private Const ERROR_NUMBER = vbObjectError + 0
Private Const APP_ERROR = -2147467008

'''''''''''''''''''''''''''''''''''''''''''''''''''''''''''''''''''''''''''''''
' UpdateStringColumn
'''''''''''''''''''''''''''''''''''''''''''''''''''''''''''''''''''''''''''''''
Public Function UpdateStringColumn(ByVal strConnect, ByRef strResult As String) As
Integer
    Dim strStmt As String
    Dim rc As Integer
    Dim adoConn As New ADODB.Connection
    Dim adoRS As ADODB.Recordset
    Dim longNumber As Long
    Dim stringString As String
    rc = 0

    ' Obtain the ADO environment and connection
    On Error GoTo ErrorReport
    strStmt = "ADO Connect with Connection String " + strConnect
    adoConn.Open strConnect
    ' Select Rows
    strStmt = "Select number,string  from db2mts"
    Set adoRS = adoConn.Execute(strStmt)

    If adoRS.EOF Then
        GoTo ErrorEmptyTable
    End If

    ' Update Rows
    longNumber = adoRS.Fields("Number").Value
    strStmt = "Update db2mts set String = 'S" _
            + Trim(Str$(longNumber)) + _
            "' where number = " + Str$(longNumber)
    adoConn.Execute strStmt

    ' cleanup
cleanup:
    On Error GoTo 0
    If Not adoConn Is Nothing Then
        If Not adoRS Is Nothing Then
            adoRS.Close
            Set adoRS = Nothing
        End If
        adoConn.Close
        Set adoConn = Nothing
    End If

    If rc <> 0 Then
        GetObjectContext.SetAbort
```

```
          Err.Raise rc, strStmt, strResult
      Else
          GetObjectContext.SetComplete
      End If
      UpdateStringColumn = rc

Exit Function

ErrorReport:
      rc = Common.GetError(adoConn, _
                          "Execution of: " + strStmt, _
                          strResult)
      Resume cleanup
' End ErrorReport

ErrorEmptyTable:
      rc = Common.GetError(adoConn, _
              "db2mts table is empty. Transaction aborted", _
              strResult)
      Resume cleanup
' End ErrorEmpmtyTable

End Function



,.............................................................
'
'   Project DB2COM.vbp
'   Class VerifyUpdate.cls
Option Explicit

Private Const ERROR_NUMBER = vbObjectError + 0
Private Const APP_ERROR = -2147467008
'..............................................................
' VerifyUpdate
'..............................................................
Public Function VerifyUpdate(ByVal strConnect, ByRef strResult As String) As Integer
      Dim strStmt As String
      Dim rc As Integer
      Dim adoConn As New ADODB.Connection
      Dim adoRS As ADODB.Recordset
      Dim longNumber As Long
      Dim strTest, strString As String
      rc = 0

      On Error GoTo ErrorReport
      ' Obtain the ADO environment and connection
      strStmt = "ADO Connect with Connection String " + strConnect
      adoConn.Open strConnect
      ' Select Rows
      strStmt = "Select number,string  from db2mts"
      Set adoRS = adoConn.Execute(strStmt)
      ' Verify row
      strStmt = "Verify Update"
      longNumber = adoRS.Fields("Number").Value
      strString = adoRS.Fields("String").Value
      strTest = "S" + Trim(Str$(longNumber))
      strResult = "Row: Number=" + Str$(longNumber) + _
                      ";String =" + strTest
      If strString = strTest Then
          strResult = strResult + ".  Verification Successful"
          rc = 0
      Else
          strResult = strResult + ".  Verification failed"
          rc = -1
      End If

  ' cleanup
cleanup:
      If Not adoConn Is Nothing Then
          If Not adoRS Is Nothing Then
              adoRS.Close
              Set adoRS = Nothing
          End If
          adoConn.Close
      End If
```

```
        If rc <> 0 Then
            GetObjectContext.SetAbort
            Err.Raise rc, strStmt, strResult
        Else
            GetObjectContext.SetComplete
        End If
        VerifyUpdate = rc
Exit Function

ErrorReport:
        rc = Common.GetError(adoConn, _
                            strStmt, _
                            strResult)
        Resume cleanup
' End ErrorReport
End Function
```

APPENDIX C

Related Publications

The publications listed in this section are considered particularly suitable for a more detailed explanation of the topics covered in this book.

- *DB2 UDB for Windows, Quick Beginnings*, GC09-2971
- *DB2 UDB Installation and Configuration Supplement*, GC09-2957
- *DB2 UDB SQL Reference, Volume 1*, SC09-2974
- *DB2 UDB SQL Reference, Volume 2*, SC09-2975
- *DB2 UDB Command Reference*, SC09-2951
- *DB2 UDB Application Building Guide*, SC09-2948
- *DB2 UDB Application Development Guide*, SC09-2949
- *DB2 UDB Call Level Interface Guide and Reference*, SC09-2950
- *DB2 UDB Administration Guide: Planning*, SC09-2946
- *DB2 UDB Administration Guide: Implementation*, SC09-2944
- *DB2 UDB Administration Guide: Performance*, SC09-2945
- *DB2 UDB System Monitor Guide, Version 6*, SC09-2956

The following Web sites are also useful:

- IBM Data Management Home Page:
  http://www-4.ibm.com/software/data

- DB2 Product and Service Technical Library
  http://www-4.ibm.com/software/data/db2/library

- Application Development with DB2 Universal Database
  http://www-4.ibm.com/software/data/db2/udb/ad

- DB2 Universal Database & DB2 Connect Online Support
  http://www-4.ibm.com/software/data/db2/udb/winos2unix/support

- DB2 Maintenance - Fixpaks for DB2 UDB:
  http://www-4.ibm.com/software/data/db2/db2tech/indexsvc.html

Index

Instance : DB2

Database: DWCTRLDB

Schema : IWH

Database user name: db2admin

Password : xp193193 Pbts

Back	Forward	Home	Reload	Images	Open	Print	Find	Stop

http://www.phptr.com/

What's New?	What's Cool?	Destinations	Net Search	People	Software

PRENTICE HALL

Professional Technical Reference
Tomorrow's Solutions for Today's Professionals.

Keep Up-to-Date with
PH PTR Online!

We strive to stay on the cutting-edge of what's happening in professional computer science and engineering. Here's a bit of what you'll find when you stop by **www.phptr.com**:

Special interest areas offering our latest books, book series, software, features of the month, related links and other useful information to help you get the job done.

Deals, deals, deals! Come to our promotions section for the latest bargains offered to you exclusively from our retailers.

Need to find a bookstore? Chances are, there's a bookseller near you that carries a broad selection of PTR titles. Locate a Magnet bookstore near you at www.phptr.com.

What's New at PH PTR? We don't just publish books for the professional community, we're a part of it. Check out our convention schedule, join an author chat, get the latest reviews and press releases on topics of interest to you.

Subscribe Today! **Join PH PTR's monthly email newsletter!**

Want to be kept up-to-date on your area of interest? Choose a targeted category on our website, and we'll keep you informed of the latest PH PTR products, author events, reviews and conferences in your interest area.

Visit our mailroom to subscribe today! **http://www.phptr.com/mail_lists**